The Poetics of Ancient and Classical Arabic Literature

Through analysing ancient and classical Arabic literature, including the Qur'an, from within the Arabic literary tradition, this book provides an original interpretation of poetics, and of other important aspects of Arab culture.

Arabic literature is a realm of poetry; prose literary forms emerged rather late, and even then remained in the shadow of poetic creative efforts. Traditionally, this literature has been viewed through a philologist's lens and has often been represented as "materialistic" in the sense that its poetry lacked imagination. As a result, Arabic poetry was often evaluated negatively in relation to other poetic traditions. *The Poetics of Ancient and Classical Arabic Literature* argues that old Arabic literature is remarkably coherent in poetical terms and has its own individuality, and that claims of its materialism arise from a failure to grasp the poetic principles of the Arabic tradition. Analysing the Qur'an, which is known for confronting the poetry of the time, this book reveals that "post Qur'anic" literature came to be defined against it. Thus, the constitution and interpretation of Arabic literature imposed itself as a particular exegesis of the sacred Text.

Disputing traditional interpretations by arguing that Arabic literature can only be assessed from within, and not through comparison with other literary traditions, this book is of interest to students and scholars of Islamic Studies, Arabic Studies and Literary Studies.

Esad Duraković holds a PhD in the field of Arabic literature from the Faculty of Philology in Belgrade and is Professor of Arabic Languages and Arabic Literature at the University of Sarajevo. His research interests focus on literary interpretation from Arabic.

Culture and Civilization in the Middle East
General Editor: Ian Richard Netton
Professor of Islamic Studies, University of Exeter

This series studies the Middle East through the twin foci of its diverse cultures and civilisations. Comprising original monographs as well as scholarly surveys, it covers topics in the fields of Middle Eastern literature, archaeology, law, history, philosophy, science, folklore, art, architecture and language. While there is a plurality of views, the series presents serious scholarship in a lucid and stimulating fashion.

Previously published by Curzon

The Origins of Islamic Law
The Qur'an, the Muwatta' and Madinan Amal
Yasin Dutton

A Jewish Archive from Old Cairo
The History of Cambridge University's Genizah Collection
Stefan Reif

The Formative Period of Twelver Shi'ism
Hadith as Discourse Between Qum and Baghdad
Andrew J. Newman

Qur'an Translation
Discourse, Texture and Exegesis
Hussein Abdul-Raof

Christians in Al-Andalus 711–1000
Ann Rosemary Christys

Folklore and Folklife in the United Arab Emirates
Sayyid Hamid Hurriez

The Formation of Hanbalism
Piety into Power
Nimrod Hurvitz

Arabic Literature
An Overview
Pierre Cachia

Structure and Meaning in Medieval Arabic and Persian Lyric Poetry
Orient Pearls
Julie Scott Meisami

Muslims and Christians in Norman Sicily
Arabic-Speakers and the End of Islam
Alexander Metcalfe

Modern Arab Historiography
Historical Discourse and the Nation-State
Youssef Choueiri

The Philosophical Poetics of Alfarabi, Avicenna and Averroes
The Aristotelian Reception
Salim Kemal

Published by Routledge

1 **The Epistemology of Ibn Khaldun**
Zaid Ahmad

2 **The Hanbali School of Law and Ibn Taymiyyah**
Conflict or concilation
Abdul Hakim I Al-Matroudi

3 **Arabic Rhetoric**
A pragmatic analysis
Hussein Abdul-Raof

4 **Arab Representations of the Occident**
East-west encounters in Arabic fiction
Rasheed El-Enany

5 **God and Humans in Islamic Thought**
Abd al-Jabbār, Ibn Sīnā and al-Ghazālī
Maha Elkaisy-Friemuth

6 **Original Islam**
Malik and the madhhab of Madina
Yasin Dutton

7 **Al-Ghazali and the Qur'an**
One book, many meanings
Martin Whittingham

8 **Birth of The Prophet Muhammad**
Devotional piety in Sunni Islam
Marion Holmes Katz

9 **Space and Muslim Urban Life**
At the limits of the labyrinth of Fez
Simon O'Meara

10 **Islam and Science**
The intellectual career of Nizam al-Din al-Nizaburi
Robert G. Morrison

11 **Ibn 'Arabî – Time and Cosmology**
Mohamed Haj Yousef

12 **The Status of Women in Islamic Law and Society**
Annotated translation of al-Ṭāhir al-Ḥaddād's *Imra'tunā fi 'l-sharīʿa wa 'l-mujtamaʿ*, with an introduction
Ronak Husni and Daniel L. Newman

13 **Islam and the Baha'i Faith**
A comparative study of Muhammad 'Abduh and 'Abdul-Baha 'Abbas
Oliver Scharbrodt

14 **Comte de Gobineau and Orientalism**
Selected Eastern writings
Translated by Daniel O'Donoghue
Edited by Geoffrey Nas

15 **Early Islamic Spain**
The history of Ibn al-Qū.tīya
David James

16 **German Orientalism**
The study of the Middle East and Islam from 1800 to 1945
Ursula Wokoeck

17 **Mullā Ṣadrā and Metaphysics**
Modulation of being
Sajjad H. Rizvi

18 **Schools of Qur'anic Exegesis**
Genesis and development
Hussein Abdul-Raof

19 **Al-Ghazali, Averroes and the Interpretation of the Qur'an**
Common sense and philosophy in Islam
Avital Wohlman, translated by David Burrell

20 **Eastern Christianity in the Modern Middle East**
Edited by Anthony O'Mahony and Emma Loosley

21 **Islamic Reform and Arab Nationalism**
Expanding the crescent from the Mediterranean to the Indian Ocean (1880s–1930s)
Amal N. Ghazal

22 **Islamic Ethics**
Divine command theory in Arabo-Islamic thought
Mariam al-Attar

23 **Muslim Fortresses in the Levant**
Between crusaders and Mongols
Kate Raphael

24 **Being Human in Islam**
The impact of the evolutionary worldview
Damian Howard

25 **The UAE and Foreign Policy**
Foreign aid, identities and interests
Khalid S. Almezaini

26 **A History of Early al-Andalus**
The Akhbar Majmu'a
David James

27 **Inspired Knowledge in Islamic Thought**
Al-Ghazali's theory of mystical cognition and its Avicennian foundation
Alexander Treiger

28 **Shi'i Theology in Iran**
The challenge of religious experience
Ori Goldberg

29 **Founding Figures and Commentators in Arabic Mathematics**
A History of Arabic sciences and mathematics, volume 1
Roshdi Rashed, edited by Nader El-Bizri, translated by Roger Wareham, with Chris Allen and Michael Barany

30 **The Muslim Conquest of Iberia**
Medieval Arabic narratives
Nicola Clarke

31 **Angels in Islam**
Jalal al-Din al-Suyuti's *al-Haba'ik fi akhbar al-mala'ik*
Stephen Burge

32 **Theological Approaches to Qur'anic Exegesis**
A practical comparative-contrastive analysis
Hussein Abdul-Raof

33 Ibn al-Haytham and Analytical Mathematics
A history of Arabic sciences and mathematics, volume 2
Roshdi Rashed, translated by Susan Glynn and Roger Wareham

34 Ghazali's Politics in Context
Yazeed Said

35 Orientalism Revisited
Art, land and voyage
Edited by Ian Richard Netton

36 Ibn al-Haytham's Theory of Conics, Geometrical Constructions and Practical
Geometry
A history of Arabic sciences and mathematics, volume 3
Roshdi Rashed, translated by J. V. Field

37 Science and Religion in Mamluk Egypt
Ibn al-Nafis, pulmonary transit and bodily resurrection
Nahyan Fancy

38 The Qur'an in Christian–Muslim Dialogue
Historical and modern interpretations
C Jonn Block

39 Arabic and Hebrew Love Poems in Al-Andalus
Shari L. Lowin

40 Religious Scholars and the Umayyads
Piety-minded supporters of the Marwanid Caliphate
Steven C. Judd

41 Skepticism in Classical Islam
Moments of confusion
Paul L. Heck

42 Free Will and Predestination in Islamic Thought
Theoretical compromises in the works of Avicenna al-Ghazālī and Ibn ʿArabī
Maria de Cillis

43 Ibn al-Haytham, New Spherical Geometry and Astronomy
A history of Arabic sciences and mathematics, volume 4
Roshdi Rashed, translated by J.V. Field

44 Classical Mathematics from al-Khwārizmī to Descartes
Roshdi Rashed, translated by Michael H. Shank

45 Legal Authority in Premodern Islam
Yaḥyā b. Sharaf al-Nawawī in the Shāfiʿī School of Law
Fachrizal A. Halim

46 Ethics in Islam
Friendship in the political thought of Al-Tawḥīdī and his contemporaries
Nuha A. Alshaar

47 The City in the Muslim World
Depictions by Western travel writers
Edited by Mohammad Gharipour and Nilay Özlü

48 Moral Rationalism and Shari'a
Independent rationality in modern Shīʿī *Uṣūl al-Fiqh*
Ali-Reza Bhojani

The Poetics of Ancient and Classical Arabic Literature

Orientology

Esad Duraković
Translated by Amila Karahasanović

Routledge
Taylor & Francis Group
LONDON AND NEW YORK

First published 2015
by Routledge
2 Park Square, Milton Park, Abingdon, Oxon OX14 4RN

and by Routledge
711 Third Avenue, New York, NY 10017

Routledge is an imprint of the Taylor & Francis Group, an informa business

British Library Cataloguing in Publication Data
A catalogue record for this book is available from the British Library

Library of Congress Cataloging in Publication Data
A catalog record for this book has been requested

ISBN: 978-1-138-85467-3 (hbk)
ISBN: 978-1-315-72094-4 (ebk)

Typeset in Times New Roman
by Wearset Ltd, Boldon, Tyne and Wear

Printed and bound in the United States of America by Publishers Graphics, LLC on sustainably sourced paper.

He created man;
He taught him the power of expression
(*Qur'an*, 55:3–4)

Contents

Preliminary considerations xiii
Preface to the English-language edition xxx
About the author xxxiii

Introduction 1

1 **Poetics of the Arabesque** 4

2 **The deductive poetics of the *Qur'an*** 21
Intertextuality and contextualisation 21

3 **The Qur'anic Text's advance on tradition** 29
The Qur'an *confronting poetry at the level of ideology 30*
The Qur'an *confronting poetry at the level of form 53*

4 **The simile in Old Arabic poetry: a world at a distance** 87
Prologue: the realism or "materialism" of Old Arabic poetry 87
Figures of description and the profusion of themes in poems 88
Obviousness and transparency of the world and the necessity of distance 92
Segmentation of textual space 95
Gradation of textual time 99
Concentration on the flatness of the physical 103
Typicality before description 107
Constituents of the simile as architects of positivity 111
The simile and the travelogue airiness of the world 113

5 **The Qur'anic metaphor: the world within** 118
Descent of the metaphor into the world and the metaphoric revolution 118

The Text unveiled in language and stylistics 123
Realism of the simile and transfer of the metaphor: poet's belle and houris in Jannah 129
Past time of the simile and processuality of the metaphor 136
Transparency of the world in the simile and the metaphoric vertical world order 142
The simile undertaking segmentation and centripetal forces of the metaphor 145

6 Maturation of post-Qur'anic poetics and literary tradition 149
Normative poetics and the difficulty of literature periodisation 150
The Qur'anic text as a generator of changes in tradition 154
Philology as impetus and a trap 158
Philology: text's authenticity and author's originality 164
The authority of philology and Shu'ubiyyah *169*
Tradition as a reservoir of motifs and poetic technique 170
Poetic theme not necessarily sublime 174
The origin of poetic motifs in Arabic antiquity 179
Motifs as commonplaces or topoi 183
Triumph of philological poetics: spreading across the entire Islamic cultural community 186
Form as a technique or philotechnic poetry 192
Prevalence of artistic form and the servility of criticism 196
Poetic inspiration and technique 201
Universalism of philological poetics: tradition as inspiration 202
A reservoir of motifs and the legalisation of "literary theft" 207
The artistically beautiful and literary theft: contrasting the sacred text and poetry 215
Isolation of tradition: the lack of influence of Aristotle's poetics 219
The dawn of a new age 227

Bibliography 238
Further reading 246
Name index 248
Subject index 251

Preliminary considerations

The study of Oriental-Islamic culture is often burdened by the ideological position of the researchers, be they those in the Islamic world or outside it. In general, on one hand, this culture understands itself from within and presents itself to the world from such a position. On the other, there is a well- and long-established discipline called *Oriental studies*, which – mainly from the vantage point of Western culture – interprets and evaluates the Oriental-Islamic culture and presents it not only to the West, but also to the Oriental-Islamic world itself. These two approaches often do not entail any correspondence in their methods and conclusions. There is even no closeness at times, but rather an emphasis on diverging conclusions. This fact indicates that the study of Oriental-Islamic culture is historically changeable, and this underscores Barthes's idea about the need for the history of history and history of philosophy – and thus, of course, history of literature, as he clearly indicates – to be recreated over and over, in order to make a past object always a complete object.[1] Barthes, of course, speaks in light of the European tradition, invoking the claim made by Lucien Febvre and Merleau-Ponty: he varies and reinvigorates the European constant on the necessity of doubt and permanent re-examination, which is the basis of progress in science in general. This need is also evident in light of the fact that there is a "third approach", somewhat different from the former two: the Russian Oriental "school", which can be presented in this context by referring to several notable Russian Oriental scholars: И. Ю. Крачковский, И. М. Фильштинский, А. Е. Крымский, etc.[2] Consequently, what transpires from this is that Oriental studies need the same thing premised by the West in science in general – constant re-examination, with valid methodology and argumentation.

Oriental studies, which refers here to the Western study of the Oriental-Islamic world, and particularly of its culture, is to be objectively credited in the Oriental-Islamic world, since many Oriental scholars worked hard to promote many of its values by uncovering them to the Western world, and did so in certain aspects it had failed to observe by itself. It seems that one of the greatest contributions of Oriental studies is its philological part, with the least amount of ideological deviations, since Oriental *philology* – in terms of being exact in a particular sense – is the closest to an ideologically neutral position, i.e. that which can be described as scientifically necessary objectivity. It is almost impossible to imagine this field of study today, had it not been for the enormous and beneficial activity of Oriental philology, which uncovered and published (i.e. revealed) an impressive part of Oriental-Islamic cultural and scholarly heritage: entire libraries of fundamental works of this culture were uncovered by Western philosophers, who prepared numerous critical editions – from the United Kingdom, through France and Germany, to faraway Calcutta. Russian Oriental philology (particularly in the Soviet era) should not be neglected. German classical philology, for example, made an immense contribution to the development of Oriental studies; this is not only in reference to German philologists, but also to the German school of classical philology, which had, in terms of methodology, spread to other countries and other languages.

Oriental philology thus created a solid basis for Oriental studies in the wider sense. However, once that basis, created by philology, is used to approach interpretations of Oriental-Islamic culture or its fundamental works, once one ventures into the ever so sensitive and historically unstable area of valuation, certain problems appear – as scholarly disagreements, sometimes disputes, etc., although it is the same area, or "object" of scholarly interest. The tradition of Oriental studies is well acquainted with such differences in interpretation and value judgements. The entire history of Oriental studies is a testament to occasionally different or diverging approaches and judgements related to Oriental-Islamic culture. They seem to be particularly evident in the modern era – in what we call postcolonial criticism.

In light of the scope of production of Oriental studies – be it burdened ideologically in relation to the culture it studies, be it apologetic towards it, or somewhere between the two opposites – it is simply impossible to include here all the authors and their works. The aim of this study is not to be apologetic or critical towards any Oriental studies method or its results, but rather an autonomous step into this vast culture, hoping to deliver new results. With these preliminary considerations I want to indicate, at least in summary form, some of the typical phenomena appearing in approaches to Oriental-Islamic culture, to be substantiated by certain names in Oriental studies, which, in turn, justifies the need for new research over and over. It is these phenomena that moved me to produce this study. There are among them those that instigate scholarly opposition and presentation of different views; well-informed readers will recognise my opposition, even when I do not debate directly (while citing names and titles), for this is not a critical study in that sense, but rather an exploratory one. On the other hand, Oriental studies bibliography offers methodological approaches and research results that overcome successfully the ideological burdens of some other Oriental scholars, or rather the type of rigidity in positioning themselves as the Other, which is an expression of disastrous prejudice. I believe that support is required to overcome such extreme positions. We simply work in a relatively sensitive area, whose history testifies to sharp ideological confrontations, so much so that in some oeuvres this field of study has been turned into an "ideological science" and can sometimes become servant to politics. A particular problem arises from the fact that in some cases, the authority of certain canons of Oriental studies, or

Oriental canons, is proportionate to their ideological potential. One should separate Oriental studies from any domination of ideology over it – and this is a tall order, be it in the so-called Western approaches, or the ones within the Oriental-Islamic world.

The fundamental texts of Oriental-Islamic culture are the *Qur'an* and poetry. That is why these two corpuses are at the core of my research, just as Oriental studies in general afford them the greatest attention – justifiably so. These two corpuses have a clear and strong link, despite the fact that they negate each other in certain aspects and they do so in very complex ways – for the *Qur'an* used literary devices only to show its superiority over poetry (much loved by ancient Arabs), i.e. it used literary devices to set itself in relation to literary expression in general as entirely non-imitative. Noting the enormous significance of the *Qur'an* and poetry in Oriental-Islamic culture, which developed so powerfully in poetry, but also under the influence of Qur'anic text in the Arabic language and in the *context* of the then present literary traditions – scholars have generally been very attentive to those texts, be it as autonomous corpuses, be it as texts that influenced significantly the creation of a wider cultural context. Such scholarly research presents two principal directions: the one created by scholars in the Oriental-Islamic world, and the one created within Oriental studies, noting that there are dissonant voices in the latter, as well as particular positioning towards Oriental-Islamic culture as the *Other*. The key role in this – on "both sides" and primarily – was played by ideological positions for approaching fundamental texts and values of the Oriental-Islamic cultural realm. I will substantiate this with examples of certain approaches and conclusions regarding the *Qur'an* and ancient Arabian poetry.

The category (or the doctrine, as it is often referred to in referential sources) of *'i'jāz*, understood as the supranatural and non-imitative nature of its texts, is, according to Muslim belief, one of the key aspects in approaching the *Qur'an*. The complexity of this issue rests not only on how the supranatural in it is to be elaborated and interpreted, but also in the fact that this issue, irrespective of conclusions, has far-reaching consequences for the approach to the entire Oriental-Islamic culture. Since the *Qur'an* is the fundamental text of the culture considered here, the conclusion as to whether it is supranatural/non-imitative or not indicates the position of the researcher – whether it is immanent in the sense of studying the culture from within itself (usually though not solely Muslims) or distancing in the sense that the study is conducted from the position of different traditional experiences and ideological (i.e. religious too) constellations. This is a matter of method(s), which always condition the research results. Consequently, another question arises from this, of a rhetorical nature: how well can a vast culture be understood and presented by the researchers who do not accept the postulates articulated as such by that same culture? The question of an immanent approach thus sharpens. In other words, we have a situation whereby the Oriental-Islamic culture postulated this sacred text as its fundamental text (and the entire culture is primarily a Culture of the Word), meaning that it developed deliberately *in harmony with such a postulate*. Is it possible or scientifically justified to ignore such an important fact?! Ultimately, it seems irrelevant in this context whether the Qur'anic text is supranatural/non-imitative or not; what is important is how much can either belief allow for a valid study of that culture. It is natural and legitimate for non-Muslims to consider it divine, non-imitative, etc., for they would otherwise accede to the fact that they have accepted Islam. It is also natural – and legitimate – for the principal creators of Oriental-Islamic culture throughout its history and in its present time to consider the text supranatural – thus also that its *'i'jāz* is beyond doubt. I believe that this complicated situation can be "resolved" in the following way.

Namely, scholars outside the Islamic world, i.e. those who are not Muslim, cannot accept *'i'jāz* as a kind of axiom, in view of their position: it is understandable, but scientifically unjustified, as stated above, to study a culture while disregarding the fact that it was the culture itself that posited the *Qur'an* as its fundamental text and developed in compliance with that. Ultimately, those scientists who are unable to accept this fact about the self-positing of a sacred text in Oriental-Islamic culture act in the name of another ideology and *against* the one contained in the *Other*. Science is thus powerfully ideologised, and such an orientation is damaging to both the science and the ideology. The burden is comprehensive. For example, in his book *La letteratura araba* (Milan, 1967), in the chapter entitled "The *Qur'an*", the Italian Arabist Francesco Gabrieli says that the *Qur'an* is the most difficult book to understand "for a modern man from the West", and that this text "seems *to us* [my emphasis] to be spiritually poor, repeating endlessly a set of basic motifs, harsh and confused in exploration, chaotic in the actual sequence – in short and honestly, *boring*", and that, as such, it was "the guidance and light for a large part of mankind".[3]

These categorical positions and a host of other negative qualifications presented in just a sentence or two are accompanied by no explanation or argumentation whatsoever, but the author thus created the preconditions for disqualifying a huge culture, even a large part of mankind (!), since that part of mankind finds "guidance and light" in a book that is difficult to understand, chaotic and even boring, etc. Unfortunately, Gabrieli said this on behalf of the Western man. His position is clearly ideological and negativist, even conflicting in relation to the culture it represents, as well as the principles of science in general. Naturally, there have been different approaches in Oriental studies.

Yusuf Rahman is one of the authors who have presented important works dealing with the issue of *'i'jāz* of the *Qur'an*. He presented key authors who had dealt with the issue of *'i'jāz* (al-Bāqillānī, Abū 'Ubayda, Ibn Qutayba, Abdul Aleem, 'Abd al-Jabbār, etc.).[4] One of his important conclusions states: "One might be correct in assuming that in Muslim works dealing with miracles and, especially with *'i'jāz al-Qur'an*, the author's primary aim is always 'practical,' that is to defend and to prove the prophethood of Muhammad."[5]

Al-Bāqillānī is also underscored and his position is summarised as a presentation of three key aspects of reflection of *'i'jāz*: (1) knowledge of the invisible (how the *Qur'an* presents the invisible); (2) the Prophet was illiterate and could not have produced such a body of text; (3) the composition of the text is fascinating.[6] The Oriental-Islamic tradition is dominated by the studies that base the *'i'jāz* in the *Qur'an* on exactly what al-Bāqillānī said, but it seems to me that Mustansir Mir was right, to a large extent, when he said that, strictly speaking, the challenge of the *Qur'an* should be understood as a literary challenge addressed to Arabs of Muhammad's era, with little relevance for post-Qur'anic generations, be they Arabs or non-Arabs, Muslims or non-Muslims.[7] The *Qur'an* is a book of the context and as such it was determined to demonstrate to the then speakers of the Arabic language that it was, first and foremost, superior to the found tradition of using literary devices. Traditional Muslim exegesis was focused on studying *'i'jāz* in a host of devices of literary expression, such as alliteration, assonance, rhyme, ellipsis, etc.[8] The same author states that until the twentieth century, the study of *'i'jāz* was based on an atomistic approach to *Qur'an* – ayah by ayah, surah by surah. Little attention was focused on the internal structure of the surah, particularly so in terms of coherence within the surah themselves.[9]

This dominant orientation towards the literary aspects of *'i'jāz* is historically justified, as Mir confirms, and it is, I believe, mainly a consequence of two things. First, the *Qur'an* was explicitly in competition with poets, trying to prove its divine superiority, i.e. that the Prophet himself was not a poet, as often described by opponents who were his contemporaries. So, in the Prophet's time, within that context, *'i'jāz* was primarily founded on its literary expression; hence the effort to prove *'i'jāz* within that aspect. Second, as stated earlier, Arabian and also the entire Oriental-Islamic culture was such that it expressed itself very successfully in the Word; it is thus understandable that even so long after the Prophet the supranatural nature of the *Text* is proved by placing it against other *texts*. This kind of action by inertia was necessary.

With due respect for the results reached by this type of studies, since they did indeed provide a major contribution, I think that it is necessary at this time to take a step further in interpreting the "*doctrine of 'i'jāz*". This is one of the aims of my study, and the public will judge the results. Literary approaches to Qur'anic text, just like linguistic, stylistic and other so-called traditional approaches to this very influential text, will remain important, with a possibility to further contribute with valid research results – i.e. provided they do not fall within the area of mere compilations and epigonism. It is particularly important for scholars in the Islamic world to resist this type of traditionalism. Approaching the *Qur'an* from the vantage point of the scientific areas I have just mentioned makes sense and has future perspectives in line with the well-recognised fact that these fields of study also continuously expand their horizons, and that the text itself simply makes itself available to modern scientific disciplines. For example, I believe that interesting results may arise from studying the *Qur'an* from the vantage point of semiotics, or cognitive stylistics, which seem to be – with good reason – very attractive modern fields of scholarly research. However, in principle and without diminishing the importance of specialist approaches that Johns called atomistic,[10] the *Qur'an* should be analysed in a way significantly different from the traditional "atomistic" approaches, although they are in no way contradictory – on the contrary. Namely, what Mir called "a holistic approach"[11] takes courage, although the notion itself may be discussed within this context. Such an approach is a huge step forward compared to al-Bāqillānī's consideration of *'i'jāz*, as well as that of many authors in the long tradition of studying the *Qur'an* and particularly its *'i'jāz*.

I am of the opinion that this text should be considered as the Text in the entire Culture. This expands the different aspects of *'i'jāz*. Namely, this text comprises a "range of meanings", to use a term referring to Barthes, if observed within itself; however, meanings multiply when observing the *Qur'an* in a culture that, as a whole, may be named the Text. In other words, the text functions on its own at one level, and it functions differently, or at another level, when introduced into the Context/when observed as an important part of a highly functional whole (and I use the term *holistic approach* in that sense). The text and its context are thus clearly and lastingly mutually dynamicised. The conservationist, traditionalist approaches and their results are thus permanently *overcome*, and this word indicates that the results of traditional ("atomistic") approaches have not been annulled or negated, but rather built on further. And it is this approach that is immanent to the *Qur'an*, for it is a highly contextualising text. (In this sense, let us recall at least the notion of derogation in the *Qur'an*: derogating own decisions in changed circumstances, or, for example, the category of *sabab al-nuzūl* – the occasion for revealing certain ayahs, etc.) The *Qur'an* contextualised itself not only by its relationship with poetry: its contextualisation is quite comprehensive, down to the aforementioned category of derogation, for example. On the other hand – and this is particularly interesting about Qur'anic text – at the same time, it *created* a new context: a new society and enormous complexity of relations within it, a new religion with all that it brings with it, new aesthetic and poetic postulates in literature, etc. It is explicit in that its aim is to create a new context at the most comprehensive cultural level, but it also – seen historically – gradually added to the context of many important aspects, probably in order to reach the optimum in terms of communication. Finally, it managed to create a new context – an entirely new circle of culture and civilisation. That is why I used the title of my study to define the Oriental-Islamic culture as the universe of the sacred text; at that, in the word *universe* I want to underscore the very dynamism of all its parts for the purpose of functionality of this giant whole. Any ideological bias from a distance becomes inappropriate. The immanent approach allows for immeasurable advantages. Therefore, I believe that scholarly research should indeed use this kind of holistic approach. Moreover, in light of that, there is a repeated confirmation of the belief that the literary challenge of the *Qur'an* for Muhammad's contemporaries (the *shā'ir*, the *kāhin*) has been resolved, since this context has been essentially overcome, and it is better to observe the text – very powerful in a significant part of mankind – in a new context, or contexts, or in the universe of culture it defines. This is also an important part of the immanent approach.

Should we opt for this approach to the *Qur'an* – as an undoubtedly significant text in an important historical and current context – then the category of *'i'jāz* is seen in a new light, with an understanding that is truly different, innovative when compared to the traditionally established aspects of *'i'jāz*, which see it predominantly as a historically delineated text. Contrary to that, it is its continuous contextualisation (which entails the creation of context) that makes it a permanently open and dynamic structure, and since *'i'jāz* is considered (in the Islamic world) to be its inseparable feature, this means that *'i'jāz* is just as dynamic and just as contextualised. In my opinion, it is obsolete to see *'i'jāz* only in terms of knowledge/speech about the of-the-other-side invisible or non-imitative stylistic expression. Studying this text in *context*, it is not difficult to find reasons for the belief in its supranatural nature (*'i'jāz*) in terms of the great powers it demonstrated in the creation of history (as a "context unto itself"), which we can see today, as well as in terms of influence over a considerable part of our contemporary times. This understanding of *'i'jāz* is unusual when compared with the traditional *ulama*-based one – which seems quite reductionist from this vantage point – but I am convinced that there is a basis to see *'i'jāz* in that light, and that such an approach can deliver new results. Since this relationship between text and context is important regarding the *Qur'an*, it arises from this that *'i'jāz* is a kind of process, rather than a finite given. This does not escape the immanent approach.

Scholars who deal with the issue of *'i'jāz* are – as I have already mentioned – prone to establishing it only within the realm of literary expression. Any research into this issue must bear in mind that there is almost a consensus on this in the Islamic world: this fact has greatly influenced the entire Oriental-Islamic culture.

The focus of Oriental studies is usually on Arabian poetry, carefully considered by the *Qur'an* itself, by basing an important aspect of its *'i'jāz* on the aspect of stylistic and general literary supremacy – to the level of supranatural, as Muslims believe. So, poetry is particularly important, as this importance was assigned to it by the *Qur'an* as the fundamental text of the entire culture and, on the other hand, history testifies convincingly to the fact that Arabians, and then the entire Oriental-Islamic culture, expressed their genius very successfully through poetry. Studying the relationship between these two important textual corpuses of culture, there is some controversy or disagreement, as a consequence of (I must repeat this here) different approaches – the "inner" and the "outer" one, the ideologically burdened and the ideologically unburdened one. Since I started this chapter by speaking about the *Qur'an* through indicating the clearly ideologically contaminated positions by the Arabist Gabrieli, it would be appropriate to cite his judgement of Arab poetry, indeed a judgement in keeping with his positions on the *Qur'an*, which he, just like his positions on poetry, presents "in the name of the Western man". This intervention "on behalf of the Western man" or "Western culture" is erroneous on at least two counts. First, Oriental studies include a considerable number of scholars who have expressed views quite different from those of Gabrieli, and I will mention just some of them at a later stage. Second, any initial emphasis on affiliation with Western culture (or any other culture) when approaching another culture expresses an a priori position of a "researcher" who will do anything in his power to interpret the culture which is the subject of his "research" in accordance with the a priori pre-set criteria and models: the object of his "expertise" must be assessed negatively, just because it differs from the works in his own culture. Such positions compromise the entire area of study where the "researcher" works; it equally compromises science in general.

In light of the above, it is not surprising – though it is methodologically unacceptable – that Gabrieli concludes, in his *La letteratura araba*, that "it is futile to search in Arab poetry for any dense construction or inner coherence of classic or modern Western poetry".[12] On the very next page, he concludes, after referring to the authority of T. Nëldeke, that "no pre-Islamic *qaṣīda*, and perhaps no Arab *qaṣīda*, may be called complete poetry".[13]

As for the relationship between the *Qur'an* and poetry, we should recall the opinion of Robert Irwin.[14] Irwin emphasises rightly that the *Qur'an* influenced significantly all the literary forms used by Arabs.[15] I would like to expand this statement, basically accurate and as such useful when studying the *Qur'an* and Arab literature, by stating that the *Qur'an* not only influenced all the literary forms used by Arabs, but also generally had a strong influence on a vast empire of literature created in Oriental-Islamic languages (Arabic, Persian and Ottoman Turkish). Therefore, the *Qur'an* first influenced literature in Arabic, and then this literature strongly influenced the entire literary creation in the Oriental-Islamic cultural realm. In the classical period, literature in Persian and Ottoman Turkish applied the terminology of the Arab tradition and accepted most of the poetic postulates and aesthetic principles – down to the perception of beauty and the notion of creativity as defined in relation to Divine Creation.[16] Classical Oriental-Islamic literature, in fact, belonged to the same poetic system, notwithstanding the fact that it was created in three different languages, and subsequent ethnocentric approaches to this literature are thus unfounded in terms of poetology.[17] Thus, poetological studies of classical literature in these languages shows beyond doubt that the *Qur'an* influenced strongly this entire universe – through the Arabic language and literature, rather than just Arab literature.

Some of Irwin's positions that my study deals with as well may be open for discussion, with full respect for the author. For example, Irwin states:

> As can be seen, the *qaṣīda* moved from topic to topic and much of the poet's skill lay in his ability to make the necessary transitions. Even so, a typical *qaṣīda* is likely to strike a Western reader as lacking all formal unity. It can be, as often was, compared to a loosely threaded string of beads. The earliest Arab poets expected their audience to recognize the scenes and sentiments they were evoking. There was little scope for fantasy in the *qaṣīda*, for it reflected the perceived realities of existence in the desert.[18]

This observation should be followed by a detailed elaboration, in order not to create an impression of a negative valuation of ancient Arab poetry, because of what was unusual to Western recipients. My study tries to prove, using methods of stylistics and poetology, that ancient Arabian *qaṣīda* was pronouncedly realistic, since it was dominated by comparison as the most appropriate stylistic device for presenting the physical and the visible world, as that of the Bedouin was. Only the powerful Qur'anic metaphors would revolutionise the Arabian literary expression, and I established, I hope, a clear link between the predominance of these two stylistic devices in two epochs (pre-Islamic and Islamic) and in the two corpuses with their different perceptions of the world. And it is only in this sense – conditionally, that is – that one speaks about the absence or of the limited presence of imagination in ancient poetry. It is pronouncedly realistic, but not entirely unimaginative, for poetry does – of itself and always – entail a certain degree of imaginativeness, as it is unimaginable without transposing procedures and effects. Any denial of imaginativeness in ancient Arabian poetry would mean that we accept it as a mere biographic or factual notation, which equals an attempt to deny *qaṣīda* as a poem, i.e. as an artistic entity. In fact, the very notions of *shi'r* and *shā'ir* semantically indicate knowledge, as noted by Irwin. However, it is knowledge different from the kind contained in the notion of *'ilm*: *sha'ara* means *to learn by sense, by imagination*.[19] In ancient times, *shā'ir* was the one who learned about the metaphysical, the of-the-other-side, by the very power of imagination and emotion. Therefore, this ability and this quality of a poem are contained in the very notions of *shi'r* and *shā'ir*, which are, in essence, poetological terms. And I focus on this in my study.

Ancient Arabian *qaṣīda* is indeed unusual to a Western recipient. But the question is: what does that actually mean? Is that a value judgement?

Whenever faced with old texts, particularly classical ones, we are faced with a manifest problem of the *vantage point of the present* and the *vantage point of the past.* When studying poems from the sixth or the seventh century in our time, in the twenty-first century, we must count on certain difficulties and peculiarities, particularly so since they were created in a different language, in different poetics and a different culture. In any encounter with ancient texts, be it through reading or interpretation, we face a serious issue that I will refer to here as *the lost context.* This is our severe and unavoidable handicap and it is thus recommendable to try – as much as possible, for we can never be entirely successful – to reconstruct the context of the poem. This also says something relevant about us in the twenty-first century, but we must bear in mind that the poem was written in the sixth century, for example. This kind of caution will add validity to our judgement of ancient poetic work. And it is in this sense that one should consider yet another position by Irwin regarding ancient Arabian poetry, which requires elaboration and observance of different types of contexts. I add this only as a possible illustration of how to observe a particular poetic creation, i.e. the need to contextualise it. Moreover, a certain measure of contextualisation (and I reiterate: it cannot be completed, but one must not give up the attempt) is necessary for the purpose of the immanent approach, the "approach from within". Irwin states that ancient Arabians treated women in the same manner as other material goods and that their descriptions of women were similar to descriptions of camels:

> The *nasīb* dominates the rest of *qaṣīda* and is heavy with an earthly sensuality. The fleshiness of the women is tacitly echoed in the poet's description of the frilled lumps of meat from his slaughtered riding camel, which the women are engaged in cutting up.[20]

To a modern Western reader, this kind of explication is undoubtedly a negative, or rather a very negative recommendation of this poetry, and the consequences are almost immeasurable: ancient Arabian poetry (particularly the *Mu'allaqāt*) are the most important corpus in Oriental-Islamic literature in general, and this statement suggests – perhaps unintentionally – a negative recommendation for this entire poetic tradition.

Such presentation of the ancient Arabian treatment of women illustrates the loss of several types of context or several of its levels. First, it is a matter of the aforementioned *vantage point of the present* and the *vantage point of the past.* Second, this indicates disregard for the fact that this is a work of poetry, not a scholarly or a historical record, which means that the "mechanisms" of transposition and stylisation of reality, the very essence of a work of art, are simply ignored. Third, most importantly, there is disregard for the social context wherein the cited description of a woman was created in a work of art. Descriptions of women using certain attributes of camels do indeed exist in ancient Arabian poetry, but it is necessary to bear in mind that the value of a camel to us today is indeed very different from what it was to an ancient Bedouin. It is a matter of the *sum of values* in the given social ambience, and not the literal elements of description. For a pre-Islamic Bedouin, a camel was one of the primary values in life. If understood in this way – and history indicates that it should be – then the Bedouin's comparison of woman to a camel becomes the opposite: it is clearly positive, because with such a description the Bedouin presents women as the sum of values of importance for life itself, precious to both him and his wife. It is terrifyingly wrong to ignore this kind of context, for the consequences are dramatically negative: nothing is as wrong as a literal interpretation of works of art, particularly of those that were created and "acted" in very different contexts. (Thus, for example, *Jannah* is represented as an oasis: it is wrong to see it literally as a garden full of women and other "hedonist props"; *Jannah* is represented metaphorically – as the sum of the most precious goods a Bedouin could have imagined, i.e. an oasis.) Finally, one is surprised by the sentence: "There is no sign that Imru' al-Qays was interested in the personality of the women he pursued and whose conquest he then boasted of."[21]

This opinion ignores a capital fact, the one I have mentioned before – that a poem cannot be reduced to a biographical note, and that it is degrading for a work of art to try to find any kind of evidence (back in the sixth century, no less!) whether Qays was or was not *interested in the personality* of women he wrote about. Besides, the minute she "moves" to a work of art, a woman stops being a personality: she then transforms into a character, transposed from reality into a different kind of reality.

As for the earlier statement that ancient Arabian poetry is unusual for Western recipients, something else needs to be added here, something that re-emphasises the importance of context. Namely, Westerners are distanced from this poetry in more ways than one (which is quite normal), for it is simply a matter of two different worlds, but it should be noted that the complex context of their ancient poetry is lost to modern Arabs too: it is distant to them in several aspects – poetic, social, even linguistic, since it is, after all, an ancient language.[22]

One of the fundamental questions regarding the relationship between the *Qur'an* and poetry emphasised by some scholars is the question of structural changes in the *qaṣīda* in the so-called interim period (*muḥaḍramūn*). James Montgomery thus wonders if the structural changes in the *qaṣīda* noted, for example, in the work of al-Aʿshā and Labīd, are the consequence of influences of the *Qur'an* or just natural poetic evolution.[23] He focuses in particular on the poetry of Kaʿb Ibn Zuhayra when considering structural changes in the *qaṣīda*.

This issue is both important and complicated. It is hard to assume that structural changes in the *qaṣīda* (change of position of certain themes, or exclusion of some of the themes of the pre-Islamic *qaṣīda*) happened through spontaneous poetic evolution. Historical facts strongly oppose such an assumption. Namely, as poeticised text, the *Qur'an* affected strongly the found literary tradition. It confronted poetry explicitly and implicitly: on one hand, it emphasised numerous times that the Prophet was not a poet, that what it presented to people was not poetry in the sense in which poetry it had found, but rather – it explained – words of God; on the other hand, and at the same time, the *Qur'an* cherished the value of its own literary expression, trying to overshadow the values and the influences of the poetry it had found and of the *saj'*. Moreover, it is beyond dispute that one of the fundamental aspects of *'i'jāz* has been proved in the domain of the supranatural aspect of the Qur'anic literary expression. In light of these historical facts, then, one cannot speak about a natural or a spontaneous poetic evolution, in a sense that it did not come about independently from Qur'anic text. I believe that the antagonism of the *Qur'an* towards one type of poetry (the type will be discussed later) intervened strongly, even dramatically, in the poetics of the found poetic tradition, specifically in the domain of structure of the *qaṣīda*, or rather in its ideological aspect. This poetic aspect requires attention: this study does exactly that. In short and moving forward from Montgomery's reasoned assumption, poetry did change in the time of the Prophet, or rather the time of *muḥaḍramūn*, but this change was brought about by intervention of the *Qur'an*, and not by natural evolution, independently from it. The *Qur'an* intervened in poetry in terms of content, or rather in terms of ideology, since it condemned the primary task of pre-Islamic poets, considered a medium between fellow tribesmen and metaphysical forces, and using poetic, rhymed and rhythmical words for that purpose. This was radical reorganisation of poetry in the area of poetics. Poetry dwelled in this state for a short while and after that, particularly during the Umayyad and further on in history, it blossomed in the true sense of the word. Scholars noted rightly that pre-Islamic poetry – in the form that reached our times – did not contain any traces of pre-Islamic beliefs, which is a paradox in light of the fact confirmed by the *Qur'an* many times, that a poet was considered a medium between humans and supranatural forces. What happened with that part of ancient Arabian poetry?

Here too, a logical supposition is linked to the position of the *Qur'an* in the universe that was being created at the time. Namely, for a long time, pre-Islamic poetry had lived in oral tradition and its written record started in the eigth century, which was relatively late in terms of the strong and constant opposition between the *Qur'an* and the poetry often referred to as *pagan* from the vantage point of Islam; it is thus normal to assume that early philosophers, who started recording poetry, de-paganised this corpus in a way. There are historical records by Arabs themselves, for example, Khalaf al-Ahmar (d. 796), who were prone to forging ancient poetry. A similar, interventionist approach was present on other occasions, and also in other cultures.[24] In any case, there is an evident problem of authenticity of pre-Islamic Arabian poetry (Ar. *ṣiḥḥa al-shi'r al-jāhilī*), with a plethora of referential works written about this in the Arab world and in Oriental studies.[25] This fact obliges us to be fairly cautious when it comes to the structure of pre-Islamic poetry and the influence of the *Qur'an* over it. In fact, it was thanks to the *Qur'an* that this poetry has been preserved, though not in its authentic form. The fundamental if not the only motive for recording this poetry was the exegesis of the *Qur'an* in the aspects of language and style: scholars, theologians in particular, needed a linguistic, or rather a literary "background" for interpreting the *Qur'an* and, at the same time, proving its supremacy (*'i'jāz*) in the field of language and the use of literary devices.

As for the relationship between the *Qur'an* and poetry, there is another "place" of particular contestation in Oriental studies that deserves full attention. It also negates indirectly the claim about an alleged fabrication of pre-Islamic poetry. This contested place relates to the alleged anathema/prohibition of poetry in Qur'anic text, ensuring an important precondition for a negative attitude towards the *Qur'an* – for what kind of a book is it that banishes poetry from a culture, despite the fact that this very poetry was the most successful form of artistic expression in that culture?! At that, interpreters base their conclusions regarding the *Qur'an* and poetry on ayahs 224–227 at the end of Surah 26 (*The Poets*). For example, Irwin, whose study I have cited here, ends his presentation of the *Qur'an* with ayahs that, according to him, openly condemn poets. It is almost incredible that Irwin cites ayahs 221–225, and leaves out the crucial ayah (227) wherein the *Qur'an* exempts one type of poets, and Irwin thus draws an erroneous conclusion about the overall attitude of the *Qur'an* towards poets. I will expand on ayah 227 in the text that follows.

It is interesting, for example, that Goethe understood the end of Surah 26 as a *humiliation* of poets, and inspired by it, on 7 or 8 March 1815, he wrote the poem *Indictment*.[26] Goethe's opinion on this is particularly important, since he is one of the most important minds in the entire human history. As such, he developed particularly close contacts with the Oriental-Islamic culture (and the *Qur'an* and poetry in particular), which contributed to extraordinary achievements in his work, and through that in European culture in general. It seems to be reckless to refer to this ennobling contact as *influence* of either "side", since the very word *influence* seems one-sided and simplistic: it is incapable of expressing the complexity of beneficial relationships and results engendered through encounters of truly great minds such as, for example, Goethe and Hafez.

In any case, the claim that the *Qur'an* prohibits or condemns poetry is incorrect and has, as such, far-reaching consequences in terms of understanding the *Qur'an*, the vast poetic tradition and the Oriental-Islamic culture as a whole. If such a claim is to be accepted – and I will demonstrate how wrong that would be – there would then be a reason to ask the question cited earlier: What kind of fundamental text of an entire culture is it if it forbids poetry?! Consequently, there would be a conclusion on ethical disqualification of Muslims in general as hypocrites, since for hundreds of years, despite the alleged prohibition by the *Qur'an*, they cherished poetry en masse as their supreme art. Therefore, one could say that the *Qur'an* condemns poets and hypocrites, but Muslims too are hypocrites, since they cherish poetry despite the Qur'anic prohibition.

It is sufficient to read carefully and without prejudice ayahs 221–227 to reach an unambiguous conclusion that the *Qur'an* condemns the pre-Islamic poet as the *shā'ir*. Understanding the *Qur'an* is based on context. From the point of view of Islam, the pre-Islamic poet was a pagan poet, since he introduced himself as a medium of metaphysical forces and used the poetic verse to that end. The *Qur'an* condemns that kind of poetry: *And the poets, only the deviators follow them/Do you not see that in the valley they roam/And that they say what they do not do*. This is a serious ethical disqualification of the pre-Islamic poet who claimed to be in contact with the metaphysical forces, to be acting in accordance with that, thus a very respected though not the most respected member of his community. In many other instances, the *Qur'an* supports these very ayahs, insisting that what the Prophet says are not words of a poet, but rather the pure, divine truth.

Such critical attitude of the *Qur'an* towards this status of the poet in his community is not unique in history: allow me to recall Plato, although there have been many similar philosophical stands on poetry after him. Plato – and this is a general point of reference – banished poets from his ideal republic (the famous Book X) because they arouse emotions and, allegedly, act irrationally, thus "clouding reason" and obstructing the philosophers who are supposed to run the state.

It is unusual, to say in the least, how interpreters of the relationship between the *Qur'an* and poetry overlook the last ayah (227) of this Surah (26): "… save those who believe and do good works, and remember Allah much …". Thereby the Qur'anic disqualification excludes poets who behave and act as Muslims. From the vantage point of this ayah – the final, or the concluding one on this topic – things look quite different: implicitly, this is a recommendation of the poetry that disowns the prerogatives of pagan ideology, as borne by the pre-Islamic *shā'ir*. This is quite clear in this ayah, and this can be overlooked only by those who are, as researchers, reckless and unconscientious, or wish to render a biased interpretation. In that sense, Montgomery questions the common opinion that the *Qur'an* adopts a negative stance on poets. At that, he cites authors who claimed, justifiably, that the *Qur'an* did not condemn poetry in general, but rather that through these ayah it criticised particular poetic genres. Such authors include Margoliouth, Blachère and Zwitter, and in the Islamic world the authoritative al-Zamahsharī.[27] And finally, in an act of particular importance for the history of Oriental-Islamic literature, Prophet Muhammad affirmed poetry compliant with Islamic norms, i.e. poetry that is, in compliance with the *Qur'an*, free from pre-Islamic religious content. Namely, when Ka'b Ibn Zuhayr recited to him a panegyric that started with the words "*Bānat Su'ād* ..." (that is, a panegyric to the Prophet and thus to Islam), the Prophet removed his mantle and wrapped it around the poet's shoulders. This was a clear sign of reciprocal praise to the poet.[28] In terms of literary history and poetology, this robe – as an expression of the highest praise, particularly at the level of the sacred – did not wrap the poet personally, but rather his poem (figuratively, of course) as the poetic guidance to new poetry – the poetry of the Islamic era. This historical fact should not be interpreted as an act of the Prophet's protection of panegyric poetry, or a possible guidance on how Islam places poetry in the service of its own promotion. Kaʿb's poem had numerous elements of the traditional *qaṣīda*, but the most important thing for the Prophet was – in compliance with the *Qur'an* – that poets did not convey pre-Islamic religious cults and beliefs, but rather that they recognised him as the religious authority. The *Qur'an* intervened at this watershed of epochs and, in particular, at this watershed of poetics, allowing a poetically redesigned poetry, which blossomed already in the Umayyad period. The *Qur'an* thus confirmed to the Prophet its own superiority in the realm of literary expression, and reaffirmed its own religious prerogatives as well, granting enormous space to poetry, provided it did not collide with Islamic norms. Is it possible today to even imagine the Oriental-Islamic culture – vast in both space and time – without its literature, primarily its poetry?!

In general, the Oriental-Islamic culture has relatively exciting scholarly discoveries waiting further ahead; by that I mean new research successes, largely dependent on methodological approaches. I believe that innovativeness definitely lies ahead, and I draw this belief from the knowledge about current results of research in the Oriental-Islamic culture, which come from the two approaches I presented briefly. I say this in general terms, aware of the risks arising from generalisations, exceptions notwithstanding. Allow me to refer to such an exception, but first I must specify the two types of approach to the Oriental-Islamic culture. With that I return to the starting point of this chapter.

In the Oriental-Islamic world itself, the dominant methods of study of the Oriental-Islamic culture are those that are pronouncedly traditionalist. In this study, I illustrate this point through traditionalist approaches to *'i'jāz* and ancient Arabian poetry. Namely, there is in the Oriental-Islamic world a myriad of traditional studies that are a deviation of sorts of the immanent approach: there has been a transition from immanence to hermetic closure, and this kind of approach is doomed to collapse. When traditional approaches become traditionalist, horizons of science become restricted. One needs to re-read al-Baqillānī, or al-Zamahsharī, but not to define their oeuvre in this time as *non plus ultra*, but rather to be an incentive towards *plus ultra*. At that, it is important to take into account, most seriously, the methodology that has been well developed in the West, although its application in Oriental studies is often problematic. Requirements include full methodological competence, coherence and consistency.[29]

On the other hand, some Oriental studies approaches have been burdened by the fact that they completely ignore the advantages of the immanent method; not only that – they often take the very fact of differentiation as the basis for promoting their own cultural supremacy in relation to inferiority of "others". This antagonising approach is wrong. A culture is to be studied from within itself, and differences are to be promoted for what they are – as the richness of "world culture" (to paraphrase Goethe's notion of *world literature*), rather than antagonising them or deducing any conclusions abut alleged supremacy.

An example I wanted to underscore in this context is a text by Margaret Larkin. She is aware of the importance of the immanent method in studying the Oriental-Islamic culture, and she states that we observe how scientific categories and scholarly paradigms devised in the West have been imposed unnaturally onto the science and culture of the Islamic world. The first challenge for a scholar in the West is to draw conclusions from the texts themselves, rather than try to adapt those texts to his or her pre-defined expectations.[30]

Indeed, good results may be achieved through the immanent method, using impressive methodological experiences accumulated in the West, but with no, or anyone's, ideological burdens, for they impede valid scientific results. Ronald Barthes (with whom I started this chapter) was right – to paraphrase him: one should read the classics over and over again, and be prepared for re-canonisation.

Notes

1 Roland Barthes, *Critique et vérité*, Édition du Seuil, 1966. I used this book in Bosnian translation: Roland Barthes, *Kritika i istina*, translated by Lada Čale Feldman, Algoritam, Zagreb, 2009, p. 33.

2 Their oeuvres are large and very important for the field of science discussed here. See the titles in the Bibliography.

3 I used this work by Gabrieli in translation into Bosnian: Francesco Gabrieli, *Arapska književnost*, translated by Milana Piletić and Srđan Music, Svjetlost, Sarajevo, 1985, p. 59.

4 Yusuf Rahman, "The miraculous nature of Muslim scripture: A study of 'Abd al-Jabbar's iʿjāz al-Qur'an", *Islamic Studies* 35 (1996): 409–424.

5 Rahman, op. cit., p. 413.

6 Nasr Abu-Zayd, "The dilemma of the literary approach to the Qur'an", *Alif: Journal of Comparative Poetics* 23 (2003): 14.

7 Cf. Mustansir Mir, "Some figures of speech in the Qur'an", *Religion & Literature* 40, 3 (Autumn 2008): 32.

8 Cf. Anthony Johns, "A humanistic approach to i'jāz in the Qur'an: The transfiguration of language", *Journal of Qur'anic Studies* 13, 1 (2011): 81.

9 Ibid., p. 81.

10 Ibid., p. 82.
11 Ibid., p. 32.
12 Ibid., p. 26.
13 Gabrieli, op. cit., p. 27.
14 I am also familiar with his work entitled *The Arabian Nights: A Companion*. It has been translated into Bosnian: Robert Irwin, *1001 noć na Zapadu*, translated by Enes Karić, Tugra, Sarajevo, 1999. This work was interesting also in light of the fact that my translation of *A Thousand and One Nights* was published in Sarajevo in 1999; this is so far the only integral translation of *Nights* into any of the languages of former Yugoslavia directly from the original Arabic.
15 Robert Irwin, *Nights and Horses and Desert: An Anthology Classical of Arabic Literature*, Anchor Books, London, 2002.
16 The perception of *beauty* and the notion of *creation* in relation to God's creation in classical Oriental-Islamic literature are very similar to those in medieval European literature. See Rosario Assunto, *Die Theorie des Schönen im Mittelater*, Verlag M. DuMont Schauberg, Köln, 1963. See also Ernst Robert Curtius, *Europäische Literatur und Lateinisches Mittelater*, Francke Verlag Bern und München Dritte Auflage, 1961.
17 I have just (2014) written a study on this, entitled *Poetika klasične književnosti na orijentalno-islamskim jezicima* [Poeticism of Classical Literature in Oriental-Islamic Languages].
18 Irwin, op. cit., p. 5.
19 Cf. *Qur'ān*, 2:154.
20 Irwin, op. cit., p. 12.
21 Irwin, op. cit., p. 13.
22 Since I published an integral translation of *The Seven Odes* (*Sedam mu'allāqa*, Sarajevo, 2004), I have had numerous opportunities to observe a positive surprise even by Arabs with sound knowledge of literature, stating that those are poems that even they cannot understand without well-elaborated annotations, and that they too find them unusual.
23 James Montgomery, "Sundry observations on the fate of poetry in the early Islamic period", in J. R. Smart (ed.), *Tradition and Modernity in Arabic Language and Literature*, Richmond, Curzon Press, 1996, p. 51.
24 For example, the work *Kalila and Dimna*, assigned to the translation work by 'Abdullāh Ibn al-Muqaffa' (d. 756.), went through a kind of Islamisation: this notable piece of *adab*, al-Muqaffa' introduced the noun *Allah*, and even quoted the ayahs, and we know today, on the basis of translation of this work into the Syrian language, as well as from other sources, that it originates from Indian literature in Sanskrit, and that al-Muqaffa' transposed it into Arabic from the Pahlavi language of the pre-Islamic period. Moreover, *A Thousand and One Nights* reached eighteenth-century Europe in translation by the French Arabist Galland, who was so inventive that, when observed today, the original is barely recognisable when compared with Galland's translation.
25 There are even radical hypotheses, which I find unacceptable, that the entire pre-Islamic poetry was invented in the Islamic era and assigned to invented poets. Even Taha Hussein once put forward such a hypothesis (in his work *Fī al-shi'r al-jāhilī*, 1926), but he subsequently revised it considerably, in *Fī al-adab al-jāhilī*.
26 Katharina Mommsen, *Goethe under der Islam*, Insel Verlag, Frankfurt am Main and Leipzig, 2001. I used this book in its Bosnian translation: *Goethe i islam*, translated by Vedad Smailagić, Dobra knjiga, Sarajevo, 2008, p. 279.
27 Montgomery, op. cit., pp. 51–53.
28 That is why history of literature knows this poem as *Qaṣīda al-burda* (Qasida of the Mantle). For a very long time, this poem served as an inspiration to other Muslim poets, notably al-Būṣīrī (b. 1212).

29 Thus, for example, the interpretation of *'i'jāz* includes a very problematic view, that superiority of the *Qur'an* rests on its content, and not its style. Cf. Abu-Zayd, op. cit., p. 11. In a literary text of high aesthetic values, it is impossible to determine its superiority by breaking it down into content and style/form in this way: the work exists as an entity – content and form combined.

30 Cf. Margaret Larkin, "The inimitability of the Qur'an: Two perspectives", *Religion & Literature* 20, 1 (Spring, 1988): 23.

Preface to the English-language edition

This book, published in the Bosnian language in 2007, was immediately well received by the academic community of Bosnia and Herzegovina, and was declared the country's best scholarly work of 2007 by the Publishers' and Bookseller's Association of Bosnia and Herzegovina. It was not long before the author was being urged to publish the book in English translation.

Since readers of English and Bosnian approach a text in different ways, a brief introduction to the method and aims of the work is needed for those who are reading the book in English, even though both are seen as its potential audience.

My basic aim in writing the book was to propose a new reading of ancient and classical Arabic literature, which in my view is not properly presented in the majority of orientalist works. I also believe that we need a scholarly approach to and analysis of the very complex relations within Eastern Islamic culture that constitute its literature and the Qur'anic text. Even the periodisation of Arabic literature has yet to be properly determined, both in Oriental studies and in the Arabic world, given that it has always been studied using methods that are non-immanent, do not pertain to literary studies or are ideologically heavily loaded. A valid periodisation of literature derives from methodological competence and a thorough knowledge of the material. The non-literary, "extraneous" approach to Arabic literature is an obstacle that needs to be overcome.

Ancient and classical Arabic literature, which constitutes the central focus of my research, differs greatly, poetically speaking, from ancient Greek and medieval European literature, which has led many of those studying this literature to view this very difference as traditional inferiority. Though not alone in doing so, the late Edward Said, a highly regarded scholar, unmasked the ideological lens of orientalism.

As a professor of Arabic literature at the University of Sarajevo, I am aware of the merits of orientalism, but also of its shortcomings as regards the study of ancient and classical Arabic literature. I also know that literature is the kind of material about which no final judgement can be made, no definitive system of values can be established, because *as value* it is realised in relations, not as a succession of immutable, objective facts.

Seen from these critical positions, I could have written a book contesting the methods and value judgements that appear invalid to me when applied to Arabic literature and its place in the universe of Eastern Islamic culture. This approach would have meant embarking on direct polemics with recent works in Western oriental studies; and it would also have required a much longer book, perhaps even several volumes. In any event, it would have had to be a very different book from this one.

In rejecting this option, I felt the need to write a book that was neither a compilation of Western thinking in this field nor a direct reference to the literature in question. Quite simply, I believe that we need a new reading, a new interpretation and assessment of ancient and classical Arabic literature, but from within that literature itself, not against the background of the findings of recent works in oriental studies or the study of Islamic literature. I did not want to burden *my own reading* of the literary material with works with which I am familiar but which would have led me into direct confrontation or (compilatory) approval. This is why my book disregards the dominant Western thinking in this field. By adding to *Further reading* in English, I wish to offer readers the opportunity to compare or contrast my findings with the works in this field with which I am familiar – and, of course, with many others.

I have been teaching Arabic literature at the university for almost forty years, during which time I trust I have acquired sufficient methodological competence and familiarity with this field to be able to address it by the immanent method. This entails a direct approach to the material, unmediated by the writings of orientalists and Arabists on the subject, and even without translation. I believe that this is a good way to present ancient and classical Arabic literature from within, since this approach paves the way for potential new findings. As well as works of literature as such, I also include among original material works of classical *Arabic* philology, in order to focus my research with optimum effect on the literature that is the subject of study as well as on *classical Arabic* writings on that same literature. The aim is to propose a new reading for our day, based directly on that material. This is the essence of the method I call immanent.

My approach to the Qur'anic text is the same – I seek to interpret it from within, immanently, without feeling bound to consult the vast opus of exegetic works, which would be a dangerous path towards compilation and epigonism. I believe that in placing the Qur'anic text as the pivotal text of this culture, I am not making this a work of theology (that is for the reader to judge) but, which is my intention, a scholarly work, for it seeks to demonstrate, using the methods of literary criticism, how great the influence of the Qur'anic text on Arabic literature as a whole has been. There is valid literary historical and poetological evidence for this, which I seek to outline in a new reading.

Roland Barthes has aptly remarked that no age has the right to "believe that it alone holds the canonical meaning of a work."

> We should not be surprised that a country should periodically review … the things which come down from its past and describe them anew in order to find out *what it can make of them*: such activities are and ought to be normal assessment procedures.
>
> (Roland Barthes, *Critique et vérité*, translated as *Criticism and Truth* by Katrine Pilcher Keunemann, The Athlone Press, 2007 edition, pp. 25, 1)

It is this very need that prompted me to write this book.

The author

About the author

Dr Esad Duraković (b. 1948) is a full-time professor of the Arabic language and Arabic literature at the Faculty of Philosophy, University of Sarajevo. He is a full member of the Academy of the Arabic Language in Damascus, the Academy of the Arabic Language in Cairo and the Academy of Sciences and Arts of Bosnia and Herzegovina. He is a world-renowned scientist and translator who has won numerous awards in Bosnia and Herzegovina and across the world, among which is the very prestigious Sharjah Prize for Arab Culture (2003) awarded by UNESCO. The general public also know him for his inspired and exceptional translations of the key works in Arabic literature – *One Thousand and One Nights* and *al-Muallaqat*, and the particularly appreciated translation of the *Qur'an* that, in terms of stylistics, represents a major breakthrough compared to the previous translations into Bosnian. No less valuable are his translations of works belonging to contemporary Arabic literature, from Gibran to Jabra, from poetry of the twentieth-century Arabic East to Hanan al-Shaykh. With regard to Duraković's academic work, which perfectly complements his translations, one should certainly mention the following: *Poetics of Arabic Literature in the USA*, *Arabic Rhetoric in Bosnia*, *Ahmed son of Hasan Bosniak on Metaphor*, *Prolegomenon to Literary History of Oriental-Islamic Circle*, *Style as an Argument*, *Over the Text of the Qur'an*, *Qur'an: Stylistic and Mathematical Miracle.* Numerous stylistic interpretations of the Qur'an, a true novum in this field, motivated the author to write his Routledge edition of *The Poetics of Ancient and Classical Arabic Literature: Orientology*.

Introduction

This book is largely and essentially on the poetics of ancient Arabic literature. However, consequent research of this huge system entailed studying some other aspects of Oriental Islamic spirituality as well, primarily those poetic postulates recognisable in Oriental Islamic arts in general – as principles of creativity in an impressive system that, on the historical vertical, stretches from pre-Islamic Arabian poetry to the Renaissance of the eighteenth century and, in the "spatial dimension", from the same poetry in ancient Arabia to Bosniak authors in Oriental languages in the fifteenth, sixteenth or seventeenth centuries.

Ancient Arabic literature is a realm of poetry. Prose literary forms emerged rather late, and even then remained in the shadow of poetic creative efforts. Therefore, even today it is not surprising that the Arabic language has no other term for *poetics* than *the art of poetry* (*fann al-shi'r* or *al-shi'riyya*). Naturally, this fact affected the content of my book: it is based on the poetics of Old Arabic poetry encompassing the epoch of Classicism, which tends to be inadequately denominated by literary historians.

It was actually the problem of the periodisation of Arabic literature that instigated my research. In the Arab world, as in Oriental studies in general, there has been no immanent periodisation; rather, it is derived from and denominated according to political epochs in the history of the Arab-Islamic world (*Umayyad literature*, *Abbasid literature*, etc.). Such an approach suggests that Arabic literature, having developed in a vast territory over centuries, is not treated immanently and as a system but is rather parcelled into separate periods, revealing nothing about the literature itself.

During some three decades of studying Arabic literature as a university professor, I have always been deeply dissatisfied with the approaches to Old Arabic literature that presented it in positivist terms – as a chronological account and a philologically ordered overview positioning this striking production within various strictly delimited historical and *political* periods. This literature has had the misfortune of having been mostly dealt with by philologists (Arab and Orientalist ones): while they deserve great credit for discovering and presenting sources in philological terms, because of the nature of their discipline philologists cannot grasp literature as *artistic value* being realised, expressly as a value, in extremely dynamic relations towards other works and other literary – not political – epochs.

In order to grasp and present this impressive literary tradition precisely as a tradition – and, consequently, as a continuity maintained through both reproducing and transcending already created values – its poetics must be established as a very broadly conceived system that reasonably discards unfounded parcelling and incoherent denominations.

This profusely rich tradition must evidently be grasped from within, from the tradition itself, and the poetic postulates of Old Arabic literature must be marked and explicated by means of proper scientific methodology pertaining to poetics. It is equally necessary to establish the degree of their persistence in tradition, or their ability to modify in order to keep the tradition vibrant. Only such an approach will fully expose the inadequacy of the generally accepted periodisation of Old (and Classical) Arabic literature.

At the same time I must point out that, using the term *orientology* – which assumes the great responsibility of a title – I must strongly distance myself from the ideologically contaminated terms *orientalism* or *oriental studies*; using the term *orientology*, I wish to indicate a scientific, non-Eurocentric method in approaching this field of research, as well as the immanent nature of analysis and value judgements. In addition, despite their being amazed, a careful reader can also discover a number of other connotations or contents in the term *orientology* – including a specific communication with, for instance, the works of Edward Said and Jacques Derrida.

My research has led me to conclude that Old Arabic literature is a remarkably coherent system in poetical terms, that it has its own individuality which is, in many aspects, explored in this book, and that certain conventional notions of and judgements about it – such as a negative judgement about the "materialistic nature" of ancient Arabic poetry – arise from failures to understand the poetic principles of this tradition. In general, many phenomena in this literature assume quite a different appearance when, employing an immanent method, they are presented in a living poetic system. Moreover, a proper definition of constituent poetic elements and a careful analysis of their function within Arab-Islamic culture reveal the high degree of their universalism. Namely, on the one hand, they appear self-confident and powerful enough to form a separate system beyond Arabic literature – even beyond the literatures of other Islamic peoples in their pre-modern development. On the other hand, these poetic elements are revealed as constituents of other artistic forms – from the ornamental arabesque to other forms. This actually portrays poetics, which is universalised in the Arab-Islamic world, as a very broad system of artistic creativity in general.

A parallel between Old Arabic literature and that of ancient Greece and Europe will strongly impose itself on a reader unfamiliar with the former. Although these literatures developed independently, it must be acknowledged that the cradle of Arabic literature is its antiquity (so-called Pre-Islamic literature), and that this antiquity influenced later Arabic literature in a way similar to how ancient Greek literature influenced what would become European literature, or medieval Latin literature. Certainly, there are considerable differences between them, but their similarities are many and can be of interest to comparativists.

Consequent research into the poetics of Old Arabic literature has led me to an unexpected conclusion. Namely, the Qur'anic Text appears to be the pivotal text of this literature, although it developed hundreds of years after the Text's advance on history. It is well known that the *Qur'an* directly confronted the poetry of the time, but research into the poetics of Old Arabic literature reveals that all the "post-Qur'anic" literature, especially poetry, came to be defined against it. The force of the Text proved to be unpredictably powerful; this force is brought to light and given full meaning by an immanent study of literature as a poetic system. Thus, quite unexpectedly, the constitution and interpretation of Old Arabic literature also imposes itself as a particular exegesis of the sacred Text. Given the pivotal position of the Qur'anic Text, I must caution the reader about something important.

My analysis of the *Qur'an*'s relationship to poetry at the level of ideology and of form – in all the aspects of their ideological and poetic juxtaposition – may sometimes seem a priori or an analysis tendentiously promoting an exceptional position of the sacred Text in relation to other forms of the tradition. I am aware that no tendentiousness befits the science that this book aspires to. Appreciating, therefore, that poetics, as a coherent system established on the principle of immanence, cannot tolerate any form of prejudice whatsoever – which also applies to science in general – and being aware that poetics cannot be articulated in this manner, I must draw the reader's attention to the fact that my methodological approach is immanent in nature. This means that the book offers a consistent interpretation of the immanent poetic postulates of the *Qur'an*, on the one hand, and of poetry, on the other, as well as an interpretation of their relations also implicit in the tradition itself. Thus, a reader who is outside this tradition and is not quite familiar with the *Qur'an* as its fundamental Text may, on occasion, have the impression that I am constructing a prejudiced position. Furthermore, one cannot exclude the possibility that such a perception may result from the reader's a priori attitude. Being aware of the danger of possible objections along these lines, I have always made my analysis and drawn my conclusions from the position of the Text, free from any prejudice. It is always about the position of the Text. The influence of the Text in this tradition is truly strong and diverse, so that in many aspects it also represented a discovery I was led to by consistency in this immanent approach. Because of this I believe the results of this research will be all the more interesting.

1 Poetics of the Arabesque

Literary traditions of the two great cultural circles – Western and Arab-Islamic, including Oriental-Islamic – have always co-existed under a particular type of aesthetic and poetic misunderstanding.

The leading works of Arabic-Islamic culture are not perceived in the same way in the West as they are in the East. This is best illustrated by representative works, or corpuses. The corpus of *Seven Golden Odes of Arabia* (*al-Mu'allaqāt*, sixth century) is a brilliant representation of ancient Arab-Islamic writing, and whose authority in this tradition cannot be compared to any other poetic corpus. However, in the West – in integral translations, whose frequency does not correspond to the significance of the corpus, yet another illustration of inadequate interest in it – over the centuries, it has failed to depart from the circle of interest of specialised philologists or from narrow academic circles. This is, of course, "damaging" to both traditions: the Arab one is deprived of being represented to another tradition in one of its most extraordinary forms, and the Western tradition is deprived of an adequate encounter with the most authentic corpus of the ancient period of a culture of global importance.

There is an even greater misunderstanding in the reception of the *Qur'an*. In the Arab-Islamic East, the *Qur'an* is not merely the absolute and self-sufficient source and fountain of religion, but it is also, at the same time, the Miracle of the Word, so that in this tradition it has a very strong effect as a true miracle of language and composition: its power and authority rest not only on the argumentation of ideology, but also on its aesthetics. Western culture may speak abut general agreement or denial of the *Qur'an* at the level of ideology, but this perception generally fails to take into account its superb literary and aesthetic values, which, in the realm of the Arabic language, use divine *aesthetic argumentation* to demonstrate its literary, aesthetically, stylistically and linguistically supernatural nature. For students of Arabic are aware of the fact that the literary and aesthetic level of the text of the *Qur'an* cannot be translated in full, or at least to a large extent, to any other language: it remains the Miracle of the Word in Arabic. That is why the *Qur'an* reads differently in every translation – and the West only knows it through translation – which is why its perception in this very important aspect remains inadequate.

There is, however, a different key example.

In the West, ever since Galland's first introduction of it to Europe in the early eighteenth century, *One Thousand and One Nights* has been admired by all generations, from all social strata and intellectual levels: this is writing valued as a miracle of narration and composition, as a principal work in the history of culture. At the same time, *One Thousand and One Nights* is perceived differently in the East: in the golden era of the Arabic-Islamic culture. It was not even included in the realm of the *adab* (literature in the widest sense of the notion); it was, instead, left to popular tastes and entertainment. Even today, in the pronouncedly Said-based orientalisation of the Orient, *One Thousand and One Nights* fails to win the status of a work of art of special value, although Arabic writers, educated in the West and themselves good, perhaps excessively good connoisseurs of its literary tradition, try to promote *One Thousand and One Nights* and seek inspiration from it. In the East, it is read differently.

Other examples from the history of literature could be offered to confirm this rule, though it is sufficient to list works and corpuses from the very foundations of the tradition. Two important differences between the Arab-Islamic tradition and the Western one should be added to this.

First, the Arabic literary history is dominantly lyrical. There is no epic in the tradition; this is a literary and historical fact requiring separate elaboration.

Second, this tradition has no plays. Drama was introduced into Arabic literature only in modern times, though its artistic value, its modest production and its relatively reluctant reception keep it much more an *import* from Western tradition rather than an authentic Arab-Islamic artistic expression. This tradition ignored Aristotle's *Poetics*, although it was translated several times and Aristotle did leave a considerable legacy in philosophy.[1]

It is evident that there were two-way contacts between the two traditions quite early, but their more impressive and fruitful communication did not take place on a larger scale, or in the way it happened in some other spiritual areas. There are exceptions, particularly more modern and quite notable – such as Goethe on one side, or Ghubran (Jubrān Khalīl Jubrān, 1883–1931)[2] on the other – but these are still just exceptions and individual oeuvres, whereas literary traditions as such remained historically separated.

The reason for this delineation of traditions is manifold: the phenomenon is too complex and too deeply rooted in history to be explained with a single or a simple reason. The basic reasons for such persistent separation rest in the different sources of Arab-Islamic tradition, wherein there are certain key factors, firmly interconnected: the philosophy of time and the understanding of man's position in the world, and the peculiarity of Arab, as well as Arab-Islamic poetics.

The poeticism of the arabesque is the principal structural and aesthetic principle, always dominant in Arab-Islamic art, as well as Oriental-Islamic art in general – particularly so in literature, which is the form of art where the Arab and Arab-Islamic genius found its most authentic expression and greatest amount of reasoned self-confidence. The astonishing difference from the literature of the Western culture originates, in fact, from the Arab-Islamic poetics of the arabesque, which is incapable – or self-contentedly unwilling – to adapt to any tradition based on different poetic postulates. This, of course, engenders different perceptions of supreme artistic values, for what is highly valued in one tradition may not be subject to the same value judgement in another.

As manifestly normative, the poetics of the arabesque was promoted in the earliest stages of artistic literary production of this tradition – in the pre-Islamic Arab period, i.e. in the *Golden Odes* as the most prominent poetic corpus and poetic expression of Arab-Islamic tradition as a whole. Arabesque as an ornamental form was promoted in the ninth century, in the arabesque of Andalusia, and was later perfected in the Oriental-Islamic world. However, a kind of arabesque that cannot be reduced to a typically Islamic *ornamentation* did exist much earlier – as a constructive and aesthetic principle – in the best pre-Islamic poetry, in the *Qur'an*, and in an entire series of significant works, including *One Thousand and One Nights*, dominated by this very principle of construction and aesthetics. Ornamental Islamic arabesque is just one expression of this aesthetic principle, which also determined the art of the word as the dominant feature of the overall tradition.

Although the ornamental arabesque is well known, a reminder should be presented here, however sketchy, of its main features, in order to facilitate further observations on the structural effects of the same principle in literature.

The arabesque is usually a floral ornamentation, with the stem branching out in a particular rhythm and with elements of repetition, with added leaves neither cut off nor isolated; however, they do not simply grow out of the stem. Namely, the stylistic form realises a very important element of the arabesque, that elements complement each other, penetrate each other, merge with each other, etc., so that the branch, for example, as the superficial "axis" or "dominant element" of the arabesque, withdraws itself in order to realise the principal idea – interweaving and mutual penetration. Leaves of the arabesque are more than leaves on a branch: they do not shoot out of the stem, but rather they grow into it, envelop it and give it aesthetic quality. Upon noting a segment in it and beginning to follow it, an observer of the arabesque notes that this segment becomes repetitive, with less pronounced modifications, as one seemingly dominant motif suddenly withdraws before another motif or a group of motifs, also later vacating the space for another. With this rhythmically harmonised repetition, this constant "branching out" and "leafing out", the arabesque leads the observer's eye on a quest for its end and imposes sudden awareness of some of its features.

First, the observer starts from a detail itself not decisive for the aesthetic experience of the work (which will prove to be important for a later analogy with literature) and observes very quickly that the details strive to be repetitive ad infinitum. Thus the segmentation of elements and their repetitiveness are determined as the key structural principle of the "lower level". Fragments are initially self-sufficient; the segmentation of the arabesque shows that a *single* element is what it is, but it purposefully and unnoticeably moves into *another*, aesthetically devising *itself* and *the other*, i.e. devising itself as the other and vice versa, so that in a huge sequence, the specificities overcome the *entirety* of the particularities. The charm of ornamental Islamic arabesque is mainly in the fact that in their permanent swings, the repetitive elements overcome their own segmentation and similarity, as well as their permanent repetitiveness, incorporating all of it into a superb form, a whole that gives them their ultimate meaning.

Second, the segmentation of the arabesque incorporates individual segments into the work in such a way that there is an evident tendency to cover the entire space or the entire surface: the artist does end his work at a certain place – usually after the arabesque has mastered the set space – though he could have easily ended it elsewhere, in a different "volume", had the space requested so; he could have easily "branched out" further, until he has conquered the space. The feature of the arabesque is, thus, the desire to master the space, and its principle of repetition of elements allows it to do so.

Third, and related to the above, the arabesque typically has no pronounced beginning, middle or end: it does not have a *linear* spread, but rather it does so by repeating its segments to master the surface *circularly*, i.e. owing to the principle of connections between its segments, one may start observing the entire work from different angles. It does not evolve linearly, which would necessitate single-direction perception and create a certain tension in the structure starting from the *beginning*, through the *middle*, all the way to the *end.* The arabesque prevents any tension, among other things, by means of its calmness expressed in a particular type of circular, non-linear structure.[3]

This establishes certain common traits and delineations in relation to Western poetics. In his structuralism-influenced *Poétique de la prose*,[4] Tzvetan Todorov holds that most texts are organised under the principle of a temporal or logical (cause-and-effect) sequence, and rarely under the principle of *spatial sequence.* Journals, chronicles and diaries are thus dominated by temporal sequence, and cause-and-effect links are dominant in the speech of lawyers or scientists. However, some works are organised in a temporal sequence, whereas the other two levels are suppressed. This is typical of poetry, and it is most superbly manifested in so-called "concrete" poetry. Todorov believes that Roman Jakobson's analysis of poetry indicates that in literature, on different levels, all the units of language fit into a complex system of symmetries, gradation, contrasts and parallelisms, almost as if making up a spatial structure. This, in a way, points to a fundamental principle governing the poetics of the arabesque in its need to *master the space, to cover the space*. The coverage of space is an exception in Western literature, always unusual and stylogenic, sometimes even perceived as artificial, unlike the poetics of the arabesque, which are always marked predominantly by a *circular* mastering of space.

The above-mentioned features generate yet another feature of the arabesque. Namely, it does not awaken passion, and it does not promote it, as it does not originate from it. In fact, the arabesque promotes calm joy. Oriental-Islamic arabesque is typically devoid of strong motion: no "swirling winds", no harsh bends and turns, no confrontation of elements in order to dominate the structure. On the contrary, the arabesque is about mild meanders, its elements do not collide, but withdraw quietly at the right moment, giving way to others; they are an optimal display of *parallelism and blending* in all directions. The effect of contrasts and dynamics are eventually attained by the different density of elements (leaves, for example), i.e. by means of more intense introduction of elements that continue to cooperate under the general principle of harmoniousness. Adding to the most frequent ornamental motifs of vegetation, it becomes even more evident that the arabesque is a piece of work that may easily be called an ode. There is no tempestuousness in it, or extract, or lust – it is the quiet joy, the triumph arising from the artist's awareness of the divine harmony of the elements of the world and man's constant joyous adjustment to it.

This structure of the arabesque and the dominance of its aesthetic principle in other works of art, particularly in literature, are closely related to the Arab-Islamic understanding of the notion of time, which is quite different from that of Judeo-Christian culture. This difference has almost become a general point of reference.[5] Namely, in Arab-Islamic *culture*, time is understood as cyclical or circular (*al-zaman al-dā'irī*), composed of individual moments. De Vitray-Meyerovitch refers to time in Islamic philosophy as "vertical" or "atomistic".[6] The term "atomistic" seems more adequate, as the meaning of "vertical" bears several meanings and elaborations in Islam, as communication between God and the World takes place by means of revelations along a vertical line, in the specific meaning of the word, surpassing the competence of a successful metaphor. However, the Arabic term *al-zaman al-dā'irī* denotes circular or cyclical time, "*atomistically*" comprising an endless repetition of sequences. This understanding is strongly differentiated from the understanding of time in Judeo-Christian culture, which is linear (Ar. *al-zaman al-ufuqī*): it flows from a beginning, to a certain end, and it does so *in continuo* and linearly. These different interpretations of time establish different relations towards it, be it historical time, or the temporal orientation of individuals within it. It is important to note that Easterners and Westerners measure time differently; not astronomically, but rather in terms of value. Accordingly, within a linear understanding of time, the awareness of time as such requires faster movement from the *beginning* to the *end*, reflected not only in the cultivation of longing for the reception of a piece of writing – which is the purpose of this study – but also in all the other aspects of a culture as a whole, where the speed of all the aspects of the expression of spirit has, in our time, turned into mere plummeting. At the same time, the notion of "atomistic" time, of its circular repetitiveness, indicates a certain sense of comfort and relaxation – it certainly prevents the fierceness and dramatic inertia of a linear understanding of time.

Not venturing further into this type of differentiation between two notions of time, it is evident that the Arab-Islamic non-linear understanding of time found its full and optimal expression in the arabesque.[7] Its structural principle of repetition of segments, its rhythmical alternation, its mutual merger of structural elements, etc., as detailed above, are quite concordant with a circular understanding of time consisting of a series of repeated sequences. It is important to note the absence of a pronounced beginning, middle or end, and, accordingly, the desire to cover the entire space or surface by *non-linear* expansion. Time is, in fact, like an arabesque, and the arabesque is an expression of time. Consequently, this leads to the conclusion that the result of this linear movement is the longing that creates a particular kind of tension and anticipation – or tension in anticipation – whereas the result of circular movement is satisfaction as a particular form of calmness; the first is realised through the restlessness of tension, the latter in the joy of resignation. This conclusion will be instrumental in the literary analysis that follows.

The Arabian, and later the Oriental-Islamic understanding of time, is inextricably linked with an understanding of man's position in the world, and thus with an understanding of art in this tradition. Generally, in Arab-Islamic philosophy and culture the world is understood as the emanation of God, which is perfect as such, and the only task of man is to uncover this perfection and to adjust everything else to it. There is no creative intervention by man, as the only creator in the world is God. Accordingly, there is no drama(tic) realisation of the inner self on the outer world, no sense of the interventionism that is largely evident in Western culture. The inner self of the Oriental-Islamic man, just as that of the Arabian before him – unlike the Western realisation in the outer world – is revealed in full harmony with the outer world. Thus enlightened from within by the divine organisation of the outer world, the Oriental mind is open to a compulsory effect in return: like a strong reflection, this glow of the outer world returns to his open and bright soul. This is a state of extraordinary lyricism. The Hegelian "descent of the spirit into its subjective inner self" is not typical for the Arab-Islamic East; there is, in fact, an evident expansion of the mind, a departure of the spiritual into the outer world, where it enters a state of joyful merger with nature and its (re)actions. The Arab-Islamic spirit is thus inevitably and primarily lyrical. However, referring to it as merely lyrical is insufficient – it is necessary to know that this predominantly lyrical tradition is *ruled by the ode*. Arab tradition is unfamiliar with pessimistic poetry as a particular form of self-effacing spirituality. In fact, due to the understanding of time and man's position in time and in the world that was described above, the Arab-Islamic tradition could only express itself as lyrical, in particular genres. In addition to odes, this poetic tradition is also dominated by the genre of self-praise (possibly described as an ode to the Self in expansion, rather than in self-effacing), as well as descriptive poetry. Love poetry (*ghazal*) remains specific as it expresses the poet's joy at the *manifested attractions* of the loved one, indicating also the permanent expansion of the mind towards the divine beauty of the outer world.

In addition to this privileged status and the special nature of lyricism in the Arab-Islamic world – which will be discussed in greater detail later – it also becomes obvious that the arabesque can only come to be where it did indeed: with its non-linear expansion and merger of elements, there is a clear intention of the arabesque to express its calmness in harmony, to prevent any idea of a whirlwind, or any tension expressed in breaking lines.

The culture that opted so substantially for a circular understanding of time and for the understanding of the world as the emanation of Perfection, always revealing itself joyfully while never correcting itself dramatically, developed its art in accordance with this principle of arabesque structure, an understating of art different from that of Western culture. This is confirmed not only by artistic production, but also by basic theoretical terminology. For the purpose of this analysis, it will be sufficient to provide solid evidence of the substantially different meaning of the Arab terms for *creativity* and *art*.

In the Arab-Islamic tradition, the world is understood as divine creation, in which man does not create, but rather merely uncovers what has already been created. This tradition never "found" words for *creativity* and for *art* to correspond to our terms: it never had any need to search for them, for the terms already available in it are an optimum expression of the understanding of artistic work, and reflect its understating of time and man's position in the world.

Namely, the Arabic language uses two words to denote *creativity*, both in the same semantic field: *ibdā'* and *ibtikār*. Neither entails the meaning of creation *ex nihilo*, but rather of *innovation*, *invention*, *creation-from-what-is-already-there*, etc. This is a superb confirmation of the artist's joy of discovery of the created world, rather than the dynamism of one's own realisation in it; by "re-creating" the created, the artist affirms and *innovates* it within humanly limited powers, but does not create it. Therefore, in this correlation, his spiritual dedication and joy are understandable and possible only through a specific comprehension of the aforementioned terms, which expands into an extroverted openness towards the beauties of the world.

The term used to denote *art* is elegantly congruent with the two terms for *creativity*. Namely, the Arabic term for *art* has always been *fann*, meaning, in fact, *ability*, in the sense of *skill*, *mastery*, *technique*, etc., rather than in the sense of pure creation. As the "artist" (by now requiring quotation marks!) does not create, but rather innovates and invents what has already been created, he is presented and revered as a *master craftsman* of the highest order. This is one of the fundamental reasons why Arabic art, and particularly poetry as its supreme expression, is indeed so obsessed with form. In the artists' work, substance is not of primary importance; what is, rather, is its constant re-shaping into a new appearance, or a new form – in poetry, developed to perfection as early as the pre-Islamic period. Consequently, the task of the artist's work is to announce joy, rather than anxiety, and to invoke the same feelings in those who listen to poetry; in such an understanding, poetry is always moving towards the outer world, rather than the poet's inner self. This is firmly linked with the fact that for hundreds of years – that is, in the decisive period of its poetic shaping and aesthetic weighing – poetry has lived through oral tradition: the need to convey it orally was so great that since the earliest times and at a relatively low level of societal development, there was, in this tradition, a special "class" of *professional* narrators, or rhapsodes (Ar. *ruwāt*), who enjoyed the great respect of their fellow countrymen. Namely, poetry was aimed at hearing, a channel into the heart, more than at any other kind of reflection. Of course, its focus on these "organs" of perception gives preference to form, with sound as an important element, and which, in itself, contains a series of its own elements. For poetry is not experienced in the same way when recited and when read in silence: in the former case, pronunciation and sound in the widest sense, along with a multitude of elements working with it, come to the forefront; in the latter, reflection comes first. It is no accident that a poem that relies (too) much on form makes a dedicated reader recite it, listening to the murmur of its silky fabric. Given the dominance of this principle in the entire tradition, this phenomenon becomes all the more important. The phenomenon itself is, of course, the consequence of a basic requirement of perfecting the form, as the tradition itself – just to give a reminder – does not know creativity *ex nihilo* and determines *art* as a *skill*, which is, in turn, derived from the philosophy of non-linear time and man's position as the one who discovers or uncovers.

On the basis of the above, it is evident that it was not possible for the arabesque *not* to appear as typically Oriental-Islamic ornamentation. Its late appearance may be subject to discussion, as there had been conditions for its appearance much earlier. However, such a discussion is made redundant by the fact that this understanding of time and the world was realised in full in brilliant literature, long before the appearance of the ornamental arabesque.

Namely, it has been mentioned before that the poetics of the pre-Islamic tradition (particularly *al-Mu'allaqāt* as its most prominent corpus), as well as that of the entire subsequent Arab-Islamic literary tradition, is the poetics of the arabesque. Poems of some one hundred or so couplets are composed in such a way so that one or two couplets are autonomous units of meaning. A series of such units in one poem make up a unit of meaning of a "higher level" – a theme or a motif, and more of such themes or motifs make up a poem. All are kept together by the decisive factors of form – unique metre and rhyme.

In this tradition, the basic feature of a poem is obviously a kind of "atomisation", a parcelling out from the level of micro-structures to the highest structural units. It should be borne in mind that this segmentation is characterised by a *parallelism* of elements. This exemplifies the poetics of the arabesque. The unique rhyme and metre of a poem resemble the stem of the arabesque, as the "axis" – for want of a better word – of the structure is just an illusion. In view of this segmentation and parallelism, as well as the specific, arabesque-like "weaving in" of details into the whole, it can be deduced that the positions of elements are not fixed in such a way as to make them unchangeable. That is why it was common, and therefore not particularly striking, in traditional Arabic poetry (and in many other traditions of the Oriental-Islamic circle) for different versions or edits of one and the same poem to exist, with the positions of verses changed and each position considered equally valid. This is possible only in the arabesque structure, where sense is captured and self-sufficient in its micro-structures and elements of form are not the cohesive factors of the kind that would require absolutely identical sequences of micro-structures at all times. There are frequent cases in this tradition where one edit of a poem "misses" several couplets that we find in another edit, but the poem remains unscathed – it is self-seductive and careless thanks to its arabesque structure.

Consequently, such a poem is indifferent to any *linear* structure: what the Western tradition prescribes as the *beginning–middle–end* of an artefact is made relative here, even irrelevant, and the consequences of such poetics are so great that they can hardly be grasped: they fall between the so-called Western and Oriental-Islamic traditions; hence the different perceptions, as discussed above. However, the Arabic ode did have a traditional pattern of theme or composition (it opened with a lovers' lyrical prelude – *nasīb*, and it ended in, for example, self-praise – *fakhr*), but this is a matter of a rationalist *norm* in poetics, rather than of the poetics itself. One and the same poem could have opened with verses of self-praise – it is indeed quite possible to re-arrange its motifs and micro-structures differently, with no consequences for the poem itself.

It is interesting to compare this role and structure of repetition with repetition in the poetry of other cultures and peoples. Jakobson indicated the existence of parallelism in Russian folklore poetry, in ancient Indian poetry and in Ugro-Finnish folklore, as well as in Chinese and Biblical verse.[8] He focused on grammatical parallelism and contrasts, the same tools that Souriau also believed to have had the same role that the method of utilisation of structures plays in other arts. This redundancy of sorts performed different functions: sometimes it served the purpose of easy memorisation, sometimes that of the creation of a humorous motif in a kind of tautology, sometimes a binary grammatical parallelism becomes the driving spring of the action. Repetition is also one of the fundamental features of narratives in cultures that know no literacy, and one of the fundamental aesthetic procedures (perhaps the dominant reason is, in fact, mnemotechnics). Different alliteration, repetition of syllables in a rhyme, metric phenomena – all of this is the basis of poetry in general, wherein individual verses are reflected in one another and repeated in different patterns. That is why Todorov rightly referred to the spatial organisation of poetic discourse as its dominant element. However, there are certain specific features of this in the poetics of pre-Islamic tradition: we do not encounter the same type of repetition, and certainly not any contrast of grammatical categories. Couplets are mutually replaceable and are not built in opposition. As we have seen, it is a matter of even-number organisation into couplets, brought together by meter and rhyme, though with no redundant verbal repetitions. Of course, here too the rhyme is used as a cohesive element, bringing together different segments and facilitating the memorisation of poetry. It is this very example that best illustrates the arabesque nature of Oriental-Islamic poetry, where different parts may be easily moved and interchanged, and where different standard motifs can be found in different poems, such as the odes, i.e. the *al-Mu'allaqāt*.

The absence of the pronounced *beginning–middle–end* linear structure is the decisive poetic principle due to which the traditional Arab-Islamic work of art cultivates joy rather than longing. The poetic principle of *beginning–middle–end*, so convincingly established by Aristotle and so dominant in the Western tradition for so long, is indeed particularly important in drama – traditional drama is inconceivable without it and this is one of the principal reasons why the Arabic tradition has had no drama. It is incompatible with Arab-Islamic philosophy, with the spirit of that world and with its tradition. By even hypothetically accepting Aristotle's poetic postulates, this abundantly rich tradition, self-sufficient and self-content, would have committed a sort of suicide. History has shown that in its self-isolation, this tradition made a "common-sense, reasoned" choice in favour of traditionalism rather than self-annihilation.

After having worked hard on promoting Aristotle's *Poetics*, al-Qarṭājannī's complaints (thirteenth century) begin to make sense, as Aristotle had not known the Arab-Islamic poetic tradition; he would have had much to learn from it and could have thus "enriched his own rules".[9]

It is, of course, necessary to note that in Aristotelian poetics, the Arab-Islamic tradition remained in infertile desert ground, both because this tradition emphasised man's conciliation with the world, his harmony with it, but also because there was such a strong perception of man's non-intervention in terms of creation. It has already been mentioned that the Hegelian orientalist interior is not realised in the exterior, but is, rather, revealed in it in full harmony. It should also be said that in Arabic history – in the ancient heroic age of this culture – there were no semi-gods as the highest expression of man's desire to intervene in the realm of God's and divine competences. These seem to be the principal elements of differentiation of the modern world as well: the West effects radical interventions in the world, clearly challenging its very survival, whereas the East still dreams about its own renaissance, helpless in the face of the global cataclysmic interventionism of the West.

However, returning to the basic issue of the dominance of arabesque poetics, two pieces referred to at the beginning of this chapter should be considered here as well.

The principle of the arabesque structure led the *Qur'an* to unsurpassable perfection. Each surah, each verse in it is self-sufficient and comprises, at the same time, a series of (parallel) micro-structures. Moreover, the order of the verses is conditional, the work of man, rather than of the Sublime Author. There is no doubt that a different sequence of verses could have been made, with no impact whatsoever on the *Sense* of the Revelation. However, the *Qur'an* is extraordinary in any case, because – unlike other works in the realm of Arab-Islamic art – its form is so rich in content that it barely manages to carry it. Nowhere else is there – as there is in the *Qur'an* – such magic deployed to overcome the particularity of individual segments and incorporate it into the magnificent Entirety, just as there is nowhere else in that tradition such a superb *content–form* inversion.

The structure of the Arabic language is particularly conducive to the poetics of arabesque. There should be a separate analysis of that level, as this phenomenon is certainly worthy of it, but only a few things will be elucidated here.

Namely, the Arabic language, particularly classical Arabic, is characterised by a relative underdevelopment of complex dependent subordinating clauses. The language is dominated by sentences comprising independent clauses. The loose connection between such clauses is established by coordinating conjuncts that, in effect, emphasise their parallelism. Adding to that the extraordinary capacity of the Arabic language to effect juxtaposition on any syntactic level, it is clear that the parallelism and fragmentation of the arabesque is at the very heart and soul of this culture. As for its morphology, words originate from three-consonant root words, spreading circles of lexical wealth across the semantic field by way of precise flexions and inflexions. It is always a triumph of one and the same principle.

The principle of arabesque wove the fabric of *One Thousand and One Nights* – the piece poetically representative of the Arab-Islamic tradition, but also of the different perceptions in the two traditions. In the Arab-Islamic literary tradition, dominated by poetry, *One Thousand and One Nights* was considered second-rate at best, whereas its position in the system of values of the Western tradition was quite different – very high, in fact.

One of the principal reasons for the general popularity and high academic acclaim of *One Thousand and One Nights* arises from its structure, or rather its narrative nature, which mesmerised the West immediately and infinitely, whereas its arabesque structure, the peak of which is *One Thousand and One Nights*, was quite natural to the Arabic language and its literature, and hence devoid of any exotic qualities: what mesmerises the West is omnipresent in Arab-Islamic culture, evident in the very essence of its culture and philosophy. Discussing *One Thousand and One Nights*, Sandra Naddaff tries to establish a parallel between the ornamental arabesque as a stylisation of its own, an escape from representation of human images and from representative art in general, and the narrative arabesque as an escape from representation of the "real world", with the creation of a *narrative universe* as a stylisation of life. She thus cites a deviation from the *mimetic principle* as an important feature of arabesque art, ornamental or literary.[10] The arabesque does not refer to an external element, but rather relates the "burden of meaning" to the relation between each element and the elements preceding or following it; the arabesque is, in essence, fundamentally *self-referential*. The arabesque stylisation is recognised for its antimimetic principle, where the narrative discourse establishes the actual location of textual reality; it is thus no surprise that Western post-structuralism and postmodernist literature, themselves abandoning *mimesis* in favour of *diegesis*, were to be so enchanted with *One Thousand and One Nights* and what it represents. However, there is something else related to it worthy of attention.

In the West, *One Thousand and One Nights* is read like a piece that cultivated to the maximum extent the Aristotelian poetic principle of *beginning–middle–end:* at the beginning, there is Shahrayar's cruelty, a direct threat against Shahrazad's life, and the reader rushes through one story after the next towards the *end*, i.e. *towards a resolution*. This is the habit of linearity, which engenders suspense and desire.

A brilliant illustration of this concept of desire in Western poetics is *Reading for the Plot* by Peter Brooks. For Brooks, the narrative itself is a form of human desire, and the need to tell it is a primary human need, there to mesmerise, seduce and even subordinate the listener. It is no surprise that this author sees *One Thousand and One Nights* as the story of all stories, because the narrative is, according to him, presented as life-giving, as it arouses and sustains desire, delaying the moment of its fulfilment.[11]

It is interesting to see how much the poetic tradition conditions the different reading of one and the same work in the West and in the Arab-Islamic civilisation. It should be reiterated that this refers to reading not only by theoreticians and students of poetry, but also by an average reader. This leads back to Brooks and the title of his book, which clearly presents *reading for the plot* (which is, in fact, reading *because of* the plot), i.e. in order to resolve the desire for the end and thus attain satisfaction. Brooks is thus primarily interested in issues of temporal sequence and progression, i.e. *the forward movement of the plot*, towards the end. He is interested in the outer borders of the text, its edges and lines of demarcation (and it will become evident that Roland Barthes has a different outlook on this and his concept seems to be closer to the Oriental-Islamic poetry). There is, however, no such clear progression in the poetics of the arabesque, because of non-linear time, and because the aim of its composition is not to attain a clear linear progression.

Thus, Arab-Islamic poetics implies a different reading: the kind of reading where every single moment is enjoyed, where the aim is not to reach the end, but rather to feel the pleasure and the serene joy of different parts of text.

It is due to this principle of arabesque structure that *One Thousand and One Nights* can be read the way Brooks suggests. Moving from the "beginning" to the "middle", the reader realises that each story is (an autonomous) whole, but also an integral part of another whole, as in an arabesque. Moreover, themselves accustomed to this structural principle, readers occasionally – though evermore frequently – forget Shahrazad's fate as they are captivated by an endless series of other fates. The initial desire is thus transformed into joy, as the reader realises, quite far into the text, that he may interrupt the reading at any point with a sense of satisfaction and completeness. There is no doubt that during most of the reading, the reader of *One Thousand and One Nights* will suppress the anticipation of Shahrazad's fate. It ultimately becomes a kind of structural and narrative "deception". Namely, the structural principle is so strong and persistent that the original linearity is overpowered, even transformed into an opposite of itself: Shahrazad's "path" or "fate" becomes a huge circle, with an endless series of other concentric circles within it; the importance of "fate" is relativised by its ideal incorporation into the form of the arabesque. And once Shahrazad's fate is known, it no longer impresses the reader as strongly as one may expect in view of the "beginning". This is not the kind of writing read in the same way as one with consistent Aristotelian structure: from the beginning through the middle to the end.

Arabs read *One Thousand and One Nights* differently – to them, it is the (non-linear) arabesque that imposes its concentric control over the entire "narrative space", not cultivating desire, but rather affirming pleasure. As it turns out, the joy is not in the *resolution*, but rather in the *journey* across endless narrative landscapes.

Let us now examine how the beginning and the end of a narrative text is seen in Western poetics and in modern literary theory. For Brooks, the end is always related to mortality. Narrative desire is, in fact, the driving force (which always asks, *What happens next?*), which pushes forward, towards the end, which is also a desire for fulfilment (the end of the narrative) and also a constant postponement of the end, postponement of fulfilment. That is why any ending of a narrative is also a *death* of sorts: "The desire of the text is ultimately the desire for the end, for that recognition which is the moment of death of the reader in the text"; and yet, recognition does not diminish the middle of the text, as repetition towards recognition is the truth of the narrative text.[12] Constant excitement and fear accompanying movement towards the end of the text is indeed important, as a premature end or "the wrong end" is unbearable – hence the eternal fear of non-fulfilment, non-satisfaction of desire. Postmodernist literature, particularly metafiction, plays with the end, always on the verge of non-fulfilment and reawakened desire, playing on the desire for the right end (such as, for example, John Fowles' *The French Lieutenant's Woman*, which offers two endings for the reader to choose). All that we in the West perceive as unusual, mysterious, hence stylogeneous as well, is in *One Thousand and One Nights* simply an expression of a particular poetic tradition. This tradition derives from the principle of the arabesque; hence the work itself has no definitive end. There were, therefore, frequently stylised versions appearing later: 1002 nights, 1003 nights, "sequels" that opened new circles, new pages, as if trying at the same time to enclose the original piece into a final whole. On the other hand, the Russian Arabist Krymskij states that in the Arab East, even today, oral tradition keeps developing *One Thousand and One Nights*, spreading it in concentric circles towards infinity, so that the work itself is its own kind of process ad infinitum.[13]

For Western readers, the end is supposed to meet their expectations, to be "good" and "logical" – according to the English novelist A. S. Byatt, it is supposed to make us say "Ah, yes, of course!" – for all the threads of the storyline have been connected, after suspense and anticipation, a sense of ease and relaxation is finally there. Therefore, there is very strong potential in the effect of failed expectation, particularly in postmodernist literature that, just like postmodernist theory, abandons many of the Aristotelian poetic postulates (such as the mimesis and diegesis). Within that context, it is sufficient to recall the repetitively failed expectations in Italo Calvino's novel *If on a Winter's Night a Traveller*, which become the key feature of the style of the entire novel. For an average reader, the end that fails to meet the expectations and fulfil the desire is simply "wrong". This is again well illustrated by A. S. Byatt in *The Whistling Woman*, when Agatha, the novel's heroine and an author of children's novels and stories, reads the end of her novel and the entire audience, children in particular, are in utter shock: "There was no satisfaction at the end of the story. It was as if they had all been *stabbed*" (emphasis added).[14] Here too, the end is a kind of death, though a more difficult one, as it was not accompanied by a sense of satisfied, contented desire.

The principle of arabesque functions quite differently, both in fine art and in narrative texts. Instead of the idea of ending, finitude and death, i.e. mortality in general, the arabesque brings with it the idea of endlessness, of transcendence of the limited earthly existence, and of movement towards divine infinity and potentially eternal presence, everlasting repetition.[15] The concept of the existence of a single beginning and a single end of the arabesque as an ornament, as well as a narrative arabesque such as *One Thousand and One Nights*, is simply lost.

From this point of view, of all the Western theoreticians of narration and semiotics, perhaps Barthes is the closest to Arab poetics. For him, text (particularly written text) is *a galaxy of signifiers* rather than a structure of signifieds; *the text has no beginning*; *it is reversible*, and we gain access to it by several entrances, none of which can easily be declared to be the main one. Therefore, there are no strict limits of the text, as Brooks sees them (the beginning and the end), but rather there is an openness that only the arabesque can create. Instead of seeing text as a classic plot triangle – an opening exposition, a conflict with a climax and a resolution – Barthes understands narrative as a kind of *constellation*.[16] It is this concept of constellation that is perhaps the closest to the concept of the arabesque, as neither of the two notions implies a triadic or any other limited structure: theoretically, an arabesque may always be extended further. An even more interesting feature of the arabesque is the issue of how its different pieces dovetail, how they interlock, what sense and meaning is generated at the "seams", at places where they connect. Each such seam or border of a text is a place of particular significance, both because it is the place where connection is effected and where different pieces become independent – it is the place of connection and separation. Barthes's *multivalence of text* allows readers to see the text not as a mere narrative flow, but rather as a constellation of interfering and overlapping meaning. Still, it should be said that his model, however attractive, cannot be easily and naturally applied to Western narrative texts, at least not to those that do not consciously imitate the arabesque structure. Perhaps an example of a (sub)conscious approximation of Western literature to the construct of the arabesque may be a particular kind of *fragmented poetics* seen in modern Western literature, particularly in plays and their staging. This form of poetics also constructs text on the principle of a series and combinations of atomised segments, i.e. fragments. It is always more or less *style-generating* and *wonderful*, and additional meaning is generated at the places where those fragments meet and where the different combinations, repetitions and differences are recognised. This style-generating ability of fragmentation demonstrates that it is not an inherent feature of the text, as is the case in Oriental Islamic literature.

One Thousand and One Nights delivers a unique branching out of stories, complex constructions with concentric circles expanding over and over again, only for some motifs, plots or characters to be repeated in a typically arabesque interweaving, fascinating time and again with its construction. And therein lies a wealth of unexplored issues of structure in this text: what is the actual relationship between the repeated motifs, plots or types of characters? How do such repetitions influence the overall narrative structure and the structure of individual narrative levels or the concentric circles that they appear in? Can such repetitions always be recognised as mirror-images, thus influencing one another retrospectively or prospectively? Just as in the case of the ornamental arabesque, beauty and aesthetic impression always arise from the mystery of interference and never fully discerned structure.

Using this distinction of the two types of poetics, it is easier to understand the differences in the Western understanding of other Arab-Islamic texts. It is sufficient to mention the numerous misunderstandings of the structure and style of the *Qur'an*: whereas Western poetics sees yet another deviation from the usual, the expected and predictable temporal sequence and progression, in the Arab-Islamic poetic tradition, the pattern of the *Qur'an* bore a strong influence on the style and poetics of other texts. Western theoreticians have often been confused by the different lengths of the surahs, the repetition of certain segments of text, sometimes as motifs, sometimes as chorus segments, and not in regular intervals as one may expect. Formally, the text of the *Qur'an* is centred on rhythm, rhyme and numerous vocal repetitions, which make the text coherent. This is the branch that all other segments of the arabesque spring from, always surprising with their distribution and repetition. Different elements are repeated in the *Qur'an*, both in terms of theme and in terms of language and style (refrains, parallelisms ...); sometimes unexpectedly, just like a leaf of an arabesque unexpectedly repeated at a particular place.

Such repetitions are neither redundant nor an expression of a "mistake", as Francesco Gabrielli claimed; they are, in fact, the reflection of an atomised image of the world and the absence of a linear understanding of time, as well as of even movement from the beginning to the end of the text. The arabesque implies the existence of a whole, made up of different parts; it is this very connection of different parts making up a whole and their particularity that make the structure and style of the *Qur'an* so specific and unique. Recalling that the arabesque is also a form that transcends any finiteness, spatial or temporal, and that it can be understood as an expression of movement towards the eternal and the divine (Naddaff), it is quite clear why the principle of arabesque construction is immanent to the *Qur'an* – this principle, in fact, seems to be the only possible one. On one hand, in its superb arabesque structure, enriched by Sense, it strongly resembles the well-known structure of the Universe in a state of endless expansion, and on the other, it promoted and advanced the arabesque as the ultimately meaningful way of incorporating the particular into the meaning of the whole, and did so in a way never repeated by any work of Oriental-Islamic tradition before or after it. That is why it is perhaps inadequately understood in the Western tradition – precisely in view of its poetics and its unique style.

Any approach that is based on habitual linear practice and insistent upon it and nothing else is inadequate for the works of pronounced arabesque poetics. It would be equally wrong – as much as any intolerant insistence is – to deny, for example, the validity of the Western perception of *One Thousand and One Nights*. It is a matter of two significantly different traditions and perceptions that should be encouraged to enrich each other through dialogue. It seems clear today that dialogue is a means of finding the Third Place, which enables a Meeting with the Other. This chapter is thus a Third Place of its own kind, which includes the views of both Western and Oriental-Islamic poetics, with no image distorted by lenses with a blind spot for the Other and the Different.

Speaking of circles – in this case, the two circles of culture and civilisation that we started with and will end with – it would be creative, or rather it would have the effect of Lotman's explosion in Culture, to remove them from the state of parallelism and place them into a relation of concentric, arabesque-like interweaving, and aesthetic and notional development ad infinitum.

Notes

1 Aristotle's *Poetics* was presented in Arabic as early as in tenth century, and one of the early notable translations was by the famous Ibn Rushd (Averroës, d. 1198).

2 The transcribed names of Arabic authors, as well as the years of their birth and death, will be given only when first mentioned in the book. The Index of Names will offer the Arabic names in phonological transcription as well as their English version.

3 This is also the argument that the idea of the arabesque is the basis of all art, as E. Souriau tried to establish in *La Correspondance des arts* (*Odnos među umjetnostima*, Sarajevo, Svjetlost, 1958). However attractively presented, it cannot be fully accepted in relation to poetics. Namely, just one aspect suffices: Souriau speaks about novels as arabesques with a *linear sequence of sentences, headings and chapters* and about *straightening the linear arabesque of a story* (ibid., pp. 128–129). Our elaboration demonstrates that the arabesque *does not know* any linear principles or sequence, and that it is based on circular series and parallel, parcelled elements that form a complex construction.

4 Tzvetan Todorov, *Poetika* [orig. *Poétique de la prose*], Filip Višnjić, Belgrade, 1986, pp. 50–57.

5 A notable essay on this point was written by Eva de Vitray-Meyerovitch, "Poetika islama" [Poetics of Islam], in Julia Kristeva, *Prelaženje znakova* [*La Traversée des signes*], Svjetlost, Sarajevo, 1979.

See also the distinguished Arabic writer and literary theoretician Ibrāhīm Jabrā (1920–1994), who wrote on Judeo-Christian and Oriental-Islamic notions of time (see: *al-Mawqif al-adabī*, No. 173–174, Damascus, 1980). He explained that it was this differentiation that he used as the principle of poetic construction for his novel *al-Baḥth 'an Walīd Mas'ūd*, one of the most significant works of artistic prose in Arabic. (The novel was also published in Bosnian translation: Ibrahim Džebra, *U potrazi za Velidom Mesudom* [*In Search of Walid Masoud*], ZID, Sarajevo, 1995, translation and commentary by Esad Duraković.)

6 De Vitray-Meyerovitch, op. cit., p. 199.

7 A distinction between the notion of *time* as a purely theological and cultural category and a poetological one should be introduced here. Namely, in Islam and Christianity as religions, *time* is essentially linear, as it unfolds from the creation of the world towards its end and transition to eschatological eternity. However, this text refers to time as a poetological category that differs in the two cultures and civilisations.

8 Roman Jakobson, *Lingvistika i poetika* [orig. *Linguistics and Poetics*], Nolit, Belgrade, 1966.

9 Al-Qarṭājannī, *Minhāj al-bulaġā'*, s. l., s. a.

10 Sandra Naddaff, *Arabesque: Narrative Structure and the Aesthetics of Repetition in the 1001 Nights*, Northwestern University Press, Evanston, IL, 1991, pp. 117–119.

11 Peter Brooks, *Reading for the Plot: Design and Intention in Narrative*, Harvard University Press, Cambridge, MA, London, 1996.

12 Ibid., p. 109.

13 Крымский, *История новой арабской литературы, XIX – начало XX века*, Москва, 1971.
14 A. S. Byatt, *A Whistling Woman*, Vintage, London, 2002, p. 10.
15 Naddaff, op. cit., p. 113.
16 Roland Barthes, *S/Z: An Essay*, Hill and Wong, New York, 2000.

2 The deductive poetics of the *Qur'an*

Intertextuality and contextualisation

The *Qur'an* is a work of context. It was revealed (in)to the tradition in form and content that established complex and dynamic relations with tradition in the most comprehensive sense of the word. At the level of ideology, the *Qur'an* constituted a sea change in its reach and force typical of those that occur only a few times in history: it converted a people from heathenism to pure monotheism, inspiring them with strength and arming them with an ethical system. Provided with these, its adherents would, in an astonishingly short period of time – a historical flash, as it were – conquer a significant portion of the world of that time, including parts that, before the *Qur'an*, had been incomparably more advanced than the Arabians. However, this decisive period in the history of civilisation belongs to a different kind of research. I mention it here in passing to point out this particular dimension of the *Qur'an*'s contextuality. Through this dimension, it asserted its overwhelming superiority over the previous tradition and phased out many of its forms so as to underline the importance of graduality on the one hand and, on the other, to demonstrate that tradition is essentially respected as a value even if some of its forms must be eliminated or left behind. At the same time, the Text was yet another way of promoting tradition as such: as a continuity of values, regardless of the need for its constant regeneration or for the "rejection" of certain forms, which were only transformed so as to be barely recognisable. Although remarkable, this way of promoting tradition as a particular kind of continuity sometimes fails to be noticed or to be sufficiently emphasised; on the contrary, it is often stated that the Text rejected tradition entirely. In fact, the relations between the Text and tradition are far more complex.

Although this Text is original in its entirety (previously, it did not exist in an integral form), it is uniquely repeated in history and thus realised within a transhistorical continuity and in the context of history in its entirety. This is the absolute immersion of the Text in Context. It is necessary to present this position of the Text.

The self-repetition of the Text does not lie in its literal and complete repetition, in its form and content, throughout history. As a work, it is authentic;

however, at the level of ideology, or in the sphere of its content, it reiterates and elaborates the same essential Meaning (its form of monotheism), even asserting that there is to follow the final *attestation* of the same Meaning and Content communicated and interpreted by God's prophets through an unknown number of centuries, back to the dawn of mankind. Therefore, the Text enters its Context at the highest level while fatefully creating this Context itself. For the Text explicates that its Idea, its entire Meaning, is not new; the Text only provides a sort of divine revision and revitalisation of history: according to it, Islam was not created with the *Qur'an* but has existed since the First Man, except that the essence of Islam has become deformed through history so that its *original* forms must be restored. This "textual fact" is important and should not be overlooked if the Text is to be properly and immanently interpreted. However, many still overlook this fact, believing that Islam emerged only with the *Qur'an*. Such an oversight of the Qur'anic explication is inconceivable – hence inadmissible as well – regardless of the religious or ideological position of the researcher: such a researcher has initially abandoned the advantage of immanent interpretation of the Text and is therefore not able to understand the position of this Text in history, a position that is revealed in several important aspects.

Namely, the involvement of the Text in tradition and the virtue of its contextuality are explicated through the conservation and *gradual* superseding of some forms of the tradition (in *tafsīr*, this is known as the principle of *derogation*). However, its transhistorical continuity is also explicated through continual assertions that, in essence, the Text only confirms what was already revealed and explained in different forms throughout history. Through this, its continuity and contextuality acquire the attribute of absoluteness that the Text perpetuates as its own very being. This is important not only at an ideological level but also in terms of the relation between the form and content of the Text, or a number of its poetic postulates.

Asserting that it brings the very same Meaning that had been brought by all the prophets before the Last Prophet, the Text emphasises something extremely important from the position of poetics: the Text thus distinguishes itself from claims that it represents art.[1] For a work of art exists in its originality, in its unimitated and inimitable essence, expressed through the oneness of its form and content. The *Qur'an*, conversely, insists that its content has repeated itself throughout history and that the same content was now revealed in a new form associated with the highest literary and aesthetic values. Moreover, to understand its originality as determining and adorning its art (and therefore, non-repetitive) would be contrary to its being, as then its Content would become deformed: it would suggest that there had been no Islam until a certain point in history (the early seventh century), which would imply that God had delayed introducing the World to the Truth about Himself, and which in turn would cast doubt on the faith's very foundation. Therefore, the category of artistic originality is here entirely precluded; or, more precisely, originality is displaced from its artistic concept because it inheres in God as the Author, where the word *Author*, likewise, should not be interpreted to have the meaning it assumes in literary art.

Divine and human authorship, or divine and human originality, are inherently incomparable, and hence belong to entirely different orders of creative power. Consequently, any claim of the originality of the Text in the unity of its content and form strongly implies that the Text is the Prophet Muhammad's work, and that the Text and its Meaning appeared at an identifiable historical point for the first time. This claim – now seen from the Text's position – constitutes heresy.

Having thus defined its contextuality, the Text obtained a key argument for its position among other religions. Namely, it sees all other religions as being close to conceiving of originality as man-made transposition or stylisation. In this context, it is interesting to remember that the *Qur'an* recognises the so-called "People of the Book" (*ahl al-kitāb*), i.e. it mentions that all the major monotheistic religions have resulted from fateful distortions of the very same Revelation that the *Qur'an* verifies. In other words, these religions represent a sort of "creative distortion" of the primeval Revelation, where the concept of creativity – from the semantic field of *originality* – is defined negatively in relation to its Truth. At the same time, the authenticity of the sources of these religions is shifted from the level of Divine Authenticity to one of human authenticity – to different revisions of these sources. (Of course, I am referring to immanent judgements and views, those revealed from the position of the Text.) These two levels are simply impossible to compare, and exist in opposition: the authenticity of Divine creation is of one order, while the authenticity of human creation is of quite another.

The content of the Revelation, as the Text says, is no (artistic) transposition of reality, but an essential and absolutely authentic account of it. Hence it is not possible, adds the Text, for this reality not to have always been revealed as essentially the same Content or Meaning. A rich diversity of texts belonging to the "People of the Book" and to other religions indicates their aspiration towards originality or authenticity in many fundamental aspects of the Content, which, in turn, indicates a relative departure from its Authenticity.[2] It follows that all other religions and their texts, in the widest sense of this concept, are original in terms of human originality.

Therefore, the Text appears with clear pretensions to continuing history, which adds multiple meanings and aspects to its contextuality. In fact, this contextuality is absolute, since it takes the entirety of history as its broadest context, on the one hand, and simultaneously creates the same context, on the other. This aspect gives rise to the impressive "poetic consequences" of the Text.

Namely, the Text establishes a kind of dialogical relation with existing cultures and religions generally, and not only with those of the Arabian Peninsula; it is dialogical both diachronically and synchronically. This is the origin of its essential feature, which in terms of contemporary science can be called citationality and intertextuality. The *Qur'an* abounds in dialogue, starting, for example, from the creation of the First Man (when God enters a dialogue with the angels and Iblis about His decision) to addressing the Prophet Muhammad. In between are a number of stories – such as those of the Prophet Joseph (Yūsuf) or the Prophet Moses (Mūsā) and the pharaoh – where the Text cites prehistoric protagonists as well as prehistoric and historic "corpora", such as those in the *Torah* (Tawrāt), *Gospel* (Injīl), etc. Of course, such a relation can be called citation only conditionally, since the Text does not quote these corpora literally or as authorities, but profoundly transforms, reorganises and builds them into its own structures, at the level of both ideology and form. Implicitly, from the Text's position, it does not cite in the true sense of the word, but aspires to revise the "citations" using the power of argument. However, as the focus here is on the Context and the fact that history comprises the different corpora the Text communicates with, we can still talk about its citationality, even if it is understood conditionally. This is important from the aspect of poetics, as a large portion of the Text's content and structure is based on this type of citationality. In fact, such citationality works in intertextuality, where intertextuality cannot be entirely reduced only to the Text's relation with other sacred corpora in the contemporary meaning of the term. Nonetheless, in a poetically coherent way, the Text incorporates a number of other texts, whereby I refer not only to the literal meaning of "text" – as a written text – but in the widest sense explained earlier. The intertextuality of the *Qur'an* is remarkably impressive, as it incorporates the most relevant sacred texts in history. Within this intertextuality, however, its citations can be regarded in two ways. First, if its citationality is regarded from the position of strictly literary and cultural research – and not from a *religious* (Muslim) standpoint – it then emerges as citationality in the usual sense: a citational relation to other texts whose authenticity is not questioned. Second, if its citationality is regarded from the position of a Muslim-believer, then it ceases to be citationality in the usual sense and becomes *autocitation*. Namely, the Text builds its citation in relation to other texts/sources by considering them to be inauthentic and, as such, unworthy of its ideological genuineness. Unusual as it may seem, the Text actually cites itself, or the prototext, for this is a condition of its divine authenticity. Since it is established as the Revelation that, for the last time, rectifies the deformities of earlier prophecies, it restores citations in their authenticity, using this type of citationality to define other texts as apocryphal. This is a remarkable form of divine autocitation that serves to preserve authenticity. Such autocitation is, of course, unacceptable from the position of the other texts positioned throughout history, but the Text is not concerned with this. Moreover, autocitation is presented as one of the Text's main goals, since this is a means to establish the quality of its relations to other texts. The principle of contextuality is thus raised to the highest possible level.

By maintaining such intertextuality and citational relation to other sacred texts, the Text uniquely "reinforces" hierohistory and history, translating them into a continuity of the highest order. It regards so-called hierohistory and history as a continuum parcelled by other texts in history that become demarcated by their revelation dates. The Text uniquely incorporates into its own structure texts from the so-called revealed religions that preceded it. For instance, it abounds in citations about Moses, Abraham (Ibrāhīm), David (Dāwūd) and other prophets, and communicates with all of these texts in a unique style, while these texts do not maintain the same level of communication among themselves, and particularly not with the *Qur'an*; this is because the *Qur'an* succeeded them, and history became parcelled in proportion to the inability of these texts to mutually communicate. For example, in addition to a number of structural and ideological purposes, an important task with which the paradigmatic story of Moses is charged is to underline the continuity of both the Revelation and history itself, all of which is accomplished by means of intertextuality.

Having thus become a Hypertext, it, among other things, emphasises two important points.[3]

First, the texts it communicates with in terms of citations and intertextuality do not have the capacity for intertextual organisation of its own rank – diachronic and synchronic – as they do not have the same relation to the recognition of other texts as the Hypertext does. Certainly, they too are well familiar with the principle of intertextual architecture, but in a considerably narrower scope than the Hypertext. As I have already mentioned, the Hypertext absorbs texts from all directions following the peculiar principle of autocitation. This type of architecture yields enormous results at the level of ideology. The Text thus establishes a vital prerequisite for arguing its divine universalisation – that its authenticity is eternal and everlasting.

Second, following the same principle, the Text uses its particular intertextuality to differentiate the level of its contextualisation from the contextualisation level of other texts. Namely, other texts have a reduced degree of contextuality, in proportion to their delimitation in history that they thus parcel, influencing its course only upon being carved into it. Therefore, the Hypertext successfully overcomes this reductionism through the intertextuality discussed so far: resolutely and explicitly, it spreads its net over the whole textual and sacred history.

A possible objection to my understanding of different levels of intertextuality might be based on the fact that other texts (such as the *Bible*, for example) also have command of the principle of intertextuality, for they employ citationality to establish connections with earlier historical texts. This is an incontrovertible fact – as is their intertextuality – yet the difference, however, lies in the "scope" and "quality" of their intertextuality, which, in turn, leads to other consequences. Namely, the Hypertext has the definite advantage of coming last in the course of history and can use this privileged position to establish a relation with all previous texts – back to the Text/Dialogue about the creation of the First Man – by defining the degree of their authenticity and trans/historic accomplishments. In doing so, it also explicates its "stretched-ness" back to the beginning of time, using intertextuality to support this explication at the same time.

The citationality and intertextuality of this Text have multiple functions that are performed simultaneously and always in the same direction. I am here primarily interested in their poetic function. Namely, the citationality and intertextuality of the Text do not operate solely at the level of literary structure: they do fulfil their task at this level too, but taking it only as a sound basis for further pursuit of the final end – an ideological one. This sacred Text is not confined to the aesthetic sphere only; through it and enriched by it, the Text proceeds to the sphere of ideology, to cast particular light from this perspective on the whole road behind, and on its literary and aesthetic structure. However, before explaining the importance of such illumination, I should point out that the whole "set of poetic instruments" in the field of citationality and intertextuality serves the Text's determination to affirm *the idea of its continuity and its transhistorical authenticity*. This is one of its key aims. Furthermore, this is also important from a poetic perspective. Reading the story of Moses, one can appreciate it on a literary level, being amazed at its arabesque structure and its distribution across different parts of the Text; however, the Text does not stop at this level of reception, as it says: "Therefore, recourse to the narratives of suchlike persons so that they may hopefully pause to think."[4] It means that the Text requires that the literary and aesthetic reception be transcended, while imposing another requirement – one of an epistemological nature. In other words, there are stories narrated in the Text, but their task is to present the Idea represented by the whole Book. In this process, citationality and intertextuality operate in two different ways. On the one hand, they are the key elements of the narrative texture, which makes them vitally active in the literary and aesthetic organisation of the Text. On the other hand, however, citationality and intertextuality have the task of supporting the argumentation of the Text at an ideological level: of presenting the decisive and vital role of Islamic monotheism, apostasy, violence, etc. From the position of the Text, this comprises the whole and essential *history*, not its (artistic) transposition into a *story*.

I have already said that, from its highest platform, namely its ideological level, the Text casts an extraordinary light on the whole road behind it, as well as on its literary and aesthetic structure. This is how it seems at first glance. More precisely, such a direction – from narration of the story towards its ultimate meaning – feels natural to the reader, which makes it all the more effective, for a very important *realisation* awaits the reader beyond *narrativity*. Citationality and intertextuality do, indeed, serve a full affirmation of this direction. Such a direction and structure make a story interesting, providing it with the vitality of its plot. However, the direction is quite the opposite of the Author's position. Namely, the Author uses the form to embed in it the Idea the reader is to adopt. In other words, the Idea is the Author's primary concern, it is pivotal to the whole procedure, and He descends from the Idea towards the form. Taking the road of deduction, the Text brought about a reversal of the Arab-Islamic tradition, which had been governed by inductive poetics for centuries. It also becomes evident that, moving from the Idea towards the form, the Text ensures the perseverance of the Idea throughout transhistory, of the Idea that is only revealed in different forms appropriate to different contexts – from the Idea, for instance, contained in the Text of the *Tawrāt* to the Qur'anic Revelation. These forms, however, had not been entirely abandoned, or had not been entirely repealed. This is a notable fact. Namely, the forms had only been modelled in different times, but – from the position of the Text – there can be no mention of their obliteration. A certain sense of continuity had always existed, regardless of the *diversity* of forms, precisely because of the power of the Idea that, having remained essentially unaffected, held in its orbit all the forms of its revelation. This is an absolute advantage of the Text's deductive poetics. For other texts or forms in which the Idea had been revealed were constantly exposed to centrifugal forces – until their possible evanescence in the depths of the past – whereas the Idea exerted a centripetal force; thus, in critical periods of text deformations, it was always revealed in a new form, establishing such close relations with other forms and texts that it developed a universe, or a strong historical continuum. Giving a preference to a certain form, or employing poetic inversion, would never yield such a result. Intertextuality is of the utmost importance here. Namely, the gravitational field of the transhistorical Idea encompasses a number of its forms/texts, so it is only natural that the text of the *Qur'an* should use intertextuality: it is a distinct way of highlighting the power, importance and perseverance of the Idea, and to articulate One Voice over the dissonance of texts. Consequently, it follows that intertextuality is in the very essence of the Text.

However, there is something unusual running through the intertextuality of the sacred Text, something that differentiates it from many other texts also characterised by intertextuality, particularly from those of literary postmodernism.

Namely, in literary art, citationality and intertextuality uphold or contest texts being built in a new work of art. At the same time they, for their part, uphold the emerging work. Hence, a relation of approval or disapproval comes into play here, through a relation maintaining the continuity of tradition and bringing the entire culture into the foreground again, rescuing it from self-oblivion or disintegration in space and time. The aim of intertextuality in this sacred Text, however, is to designate other texts as falsified, inauthentic, plagiarised, deformed, etc., and to establish its own position against the characteristics of such texts. Other texts, therefore, have a different value here: in the form they were found at the time, they represent a deformity unacceptable to the Text, which aspires to absolutely establish the truth. These texts certainly are part of a tradition, of culture in history, but important parts of their content are negativistic with regard to the content of this Text, in which they are incorporated through intertextuality only to be differentiated in accordance with their relationship to the Truth. This evidently implies quite a different relationship to citationality and intertextuality from that found in literary works. The difference lies in the quality of their relationship. In a literary text based on the principle of citationality and intertextuality, truthfulness is irrelevant and transfiguration of citations becomes a necessary principle for such an intertextual edifice to achieve efficient and aesthetically effective fusion with the new structure that, as a result, seems like a firm fabric. Form is of extreme importance here, in proportion to indifference towards the kind of Authenticity and Truth promoted by this sacred Text. The sacred Text does not pursue tradition, or culture in history, as its primary or ultimate goal (which is the case with literary texts) but, rather, upholds the Idea along the continuum of tradition, or for that matter culture. The entire culture has always toiled in an effort to convey the Idea. The history of the world is largely the history of these efforts and toil, just as distinctive qualities of cultures stem from different relations to the Idea.

Hence, the sacred Text analysed here is realised through deductive poetics and it exists to reveal the Truth, not to inspire imagination, aestheticism or the *utmost* indulgence in the allure of the form. It does not regard itself as art. Its transformation of other texts does not, therefore, end in the domain of the aesthetic – though always recognising its huge importance – but in the domain of the ethical: it employs citationality to "subject" other texts to its Truth, not to artistic fiction. For example, in the story of Moses we can recognise many elements of the same story from other sacred texts (and a number of non-sacred texts); however, the Text "espouses" them not only to fulfil the aesthetic and entertainment functions of the story (although the reader finds these functions precious as well) but, in the first place, to bring them to the intense light of its Truth.

There is something else rather interesting about citationality and transfiguration. Namely, the Text sometimes quotes itself as well, but always uses transfiguration when doing so. Let me turn to the story of Moses again: the Golden Calf motif, for example, recurs six times (some motifs recur even more frequently) but is always transfigured in a new textual environment. Citationality is thus twofold here: on the one hand, it relies on other sacred texts while, on the other, it also resorts to autocitationality – partial repetition of the same structures within the same motif.

One can only conclude that the contextuality of the Text is comprehensive. It manifests itself at many levels: the religious, sociological, literary, etc. Citationality and intertextuality are irreplaceable "instruments" for maintaining its total contextuality.

However, special attention should be devoted to the kind of Qur'anic Text contextualisation realised in the literary tradition to which the *Qur'an* builds a very interesting and dynamic relation in terms of ideology, in particular influencing the poetics and production of the entirety of Old Arabic literature.

Notes

1 The text is constantly distinguished from art in different ways which I am going to present at different points, as this is the fundamental postulate of its poetics.

2 I use the capitalised noun *Text* to refer to the text of the *Qur'an*. However, I use the noun "text" with reference to other religions in a very wide, non-literal sense of the word: this meaning belongs to the fields of semiotics and philology; "text" in lowercase letters refers here to every revelation or every religious source, whether oral or written. After all, the *Qur'an* was revealed to the Prophet in an oral form and only subsequently became shaped as a text in its literal meaning.

3 The term hypertext is used with a different meaning today – as "a separate aspect of intertextuality, in fact, its utmost technological realisation" related to the use of information technologies. (Further reading: Marina Katnić-Bakaršić, *Stilistika*, Ljiljan, Sarajevo, 2001, p. 296 onwards.) However, I believe this term can be used here in the sense I explain.

4 *Qur'an*, 7:176. All the quotations from the *Qur'an* in the English version of the book are taken from the translation of the *Qur'an* into English by J. M Rodwell, Phoenix, Orion House, London, 1994.

3 The Qur'anic Text's advance on tradition

The *Qur'an* found a rich literary tradition in Arabic, which had already achieved a degree of technical perfection. The corpus of the *Seven Golden Odes* represented the gilding of this tradition at the historic moment of the *Qur'an*'s advance towards it. The Arabian people had expressed their genius in poetry through production and quality that inexplicably exceeded their general level of culture and civilisation at the time. Arabian culture was a Culture of the Word that found its expression in technically perfect poetry as early as the fifth or sixth century. However, it did not only represent an art that met the Arabians' aesthetic needs, transposing reality as art usually does: on the Arabian Peninsula poetry represented "a general state of mind", so that it profoundly influenced the reality and history of this heroic age in which poets were heroes of the highest order. Tribal leaders and herdsmen were equally enchanted with poetry, took pride in it equally and could compose poetry of equal quality. This was something not observed in other peoples: Arabian and, subsequently, Arabic poetic elitism was all-embracing. Furthermore, in this world the Word demonstrated its outstanding importance at yet another level, which was only natural considering the general appreciation of its majesty. Namely, the Beautiful and the Word in which it is revealed were raised to the level of religion and magic at the same time, so that the total dedication of the whole people to the Word came as no surprise. Given his exceptional intimacy with the Word, the Poet acted as the tribal soothsayer (*kāhin*). The authority of poetic word obtained for him a special status among his people – that of the medium between the recipient and supreme forces. In this context, it is reasonable to talk of the magic of words for pre-Islamic Arabians and, subsequently, of the privileged status of poetry against all other arts. Such a special status for poetry has never been superseded with Arabs, regardless of the fact that the *Qur'an* firmly cut into tradition at this very spot. Furthermore, its perseverance shows that tradition will never completely fade away, regardless of the power of the explosion that texts of immense strength, such as the *Qur'an*, can cause within it. Even after the *Qur'an* appeared on the scene, poetry remained an unparalleled form of artistic expression with Arabs. It is true that poetry had to surrender its medial sacerdotal function, but it still kept the status of cult art; the cult of the Word, especially the poetic word, is still evident in the Arab world. Therefore, adjusting to the new situation created by the *Qur'an*, the tradition managed to make its way around this dawn of Islam; hence, it is only legitimate to talk about the transformation of Culture and the reorganisation of certain positions, and not in any way about the evanescence of Tradition as such.

Very powerfully, and with the determination of monotheism, the *Qur'an* cut exactly into this vital part of the Arabian being from several angles. Its Text expresses an attitude to poets and poetry in a number of places, making it legitimate to ask why a sacred Text of such enormous importance is explicitly and implicitly concerned with poetry to such an extent.

Although the previous passages already suggest an answer, this position of the *Qur'an* should be elaborated further, since it concerns a fateful confrontation with tradition as found by the *Qur'an*, as well as for the tradition to be shaped over hundreds of years in the gravitational field of this Text.

The relation between tradition and the *Qur'an* should be considered at two levels: at their ideological (content) level, and at the level of the form in which their content is communicated. Clearly, these two levels are not mechanically separated, but rather realised in unity, both in the Qur'anic Text and in the highest traditional values. The confrontation was so dramatic that the entire tradition, all but rhapsodic and self-sufficient until then, fell silent for some decades, devising a way to survive. From the broad vantage of the present day, we now know that tradition has survived, quite resourcefully so, although it had to abandon certain poetic postulates from before the poetics of the *Qur'an*.

The *Qur'an* confronting poetry at the level of ideology

Poet possessed and Prophet faithful

The poetry of pre-Islamic Arabians was not art for art's sake, nor was it art for the sake of aestheticism, though it was so obsessed with form that it is legitimate to talk of a certain philotechnic component of this poetry: it was fascinated by its own form, and with good reason, since it had developed its form to perfection. However, this issue will be discussed in more detail in the next chapter. Let us only say for now that the primary cause of the *Qur'an*'s serious confrontation with poetry was not its form – although the *Qur'an* establishes its superiority to this aspect of poetry as well; the confrontation between the Text and poetry, on the contrary, primarily took place at the level of ideology. The Qur'anic Text – according to its explications – did not surface in history to abolish the Arabian poetic form, but to defeat the ideological dimension of poetry, while the Text assuming superiority at the level of form *too* served an "attendant" divine argumentation, to a degree where these two "poles" of the same expression could not be divided.

I have already mentioned that poetry enjoyed the status of a special medium. This defined it as eminently ideological in character: through the power of the Word in Form, the poet communicates with supernatural forces, which he can, indeed, propitiate with his art. This implies, of course, that these supreme forces are also very susceptible to the Word or, more precisely, to the Word masterfully clad in the Form. At this stage of poetry – when it was, in a Hegelian way, closely tied to religion, as a remarkable instrument of intuitive cognition – poetry had several important functions for pre-Qur'anic Arabians: it served their aesthetic needs; it fostered their awareness of personal and tribal esteem and served as effective derision of the enemy; it perpetuated their highly developed collective memory and genealogy; it cultivated great sensitivity of people who, in overly harsh conditions of their reality, managed to generate brilliant poetry as a sanctuary for their increased need for fiction and imagination. In short, poetry meant everything to them and, precisely because it meant everything to them, it succeeded in achieving its religious status from this level: the poet was the tribal soothsayer or shaman; his poetic word became divine as it represented an irreplaceable code for contacting deities who were better pleased by poetry than by anything else. Since the Arabians believed in polytheistic cults and followed pagan practices – from brutal blood feuds to burying their own female children alive – the implication is that poetry was much too closely connected with paganism, as well as that its ideological position was very strong and, consequently, deserving of appropriate treatment. This is the reason why the *Qur'an* swooped down on poetry so uncompromisingly. Thus, it cut into poetry from above – at its ideological level, knowing that by sorting out this level, through deduction, it would reduce poetry down to the sphere it belonged to, as well as shatter the belief in supernatural powers and the medial character of the poet – a belief not typical of the Arabians alone but, to a greater or lesser extent, of many other peoples and cultures as well – from Greek muses to the "Blue Flower" of Romanticism. Even today, poetry still carries in its "genes" memories of these irretrievable times.

Be that as it may, the *Qur'an* came on the scene intending to put an end to the symbiosis between poetry and religion, and to differentiate them clearly: according to the *Qur'an*, poetry is not capable of reaching religious truths and its persistence in pursuing this end is defined as heresy of the highest order; poetry must leave the path of religious illumination and search for different focuses and directions. It is only in this sense that poetry was "de-missioned" by the Qur'anic Text, though it had actually never been buried – it only dressed in new attire, took a good rest and, inspired by a new meaning, flourished in a new form in Arab-Islamic culture as one of its richest ornaments.

We learn most of the authentic ideological aspirations of pre-Islamic poetry from the *Qur'an* itself. Namely, the ideological dimension of this poetry cannot be fully grasped from it alone, since pre-Islamic poetry as we now know it is problematic in terms of authenticity: it had been handed down as an oral tradition for several centuries, only to be recorded by Islamic philosophers, who probably undertook to de-paganise it in a way.

In a number of places the *Qur'an* warns us that its text is not poetry and that the Prophet Muhammad is not a poet, implying the role of the poet in the domain of religion. The following passages offer several typical quotations.

We have not taught him [Muhammad] poetry, nor would it beseem him,[1] states the *Qur'an* decisively when disallowing the Arabians' objection that the

Prophet is a poet. The Prophet does not need poetry to communicate with God or to exert decisive influence over people. It follows from this ayah that, at that time, poetry clearly had the status I have discussed before – poets called to deities by means of the poetic word, so that poetry had a powerful influence over people in this domain. Ayahs relating to this context inform us of the nature of poetry in terms of religious illumination and religious acts in general. Namely, the *Qur'an* complements the previous statement by words leaving no room for doubt: *This* Book *is no other than a warning and a clear Qur'an.*[2] The key word in this part of the ayah, since it contrarily interprets the concept of poetry (*shi'r*), is the word *clear* (*mubīn*). This means that, in the domain of religion, poetry is designated as obscure, blurred, fictional; its perception, therefore, is inauthentic and deceptive in its obscurity, which exposes poetry itself as essentially delusive.

In another place this Text says:

> That this [the *Qur'an*] verily is the word of an apostle worthy of all honour/ And that it is not the word of a poet – how little do ye believe;/Neither is it a word of a soothsayer [*Kāhin*] – how little do you receive warning – It is a missive from the Lord of the worlds.[3]

Here we have the opposition between the phrase "*an apostle worthy of all honour*" (*karīm*), on the one hand, and the phrases "*the word of a poet*" and "*a word of a soothsayer*" on the other. The Prophet is worthy of all honour in terms of authenticity, whereas the poet – as it follows – is inauthentic and untruthful; the Prophet is on an apostolic mission, which means that his word is true in relation to its Source, whereas the poet's word is self-proclaimed and thereby inauthentic in relation to the Truth.

A point to note here is that this ayah places *the poet* (*shā'ir*) and *the soothsayer* (*kāhin*) at the same level, which confirms my previous statements. The poet and the soothsayer are at the same level in terms of their relation to the Truth. They are "functionally" equated: they are two functions identified in one person. A number of grammatical parallelisms in these ayahs support the statement by means of language and poetic syntax. With poetry as his principal instrument, the soothsayer is someone whose activity is primarily ideological, which is why the *Qur'an* is so firmly positioned against the poet-soothsayer, or the soothsayer-poet.

The attribute pre-Qur'anic Arabians used with the word "poet" (*shā'ir*) was the adjective "possessed" (*majnūn*); this attribute carries negative connotations today, but its connotations at the time were positive. Namely, the word *majnūn* (possessed) is the passive participle derived from the root *jnn*, meaning "to be possessed by jinns". It was the poet's *privileged* state of mind in which he was possessed by supernatural forces – jinns – that, allegedly, gave him superhuman inspiration. The inspiration was an unnatural state, so that the poet's word was, correspondingly, considered uncommon and supernatural. This is the Arabian version of the ancient Greek muses. As synonymous with the word *jinn*, they used the word *shaytan*; this word also carries only negative connotations today, but, at that time, a shaytan was believed to be whispering to the poet in his state of inspiration, enabling him to be an excellent poet. It is interesting that this belief persisted, though sporadically, long after the *Qur'an* was revealed, so that one of the greatest Umayyad poets, Jarir (Jarīr, 653–733), imparted his creative possession by jinns and shaytan. Following this belief, the ancient Arabians even named their offspring *Shaytan*. From today's perspective, it is difficult to think of a more heinous ideological qualifier, since the *Qur'an* defines shaytan as haughtiness, insubordination and transgression personified; from the Qur'an's perpsective, there is no greater enemy of God and man than shaytan. There is hardly anything else that underlines the ideological opposition between this poetry and the Text better than this word and the historical, or literary and historical, fact about the use of this word. When counterposing poetry, the Text most frequently offers the Truth as its argument, or the claim that, unlike poetry, it is indeed perfectly clear. Thus, in a number of places the *Qur'an* maintains that the Prophet brought the Truth. In consequence, this means that poetry as a whole does not represent the Truth, as something clear, unclouded and, as such, a warning and guide. Admittedly, since the highest literary and aesthetic values distinguish the Text itself, it also contains certain parts that are unclear and vague: *The best of recitals hath God sent down – a book in unison with itself, and teaching by iteration.*[4] This vagueness or iteration[5] refers to some of the Text's figures of speech and tropes, but does not refer to the basis of its monotheism, to its foundation and belief system, etc. In contrast, according to the *Qur'an*, poetry is entirely obscure and inauthentic when presenting the Truth in the religious sense of the word. This is the essential difference between them. Poetic language, which the *Qur'an* also uses, is always more or less suggestive and connotative, but what is crucial in this respect is the way the Idea is presented. In addition, it is important to point out the directions that both poetry and the Qur'anic Text follow. Poetry employs a number of affective means of poetic language in order to direct towards the "Truth" from the perspective of the affective and emotional. The "Truth" is then presented obscurely and subjectively precisely because of the strong impregnation of the affective. Furthermore, being often recited during certain rites, poetry represented an important instrument for increasing the emotional charge that enhanced "cognition". Therefore, poetry took a path that could be called *the path of induction*: "cognition" was realised from poetry and by poetry and, as a consequence, the degree of cognition could be concluded to have been proportionate to the degree of poetic quality. The ultimate consequence of this was poetry that shaped cognition, or the Idea, at this level – not the other way round.

It is on its reverse path that the *Qur'an* insists. It does not need poetry (the relevant ayah is quoted above) to represent the Idea: to do so it resorts partly to prose text and partly to text using rhyme and rhythm. Poetry is not essential for the Idea to emerge – the Idea is disclosed in different forms of literary language, depending on its own needs. The *Qur'an*'s reverse path of deduction is of extreme importance here because the Text is shaped according to an Idea that is relatively independent of it, or is independent of its form, as it is sufficiently clear in itself and for itself as well as powerful enough to be revealed in other forms as well. From this perspective – following the path of deduction – the Text is sheer and clear to the same extent as the Idea is clear. On an inductive poetic path, poetic language is not able to render the Idea in its fullness and clarity: it exhausts itself in constant efforts to embrace something beyond its capabilities, which is why it requires too much allusiveness, connotation, obscurity, etc. The poetic language of the Qur'anic Text is, by contrast, pregnant with content and can only just bear all the subtleties of the Sublime Meaning. Poetry endeavours to reach the Idea, whereas in the *Qur'an* the Idea pours itself out into the Text, hence the difference in their suggestiveness: while poetry resorts mostly or solely to the emotional or suggestive in order to attain the Idea, the *Qur'an* has suggestiveness less expressed in its Text, as the Idea cannot be fully expressed through poetic language.

It becomes clear from this why the *Qur'an* insists so much on sentences like *Do they not pause to think*; *Do they not understand.* Namely, poetry mainly relies on emotions, on sensibility, whereas the Qur'anic argumentation strongly relies on the mind, on reason, which results from its deductive approach. It is true that the language and style of the *Qur'an* profoundly affect believers' emotions too, and that the *Qur'an* does not exclude "imagination instruments" either, but it largely relies on human reason. In fact, while poetry appeals to only one "pole" of the human being – that implied by the term *feel* – the *Qur'an*, on the other hand, includes and cultivates both poles: *to know* and *to feel*; to reach by *the mind* and to embrace by *the heart*. Acknowledgement and cultivation of only one human ability leads to man's deformation. The following ayah is particularly meaningful in this sense: *Warn thou, then. For thou by the favour of thy Lord art neither soothsayer nor possessed.*[6] Namely, God bestowed a great favour, or a blessing, on His Prophet by sharply distinguishing him from a *soothsayer*, or the *one possessed*; it should also be noted that the noun *soothsayer* is synonymous with the noun *poet*, and that both are modified by the adjective *possessed* (by a jinn or shaytan). Both the soothsayer and the poet are, thus, depicted as entirely negative. The difference between them, as this ayah implies, is the same as the one between paganism and monotheism, for, in this ideological confrontation, the Prophet is given the greatest of blessings by virtue of his prophethood being in every aspect different from the poet's agency. Unlike the Prophet, the poet-soothsayer is beyond God's blessing, which is equated here with the Prophet's privileged position with regard to the Truth, and is condemned to delusion. The first sentence of this ayah is hence strongly stressed: *Warn thou, then.* Namely, having a mission that is, on an ideological level, entirely different from the ideological represented by the poet or soothsayer, the Prophet has the duty to warn, to advise about the Truth, to be its bearer. Consequently, this means that he must extend his mission to include warnings against the poet-soothsayer as well. Moreover, in the given context, the poet-soothsayer is the principal ideological enemy of the Prophethood presented as the Truth, which appeals to man's intellectual and rational faculties, whereas the poet-soothsayer appeals to man's sensory faculties. I have already mentioned that, to some extent, the *Qur'an* also relies on man's sensory and imaginative faculties; but within the influence of the Qur'anic Text, emotionality mostly arises as a consequence of Divine argumentation rooted in the sphere of mind and reason, whereas the poet-soothsayer goes off in the opposite direction and hence cannot have the same reach. Furthermore, the essential difference between the poet and the Prophet of God is also reflected in the etymology of these two words.

The Prophet of God is not like a poet: he is a bearer of the Truth in the light of reason

1 *The Messenger* (*rasūl*) is a person dispatched with a certain mission. His medial function is fully specified in etymologic and semantic terms, as he cannot exert (magic) influence over the One who dispatched him unless it is explicitly stated. The messenger can act in one direction only – he carries out the task of the One whose messenger he actually is, with precise instructions about his mission, and cannot, in principle, go off in the opposite direction: he does not act on behalf of those he is sent to in the direction of the One whose mission he actually carries out. The principle of the Vertical is inviolable here. God can be merciful to those who are good and considerate towards His prophet – that is exactly what He promises to do – but this is so because he is His prophet, with the stress on the word *prophethood*. God will do so only by virtue of reverence for His Own prophethood. A qualitatively different approach to the situation, or possibly placing the emphasis on the prophet's action in both directions, is not viable because it would turn such a person into a real medium, which would be quite inappropriate for *prophethood* as the realisation of the (one-way) Vertical.

2 At the same time, the word *prophet* does not imply emotionality – quite the contrary. A prophet carries out his mission highly rationally and within specific instructions; emotionality, great emotional charge and similar states are not inherent in him. He is sent with sound arguments, with which he does not interfere in order to preserve their full authenticity – which is an argument in itself and by itself. Insistence on the emotional dimension of prophethood would possibly obscure the arguments conveyed by the prophet and would, accordingly, lead to so great a semantic shift in the word *prophet* that the word would have to be abandoned and adequately replaced. If, in the people a prophet is sent to, there are certain emotions aroused with regard to prophethood-related activities, then it certainly represents a secondary phenomenon: it does not originate from the prophet himself and the act of his prophethood as their primary occurrence, but from the people's state of mind shaped or produced by the exceptional nature of arguments. It happens on different occasions – and this is something the Revelation strongly relies on – that a person, upon accepting rational argumentation, experiences exaltation that is manifested in different ways and in proportion to surprising effects produced by the argumentation. In any case, the latter reaction is secondary only; it is a consequence arising from the man's primary activity – communication with the argumentation. These two activities are not mutually

exclusive; rather, the latter comes as the attestation of the former, as its unique backing; however, while interpreting the nouns *prophet* and *prophethood*, it is important to bear in mind that emotionality is not their inherent or primary content. Of course, from the position of Revelation, it is clear that God does not send prophets in order to convince people of His existence by means of some extraordinary excitement; He dispatches a prophet with arguments, while emotional states are a consequence of the relation to God and His arguments, just as enjoying his blessings is a result of the relation to His argumentation. Even when, for instance, the prophet Musa threw down his staff that "swallowed up" all the magic creatures of the Pharaoh's magicians, they bowed and professed their faith for no other reason but argument: the Staff-miracle was the *argument* that provoked strong reactions. Anyone facing prophethood in general – whether accepting or rejecting it – must face the resultant consequences, which, naturally, are in proportion to the significance of prophethood. In the case of divine prophethood, these consequences are immensely profound, but the same principle is evident in other important forms of prophethood as well. For example, if an emperor dispatches his emissary with conditions that are dictated through him, adopting any attitude towards these conditions must have its consequences.

In any case, my aim here is to suggest a specific medial role of the prophet of God inasmuch as it is argumentative and medial as well as emotionally neutral, except that a prophet has a special relationship with the One who sends him, as – for the mission to be effective and for the prophet's authenticity to be preserved – he must be utterly loyal, rational, steadfast, etc.

Having in mind such an etymological origin and semantic field for the word *prophet*, it is clearly not just randomly added to the proper noun Mohammad and the names of other prophets in the *Qur'an*. The noun *prophet* is in constant and strong opposition to the nouns *poet* and *soothsayer* (where we should always bear in mind that the soothsayer uses poetry as his main instrument). Such interpretation of the word *prophet* aims at highlighting the qualities on account of which the *Qur'an*, as can be seen from the quoted ayahs, refuses to equate the functions of prophet and poet, defining their ideological positions as opposed. The part of this book that elaborates on the etymology and semantics of the word *shā'ir* (poet) will adequately underline their oppositeness, revealing why the *Qur'an* devotes so much attention to it. In order to achieve this goal, as well as to elucidate the deductive nature of Qur'anic poetry and the inductive nature of traditional poetics, several further warnings should first be given here.

3 *A prophet*, in general, implies the unidirectional relation of prophethood, as already mentioned. Naturally, I hereby refer to the fact that he always conveys primary content in one direction only. His feedback is secondary and, in special cases, such as a message from God, such feedback is ephemeral in terms of a possible influence on primary content modification; the ephemerality of this relation is proportionate to the power and authorship of the One dispatching the prophet, or proportionate to His independence from the reaction of those to whom the prophet is sent. Consequently – what indeed is important for my proposition – prophethood can only function in an act of deduction: the prophet's

reception of the world does not matter, nor does his relation to all forms of tradition, as his task is to bring the *deductive* Text into the World and Tradition in order for the Text to modify and create them after the Author's intentions. However, it seems insufficient to say that this is simply a matter of deduction; it should be emphasised that this is a matter of – if I may use such a term – vertical deduction, in the sense of its absolute unconditionality and, by implication, of the unpredictability of explosive reactions that the Text will cause in the World and Tradition by means of this very type of deduction. The poet follows the opposite direction.

4 *A prophet* does not create. Considering the nature of his mission, a prophet has no capacity for intervention in the domain of the content he conveys or the form in which he conveys this content. He has a medial, not a creative position. Therefore, the poetics of Revelation is entirely beyond the Prophet's influence in terms of possible changes to it. The word *Revelation* itself denotes quite a different quality from the one espoused by the poet-soothsayer: the latter does not restrict his activity to mediation/transmission of the content allegedly whispered to him by a jinn or shaytan, but uses this whispering in order to create, which, in turn, crucially influences the authenticity of the whisperer. The prophet's task is to absolutely faithfully convey the Revelation content, which is *not whispered* but *delivered* to him, for the Revelation insists on its absolute authenticity. The terms *whisper* and *deliver* must obviously be distinguished (the Arabic text uses an even better expression – that the Revelation is *descended*). The first term specifically defines the relationship between the whisperer and his medium, because whispering as such is non-resolute and essentially inarticulate; the whisperer's position is discreet, mysterious and magical, it is defensive and digressive, and it must be such so as to allow the poet-soothsayer as much space as possible for creating, modulating and modelling the whispered "material", etc. Their relationship is somewhat like a partnership. From the *Qur'an*'s standpoint, it is partnership in connection with the Revelation that is absolutely the gravest sin of all.

The differences between the poet-soothsayer and the prophet are becoming increasingly notable. The term *deliver* includes nothing of the above: a deliverer has no powers to make interventions in the "material", especially not to modulate it as a medium, but has the duty to faithfully convey what he is tasked with. Hence there are many places in the *Qur'an* explicitly stating that the Prophet is but a human being and that his whole task is to transmit the Revelation.[7] This direction from the Revelation Source to its recipients, and the quality of the Prophet's mission, are both significant for elucidating the deductive character of the Revelation and the inductive character of the poetry at the time. With regard to this shift, it is important to note one more thing.

The poet's relation is always transpositional, since he never surrenders his creative prerogatives. In this sense his poetics is inductive too. However, owing to the nature of prophethood, or the character of the prophet's mission, transposition relating to the Revelation follows exactly the opposite direction. The Revelation *descends* from the unknown beyond, from the metaphysical, through the prophet into the World. Deduction is vertical. The undivided content of the

Revelation is "transposed" from some other World into this world by way of a prophet, in the form that the World has been trying to interpret from its descent to this day, considering the fact that this form incorporates a vast and too condensed body of content. The opposite way is inconceivable: a prophet has no capacity, hypothetically, for transposition in the opposite direction that could even remotely be of the same extent and quality. It can only be done by a poet, which is why his "mission" is quite inappropriate in the domain of religion.

Another frequent word that the Text uses for the Prophet Muhammad falls within the same semantic field (although with a different root) and carries the same poetic implications. It is the term *prophet* (*al-nabiyy*), which, due to the effect of the powerful forces of the sacred context, should be translated as the *Prophet of God*. *Messenger* and *prophet* are clearly within the same semantic field and have the same position with respect to the Revelation Source in terms of mediation, creative non-intervention, poetic definiteness, etc. I will therefore not devote any particular attention to this term.[8]

The poet is not like a prophet of God: the poet stirs emotions in the hearth of magic

The etymology and semantics of the root *sh'r* and of its derivative form *shā'ir* (poet) are in opposition to the noun *messenger* (*rasūl*).[9] Among the number of meanings associated with this root, two are the most frequent and closely related. Namely, the first is *to know, (re)cognise, perceive, realise, feel*. The other is *to write/recite poetry*.[10] The point is that these two fields are in concentric semantic circles. *Knowledge* or *cognisance* expressed by the root *sh'r* is knowledge or cognisance acquired through senses, imagination, intuition, etc., or, as jargon would put it, through *a sixth sense*. The knowledge denoted by this verb, therefore, is not positive and rational knowledge, or science, but the sort of "knowledge/cognisance" gained by other means. To denote positive cognisance in scientific terms, the Arabic language uses the root *'lm*, not *sh'r*. Consequently, there is a direct and strong association between feeling and knowledge in the root *sh'r*, and these two "acts" are characterised by simultaneity in one: this kind of knowledge is gained through feeling and, in response, this kind of knowledge further intensifies feelings. As a result, this might mean that the degree of knowledge is proportionate to the intensity of feelings. It is not surprising, then, that the *poet* (a noun derived from the root *sh'r*) – following the need for this proportionality – was described as possessed (by a jinn or shaytan): this possession guaranteed the poet exceptionality with regard to eccentric – perhaps even ecstatic – sensibility in the act of creation. Modern culture distanced itself from this attribute associated with the poet – which is quite indicative – as, in the word *majnūn*, it pushed the connotation *possessed* into the background, while bringing the connotation *crazed* in the foreground; however, these two meanings have remained in a causal relation till this day.

The active participle *shā'ir* was derived from the root *sh'r* and then became completely nominalised. This participle has always been translated as *poet*, but such a translation is not the exact equivalent of *the poet*, which is something I would like to point out here. However, a different translation is impossible and the reader must always keep in mind that the noun *poet* is not an accurate translation of the Arabic noun *shā'ir*. In order to preserve the original semantics of the term, I will occasionally use the word *shā'ir* instead of *the poet*. It is quite another matter that the term has survived despite the *Qur'an*'s uncompromising attitude towards its ideological aspirations and qualifiers, for even today the Arabic language has no other word for what we call *a poet* and what we consider an ideologically neutral term. Tradition is endlessly resourceful and therefore vital: after the Revelation, the poet surrendered his ideological function but, preserving the term *shā'ir*, tradition preserved an everlasting memory of this earliest origin of poetry.

Thus, *shā'ir* is *the-one-who-knows-through-feelings*, or *the-one-who-feels-knowing*. Only this sort of "translation" can illustrate the inadequacy of our term *poet*. This is exactly the description of the soothsayer's function. Certainly, the soothsayer does not necessarily use poetry alone to invoke supreme forces, but his instrument of choice is often poetry. It is important to remember that, as was mentioned above, Arabic culture is a Culture of the Word. Consequently, in a culture like this, the soothsayer could not have chosen any other instrument of his cognisance but a word optimally immersed in emotion. There is a causal relation between the culture and cult within it; they perpetually cultivate one another.

The other meaning of the root *sh'r* I referred to – *to write/recite poetry* – becomes readily incorporated here and displays an unexpected stratification of meaning in the word *shā'ir*. Namely, in an attempt to render this stratification into a language other than Arabic, *shā'ir* could be translated as *the-one-who-knows-feeling-through-verses*, which is functional in terms of my analysis but clearly unsuitable for general and widespread usage. Therefore, *shā'ir* is "the one who arrives at cognisance through feelings aroused by his poetry and feelings that he builds in his poetry".

In order to define the word *shā'ir* as precisely as possible and to contrast it with the word *rasūl* (messenger) we should first discuss its morphological status. It is an active participle of *aspiring*, and, as many other active participles in Arabic, a nominalisation with emphasis on its aspiration: through it, participles underline their specific status. Likewise, this active participle stresses its processuality, an ongoing *intensification*; it expresses permanent activity, which is why it refuses to become a noun in full capacity, as the noun does not have the potential that the Arabic active participle has.[11]

In the following section I will draw a demarcation line between *rasūl* (messenger) and *shā'ir* (poet-soothsayer) in the domain of poetics, or the ideological confrontation of the *Qur'an* with poetry, in the same order in which I gave the attributes of a poet. These two terms are not a purely random choice so as to display a great number of nuances. My "selection" is actually the "necessity" of immanent analysis, because the *Qur'an* confronts the poet in terms of his relation to cognisance of the truth, which implies that *the poet's* positive antipode is *the prophet*.[12]

Ad 1. The prophet's mission is unidirectional – it proceeds vertically, where the prophethood cannot be amended or modified in the direction from those the prophet is sent to towards the One who sent him. The poet-soothsayer is active in both directions: he is a special medium who, on the one hand, "receives" certain messages and, at the same time, modulates them by virtue of his mediating position (poetry), influencing the degree of message authenticity; on the other hand, using the power of his medium – poetry – he initiates communication with a higher force on which he can have a profound impact: he can, for example, appease or enrage it through forms of the "supernaturalism of poetry". The strength of his "instrument", poetry, is very important here, as the effects of his act are in proportion to his poetic powers. In short, the poet-soothsayer operates in both directions, which is why his "mission" has a different angle from the prophet's – it is not vertical, no matter how much, during his act, the poet-soothsayer may direct his gaze to the sky or to the dust under his feet.

Such a relation has a magic quality to it and is, as such, absolutely unacceptable from the viewpoint of the Revelation. Since the levels of authenticity are confused here, it becomes unclear what the "message" is and what the creation of the poet-soothsayer is; "refraction" of the message through his *experience* and poetry is too involved for the "message" to be delivered as authentic. At the same time, the purity of relation – in terms of power and superiority – is also quite blurred in the case of the poet-soothsayer because he is considered an extraordinary, rare being that can use *his will* to establish special contacts with a higher power. Therefore, he never relinquishes it, but, what is more, aspires to have an unlimited influence over the source of his message. Raising its quality, this relation aims at eventually becoming a sort of partnership, which is also wholly unacceptable to the *Qur'an*, as the prophet has no such powers or ambitions whatsoever. On the contrary, God strongly emphasises that the Prophet is just a man on a mission of divine prophethood.

Poetic consequences are certainly far-reaching here. The poet-soothsayer is the author of his work, even if it is partly "whispered" to him, whereas the Prophet does not partake in the authorship at all, as it, in its absolute authenticity, belongs solely to God. This means that the poet's work is a work of art, while the Revelation is God's work that categorically refuses to be reduced to a work of art, as the latter is inconsistent with and unnecessary to it. In poetic terms, work that explicitly refuses to be a work of art, on the one hand, and work that establishes communication with something metaphysical through its artistic values and induction, on the other, each have radically different positions. I will have to refer to these positions occasionally.

Ad 2. The noun *prophet* semantically does not imply emotionality, unlike the semantics of the participle-noun *shā'ir*, which implies emotionality, or sensory perception as its essence. I discussed this in detail when I explained the etymology and semantics of this word. I also mentioned that a *shā'ir* is one who knows through feelings by means of poetry. In this regard, it is important to mention that cognition lies at the heart of the prophet's mission as well, but these two kinds of cognition are essentially different in terms of their quality. The prophet does not arrive at cognition through an act of magic but bases his cognition on reason; the prophet's cognition precedes his prophethood, whereas the cognition of the poet-soothsayer is simultaneous with his versification – in "the identity of intuition and expression". Furthermore, and what is the essence of the matter, the prophet's cognition takes sharp contours, is clearly defined and is non-subjective, all owing to the fact that the prophet's interference with the Revelation content is precluded. The case of the poet-soothsayer is quite the opposite. Since sensibility/sensitivity is the principal instrument of the poet's cognition, the contours of his cognition are rather blurred, unstable and fluid, as they depend on the intensity of sensibility/sensitivity, which is always different even in the same subject. Consequently, his cognition is highly subjective because it is reached through the sensibility of the subject and depends on subjective poetic abilities. All this is completely opposite to the faith as passed on by the prophet.[13] The poet-soothsayer cannot maintain the same quality while repeating his act, nor can he produce the same effects on the source of his inspiration. However, the content the prophet conveys and his relation to his Source are essentially supra-subjective, so that the Revelation is presented with an absolute perseverance that is even above the prophet's personality and subjectivity: it is given in an unchangeable form to each and every subject – therefore, to all times as well. The opposition to the position of poet-soothsayer is complete and fateful.

It is true that there is a sort of subjectivity relating to the Revelation, but it happens at another level and again in opposition to the poet's subjectivity. Namely, since the poet-soothsayer's communication is subjective, it is fluid, as I said, so that the content coming from his "source" is also fluid: it is poeticised, meaning that it is always changeable and inauthentic. However, the Revelation insists on its authenticity and perseverance so much that, during somewhat less than fifteen centuries – which is a scientific fact – it has remained identical in every single letter or sound; it even insists, intertextually, on its transhistorical invariability because it comes, as stated in it, to restore its authenticity, which was previously falsified by people. However, establishing its perseverance and invariability, the Revelation majestically asserted *subjectivism*, which I distinguish from *subjectivity*. The Revelation allows every subject to go into it, to understand it and establish relations with it, to search for their own hope and their own anxiety over punishment. In other words, the Revelation does not recognise either mediators or priests, but allows each subject to directly communicate with it and, obviously, with God or – as it can also be described – each subject can directly communicate with the Revelation's Universality. A more powerful assertion of subjectivism can hardly be thought of.

This having been said, there is no need to dwell on the notion of subjectivism and subjectivity with the poet-soothsayer. He promotes only his fervour and subjectivity, which cannot represent qualitative constants. Other subjects are markedly inferior in relation to him. This means that, in proportion to the exaggeration of his subjectivism, he degrades other subjects with respect to the Source of his inspiration. This happens because other subjects cannot achieve the same quality of communication with the Source as he can. He is the authoritative mediator.

Such a position with respect to other subjects essentially represents aggression against their subjectiveness; these are religious grounds for privileged status, on the one hand, or the grounds of inferiority in religion, which is, in turn, in direct conflict with the religious principle of the equality of all people. Any manifestation of privileged status represents an attack against subjectivism, which is at variance with God.

The principle of vertical deduction is, therefore, miraculous. For, any inclination of this Vertical – whether in the form of pagan or magic influences on the Source, or in terms of other sorts of inclination in some religions – necessarily results in protectionism at various levels, which represents a human attack against the divine guarantee of equality among subjects devoted to God. This is why the *Qur'an*, which does not permit clerical, divine-human or any other differentiation, reiterates not only that His prophet Muhammad is a man like other men, but also that God does not even make a distinction among His prophets.[14]

Deduction offers incomparable advantages.

Ad 3. The Prophet brings the Text into the World by means of vertical deduction, and this Text causes an explosion in culture. The poet follows the opposite direction and therefore causes no explosion. Namely, since the poet's communication is creative in nature, it implies that he himself is actually the origin of the text through which he aspires to reach the metaphysical and, at the same time, uses the text to influence the world around him.[15] This frustrates the universalism of his text: the text originates from the spirit and experience of one man, no matter how extraordinary he may be considered in his mediation; the poet's relation to the force above him is individual, personal even, but the scope of his creation in terms of influencing his recipients – perhaps his consumers even – is rather limited; it can, at best, barely reach beyond the tribal community.

The poetic path of induction is restricted by a powerful effect of subjectivity that never succeeds in reaching the universalism of deduction. The poetic path of induction is not restricted by the factor of subjectivity alone – subjective experience and abilities – but also by limited experience of Tradition. For, the poet (in this context I refer to the poet of ancient Arabian times, although throughout history poets have more or less been inclined to believe in their own uncommonness) is completely immersed in tradition whose experience he can broaden, except that he always does this on its wide horizon, or the horizon of what we believe Tradition is and should be. It is well known that passing down intergenerational experience is a highly appreciated value. Therefore, the poet's text (and act) is inductive in this sense as well; it is "horizontal" at best, as it communicates with other subjects on the basis of the experience of one subject. The poet's belief that he communicates with supreme forces is blurred since it is based on the emotional and sensory, which is essentially the source of his *illusion*. The reach of such poetics is relatively expected and non-explosive. It can even be extraordinary: it can cause dramatic shifts in the value system but it always, more or less, meanders on the horizon of Tradition, even when it considerably enriches it. Hence, we can ultimately conclude that the original poetic text – often described as epoch-marking – is in its very essence a strong and specific endorsement of Tradition, even when it transcends it.

However, a descent of the Vertical into the Horizontal causes profound changes. This is what the sacred Text does. I have already mentioned that the sacred Text respects tradition, but in a specific way and with a specific meaning. Namely, the Text acknowledges the human need to adopt novelties, particularly "new" religious injunctions, in a gradual manner (gradualism and continuity are a part of the tradition indeed, even though they may sometimes be whimsical), being aware that it strongly and convincingly argues for their rationality. However, while doing so, the Text does not aim at preserving tradition, although it may seem so at first. The sacred text actually preserves the *sacredness* of tradition. Absorbing previous sacred texts and revising them at the same time, the Text asserts that it has always existed but was, in this very tradition, deformed and falsified in certain periods of history and that it wants to restore its Authenticity. This is precisely the outstanding quality through which it is absolutely uniquely introduced as both the Prototext and the Hypertext. This is where its poetic uniqueness lies. In other words, the relation of the Text to tradition is such that it preserves the tradition of the Vertical; the tradition's diachrony is significant insofar as it underlines the importance of prophethood in continuity, as well as the importance of that gradualism precious to human nature. Consequently, the sacred Text always emphasises the fateful sharpness of angle formed by its deductive verticality and the flatness of tradition. This angle is a prerequisite for its revelation; at the moment when, from the Text's position, its impact diminishes with the course of history, and history itself begins its precipitous decline – to use the same metaphor – even in such a way that poets become "divine mediators", the Text activates the Vertical as an emergency measure and, through intertextuality, uses prototexts from tradition – that is, authentic elements of previous revelations, thus achieving extremely functional contextualisation.

The consequences of such impact of the poet on the one hand, and of the sacred Text on the other, are profound and diametrically opposite. Using the inductive method, the poet's text can never cause such tectonic movements as the sacred Text can. The impact of the poet's text can never be at the right angle because it would mean it has been catapulted out of the orbit of tradition; the poet's text can only survive within the horizon of the expectations of Tradition. However, the sacred Text preserves the sacredness of tradition, which is why its descent into the World and History at the right angle was always powerful and dramatic, so explosive that it always broke tradition into smithereens. Its universalisation is absolutely superior even to the poet's most superior subjectivity. Moreover, since this involves an ideological confrontation between the sacred Text and that of the poet, this universalisation is relentlessly confronted with the poet's subjectivity and fervour imprisoned in its aspiration towards universalisation, which only highlights its sacredness in relation to the Truth.

There is yet another aspect to the sacred Text's relation to tradition – an aspect in which the Text asserts the importance of continuity, while underlining this discontinuity, paradoxical as it may seem at first.

Namely, by the very fact that the Text insists on its being constantly expressed in prototexts as well – i.e. that it has always existed – the Text illustrates how much it perseveres with continuity and with a very strong network of intertextuality. From this aspect, the Text regards tradition as a necessary continuity constantly verified by it in the sphere of sacredness. Furthermore, its intertextuality is not only related to sacred prototexts in positive terms (to authentic revelations that people distorted over time) but to texts in general: the Text's relation to poetry, as already illustrated by the ayahs quoted, demonstrates that the sacred Text can adopt a distinctly negative attitude towards certain texts. Hence, its all-embracing intertextuality is an expression of (tradition) continuity.

However, by its very repetition through history in terms of its fundamental principles, the Text imparts that history constantly sees discontinuous rifts open up, which the Text steadfastly repairs. In other words, discontinuity as a departure from the Text's authenticity towards various other kinds of texts, even towards poetic ones, is the fate of the World in History. To go a step further, this means that human unreliability is a constant, even sacredness in relation to the authenticity of the Text onto which man "pastes" his own texts, as well as that this unreliability creates discontinuous rifts and ideological "alluvia" of texts making the angle of the Vertical evermore obtuse. Poetic texts have a strong influence on man's emotional sphere, which is why – at that stage of human development – poetry had the considerable capability of exerting adverse influence at the level of ideology. This implies that the Text is the only absolute, and therefore necessary, guarantee of continuity.

Ad 4. The prophet is neutral in terms of creation, whereas the poet is highly creative. Accordingly, the prophet is a *common* man who, to the exclusion of everything else, *reliably* conveys a certain content, whereas the poet is an *uncommon* man who establishes communication with the metaphysical through his "uncommonness" and creative abilities. In the prophet's case, something like this would be equivalent to sacrilege of the highest order. As a matter of fact, the point is that the content of the prophet's mission categorically refuses to be designated as artistic, whereas the poet depends precisely on his art and artistry. From the position of the sacred Text, its entire content is utter reality, reality in its sublime state, while poetry transposes every reality – even reality represented by the Text, modelling it in a way, which means that the poetic text works towards the very point and very direction that the sacred Text regards as its antipode. This is the area of their fundamental and irreconcilable oppositeness. Having all this in mind, the attitude of the sacred Text towards the poetic one emerges as natural – that is, the attitude according to which proclaiming the Prophet as a poet is equal to heresy and according to which, at the same time, any attempt of the poetic text to raise itself to the level of ideological prophethood is also heresy.

What I have labelled several times as the resourcefulness of tradition surfaces here as well. Tradition sought to proclaim the Prophet as poet – the Text often refers to this – risking to grant him an extremely high status in the society and ideology of the time, since it took place in an Arabian society that valued poetry the most and whose tradition was predominantly poetic. Considering the highly extensive and intense influence the Text had among Arabians, it could have realistically been expected to acquire a status of the highest poetic order. There were two reasons why tradition chose to run the risk of the "Prophet's" Text towering over all other texts, and both these reasons arose from its need for self-preservation.

The first reason was that, positioning the Prophet as poet, tradition would have legalised all poetic texts at the level of ideology, which would have been extremely important for such a powerful poetic tradition as this tradition was. Everyone in the Arabian world of the time could have been impressed by such a definition of the "Prophet's" Text, considering the high degree of its literary and aesthetic values. However, the Text was relentless, as otherwise its ideological position would have undergone a fundamental change – obscuring its Authenticity by means of art.

The other reason was that by defining the Prophet as a poet Tradition would have maintained the horizontality principle: this vast realm of poetry would have been only substantiated and supplemented with a new vital text, while at the level of ideology there would have been no revolutionary changes such as those caused by the Text's refusal to be fitted into the system of traditional poetic values. Therefore, when the *Qur'an* talks about the poet, one might get the impression that the poet is always positioned unfavourably. This is only partly true: the *Qur'an* does define the poet-*ideologist* in negative terms but, within the tradition that the Qur'anic Text permeates, the poet is a positive value of the highest order. This is why the sacred Text was able to cause a sea change that completely altered this society, thus also affecting the spiritual "physiognomy" of a substantial part of the world. Tradition was in a state of shock for a while, but then it contrived certain adaptive measures owing to which poetry still remained the dominant art form in the Arab world during the following fourteen-and-a-half centuries.

How could this have happened?

Wisdom of the **Qur'an** *and resourcefulness of tradition*

In a test of strength between the *Qur'an* and poetry, the *Qur'an* generously and wisely offered poetry an opportunity to retract, and poetry took it. Namely, a crucial passage concerning the confrontation with poetic texts can be found among the final ayahs of the surah entitled *Poets*:

> It is the poets whom the erring follow!/Seest thou not how they rove distraught in every valley/And that they say that which they do not,/Save those who believe and do good works, and oft remember God, and who defend themselves when unjustly treated, but they who treat them unjustly shall find out what a lot awaiteth them![16]

These ayahs demonstrate that poetry is condemned at the level of ideology. Through very concentrated attribution, in no more than three short ayahs, poetry is completely disqualified in terms of ideology, since the three ayahs indicate one ideological position each, all of which stand in an inherent conflict with the *Qur'an*, and each position individually is depicted as sufficiently negative for the uncompromising position of the *Qur'an*.

The statement that "the erring follow" poets represents the most severe condemnation: the sacred Text insists on its truthfulness insofar as this is important to religion – which is infinitely much, as opposed to the poetic text that leads to delusion, or misleads people directing them away from the Light of Truth. Recruiting and guiding those misled is facilitated by all those qualities of the poet, his ambitions and his way of constituting poetics that we have discussed before. This ayah comes as a résumé of our previous discussion. Still, we should remind the reader that the poet is *shā'ir* – therefore, one whose entire being and interests are based on the emotional, so exaggeratedly that he can, allegedly, communicate with supreme forces. Implicitly, emotionality without reason must eventually mislead, since it encourages one aspect of the human being, disregarding the other. At the same time – which actually is one of the messages of this ayah – poets deserve to be dealt with by this Text (which, indeed, deals only with the most important issues and phenomena) because their emotionising – to offer an unusual lexeme here – does not remain at the level of the individual. On the contrary, the poetic text always implies a recipient and, in the Arabian pagan period the *Qur'an* talks about, the poetic text first and foremost takes into account its recipients, even aspiring to make a powerful influence on the ideological level of their consciousness. Therefore, refining his emotional state by the word and in the word – the relation between the poetic word and emotional state is the relation I call the poetic text – the poet also heaves the emotions of his recipients, since his mediation cannot function without it. Moreover, his power is proportionate to his ability to emotionise. (A reader unfamiliar with the Arabic language will miss something that is very important here, and I encourage them to always bear it in mind: the word *poet* has neither the etymology nor connotations that the Arabic word *shā'ir* has.) In a hypothetical situation we could ask the following question: would the sacred Text have adopted such an uncompromising attitude towards the poetic text if the latter had not had such a wide audience it aspired to lead, or mislead? The answer to this key question is incorporated in the last quoted ayah (227) and more attention will be devoted to it a little later.

Qualifying the poet as belonging to the category of people capable of misleading others triggers certain associations regarding the position of the poetic text in relation to religion from Plato to Hegel. There is no direct influence on the sacred Text, but a comparatively similar definition of the poetic text by Plato and by many other learned men testifies to their – let us use an overly modernised term – consensus about the status of the poetic text in religion. It is a commonplace, for instance, that Plato described poetry in similar terms in *The Republic*. He banned poets from his ideal state as a category of influential people – to paraphrase Plato's reasons – who used emotions to obscure reason, and implicitly philosophical knowledge as well. Furthermore, considering their abilities, poets were regarded as dangerous and had no place in Plato's state to be run by philosophers. A similar attitude can be found with many other philosophers, all the way to Nietzsche and Hegel, according to whom – which is a commonplace – poetry is the lowest level in self-cognisance of the Absolute Spirit. It was in this sense that Hegel declared its death.

The second ayah of the quoted "block" – *Seest thou not how they rove distraught in every valley* – is a laconic finishing of the previous attitude that poets are followed by the erring. Tafsīrs offer different interpretations of the second ayah, consistent with different interpretations of the metaphor *the valley they rove* (i.e. fantasising; daydreaming; gazing absently). However, the ayah undoubtedly has a negative meaning in the given context. Namely, since it immediately follows the ayah stating that poets are followed by those that have erred, it serves to specify the previous, relatively generalised statement. For poets mislead because of or by their being able, through the effort of their emotionality and fictionality, to appear in every "valley". It should be noted that the original verb *yahīmūn* means "to get carried away by something", "become lost in reverie", "fictionally roam through a space", etc. Most exegetes believe that the word *valley* refers to poetic genres, meaning that the poet can easily switch between a panegyric and a lampoon, between a self-panegyric and an elegy, etc. Whatever the case may be, the emphasis is on the poet's (emotional) instability, his ability – developed into sacredness – to travel by fiction to any emotional state, independently from his beliefs. In a certain significant way, he is out of harmony with himself and reality around him.

Such a dominant exegetic denotation of *valley* in terms of poetic genres has its grounds, but I believe that it leaves out an important aspect of the valley metaphor in the general context these ayahs are revealed within. It is hard to believe that the *Qur'an* adopted such an attitude towards the poet simply on account of his ability to become emotionally realised in opposing emotional contexts. For it should be borne in mind that, even after the Revelation, poets extensively wrote in different poetic genres, turning their artistry into highly profitable poetry. This was a widespread practice that lasted for centuries, until modern poetry began to foster the poetic postulate of truthfulness, first and foremost in the works of the Diwan, Apolo and Mahjar literary groups.

The sacred Text always adopts a position to the poetic text primarily with regard to its poetic qualities and ideological pretensions. It is true that the *Qur'an* cannot support poetic "hypocrisy" in terms of genres, although its condemnation is not focused on it, since such poetry did survive and even thrived in centuries to follow; the *Qur'an*, however, made it a condition for poetry to adopt a different ideological position. Therefore, I believe that the statement that poets rove distraught in every valley implies their tradition of fictitious travels "through the space" belonging to shaytans, jinns and other supernatural forces, and also implies that they affected their audience in accordance with the laws of these forces and their worlds, which consequently entails a tragic departure from the Authenticity of the Truth. Shaytanic forces could thus – absolutely unacceptably for the Text – use poets to influence people in order to mislead them. At the same time, by virtue of the poet, these forces were given an opening for appearing to be divine, perhaps even to be gods. Different forms of emotional communication with these forces are the immediate cause of such an attitude on the part of the sacred Text. It is hard to believe that its cause is the poet's ability to sing a dirge for a deceased person today, and a commercial panegyric to his patron tomorrow. After all, the severity of condemnation that poets mislead is adequate to their ideological *pretensions*, not to so-called ordinary genre "instability"; the emotional wellspring of any poetic genre can be regarded as harmless unless it encroaches upon spheres of the ideological of the highest order. This is why the interpretation of this ayah as referring to genre versatility alone is a reductionist one: it is not incorrect, but it certainly leaves out the most important aspect of the ayah.

Even as a semiotic sign of space, the *valley* is polysemous. The *valley* is positioned "lower" than the ground itself, as it represents a sort of concavity on a relatively flat surface; it is something that lies below the "normal space" level. Admittedly, the *valley* can also carry positive connotations because (in the geographical space where the Text was revealed) it occasionally serves as a bed for life-giving torrents, but this positive quality is again transformed into a negative one: torrents in a valley also deposit their silt (this should be perceived as a very rich metaphor): torrents pass very quickly, leaving their alluvia but not changing the space permanently, they are raging but are also transitory, etc. The torrent-course of emotions stirred up by the poet and the "cognisance" these emotions lead to are parallel to the relation between the valley and a torrent in it. On the other hand, the *valley* can be construed as a sort of a shelter or lee, but this also implies recession from the "normal surface level" and is therefore not desirable: there is no positive circulation in it, the *real* horizon cannot be seen from it, the sun does not shine upon it as it does upon the space around it, etc. This brilliant metaphor of the Text could be developed further, but I hope that these suggestions about the semiotics of space make it evident that the *valley* corresponds to a specific deception, so that this word (together with the following ayah) heavily underlines the *deception* expressed in the first ayah. In this semiotics of space it is certainly opportune to juxtapose the word *valley* with another semiotic sign: *top* or *elevation*. With all their contrasting qualities, it should be noted that a position *at the top* is always privileged with respect to a position *in the valley*: the top offers a better and clearer view of the world, a view reaching farther than that from the valley.[17] When discussing semiotics of space, I must indicate the direction it further leads to. Namely, the poet in the *valley* has one perspective of the world; the *plane of the world* offers another perspective; the *top* from which the Revelation comes offers still another perspective. Everything else is *topped* from the top. Differentiation in semiotics of space signs is more than obvious here: it is truly impressive. I am actually trying to say that here – always in ideological terms, not in terms of genre – the *valley* as a semiotic sign automatically brings forth the other member of its binary opposition – the *top(most) point*, considering that the Revelation is defined as opposed to the poetic text. Perhaps unexpectedly – but here necessarily – the meaning of the Vertical emerges among the final consequences, in semiotics of space as well: poets are confined to valleys; the prophet's activity spreads across the infinite plane of the world and history, while God tops everything. This gives a crystal clear illustration of the inductive nature of the poetics of poetry and the deductive nature of the Revelation.

The third ayah (226) is a specific completion of the previous two ayahs: *And that they say that which they do not*. Obviously, this ayah establishes the discrepancy between the poet's words and his deeds, which is a specific type of hypocrisy, mendacity, sanctimony, etc.; in any case, this is the most severe condemnation from a religious standpoint or from the standpoint of ethics in general. The discrepancy between words and deeds suggests a fatal split in the poet's personality caused solely by his reliance on emotions as an instrument of cognition and communication. The poetic text is, therefore, an expression of the poet's world which is incompatible with his real world, or with the world of his deeds. This is in complete contradiction with the prophet's world or, in general, the world of those who follow the Revelation, as the Revelation firmly insists on absolute agreement between words and deeds, even between thoughts (intentions) and deeds, as on one of its fundamental requirements: insofar as these two are in agreement, a believer can consider his faith genuine. While the poet stresses the line that divides the world of his fiction from reality in ideological terms, the Revelation insists on an opposite process – the obliteration of this line, because both worlds represent reality for the Revelation, so that a relation to them must be established where words and deeds are in absolute agreement.

The relation between these two ayahs (225 and 226) is interesting from a linguistic aspect as well: in syntactic terms, it is an elliptical structure. That is, they can be translated as quoted above, i.e. as two independent coordinated sentences, with the coordinating conjunction *wa* (*and*) establishing a link between them. Such a translation does not necessarily mutually relate all poets' actions, i.e. it implies that the discrepancy between their words and deeds is expressed not only in the act of versification (while "they rove distraught in every valley") but that they usually say other than they actually do. However, this coordinating conjunction, followed by the personal pronoun *hum* (*they*), as is the case here, also forms a so-called "clause of state" (*wāw al-ḥāl*) which we render by means of the present participle, while the entire "clause of state", as its name suggests, expresses the state of its subject at the moment of action denoted by the verb. Hence, the following translation would also be syntactically accurate: *Seest thou not how they rove distraught in every valley, saying that which they do not?!* The coordination of clauses is now lost in favour of their subordination: Poets rove distraught in every valley *while/when* they say that which they do not. On other occasions poets need not be so. But, regardless of this, their ideological unreliability is related to the poetic text in any case, since poets are in inspirational contact with – as they can now be called from the Text's position – satanic forces. This idea is conveyed in several ayahs directly preceding those I quoted above, which can be understood as preparation for the ayahs analysed so far: "Shall I tell you on whom shaytans descend?/They descend on every lying, wicked person!/They impart what they have heard – but most of them are liars."[18] The poet's inspiration is clearly defined here: the poetic text (I always refer to its ideological layer in this pagan period) is a satanic deed because it is created after devils have "descended" to the poet and inspired him. Clearly, shaytan – always and in the deepest sense – connotes every form of evil, which makes his medium, the poet, a liar and a sinner. Shaytans secretly listen to things in the unknown Beyond – conveys ayah 223 – only to deform them as much as possible and impart them to the poet. Of course, the act of *secret listening*, as well as of *imparting whispers*, carries negative connotations. In any case, these acts which are the shaytan's only preoccupation are all the more severe transgressions since no insignificant matters can be secretly listened to in the unknown Beyond, because there are no such matters there but only matters that are fateful for man and the world, which are then distorted through a shaytanic prism and delivered/whispered to man as something crucial for his fate.

This evidently refers to poets who, owing to their art of word, appear as clergymen or *kāhins*. In this regard, we should once more resort to syntactic analysis to see how these three ayahs (221–223) apply to poets as clergymen. Namely, the syntactic relation between ayah 223 and ayah 224 is established through the conjunction *wa*: *[And] It is the poets whom the erring follow*. The conjunction *wa* is extremely frequent in the classical Arabic language. It is most often translated as *and*, although it performs much more complex syntactic functions. (In the sacred Text discussed here it serves both as a connective and as a stylistic unit realised at the level of phonetics, whose repetitiveness is quite functional in terms of style.) I have just shown how it forms a "clause of state", which is usually translated by means of the present participle. The function of this conjunction is always – more or less explicitly – the intention to express the simultaneity of actions, closeness of states, etc. It therefore need not always be translated by lexical means (though it should be in this particular case, as it represents a stylistic unit upholding the repetitiveness and stylistic form); its meaning can be rendered by a punctuation mark (the classical Arabic language did not have any punctuation): in this case it could be colon or dash: *[. . .] They impart what they have heard, but most of them are liars: It is the poets whom the erring follow*, or: *[. . .] They impart what they have heard, but most of them are liars – It is the poets whom the erring follow [. . .]*. This conjunction can sometimes be translated as *because*. Therefore, the conjunction *wa* undoubtedly serves a syntactic and semantic function to bring the preceding statements about shaytanic deeds into a strong, coordinating and causal connection with the poet's activities that are essentially magic and, as such, draw the most severe condemnation from the sacred Text.

A strong syntactic link between the two blocks of ayahs analysed here is powerfully broken by the preposition *save* (particle *'illā*) signalling an exception; the link is broken as powerfully as the Text's opening for exceptions can be saving. The negative image of poets-soothsayers is made complete in the closing ayah of the same surah (227): "[. . .] Save those who believe and do good works, and oft remember God; And who defend themselves when unjustly treated [...]" This ayah completes the attitude to poets in the only way possible for the Revelation considering everything I have already mentioned about the social and ideological status poets enjoyed in the society at that time.

Therefore, poetry is not condemned as a whole, because the *Qur'an* is a work of powerful and diversely meaningful contextualisation. It would have been all too cruel and culturally groundless to ban poetry in its entirety from the Arabian society that had brought it to perfection, while expressing its genius in this very poetry. The *Qur'an* reasonably respected this fact. However, the *Qur'an* evidently condemned the type of poetry defined prior to this exception, i.e. poetry pretending to be the bearer of religious "truths". Poets who believe and who do good deeds are excused. The relationship between religion and poetry, between the sacred and poetic text, is quite clearly defined: the poetic text in the religious domain is definitely confined in the pagan period, while the Revelation is transformed into the Text often presented as a metaphor for the light leading the world out of the gloom.

What are the possible meanings of excusing poets who believe in the last ayah?

The first meaning is that the Text condemns those poets who are on the other side of orthodox belief, or those who use the poetic word for expressing pagan or any other non-Islamic religious feelings or knowledge defined as fake.

The second meaning, naturally arising from the first, is that those who believe are allowed to engage in poetry since they, as such, will not introduce into poetry any ideological content anathematised by the sacred Text. Poetry was given its chance but with certain conditions attached to it.

The third meaning is hypothetical: it is, I believe, deliberately left unspecified through the elliptical structure of this ayah. Namely, it is certainly legitimate to examine the meaning of excusing true believers from this utterly negative context. A possible explanation may be in the fact that the poet's genuine belief is incompatible with the kind of poetry condemned by the Text, which means that he can write poetry void of such ideological content. Another possible explanation – which cannot be derived from this Text in an explicit form – is that poetry too could engage in promoting genuine belief, or in promoting Islamic dogmas and the values of Islam in general. If the quoted ayah is to be understood in this way, there are two things to be borne in mind. First, making a break with poetry of the time is explored far too much in the *Qur'an* to allow for the importance of poetry to be cancelled entirely and forever. Second, the Revelation was certainly aware that the Arabians it first came to were so positively oversensitive to the poetic word that poetry could contribute to the promotion of the Revelation. It is through this very exception that the Revelation shows it has no intention of creating a waste land in tradition. Is this not a discreet invitation for Muslims to replace (magic) poetry with rightly guided poetry but, of course, in a different sense? The Revelation denied poetry rights and capacity in the domain of religious knowledge and communication with God, which gave poetry a direction essentially different from that of poetry condemned by the

Revelation. In other words, can this ayah *also* be interpreted as an invitation to poets to sing praises of Islam, the Prophet, etc.?[19]

In this context, it may be interesting to indicate – even if giving a mere outline, as I will go into more detail later in the book – what happened to poetry after the Revelation's descent.

During several decades poetry underwent a period of severe stagnation, mostly until the establishment of the Umayyad dynasty (661–750), after which it fully thrived during the Abbasid dynasty (750–1258). There are several reasons for this. One of the most important ones is probably such a strict ideological attitude of the Revelation with regard to poetry of the time. Another reason lies in the fact that the sacred Text entered the tradition with its high literary and aesthetic values that, as generally accepted, were superior to poetry of the time, so that poets simply fell silent before it, feeling creatively inferior. I will say more about this dimension of the Text later in the book. Yet another reason is that Arabians perceived the *descent* of the Text as a superlatively powerful civilisational and cultural explosion, and that during several decades they were completely immersed in widespread dissemination of this Text in evermore distant parts of the world. Naturally, many a war was fought during this time, which was not conducive to poetry. At the same time, this predominantly poetic tradition needed some time to consolidate in the new sphere – in the new world, really – and to reinstitute itself through new forms not at variance with the Text.

In this sudden poetic quiet only a few poets spoke and only those who decided to seek fresh inspiration for their promotion. These were converts delighted by Islam and its Text, ready to acknowledge the Text's superiority in terms of form and indisputability in terms of content. Such poets – very few compared with the periods preceding and following this one – can be represented by Ka'b Ibn Zuhayr (530–627) with his famous *Mantle Ode* (*Qaṣīda Burda*) opening with the words *Bānat Su'ād*... The poem is famous for being composed as a panegyric to the Prophet and his mission, but what is indicative here is the Prophet's reaction after the poem was recited to him. Namely, without saying anything, he took off his mantle (*burda*) and wrapped it around the poet. This gesture was understood as approval or even support of poetry promoting the Prophet and Islam.[20]

However, despite such a promising gesture, panegyric poetry failed to thrive. One of the reasons may have been the fact that poetry had been related to soothsaying rites too strongly and for too long, and the fact that the *Qur'an* adopted such an uncompromising attitude to it. The associativeness of poetry is too risky, while the sacred Text is brimming over with self-sufficiency and self-confidence. In any case, it is interesting that there is no large-scale production of religious poetry in Arab history as there is, for example, in the Christian cultural community.

Poetry in the Arabic language began to flourish several decades after the Prophet's death, and flourish it did in the most elegant lyric genres. It had once and for all abandoned its pre-Qur'anic ideological pretensions and only then was poetic tradition reincarnated. Furthermore, poetry did not only desert its efforts to represent the religious truth – surrendering it entirely to the *Qur'an* – but, what is more, went to another extreme by the force of inertia, or resourcefulness. In contrast to poets' pre-Qur'anic ambitions it proclaimed "mendacity" as its poetic postulate, by which it implied the irrelevance of poetic content and the freedom of borrowing them from tradition's repository of motifs (this poetics communicates the legality of literary thefts in this regard) while, on the other hand, optimally emphasising the significance of the poetic form the poet's creation assumed. The domination of poets in the sphere of religious metaphysical matters was put to an end. In the confrontation with the *Qur'an* at the level of ideology, poetry suffered a defeat. This is why it turned to new themes and poetic postulates. Then, in this new apparel, it shone for hundreds of years.

Poets could finally be both poets and rightly guided believers.

The *Qur'an* confronting poetry at the level of form

All Arabic literature studies include the *Qur'an* but approach it from different positions and use different methods. Considering the *Qur'an* as a work that powerfully influenced the Oriental-Islamic cultural community, Orientalist studies mostly treat it as the work of Muhammad (saws). Therefore, they adopt an eminently transcendent or external approach that, as such, has severe limitations.

In the Arab-Islamic world the *Qur'an* is studied as the Word of God, so that all Arabic textbooks on stylistics abound with examples of its style. However, it may be useful to consider the Text using a method that situates it with regard to both "external" and "internal" positions. Without questioning the *'i'jāz* of the Text (a particular kind of its supernaturalism in language and style), it is sensible to regard it within the Universe of forms in tradition, and therefore not only as a handbook of model stylistic examples but as a single system that over centuries has influenced, through its *'i'jāz*, the growth of a wide variety of forms in Culture, not just in literature. In this context, we should also analyse the attitude of the *Qur'an* to poetry at the level of form.

Stylistic supernaturalism of the Text and Tradition

Condemnation of the poet as a cleric (*kāhin*) is uncompromising in the *Qur'an*, as the poet's clerical activities are in conflict with the Revelation. At the level of form, however, poetry is not entirely discarded, as in the previous case; it is rather a matter of transcending poetic tradition in a particular way. Namely, in literature the form per se does not necessarily imply *specific* ideological contents, which is why the Text establishes a qualitatively different relation to the form. Certainly, the content and its form cannot be treated as radically separate in aesthetics because they, in Crocean terms, exist as the identity of intuition and expression. This is even a powerful argument on the Text's part when it denies poetry the ability to express the highest religious content, or to get at the highest religious truths. Whether explicitly or implicitly, the Text constantly warns that poetry as a "*form* of cognition" represents a tragic mismatch between form and content; poetry as a *form*, in a wide sense, attempts, quite inadequately so from the standpoint of the Revelation, to embrace the Content, which it then deforms through its own unsuitability.

The *Qur'an* itself pays close attention to the form it is revealed in, but with a clearly redefined relation between form and content. The Text is in the form of prose characterised by rhyme and rhythm (*saj'*); therefore, it is not in the form of "pure poetry" but in a special form also called *naẓm* – an organised and structured text that will not be put in a poem but that heavily stresses the importance of the poetic function of language which is not an end in itself but primarily serves to convey certain contents. Departing from the "pure poetic form", the Text shows how important it is to outgrow the function of a *kāhin*'s poetry, at the same time demonstrating its own ability to use a different form to express the content that, until then, poetry endeavoured to express.

In many places the Qur'anic Text explicitly states its intention to express its Content in a language and form that optimally took heed of the Beautiful. There are many examples illustrating this, and perhaps the most impressive one can be found in the opening of surah 55 (*The God of Mercy*):

> The God of Mercy
> Hath taught the Qur'an,
> Hath created man,
> Hath taught him articulate speech.[21]

Optimally short paragraphs build a relationship of pyramidal structure among several themes of cosmic significance; all the themes are expressed in a strong positivity that becomes optimised by these themes inextricably drawing on one another. This order of cosmic priorities has *al-bayān* incorporated in it, in the fourth ayah, which is translated as *articulate speech* conditionally only, since the Arabic language uses the same term for *stylistics*.

It follows from an immanent analysis of these several ayahs that they express the following meaning.

At the top of everything, as the primordial originator, is the God of Mercy (God), and it is no accident that this noun phrase is used as the first paragraph. It is structurally quite significant that this single phrase constitutes the whole ayah-paragraph. The supreme token of mercy is that the God of Mercy reveals the *Qur'an*: it is the ultimate mercy on the worlds, since it leads towards the recognition of God and, thereby, to His mercy. The creation of man (ayah 3) is added to the importance of the previous two acts: the God of Mercy shows His mercy through the *Qur'an* revealed to man that He created; this is an unbreakable chain of God's activities. Finally, ayah 4 brings the point: God also taught man, whom He created and to whom He revealed the *Qur'an*, articulate speech (conditionally: stylistics) as the supreme token of His All-Embracing Mercy.[22]

Therefore, God put man's capacity for articulate expression at the top of His mercies. On the one hand, this is equal to the very act of creating man, and is related to this act, which is of immeasurably huge importance. On the other hand, this capacity of man is brought in a direct connection with the *Qur'an*, since the original uses the same verb *'allama* (teach, instruct) twice: [God] *hath taught the Qur'an*, [. . .] *hath taught him* [man] *articulate speech*. It seems that, in other places where the *Qur'an* talks about the importance of *articulate expression*, the significance of this great gift is not elevated to the highest possible level of man's abilities and God's gifts in the same way as in the opening of surah 55: what underlines its importance here is the extraordinary pyramidal structure of God's deeds and man's relationship to them, even more so as the ayahs are in a lapidary state, making the delight of their interpretative unveiling even greater. This reveals a strong link between the Text's stylistic values and man's capacity for receiving them. In certain places the *Qur'an* explicitly says that its Text is presented in the highest possible stylistic values. There are at least two grounds for this explication. First, since the *Qur'an* comes from God to man as the Text, it is natural to expect it to come in the form of an optimum arrangement. Second, in relation to the first, the Text addresses this extraordinary capacity of man for articulate expression. The connection between these two aspects now becomes obvious.

Hence, the importance of form, of highly stylised expression, is emphasised at both "poles": at the one end God emphasises the form in which He delivers His Text, and at the other end He emphasises the significance of His gift to man in this domain, a gift worthy of its "channel" of vertical communication. However, this implies an important distinction between these two "poles" – between the optimally arranged Text in terms of style and man's being exceptionally gifted with stylistics. This important distinction will be discussed later in the book but must be at least briefly mentioned here. Namely, the differences in rank are enormous. For, since God reveals the Text that deeply respects the beauty of expression, He will clearly confirm it at the highest, divine level. Consequently, in communication with man's capacity for its reception, the Text is necessarily presented as a miracle in this sphere, as it is unbecoming for it to be arranged exactly the same as it could be arranged/written out by a man. God gave man the power of speech, but the sacred Text, among other things, teaches him articulate expression, since the Text is revealed as a miracle of language and form considering the purity and perfection of its divine Wellspring. This semiotic constellation, contained in only four very short ayahs I quoted, embraces the meaning of the Text's supernaturalism that all Muslims believe in, but which is also recognised by many a non-Muslim thoroughly familiar with the Arabic language.

Another important reason I use these ayahs to demonstrate the Text's determination to place a high value on the form is the remarkable form and stylistic function of this very surah, which the majority of authorities on the Text regard as one of the most beautiful surahs; I too find this surah to be the most beautiful in literary and aesthetic terms.[23]

Thus the *Qur'an*, obviously on purpose, underlines the importance of man's divine gift for articulate expression in the very opening of the surah that is, at the same time and not by accident, the most beautiful among the 114 surahs in terms of literary and aesthetic values. This is an undeniable relation, although only implied in the *Qur'an*. The boundless profusion of its metaphors; the relatively even length of its ayahs that aims at being associative of the metric organisation of a poem, without establishing it, of course, as it is still prose, not poetry; the rhyme disciplined to the very border of a monorhyme scheme; the remarkably and very effective refrain that, successfully establishing a phonetic theme, wedges in between phrase constituents that cannot be split in ordinary language, and the refrain that is almost as frequent as half the other ayahs of the surah – all this, together with many other values of the surah, conveys an implicit message: as the highest expression of His mercy, God teaches man articulate expression and the *Qur'an*, which is the unattainable paragon of teachers, and in such *Qur'an* it is precisely this surah that is the most beautiful.

It is difficult to imagine this Text revealed in a different form. For example, it is inconceivable for it to be translated into the language of legal register, even though, on the other hand, such expectations would not be unreasonable, since the Text closely regulates man's position in the World and in the Community, his relationship to God on whom his lot in both worlds depend, etc. Hence, there is very little in the Text's content that is *thematically poetic*, such as, perhaps, the epic passages about Jannah and Jahannam – everything is too realistic and truthful to be considered a fictional world of poem. Still – can someone try to imagine the form and language of the Text transformed into paragraphs that, in a kind of administrative language, define and stipulate the matters composing the Text's meaning! This may reveal one of the Text's arguments in favour of its form: neither poetry nor prose, this Text incorporates essential elements of both thus creating its own and unique textual "reality" suitable to the singularity of the content it expresses. A more lengthy discussion of this issue can be found in the part of this book discussing the attitude of the *Qur'an* towards poetry at the level of ideology. I can say now that the *Qur'an* did not regard the form of poetry adequate for expressing religious content either. The reason behind this attitude, among other things, is the traditional orientation of poetry towards (inadequate) articulation of such content and the Text's implicit claim that poetry belongs to the realm of emotions, whereas the Text's content and messages refer much more to reason than to emotions. However, there still remains the question why the Text is revealed in a form that deliberately fosters its literary and aesthetic values – i.e. in prose characterised by rhyme and rhythm – and not in, for instance, a legal register. Among possible answers to this question, the following should be explored.

Through its form and in a special way, the Text enters the context of Tradition, with which it always establishes relations, whether conserving it, transcending it or discarding some of its forms. Namely, considering the fact that the pre-Qur'anic Arabian tradition, as well as tradition after the revelation of the *Qur'an*, was markedly poetic, it was only natural for the Text to establish a contact with such tradition through its form, where it did not opt for the poem but for prose characterised by rhyme and rhythm, which was also widespread in that part of the world at the time. Through such a form the Text, on the one hand, entered a tradition that had already been prepared for its reception, since the Arabians were highly receptive to poetry (*shi'r*) and to prose characterised by rhyme and rhythm (*saj'*). Had it come in any other form – such as in a legal paragraphic structure and amorphous administrative language – the Text would not have been met with the reception it actually had. Therefore, the Text perfectly capitalised on the experience of tradition in this domain.[24]

On the other hand – precisely because of the rich experience of such tradition – the Text was able to demonstrate, on this ground better than on any other, its superiority to this tradition. The Text's character in the domain of form is competitive, which I will discuss in more detail further in the text, dwelling on its explications in these terms as well. One of the primary aims of the Revelation is to present itself in a language and form wholly superior to tradition, even though the Arabians believed it was in this very domain that they had reached the highest level and were second to none. The language and form are the Text's (divine) argument. The Text advised the Arabians openly – as an argument should generally be presented – that it is infinitely superior even in fields they most excelled at. It should always be borne in mind that the Arabians themselves, and later the whole Islamic world subsequently created, never hesitated to agree with this argument. In other words, the advance of the Qur'anic form and language on Tradition was realised as a *mu'jiza* – as the Prophet's argument proving the supernatural nature of his prophethood. Any other linguistic register or genre would have failed to produce such an effect, not because it could possibly, from certain aspects, raise the issue of whether the Revelation could "be descended" in a hypothetically different register, but because tradition represented a field already prepared for this particular language and form of the Text. This establishes a qualitatively different relation between the Text and tradition: the Text does not discard tradition in this sense, but conserves it partly and transcends it completely. While the ideological aspect of poetry is entirely and uncompromisingly discarded, the relation to the form is, essentially, one of transcendence. In this regard, it is interesting that a substantial portion of pre-Islamic poetry, having existed as oral tradition only, was recorded in writing only in the Islamic epoch.[25] The fact that pre-Islamic poetry was, nonetheless, written down and not discarded testifies to the *form* of poetry being unquestionable from the Text's position, of its being accepted. However, this poetry makes no mention of faith in the pre-Islamic period – which, on the other hand, implies that, in the Islamic epoch – when it was written down, poetry was also *de-paganised*. This rather complicates the issue of its authenticity.

In this regard it should be pointed out that, through its form, the Text addresses an important "pole" of man's being – his need for poetic language (*articulate expression*) and his capacity for this kind of reception. For, we have just seen that God presents it as one of the supreme tokens of His mercy. It is one kind of non-poetic reality that the Text presents by means of its poetic language and form, which implies that its contents – to whose contemplation and espousal the *reason* is called dozens of times in the Text – are revealed in a form whose beauty also engages the "pole" of man's *sensibility*, or his susceptibility to beauty. The *Qur'an* thus promotes two fundamental human abilities – the reasonable and emotional parts of the human being, creating an immediate balance, as it were, since the same Text affects both "poles" at the same time. Other registers and their styles do not have such capacities. The content, on the whole, addresses man's reason, while the form addresses his sensibility. This entails the optimum "identity of intuition and expression", forged here more impressively than anywhere on the whole horizon of tradition. The history of Islam recorded accounts of bitter enemies of Islam who would, soon after Islam began to spread, sometimes sneak close to the windows of Muslims who, still covertly, recited the *Qur'an*; enthralled with its form and content, these enemies would themselves become engrossed with the *Qur'an*. It is also well known that, today, many Muslims can become ecstatic while listening to a masterful recitation of the *Qur'an*. Naturally, the primary source of such feelings is faith, but they are also intensified by the form through which the Text communicates with the listener or the reader. This also reveals another distinction of the Text. Namely, it is directed to man's capacity for the reception of form and his sensibility in this regard, but it is also, at the same time and at any moment, charged with the task of cultivating these human abilities. Since it is introduced as the Revelation, the Text aims at refining, through its own values, man's sense and powers of *articulate expression*, even obliging man to cultivate them. God honoured man with this great gift, as mentioned in the opening of surah 55, and therefore indirectly obliged him to refine this gift so as to get a finer grasp of principles of the Revelation constantly revealed to him in new nuances. In other words, the Text claims that it represents supernaturalism realised in language and form, as a proof of divine authority, and that man must constantly resort to its arguments in this domain, which he cannot do properly without refining this remarkable gift. An appreciation of the grace of form, of the beauty of expression in language, is therefore introduced as both a process and a responsibility. It is a process because it is refined through sustained contact with the Text brought into the state of perfection; it is a responsibility because an adequate perception of the significance of the Text's language and form is a specific requirement for its thorough understanding and embracing as a miracle made available to the Prophet. Ultimately, commitment to the Text through understanding its linguistic as well as literary and aesthetic values represents an act of devotion to God of a special order.

Another reason that the Text is revealed in poetic language – in prose characterised by rhyme and rhythm – lies in the generally recognised fact of the extremely high suggestiveness and connotative nature of poetic language, which in this way is unlike any other kind language. A more detailed discussion of this can be found in the part of this book concerning the Qur'anic translation of Tradition and the World from the state of Simile and Distance into the state of Metaphor and its interactional directness (see Chapter 5). However, the following matters should at least be brought up in this context focusing on the advantages of the poetic language and form over any other.

In terms of their suggestiveness and connotative nature, the language of the legal profession (taken as an example representative of the administrative register and style) and poetic language are at opposite poles. Poetic language has limitless potential for suggestiveness and connoting, whereas the language of the legal profession, in principle, seeks to eliminate them so as to preclude diametrically opposing interpretations. At the same time the language of the legal profession is quite neutral in terms of emotionality or sensibility, whereas poetic language is inclined towards the opposite pole. There are also some other differences between them. This raises the question why, then, the Text is revealed in poetic language and form.

Necessity of poetic language and form

So far quite a lot has been said about the development of potential for sensibility, which the Text insists on, with another reminder of the fact that sensibility, in association with reason, represents a particular instrument of cognisance, which can still not be self-sufficient. However, poetic language has at its disposal instruments for presenting reality that cannot be presented by any other language. This applies to matters beyond human experience, such as the transcendental, particularly to the religious reality of the Other World. An excellent instrument for apprehending this reality can be found in simile, and even more so in metaphor which, owing to its epistemological potential, is the only instrument that can depict, for instance, the state of Jannah or Jahannam, since they are completely on the other side of our experience. Admittedly, metaphor depicts them without a precisely defined "relief" and without particularly sharp contours – as metaphor generally does – but still depicts them in its own peculiar way. We cannot possibly conceive of gaining knowledge of the Other World by means of another language or form, since no other language, except poetic language with its dominant metaphor, can form the arch of knowledge towards the transcendental as metaphor can. Naturally, metaphoric knowledge is necessarily inexact and hence predisposed to subjectification or is, at best, intersubjective, but is not, however, disadvantaged because of it. Moreover, this could conveniently be interpreted as its advantage, for as faith is always, in essence, the *state of an individuum* or, as it is usually phrased, a personal act, the understanding of the unknown Beyond is thereby relatively subjectified, in proportion to the intensity and colour of the light we emit onto the metaphorical arch from within our being. No other language has such potential. This, obviously, opens up a possibility for a diverse range of interpretations, but what is important is that all these interpretations develop in a single direction, and that they are not divergent interpretations. For example, some men understand houris – beauties in Jannah – very literally, while others interpret them metaphorically as an otherworldly equivalent of the greatest (male) joy and pleasure in this world: such interpretations are different but not opposing. Similarly, there are women who understand literally the silk promised in Jannah, as well as gold and silver armlets they will allegedly wear, while other women take it figuratively. In any case, both kinds of interpretations have the same direction – always towards the highest possible positivity; they are not divergent.

Therefore, the advantage of poetic language is absolutely incomparable here, because it offers every believer a possibility of conceptualising and expecting the sum of the good according to their experience in this world. The same principle applies, of course, to the negative geography of the Other World, with its negativism being developed in the opposite direction.

Let us try to imagine that all this, and anything similar, is expressed in some other language and in some other form. It would take countless words and hours to depict the blessings of Jannah or sufferings of Jahannam so that all people in all times could perceive them as absolutely the greatest sum of good and suffering, respectively, considering that values are relative categories for different people and in different historical periods. Using another language and form would, hypothetically, make the Text too extensive, inadequate for many people, emotionally void, etc. Poetic language achieves all the effects that are contrary to these: owing to its suggestiveness and affective impregnation, it is able to meet an important requirement for terseness and ellipsis, for a particular kind of metaphorical universalisation within which individual approaches branch out; it also ensures the necessary level of emphasis, and not of understanding alone. The form is much more than just a form; it is by no means just a pure formality. The metaphoric arch is, in this case, much more efficient than any denotative description.

In the confrontation of the *Qur'an* with poetry at the level of ideology there was, as we saw, no compromise: the *Qur'an* did not invite poetry to a competition in terms of arriving at and representing religious truths, but eliminated poetry altogether in this regard. However, at the level of form, the *Qur'an* establishes a different relation with poetry and tradition in general. This Text openly invites competition several times. For instance, the surah Jonah (*Yūnus*) says the following: *Say: "Then bring a Sura like it; and call on whom ye can beside God, if ye speak truth!"*[26] In a different place, when objections are raised that the Prophet is devising the *Qur'an*, or that the *Qur'an* is not God's but the Prophet's work, God speaks to the Prophet:

> If they shall say, "the Koran is his own device", "SAY: Then bring ten Suras like it of your devising, and call whom ye can to your aid beside God, if ye are men of truth!"[27]

This challenge can be interpreted as an invitation to a competition in creating even a few surahs in the domain of both the content and the form, since these two achieve unity. Such reading is based on the commonplace that the content exists in its form. However, I am more inclined to read this challenge as a challenge to the form, since the *Qur'an,* as already explained, demonstrated that the *kāhin*'s poetic content was inadequate to the form and that poetry had to be void of such content. In other words, it follows that poetry existing at the time when the Text was revealed is not the necessary form in which the content can be revealed. Moreover, according to this Text, the content and its form can be intolerably discordant, as is exactly the case with the *kāhin*'s poetry. Following the practice of applying the principle of deductive poetic everywhere, people usually favour the view that the content always requires *its* form and that, by its very revelation in this form, the content verifies the quality or uniqueness of the form. However, identifying the discord between the form and content in the *kāhin*'s artefact, this sacred Text strongly suggests the opposite direction: the poetic form, as the dominant form of tradition, should focus on other content that is more appropriate to it. Therefore, the *Qur'an* does not put an end to poetic tradition as a whole but rather regulates it – as it regulates everything else – instructing it to reconsider its themes and its relation to the Absolute. Naturally, the Text is not concerned with individual cases on any occasion, unless an individual case is paradigmatic or is regarded as a common value. Thus, the Text never deals with individual poems, nor even with individual genres – as this would imply an unnecessary waste of strength in terms of its strong need to generalise. The Text instead "imposes order" on tradition, regulating and revising its fundamental values. Accordingly, the Text's relationship to the form in tradition should not be reduced to a demand to renounce *individual* genres or to saturate them with new content; this relation should rather be understood as the relationship to tradition in general. The history of Arabic literature confirms precisely this. Namely, the Form in Tradition survived, was even revitalised and flourished in the first centuries of Islam. While most genres survived, history dispensed with poetry concerned with religion. This fact gives us sufficient grounds for reading the quoted ayahs as a challenge to the form, since any pagan content in poetry is wholly unacceptable to the Text. The poetics of this poetry was judged inadequate, so that the entire production based on *kāhin* poetics was disqualified.

The *Qur'an* was not revealed in the form of poetry, but in prose characterised by rhyme and rhythm, which also represents a very meticulous form with the poetic function of language in the foreground. This fact that the Qur'anic form departs from "pure poetry" should, among other things, be understood as the assertion that poetry is not apt to sustain such sublime and pure content. The Revelation considers its form adequate, which brings back the deduction principle, although for a brief moment it may have seemed to be relativised by the "recommendation" to Tradition/Form to search for other content. Prose with rhyme and rhythm, and language with enormous poetic potential, all of which distinguish this sacred Text, are the most adequate form for the Revelation – so much so that it explicitly states that it is inimitable. Obviously, the poetic course of induction does not apply in this case because *saj'* (prose characterised by rhyme and rhythm), also a form existing in tradition, did not develop the Revelation as its content. It was the other way round: the Revelation was given the *saj'* form where, owing to the content it is saturated with, the form is perfected to such a degree that, according to the Text's challenge, no one is able to imitate it. The principle of deduction is evidently underlined in the content–form relationship as established by the *Qur'an*, unlike the relationship that the *Qur'an* identified in tradition.

The *Qur'an* opted for one of the forms existing in tradition because, among other reasons, this was certainly a prerequisite for communication, as the Text would have been incommunicable had it been revealed in a form outside the experience of tradition. Moreover, it chose a form through which it would intensely (emotionally and rationally at once) communicate with Tradition and with the World; in addition, a strong emphasis on a deductive course is evident from the fact that the Content, in an amazing and positive way, "deformed" the form in which it was conveyed. In other words, the experience of tradition in prose with rhyme and rhythm had not achieved a level at which it could carry the ever so rich content of the Revelation, so that the form had to be considerably transformed and adapted to the new requirements imposed on it. This represents a forceful intervention in tradition, since the *saj'* form in the Qur'anic Text was so much enriched that the Text "gained the right" to its claim of inimitability and perplexed its recipient as to which genre to associate it with: there is a considerable hesitation whether to characterise the Text's form as *saj'* or *naẓm*. The general explosiveness of the text is thus demonstrated in the sphere of form as well. Naturally, there is a strong mutual influence in the relationship between the content and form, since the extraordinary form through which the Text communicates promotes, according to its suitability, the content revealed in it – hence the tremendous excitement I mentioned with regard to reciting the *Qur'an*. In fact, in works of art as well – although this Text is considerably different from them – historic breakthroughs at the ideological level frequently result in changes in form, since a change aspiring to be expressed as a historic one must also find an expression in which it will appear as such. "Lower-rank" changes do not have such high demands. Finally, the word *Revelation* itself indicates many things I have just mentioned. It strongly suggests the vertical course of deduction. In addition, the *Revelation* indicates a specific relation to the form in a very broad sense. First and foremost, it implies, as something inseparable, the quality of Authority. Furthermore, the *Revelation* expresses the need for a form through which it can be adequately conveyed. Since this concerns God's Revelation to the World, it follows that all the stages on its "path" from the Beyondness to the World represent certain kinds of form taken, as I said, quite broadly. The act of prophethood is a sort of form that God selected to convey His Text; then, the stages of this prophethood – from the first communication in the Cave of Hira to the ayahs of the Farewell Sermon – represent graded forms through which the Revelation took its shape; its textual "performance" and recitations are also certain varieties of its form, etc. As an utterly extreme but well founded consequence, the whole World is a sort of form through which the Revelation from the World of Divine Beyondness becomes realised. For, on the one hand, the Revelation was *formed* (referring here to semantic values of the word *revelation* – *waḥy*) during the Prophet's mission but, in a way, it keeps – although the Text remains unchanged – being formed as long as the World exists, which it accomplishes by being open to occasional reinterpretations, and through the different effects it brings about in the world, by its amazing capability of contextualisation, etc.[28]

Diversity of forms

Therefore, the concept of form is inherent in the Revelation but is defined at a very high level. Since the Revelation is sent to the World as God's necessary intervention in it, then intervening in a tradition "constructed" of a number of forms must also be inherent in it. It would be inappropriate for the Revelation to embrace all traditional forms – which would give no cause for intervention – though its aim is not to eliminate all these forms either, because the Revelation needs a highly efficient communication code which can certainly be found in tradition. If we take into account that, in the region the Revelation first arrived in (the Arabian Peninsula), poetry was the dominant form of tradition, including its strong connection with religion, it becomes clear then why the Revelation is shaped in poetic language and a form with very high literary values: it intervenes in Tradition, in the territory Tradition absolutely considers its own, and through a form that would create confusion among traditional forms, forcing them to redefine their themes and goals.

One of the important types of intervention in tradition is to make the relationship between the form and its content relative, as opposed to the Text that includes no such relativisation. Namely, I have just explained that the Revelation found a form adequate for it, perfecting the form to the point of inimitability, as well as that a reversed order cannot be conceived of. However, this does not apply to forms in tradition, because these forms – according to what the Text implicitly or explicitly shows – can be imbued with inadequate content. In fact, this suggests the inductive character of the form–content relationship in tradition. Form becomes refined through tradition to the extent that it achieves relative independence, or the ability to convey quite different content. Consequently, forms are inconstant and diverse, just as are products of the human spirit and mind. The character of human inconstancy is thus indelibly marked in the form–content relationship, and hence in tradition as a succession of their changing relationships. In opposition to this, the unity of the Revelation and its form in the Text is presented as ideal and definitive, with conclusive interpretations allowed in certain places due to openness of meaning, due to its polyvalence. Since the content is fixed, its form must also be fixed for ideality to be achieved; different relations of the human and divine to changeability are proportionate to human transience and God's eternity. Namely, from time immemorial, we have regarded tradition as permanently changeable, since the human creation in it implies perpetual transcendence as its distinctive quality and value judgement. A breakthrough in tradition does not mean its abandonment; every new breakthrough, rather, broadens its experience and puts it into a comparatively new perspective. Innovation is virtue and value. And vice versa – the historical moment (and there have been quite a few) when traditional values and forms are preserved as unsurpassable at any cost brings traditionalism into the foreground, which results in a sclerosis of culture because traditionalism does not allow for regeneration, development, value shifting, etc., but turns – following the *non plus ultra* principle – the previously most creative forces and values into an epigone that gives a firm diagnosis of decay. The relative changeability of forms – to develop my metaphor further – is equivalent to their constant rejuvenation, and this changeability yields, like an elixir, the vital juices of the entire tradition.

The Text is presented completely contrary to this because it stands as a sort of origin of forms in tradition, because it creates tradition, or because it is a sort of the Absolute Form – as a pivot and epicentre of the Universe of forms that orbit around it, adjusting to it. This Text, as a unity of form and content, cannot be changeable as traditional forms are, for in that case everything would be relativised for good and there would be no Force holding everything together, even if in constant vicissitudes. Naturally, I am interpreting the position and message of the Text here. The Text's unchangeability is a condition for its survival considering its responsibility to sustain everything, just as the relative changeability of forms in tradition is a condition for the survival of Tradition. The positions of the Text and Tradition are radically different, so that their relationships to the form are equally different as well. I am going to illustrate this point in a few sentences.

For fourteen-and-a-half centuries the sacred Text – as the unity of form and content – has subsisted in its absolute authenticity, without change to a single letter or word. Through a hypothetical change in this sphere, the Text would refute its fundamental claims and would abolish itself. "Changes" are only generated in the sphere of re/interpretations coming from the perspective of the World's relationship to the Text, not the other way round. It is exactly this that makes it enduringly contemporary, omnipresent and all-embracing, despite its absolute formal and structural unchangeability. If tradition were so loyal to unchangeability, it would result in its own demise; something like this is simply inconceivable.

All other forms, however, have gone through numerous vicissitudes. For instance, Arabic poetry, since it is the subject of this discussion, has survived many things in its history – from Imru' al-Qays' (Imru' al-Qays, d. *c.*540) mu'allaqa in the gilded form of tradition to al-Bayyati's ('Abd al-Wahhāb al-Bayyātī, 1929–1999) "heretical" free verse. Many a new literary genre was begotten along the way, and a number of new kinds created in poetry. And each time, after a short period of resistance, bewilderment and assimilation, tradition always came to pride itself on these novelties. Analysing the problem from this perspective, I can enrich the interpretation of the famous end of the surah *Poets*, which says that poets "rove distraught in every valley". Staying with the essence of the previous reading, I can say that, in this context, the ayah actually identifies the character of tradition that is immersed in constant vicissitudes, unceasingly creating new forms or significantly "exercising" existing ones, which is entirely contrary to the necessary perseverance of the Idea and Form of the Qur'anic Text. At the historic moment when poetry consented to and adopted an attitude to this statement made by the Text, it ensured its own survival in forms that were necessarily changeable, while unchangeability was attributed to the Text. Of course, this was a huge gain for poetry, which it may not even have been aware of at that moment. For, only after it consented to being an art instead of ideology did poetry become free from its ideological tension, more relaxed and regenerated; only then could poetry, through the great delight of human creation, hasten towards new luxurious forms, but always secured, in a way, by the perseverance of the Great Text it orbited around with its forms. The freedom of form in diversity was saved. At the same time, the unity of form and content in the Text became supernatural and inimitable in tradition. The ayahs I quoted in this context underline precisely this status of the Text.

Namely, the Text's repeated calls to competition are obviously rhetorical: they imply that human beings are not able to compose a single surah like any found in the *Qur'an*, even if they ask for help anyone other than Allah. Therefore, this underlines Allah's authorship of the Text and lays the foundation of the faith of every Muslim, but also presents an obvious fact in tradition and literary history, i.e. something well known as *'i'jāz*, or the linguistic and stylistic supernaturalism of the *Qur'an*.

Asking for help anyone other than Allah probably refers to those with whose "help" poets created until that moment: to jinns and shaytans, those whom the *kāhin* appealed to as supernatural beings.

Different aspects of 'i'jāz

(a) The reader within the form and positioning the Text in the Universe of forms

A reader not very familiar with the Arabic language and the tradition built on it can hardly – if at all – fathom where the supernaturalism of the Text lies. Since he cannot gain an insight into the arguments about the supernaturalism on his own, the reader cannot but trust expert analyses and elaborations, as much as it is possible from his external position, and examine the coherence of such analyses and elaborations.

In any case, *'i'jāz* must be elaborated further, considering its manifold importance. We should also bear in mind the important fact I already referred to in a different context: *'i'jāz* was wholeheartedly endorsed by Arabs and, subsequently, all Muslims – that is, in the first place by those who were the most competent to make such a value judgement, since the Text was revealed in their language and in their tradition. This belief is not a result of the believer's position alone, since the Text explicitly declares its supernaturalism, but is also a factual and cultural state of the Text. Namely, we know today that history has not seen a work successfully imitating the Text in all its aspects, primarily in those linguistic, formal and ideological.[29]

One aspect of the importance of *'i'jāz* is manifest in believers. From the Text's position, this aspect is probably the most important. The Text aims at presenting itself as supernatural in order to substantiate its divine origin so as to, at the same time, encourage man's *faith*. Therefore, *'i'jāz* is one God's crucial arguments offered to a believer. Relieved by his knowledge of *'i'jāz*, and hence in a rapture typical only of the strongest faith, a believer can give himself over to the Text, letting these very elements of supernaturalism carry him like a powerful and cascading current that kindle feelings exalting him in his faith. The Text's form is, in this case, experienced from such close proximity that it can be called a *full inner experience*, where each of these three words is optimally stressed: the experience is *complete* in terms of faith; as an internal one, it is *direct* and all the more intense; and finally, it is an *experience* that (at this stage of the believer's reception) need not be accompanied by rational judgement. Moreover, owing to such closeness to the form, in this state the believer-recipient is not concerned with other forms and generally does not feel the need to compare them, despite the fact that the Text invited them, albeit rhetorically, to a competition, or a comparison. With his *faith*, the believer/recipient is entirely *within the form*, in its very core, and since it is the epicentral form for him, he is made ideally happy precisely through his awareness of its epicentral character and perseverance, as well as of the fact that all other forms are incomparable to the one to which he is given over. Other forms are actually on the most remote periphery of his consciousness, but when given over to the Text's form they are beyond the reach of his consciousness, which is ever so radiant with the merits of the Text's form. The experience of *'i'jāz* is also an outstanding experience in terms of the form. This kind of rapture is measureless.

The aspect of *'i'jāz* is somewhat different in a traditional and cultural sense. In principle, a believer is also qualified for this aspect in proportion to his level of education, or his ability to understand tradition and history. The believer's aspects and traditional aspects – if I may conditionally call them so – are not mutually exclusive, but rather complement each other, extending the knowledge of the relationships of forms and of the majesty of *'i'jāz*. Again, this extension is proportionate to the recipient's level of education.

For example, knowledge of the history of Arabic-Islamic literature – if a believer has it – makes the comprehension of *'i'jāz* quite complex, all the more so as he is more familiar with this history. Namely, since Arabic culture is a Culture of Word, the Qur'anic Text (the Text refers to itself as *Qawl* – Speech; *Kalām* – Oration, etc.) can be better understood through knowledge of this culture and its forms which the Text communicated with in different ways. For a relatively uneducated believer, or an insufficiently educated one, *'i'jāz* is a permanent "inner state", because he simply *believes* what the Text tells him, not being able to recognise or understand its true superiority in the universe of forms. An educated believer, however, can arrive at precisely this.[30] While within the Form of the Text, an educated recipient retains at least in his subconscious, sometimes even in bright illumination, for example, the polish of the legendary Arabian work *Seven Golden Odes*, marked by a form–content dichotomy, and vanity of form of panegyric excessiveness as much as of the lampoonist one; he remembers the lavish gold-streaked verse of almost all prose works; he recalls rhymed and rhythmical invocatory passages in Ibn Khaldun's (Ibn Khaldūn, 1332–1406) *Prolegomena*, for instance, and similar works, etc. Such a reader of the Text remembers, with full and precious understanding, the pre-Qur'anic *kāhin* poetry we have already discussed, and develops an ever stronger relationship with the Text. In short, he has a survey of forms in tradition, their vicissitudes and achievements, so that his *experience* of the form of *'i'jāz* is followed by a full *understanding*. Implicitly, the Text prefers his reader to be educated but also acknowledges the relationship of a relatively uneducated one. The virtue of being educated and learned is incomparable. Therefore, it is no coincidence that both the *Qur'an* and Hadith raise education and learnedness to the level of a fundamental duty, just as it is no coincidence that the Islamic world sank into a decadence – which still lasts today – at the very moment when the avant-garde in learning and education was replaced with the authority of antiquity, or with traditionalism.

Hence, the path of an educated believer to the hearth of *'i'jāz* is considerably more complex – in a positive sense of the word – since the effects of *'i'jāz* are multiplied in proportion to the level of education. Communicating with the Form of the Text, such a reader simultaneously communicates with all other forms, by comparing or contrasting them; he has the whole history of forms in a single place and in a single moment. Such a reader is not always and only within the Text, but can sometimes view the Text as well from a distance of other forms, from the platform of his knowledge of them, and these two yield a qualitatively different experience and comprehension of *'i'jāz*.

This place sees the resurfacing of the wisdom of the Text contained in the decision not to abolish poetry as a form in general, but only poetry that is ideologically too pretentious.

Namely, the rhetorical invitation of the ayah for people – "if ye speak truth" – to develop even a single surah like the Text's can be read as the effectuation of the Text's supernaturalism in a sequence of history, in a moment when the living and active Prophet was accused of being a "poet possessed" and of concocting the Text himself. This kind of contextualisation of the form is obvious and very functional. However, the rhetorical invitation has remained open throughout centuries – from the Prophet's to ours – and intends to remain so until the end of the Cosmic Day.

In what way is the universal importance of this decision of the Text reflected?

Had the Text swept other forms away – including poetry as the dominant form in general – it would have meant the catastrophic murder of a tradition, for how could we even imagine the Arab-Islamic world from the *Qur'an* to this day without the immeasurable abundance of literary as well as of many other forms; for, I have already mentioned that, following the Text, the concept of form began to branch out in terms of abundance and refinement, but always under the impression of the Text. Let us take the example of magnificent forms – in addition to literary ones – in Islamic architecture, calligraphy, miniatures, etc. The absence of these forms is inconceivable not only for the Arab-Islamic world, but also for the world in general: ultimately, the world created by the Qur'anic Text generated, among other things, Humanism and the Renaissance that the West rests on – the West that is becoming tragically ungrateful today because it is evidently following the direction of destructing spiritual and cultural values of the very same world that had afforded it, as a happy and healthy childhood, Humanism and the Renaissance.

The Text, however, preserved the forms; moreover, as we have seen, by redirecting them, it even made them considerably richer and more diverse than they had been before. It is therefore wrong to think that the Text is based on a prohibition of poetry in general, just as it is wrong to interpret *'i'jāz* as an ultimately limiting factor in the development of forms, which I will explain in the following part.

By preserving the forms in principle, the Text established its relationship with them not only in the Prophet's history, but in transhistory as well. Through the post-Qur'anic development of forms and our contemporary knowledge of these forms in history, *'i'jāz* is revealed as current and living throughout this whole period, as it never severs its relationships to them. Today's believers, as much as researchers, can explore all the nuances of this relationship and substantiate *'i'jāz*.

Therefore, the status of *'i'jāz* is not an issue that concerns believers alone, but also concerns researchers generally who study the Text in tradition and the Text's position with regard to forms. This is also a very complex cultural and historical issue, even an issue pertaining to the whole of civilisation, since the Text's treatment of other cultural forms influenced the entire development of culture.

The Text's foresightedness is expressed in its acceptance of forms as such, because its relationship to them, by power of contrast, underlines its transhistorical values. Preserving the forms around it, the Text also preserves the evidence of and testimonies to its *'i'jāz*, because these specific forms illuminate its supernaturalism, or – for those who are not believers – these forms enable its inimitable singularity to be perceived. In other words, *'i'jāz* is also meant for those who are not Muslims, because those studying the Text should bear the *idea of 'i'jāz* in mind at all times, as the aim of *'i'jāz* is to stand as an argument for embracing everything the Text contains. Hence, the form of *'i'jāz* is a missionary one. In order for this fundamental value to remain constantly active, the forms in history must be preserved so that *'i'jāz* might always stand in positive and clear contrast to them. The conciliatory attitude towards the form of poetry has, from this perspective, proved to be greatly foresighted and functional, as opposed to the uncompromising attitude towards ideological poetry.

Such subtle differentiation of *'i'jāz* yields at least three consequences, strongly mutually related.

First, the form of *'i'jāz* is optimally elliptical. *'I'jāz* is a process, not conclusively offered and closed arguments for supernaturalism. The importance of the Text's contextuality never withdraws.

Namely, existing in the universe of forms, the Text establishes its *'i'jāz* through relationships with forms that are constantly undergoing their historical development. The development of forms is not the same today as it was in the Prophet's time or the time immediately after his – the experience of tradition has grown vast, so that the arguments supporting *'i'jāz* cannot be identical, in terms of nuances, to those of the earliest period. The development of language and forms has very much improved during these nearly fourteen-and-a-half centuries, and it is only natural that scientific researchers today are trying to find proofs of *'i'jāz* in new nuances, in the spirit of these new experiences of language and forms. Moreover, if the Text is able to convince us of its *'i'jāz* despite the very lengthy period from its revelation to this day, then its ability to do so is all the more remarkable than it was in the Prophet's times; every reader observing this carefully cannot but wonder: how can it be that, during fourteen-and-a-half centuries, the Text has been generating its *'i'jāz*?! The arguments for *'i'jāz* are thus becoming evermore compelling. As a process, *'i'jāz* is realised at all times, just as the Text maintains that it is meant for all times.

Second, related to the previous point, *'i'jāz* is also an incentive to other forms, not their limiting factor, as much as it may appear as one. The Text may seem at first to discourage other forms by its own superior form, as these forms may conclude that they have no prospects whatsoever considering the Text's *'i'jāz*, and they may be expected to succumb to depression as a way of stagnation. However, the state of the matter is essentially different. The Text is interested in the development of forms, or even in their full prosperity, since this increases the possibilities for its *'i'jāz* argumentation. The avant-garde nature of forms never ceases to bring to light the Text's unattainable "Divine Avant-garde". Therefore, the Text has an important interest in a continuous development of culture and its form, as well as of science in general, since they, in proportion to the power of their beam of light, illuminate the *'i'jāz* arguments always more deeply and clearly. This is an unstoppable progression. However, there is yet another reference to be made here, albeit a passing one.

This discussion confirms that at the heart of the Text lies strength encouraging unstoppable human creation, progress, constant scientific dedication that must be avant-garde in relation to itself. Ignoring this strength is equal to ignoring the essence of the Text, which then inevitably leads to stagnation and the kind of lagging behind the Islamic world finds itself in today. For, understanding the Text in tradition, in relation to all other forms, as I said, requires constant learning, progress, changes in positive directions – this is the implied supreme command of the Text's Author. But, at the same time, this also implies a truly dedicated effort that I have just termed avant-garde in relation to itself. Namely, sometimes it is not difficult to be avant-garde in relation to others and it often does not imply that all of one's potential should be maximally engaged. The problem – and a true feat – is to be avant-garde in relation to oneself, i.e. to always make a step beyond one's own potential and ahead of one's previous step, regardless of how large the steps of others may be. This is the essential request of the Text that I have just explained and that, with continuous acceleration, leads to the values and aims set by the Text. As long as Islamic peoples were aware of this type of avant-garde, they were the most progressive in the world.

Third, *'i'jāz* is diversely reflected in the field of language as well. The traditional study of *'i'jāz* is limited to an analysis of its rhetorical unattainability and style. A vast amount of literature has been written on this. This aspect of *'i'jāz* is undeniable, obvious even, and as such it typically attracts researchers. The form *naẓm*, or *saj'* in which the Text came to be, is really unique in history, considering the lavishness of its stylistic devices, tropes, rhymes and refrains – in short, the Text is characterised by an inexhaustible array of linguistic and stylistic values and values of form in general. The Arabs' fascination with these values is perennial and well known, and to a great extent the fascination of Muslims in general, but other researchers have clearly observed this aspect of *'i'jāz* as well. Thus, one of the best translators of the *Qur'an*, A. J. Arberry, says that the *Qur'an* is "inimitable symphony".[31] Similar appraisals can be found in the works of some other Orientalists. However, this aspect is quite well explored, though not exhausted, and I would not interpret it here.

Another level of the relation between *'i'jāz* and language is quite interesting; this relation is not unfamiliar but is not as obvious as the first.

Namely, *'i'jāz* is understood not only as something created in a supernatural form and language, and as something that convinced the earliest Muslims of the divine origin of the Text, as well as those coming after them – therefore, as something given all at once, something clear and active in one period. This is the first layer of *'i'jāz* indeed, and I have just mentioned it as the traditional conception and study of *'i'jāz*. However, the second and very effective layer of *'i'jāz* is reflected through history and tradition in all its aspects. What I want to say is that *'i'jāz* is not only the *Qur'an* as *Muṣḥaf*, i.e. an *aggregate* of divine marvels that are *in* it, lodged and open to research. Furthermore, the Text "produces" *'i'jāz around* itself as well, or *beyond* itself, producing it in Time and Space in general, in the Universe of moveable forms and, while doing so, naturally emitting its entire influence on developments around itself from within itself. Therefore, it is not only that the *'i'jāz* is the sum of values found in linguistic, stylistic and formal values confined in the *Muṣḥaf*; the supernaturalism of the *Qur'an* unstoppably and continually pours out from the *Muṣḥaf* onto the World. This unending dynamism through which it influences the World represents an important aspect of the Text's *'i'jāz*. We have just seen that, despite its unchangeability and the assertion of its supernaturalism, the Text encourages the development of tradition and traditional forms that promote the Text in proportion to their refinement. We have also seen that the Text encourages the development of education and erudition as an important requirement for its understanding, promotion, etc. Hence, this effect is one aspect of the impact of *'i'jāz*. However, let us return to language.

(b) Centripetal forces of language

The obvious aspect of *'i'jāz* in language is the Text's linguistic and stylistic value. However, in the field of language, *'i'jāz* is also realised beyond this framework through heaving a history whose framework can barely be comprehended. The *Qur'an* codified and standardised the (classical) Arabic language; considering the time in which the Text was revealed, this language is amazingly regular, consistent, almost mathematically precise in the field of morphology and grammar, and is also lexically and semantically rich. In such language was the Qur'anic *'i'jāz* created. It is also a miracle that, during fourteen-and-a-half centuries, the Text has fascinated its readers with its form, style, grammaticality, etc. Try to imagine a several-hundred-year-old literary work in our mother tongue that can be understood and received in such a way! Immediately before the Text, Arabians had the brilliant *al-Mu'allaqāt* corpus – the *Seven Golden Odes* – which was irreplaceable in terms of popularity, but the corpus met quite a different fate from the Text's, even in terms of language: the *al-Mu'allaqāt* remained confined to the past, so that even educated Arabs cannot understand them today without detailed comments. Unlike this, the *Mu'allaqāt*'s contemporary, the sacred Text, is still alive today, not only in ideological but also in linguistic terms.

It should be said that, in relation to the classical Qur'anic language, the modern Arabic language has changed to a certain degree – which is only natural – in the field of lexis, syntax, etc., but these changes cannot be compared to those existing between, for instance, the modern German and Gothic language, between Old Slavic and Serbian, between Latin and a number of Romance languages, etc. The closeness of the classical and modern Arabic languages has remained strikingly strong considering that a considerably long time has elapsed. The effect of the Text is quite specific here, *'i'jāz*-like, and testifies to what I have just termed the impact of *'i'jāz* beyond the covers of *Muṣḥaf.*

Namely, the Text not only allowed but encouraged the development of forms, even language, always remaining at the centre of this cultural and civilisational universe. The Qur'anic Text simply does not let language be so transformed as to become unrecognisable against its matrix; it has a power preventing language(s) from developing and detaching in time to a point where the connection between them would be broken, which is the case with other languages. Its *'i'jāz* activity at this level is evident and truly astonishing. Moreover, modern Arabic cannot be said to be as archaic and ossified as could be expected considering the large number of centuries standing between the Text's appearance and this day. Although it may seem paradoxical at first, this linguistic core of the Arab world has an unusual strength with which it keeps the development of language "under control", preventing it from "floating away" but also from becoming obsolete beyond recognition. The Text steadfastly seeks to control all of history, including language in history.

I have often read and heard Arabists wonder: How have the strong and numerous dialects in the Arab world not become independent and developed into separate languages – as happened with Old Slavic or Latin? Such Arabists have also expressed their belief that this will inevitably happen, albeit belatedly.[32] My reply to this has always been that such views fail to grasp the principle underlying the Text's position – that something like that can never happen considering the Text's linguistic vitality, which recent centuries only confirm. Comparison with other languages fails to notice that the historical and religious circumstances of Old Slavic, Latin and Arabic cannot be compared. There are even some attempts nowadays, of which we can learn on the Internet, to market worldwide extremely large print runs of deliberately apocryphal versions of the Qur'anic Text – in order to undermine the authenticity of the *Qur'an*. However, these represent almost infantile attempts in our time, for if the Text, or even a single word in it, was not falsified in the first decades of Islam (as actually happened with other heavenly revelations), then it is impossible to falsify now. This is impossible owing to the very *'i'jāz* of language, which is a cast-iron guarantee of its authenticity. Namely, since the axiom of its linguistic and stylistic supernaturalism was established at the beginning of the Text's "descent", it ensured the Text's authenticity because, naturally, Muslims were vigilant about every single letter as the most sacred thing – and an argument of an unchangeable Divine Structure.

Therefore, the linguistic and historical aspect of *'i'jāz* is evident in its not letting the Arabic language disperse. Among the consequences of this impact is the fact that the Text, in the Arabic language, which also includes Islam both contained within it and operating from it, represents the only cohesive element of the Arab world today, which is politically so diverse, at variance even, that it would much rather irreversibly dissolve. The literary Arabic language, standardised by the Text, is a single language throughout the Arab world, while dialects, though numerous and different to the level of mutual incommunicability, are prevented from a "total separation" from the matrix. It is even realistic to expect – contrary to anticipations of the aforementioned Arabists – these dialects to be further relativised and marginalised, and the literary standard to become increasingly widespread owing to increasing mass education and the increasingly powerful influence of the media.

Certainly, owing to the centripetal forces of the Text – with linguistic *'i'jāz* as its important factor – forms of Arabic culture, or of what Orientalists call Arabic Islamic culture, bring about a certain unity in terms of culture and civilisation, despite the fact that this cultural and civilisational environment is the space of creative activity of, on the one hand, Arabs who are well familiar with centripetal forces and, on the other, foreign and non-Arab peoples. The cultural aspect of the Text's *'i'jāz* is therefore reflected in the fact that it holds the Arab world more or less together and, at the same time, makes non-Arabs gravitate towards it culturally and in terms of certain forms. The Text's aspiration to universality is evident. In a unique way it effectuates what is called the "unity of diversity". However, these are not the ultimate achievements of the Text's *'i'jāz*.

I have already mentioned that the *'i'jāz* of the Text's language and form cannot be perceived and *experienced* by those unfamiliar with the Arabic language; at the same time, it should be borne in mind that believers regard *'i'jāz* as a true miracle of God. As a consequence, this means that believers unfamiliar with the Arabic language are deprived of something very important. No translation of the *Qur'an* can adequately substitute for the original, and many believers, or those with cultural curiosity, become familiar with the original through translations. Since I too translated the *Qur'an* into the Bosnian language (published in 2004) and am thoroughly familiar with many other translations,

I know for a fact that, regardless of how brilliant the translation may be, there are substantial losses in the very field of the literary, aesthetic and semantic values of the Text.[33] *'I'jāz* is inseparable from the Arabic language.

The sense of deprivation can, to a certain degree and conditionally only, be defined as a relatively inadequate reception of the Text. Admittedly, the reception of *'i'jāz* is not a condition for belief imposed on the believer: he already has his faith and does not necessarily need *'i'jāz* as an argument. However, it is clear that his faith would be adorned with the reception of *'i'jāz*, and it is in this sense that the deprivation, perhaps even frustration, should be understood. For the experience of *'i'jāz* is indeed a marvellous feeling.

What are the consequences of this deprivation?

The fact of being unfamiliar with the Arabic language and the sense of deprivation arising from this unfamiliarity result in a far-reaching consequence of the Text anticipated through *'i'jāz*. Namely, every believer feels the need to learn Arabic, or even to have as much a command of it as possible in order to understand and experience what is known as *'i'jāz*. Furthermore, following this need, every Islamic community outside the Arab world should eventually influence the learning of Arabic by its authority and community instruments. It is well known that only Arabic is used in prayer, which is why every Muslim must know the minimum of Text required for prayer, but this still does not imply that someone has knowledge of the language, because many people utter these parts of the Text without being familiar with their meaning. However, *'i'jāz* requires learning the Arabic language as a certain mastery of language is necessary in order to understand *'i'jāz*.

Evidently, the centripetal force of language was active in the Prophet's time, and throughout history to the present moment, in which, as we have seen, it overpowers the dispersive or even divergent forces of the contemporary Arab world. However, as *'i'jāz* had its impact in the future – seen, for example, from the perspective of the early Islamic rulers, which belongs to the past from our perspective – it will, applying the same principle, make its impact in the future ahead of us. This is because *'i'jāz* strongly encourages the learning of the Arabic language. In other words, understanding the Text at its highest level requires a command of the Arabic language; implicitly, every believer is advised – though it is not a condition of his faith – to learn Arabic. This is a powerful impact of the Text in the form of *'i'jāz*. For the very same force within it keeping the Arab world together seeks to bring the entire Islamic world together, not only in religion but also in "the language of this religion". More precisely, the language of the faith of Islam is a single language – i.e. the Arabic language – but, owing to *'i'jāz*, it aspires to transcend this "knowledge" at the level of ritual, the level at which parts of the Text are uttered without their full understanding, and to reach the highest level of linguistic mastery.

A conclusion as to the consequences of this is not difficult to draw but is impressive nonetheless. Namely, it follows from all of this that, at the level of linguistic *'i'jāz*, the main aspiration is towards the linguistic unity of the world. This aspiration is realised in concentric circles: the first circle was Hijaz in Saudi

Arabia, where the Prophet was active through the Revelation; then, the circles of the world marked by Islam in the Umayyad (661–750) and Abbasid (750–1258) periods – all the way to the Bosnian territories where, for centuries, creative works in all spiritual domains were in Arabic. Finally, Arabic is also recognised as an official language in the United Nations (1972), certainly owing to the Text alone. At this moment the future of Arabic cannot be predicted, but there is no doubt that it will not, that it actually cannot, abandon its extensiveness, as is inherent in the Text.

A language and its culture cannot be treated separately. This implies that the United Nations did not recognise Arabic as an official language because the *Qur'an* had been revealed in it, but this language did become the official one owing to the richness and importance of the culture created within the framework and under the influence of the Text. This culture, as a vast range of luxurious forms, was often developed as an amalgamation. Namely, the Text drew into its orbit precious forms of other cultures – particularly of Persian and Indian cultures, for instance – but they always had to adjust to the new space, thus being modified into quite new forms of immense value.

There is no doubt – from the Text's position – that such ambitions on the part of the Text project towards the future as well. Through the impact of *'i'jāz*, the Text's language and style remain forever amazing and captivating, making the need to learn Arabic forever felt. Through its language, and certainly through its content, the Text will therefore influence – as is its intention – the culture within which it will always recognise the richness of forms, without an aspiration towards their complete unification. Moreover, the closing of the surah *Poets* implicitly acknowledges the diversity of forms – provided that there is no sacrilege of Islamic monotheism. It should be said that the Text is also accepted as a value of diversity across cultures. In this regard, the following ayah has become a commonplace: "O men! Verily, we have created you of a male, and a female; and we have divided you into peoples and tribes that ye might have knowledge of one another."[34] This ayah is so much more than tolerance related to Islam, because this is not a matter of tolerance as toleration, acceptance or co/habitation but of *an active relationship of getting to know one another in diversity*; since this is a token of God's will and mercy, it must be revered as such and, at the same time, it makes it a religious imperative to engage in every effort towards "mutual conversance" among different "peoples and tribes". Therefore, it is much more than coexistence and tolerance. The Text certainly promotes differences as a virtue and a token of God's wisdom, with the phenomenon of *'i'jāz* actively engaged in this too.

(c) Other aspects of 'i'jāz *and perspectives of forms*

There are also other aspects of *'i'jāz* that cannot be discussed in detail here but that should be at least mentioned.

Scholars of the *Qur'an* have, since long ago, identified elements of "scientific" *'i'jāz* in it, trying to prove that the *Qur'an* anticipated modern sciences.[35]

In addition, our times have recorded some serious attempts to mathematically process the Text using modern information technologies. For example, the research of Rashad Khalifa[36] is notable in this field, and a Bosnian volume I wrote together with the mathematician Lutvo Kurić has recently been distributed to bookstores.[37] Such exact research is generally interesting and I even think has a promising future. However, the study of *'i'jāz* in its traditional conception is not yet completely exhausted.

It should also be noted that, in its concept of *'i'jāz*, tradition includes the information the Text gives about the future as well. Namely, the *Qur'an* announced certain historical events with complete accuracy, which constitutes one of the foundations for building the doctrine of its supernaturalism, because the Prophet alone could not have known or foreseen these things. In essence, a large portion of the Text is indeed devoted to the future, and its supernaturalism can be verified from this aspect as well. Finally, the Text is directed towards the future in a special meaning – an eschatological future that cannot be verified yet.

With regard to the doctrine of *'i'jāz*, which was coined as a term only in the ninth century, mention should be made of another term introduced in the early centuries of Islam.[38] In their early discussions, Mu'tazilis used the concept of *ṣarf* (al-Naẓẓām in 846), which Orientalists still discuss today. The concept of *ṣarf* (deflection from a course, deterrence) expresses God's decision or a plan contained in the Text which, by divine determination, prevents people from imitating it. By a sort of an a priori or implicit decision, the Text actually diverts them from that course, deters their possible intention of imitating it, or even wards off such an intention. Even though the concept of *ṣarf* is known to exegesis, a general Muslim consensus, as far as I know, has left it aside, with a minority of commentators, supporting the traditional stylistic supremacy of the *Qur'an*.

* * *

None of the approaches to the phenomenon of *'i'jāz* described above can be regarded as essentially wrong because all of them have found their footholds in the Text, though to various degrees. Nevertheless, the traditional approach to *'i'jāz*, as the supernaturalism of the Text in the sphere of language and style, is certainly the most common and has yielded numberless results – a vast body of literature throughout the Text's history. However, the traditional approach could be regarded as satiated in one particular sense. Namely, the study of the Text's language and style undertaken over the past centuries should be invigorated with different methodological treatment, considering that the Text explicitly states that it is revealed for all times and that it poses a challenge to these times in terms of interpretation. Admittedly, the development of language and the wealth of human experience are the source of constant reinterpretation of the Text's *'i'jāz*, but I believe it is possible, or even necessary, to refresh this approach and I hope that the above analysis has made this evident.

Summarising this analysis I can say that research into the Text's supernaturalism in the sphere of language and style represents, conditionally speaking, just one stage or platform for further research. If such research is confined to the sphere of linguistic stylistics without relating it to other spheres, then such research, interesting though it may be (or even functional in terms of offering *'i'jāz* arguments), is not complex to the extent to which the Text, through its *'i'jāz*, makes a very wide impact on history and decides that its future impact will probably be even wider. Therefore, from the perspective of linguistic stylistics, a perspective validated by the entire library of works written on it, the concept of *'i'jāz* must be moved to spheres related to language and stylistics, or generally to literature, as well as to the broadest range of forms realised in the category of history we call Culture and Tradition. The knowledge and study of literature, as well as of language, is very instrumental in researching the outreach of *'i'jāz*; however, it is also illuminated by all other forms in Culture. It is wrong to regard *'i'jāz* as something stifling these forms or inhibiting their vicissitudes and expansion by its supremacy that, by virtue of its place at the level of the divine, allegedly proclaimed an intolerant relationship to the development of forms. On the contrary, it is striking how the Text promotes overall diversity (except in relation to its monotheism, as I have already said): the immense diversity of forms in literature (and of literature itself), forms in calligraphy, the unity in diversity with regard to the arabesque, to the full promotion of different colours of human skin or diversity of races. However, this immense diversity is realised in the unity of one huge framework called Islam, or within the framework created by the Text. Its *'i'jāz* is the driving force behind the prosperity of forms in the ever so rich Arab-Islamic culture and civilisation, provided that nothing produced aspires to be equal to the Text. The Text says a number of times that the essential requirement for Islamic belief is that no partner is attributed to Allah, someone who is (only apparently) equal to Him, because the Text maintains that no one is equal to God. The absolute Authenticity applies to His Text too: it is unique or, better yet, supernatural since it is God-given. Something equal to it is impossible to compose. It is unrepeatable and unrepeated in ideal terms. Even at the level of form in its basic meaning, the Text represents something quite singular in history. Namely, it is sometimes categorised under the tradition of *saj'* – prose, which is characterised by rhyme and rhythm that pre-Islamic Arabians were familiar with, but a stricter approach reveals that, though it has many elements of *saj'*, the Text often intentionally departs from this genre in terms of rhyme regularity, which is why it is then classified as *naẓm*, i.e. a genre of specially structured prose. Literary terminology is unable to fully convey its specific features. In other words, the Text encourages the prosperity of forms, remaining at the centre of the universe in which they are re/created, at a distance of *'i'jāz* from which the Text influences their "shaping", at the same time feeling comfortable but superior among them. Pre-Islamic pagan poetry, imbued with *kāhin*-generated substance, was eliminated precisely because of this substance, or more precisely, poetry was emptied of it. The Qur'anic Text competently carried the Substance, a unique Content of the highest order, which is why other forms must differ from the Text in order to even survive in the universe created by it. In these terms, there is no rivalry – nor should there be any from the Text's position. It is interesting to note in this context that the Text also affected the forms it excluded from its orbit.

Poetry survived under certain conditions but some other forms, very important in other cultures, were eliminated or hampered in Arabic culture because of their aspirations to "snatch" the Substance the Text considers its own, or to establish a partnership with the Text.

Arab-Islamic culture did not develop sculpture. In pre-Islamic tradition sculpture was closely related to pagan religion, so that the Kaaba was full of idols – *sculptured* deities. Of course, in keeping with its spirit, Islam had an uncompromising attitude to this form of Arabian creation, so that sculpture was smashed to smithereens, for all time. It never developed in Arab-Islamic culture on account of its pagan past and of the need for Islam to distance itself from other cultures that, before but also after the *Qur'an*, closely related sculpture to their beliefs. However, architecture saw unimagined development in this culture. For similar reasons painting also failed to develop. As a result, the arabesque, calligraphy and Islamic miniature thrived "by way of compensation".

Finally, music did not develop in Arab-Islamic culture as much as it did in the Christian tradition. It met more or less the same fate as poetry: popular in the Arab-Islamic world but excluded from religious service. There are no musical instruments in mosques, nor is the prayer accompanied by any form of music. There is no church music. Moreover, an individual prays within the complete silence of their mind and communicates with God, while a congregation prays partly in silence and partly aloud because of the necessary ritual communication. Some dervish rituals are not a rule but rather excesses in tradition.

Therefore, all these represent forms that could not survive alongside the Text, as they were too pretentious in terms of expressing this Substance, which is the Text's privilege.

Mosques are completely empty. The "empty" space within them is a special type of *form*. In fact, the mosque space has the "form of emptiness" because it is the most adequate for accommodating the Text and accentuating its resonance in the most effective way. The Text (here: the Word) is brought in and out of this space together with man's spirituality, because it is only in this spirituality that faith is really present. The Text, which I do not take in its literal meaning (as a written text), is self-sufficient in man's mind and spirit, which is why it becomes easily realised in any space, while this free space (it is *free* rather than *empty*) most adequately promotes the Text's freedom, its disenthrallment from visual or other forms that would reduce it in terms of identification.

The only aspect in which the Text becomes related to a type of "musical form" is *tajwīd* or the loud sing-song delivery of the Text according to strict rules (known as "recitation" of the *Qur'an* among Muslims, with the word "singing" being deliberately avoided). However, there is something interesting about it. Namely, the *Qur'an* is never recited with music or any musical instrument, the focus being on the *voice* as something absolutely individual and human. Islam is a faith of absolute individuality, with no clergy or any other physical (visual or sculptural) intercession, which is why the prayer/salat is performed in the deepest silence of privacy or is only voiced. Certainly, the Text was revealed as the *Word*, and it becomes the word to plunge into the noiselessness and depths of privacy, or it becomes the word to surface in the voice unclouded by additional instruments. *Tajwīd* is, therefore, a form through which the Word finds its perfect expression in the human voice. Man alone, without any aid or intercession, man gifted with the word and articulate expression, is fully sovereign in communication with the Text and with God owing to this full and undivided attention to the Word, whether he ponders on it in the depths of noiselessness or exalts with its resonance in the Human Voice. This is, at the same time, the *form* of utter closeness to God, and it appears to be an important motive for converts.

In terms of the promotion of *'i'jāz* in the world beyond the Arabic-speaking world there is sometimes a misunderstanding that could also be called a prejudice, and results from the Orientalist attitude to *'i'jāz*. Before I examine this prejudice, I should point out that *'i'jāz* is a matter of consensus in the Arab world – it is, therefore, not in question. However, when elements of *'i'jāz* are promoted in the West, while explaining the values of the Text's form and style, Muslims sometimes have a negative reaction to it, considering it blasphemy or a preparation for it. I myself had such an experience while I was rendering the *Qur'an* into the Bosnian language.[39] The reason behind this reflexive fear is the fact that many Orientalists sought to prove that the *Qur'an* was the Prophet's work, and an important argument in proving this kind of authorship is the assertion of the literary values of a text. Orientalists thus offered a whole set of instruments for "establishing" Muhammad's authorship of the Text. Thence came the fear among Muslims. As a matter of fact, the terms *literary* or *literary and aesthetic* values imply human authorship, and even well-educated people are often unaware of the difference between the terms *literary* and *artistic*. A text with literary and aesthetic values is not necessarily an artistic one. It is sufficient to give the example of *waqfiyyah*, which is eminently a legal document, but with an obligatory introduction written in prose characterised by rhyme and rhythm, and with a number of figures of speech and tropes. Therefore, the Qur'anic Text is pregnant with literary and aesthetic values indeed, but it is not an artistic text because these literary and aesthetic values are not its aim, as is the case with art; ultimately, the Text's style is also an argument. Even this ideal literary and aesthetic value is presented as an argument. For, in its traditional meaning, *'i'jāz* is a sum of values in language and form; it is a sum of literary and aesthetic values that do not aspire to aestheticism, "attraction for its own sake" and delight as their goal; through their supernaturalism, these values are rather an *argument* in favour of faith. It is an essential feature of the Text which differentiates it from literary art. This is why the Text demands that its literary and aesthetic values should be promoted, instead of shying away from such promotion.

* * *

Translations of the original Text arise as a particularly sensitive issue with regard to *'i'jāz*. At the same time, translations are a special type of form in the Universe created and governed by the original Text.

Every expert on the Arabic language and the *Qur'an* will conclude that *'i'jāz* is realised in the original and is, therefore, related to the Arabic language. This understanding has created two different attitudes with regard to translations of the *Qur'an*.

First, most translators abandoned the attempt of conveying the stylistic component of the original, so that their works represented aesthetically graceless philological translations. Furthermore, as the original has a lapidary style and enormous semantic indentation, translators were often forced to add to these prose philological translations bracketed interpolations, syntactic "insertions" that further aggravated the readability of such translations, thus making them create an impression opposite to that of the original.[40]

Such translators were filled with fear before the original and did not dare to even try to convey something of its stylistic splendour. Many even considered it blasphemous. In addition, such translators were mostly persons with no literary education or affinity, so that *'i'jāz* would only have been an alibi for their handicap of this kind. It is interesting that they often justified their approach by the need for literalness, the alleged need to be faithful to the original in order not to change its (religious) message, etc. Such apologies are wrong in more ways than one. On the one hand, literal translation is always the worst possible decision a translator can make, since the text does not function through its literalness but through poetic syntax and contextuality; literalness is the best testimony to absolute translating incompetence. Moreover, it follows from their attitude that a *literarily adequate* translation and *genuineness/authenticity* of the Message are mutually exclusive, which is also a powerful testimony to the translator's incompetence.[41] However, the opposite is the case: the effect of the Message is enhanced by a stylistically adequate translation; furthermore, in the previous discussion, I highlighted the fact that the sublime style and form are a very important element of the Message. *'I'jāz* is at the very heart of the Text and a translator must not ignore it, although it still is an open issue to what extent a translation can come close to it. In addition, literalness is no obligation whatsoever, since it offers no guarantee that the original content will be rendered "accurately". Namely, not counting the layers of the Text "legally" governing relationships among people, relationships on which the community (*umma*) is based economically and socially, a major portion of the Text is polyvalent, elliptical, semantically stratified, etc., which rules literalness out, as the translator is forced to select one meaning out of a multitude, the meaning closest to their understanding, education, tradition, etc. Paradoxically, the translator turns literalness into an interpretation that seems a reductionist one against the semantic stratification and elliptical nature of the original. I have therefore explained that the semantic and stylistic opulence of the original is related to the organisation of Arabic, where literalness – allegedly for the purpose of authenticity – must not be confused with one's own terminological reductionism of the original. I will illustrate this with one example, quite frequent in the original Text.

The phrase *yawm al-qiyāma* is most often translated as *the Day of Judgement*. The same applies to *yawm al-dīn*, etc. The first phrase does not actually indicate anything that would basically mean *judge*, *judgement*, *judging*, etc. The phrase means *the Day of Resurrection* and its semantics is much wider than the interpretation phase *the Day of Judgement*. *Resurrection* implies *rising* (from the grave); you rise before Someone who deserves the utmost respect; the act of standing – in addition to humbleness, and in relation to it – means expecting something (judgement, *perhaps*?) from the One worthy of rising and standing, etc. Finally, the word resurrection resounds with sacredness, and the capitalised noun *Day* gives the whole phrase extreme importance, not only in terms of universality but also of deep seriousness. Therefore, any argument of literal translators is certainly not justified, and I even consider them a counterproductive excuse for their own insensitivity to what, in the opening of surah 55, God labelled as the *articulate expression* bestowed on man.

Second, native speakers of the Arabic language do not allow for the expression "translation of the *Qur'an*" to be used; they rather talk about *tarjama ma'ānī al-Qur'ān al-karīm* – which means "translating the motifs of the Honourable *Qur'an*". In the Bosnian language the word *ma'ānī* is commonly understood as *meaning* (hence, translating the meaning of the *Qur'an*), which is incoherent and inadmissible. Following this – to use the same example – rendering the phrase *yawm al-qiyāma* as *the Day of Judgement* implies the rendering of its motif indeed, but I see no coercion for it to be translated (*sic*!) in this particular way. Therefore, native speakers can in no way whatsoever agree to a translation that, as they see it, implies some sort of partnership with the original; one can only speak of conveying the motifs, completely emptied of eloquence, stylistic means, etc.

In the minds of these people *'i'jāz* is taken too rigidly, contrary to its true function expressed in its considerable flexibility to "surrounding" forms, encouraging them to develop and multiply. The conviction that only *motifs can be translated* is an expression of a particular linguistic nationalism as the sort of supremacy that develops into exclusiveness, believing that, since the *Qur'an* in the Arabic language and in its form achieves perfection, it is blasphemous to even try to use translation for conveying at least a part of its linguistic and stylistic merits. This form of the Arabic linguistic exclusiveness is inadmissible, even without any basis in *'i'jāz*, paradoxical as it may seem.

Namely, *'i'jāz* is built in the Arab world and the culture of its language. It is indeed related to the organisation of the Arabic language and is verified in this culture. However, the transmission of the Text into other languages and cultures must not surrender all the beauties of the original. Furthermore, I consider these types of translations blasphemous, and not those attempting to convey the beauty of the original as much as possible. For the "translation of meaning" sounds repulsive and I know that such translations are only read by people forced to do so – whether they are believers or culture activists. The original has exactly the opposite aspirations and qualities, and the translator must at least indicate them, convey them as much as possible and thus gratify the reader's virtue that God gave him as the sense of articulate expression. Moreover, there is no need to worry about sacrilege here: translations can never be equal to the achievements of the original.

Readers of most translations in the world – should they judge the Text by translations – will arrive at the conclusion that there is a surprising discrepancy between the proclaimed *'i'jāz* (as the perfect expression) and what they are offered in translations; they will feel cheated in a way, which is sacrilege indeed. This is why the Text must not be translated by someone insensitive to its unique literary and aesthetic achievements, and such translation is by no means the prerogative of theologians. The heart of *'i'jāz* is outstanding beauty, which is precisely the Text's remarkable divine argument.

The Text's relationships to forms in Arabic and, subsequently, Arab-Islamic cultures, which we have discussed so far, essentially exist with regard to translation texts too. Just as the supremacy of the original is realised in a multitude and diversity of forms in Arab-Islamic culture, it is also realised in a multitude of translations in other languages and cultures. Furthermore, in their relationship to the Text, in only one special aspect, of course, translators are in a privileged position with respect to the Text's recipients in the Arab world: the Text has been given to Arabs once and for all, without the slightest possibility of changing even a single letter, while translators have the opportunity to, respecting *'i'jāz*, (re)create linguistic and stylistic values of the Text over and over again, searching for their equivalents in their own languages. They are doubly creative. On the one hand, the reception of the Text, open in the original, is always a sort of creation and, on the other, translators create conveying this reception to their language and culture. *'I'jāz* feels great in such a relationship because it becomes doubly promoted as well: through understanding in the source language and structure and, then, through (re)creation in another language and culture. According to this inertia, it obviously enjoys each new breakthrough, any progress, as its supernaturalism is thus illuminated over and over again. A good translation is always more than just a translation, particularly when it comes to texts with high literary and aesthetic value. The original and a good translation do not live independently of each other but are in constant interaction: the original always appraises the suitableness of translational creation – in accordance with its reasonable "vanity", and a translation always brings us back to the original with which it has established permanent and intense communication, provided that it is at the level of the original, because there can be no communication otherwise. This is why the communication between the original and its "translations of meaning" is overburdened with noise.

Since *'i'jāz* is the ideal form, it realises its ideality among other forms, not among poor forms but among the best and most diverse ones. This is why the Text permitted poetry as the *best* expression of the Arab spirit; it stimulated the endless aesthetic and historical meanderings of the arabesque, as well as of calligraphy that promotes the principles of arabesque structure; it encouraged the development of splendid architecture, even of philosophy, etc. This multitude of forms also includes translations of the Text; moreover, they occupy a prominent position in the universe of forms. However, translators have not adequately understood their task so far because, instead of *'i'jāz*, they have upheld the form–content dichotomy, thus desecrating the beauty of their unity in expression.[42]

* * *

I opened my discussion of the Text's relationship to forms with an analysis of its confrontation with poetry, where I made a distinction between the Text's relationship to poetry at the level of ideology and that of form. This relationship was more or less dramatic and the Text paid careful attention to it. However, the relationship to poetry should be taken as a paradigm established by the Text. Namely, to achieve clarity and produce a most powerful effect, the Text placed poetry at the centre of its relationships, since poetry was the dominant cultural, artistic and, to a degree, religious form in that region at the time. As the Text is elliptical in many aspects, it is also significantly contextual. Its contextuality is achieved through its position with respect to poetry for the reasons I have just explained. However, this implies that the Text – with intertextuality being inherent in it – generally develops such relationships with other forms too. In other words, the richness of forms is accepted, even encouraged, provided that these forms do not pretend to the Truths the Text is concerned with. The positioning of poetry in the given historical situation was realistic and literal; but, having in mind the Text's assertion that it is meant for all times and the fact that poetry, in terms of the religious function it had when the *Qur'an* was revealed, is long since dead and buried, this relationship to poetry should be understood as a particular parable.

In endorsing this positioning of poetry as a parable – because it is a Text of polyvalent meanings and tremendous achievements – close attention should be devoted to its true revolutionising of literary history, or poetics. The nature and scope of its "poetic revolutionising" can, I believe, be neatly presented through a comprehensive analysis of the simile, as the dominant figure of speech in the pre-Qur'anic style, and the metaphor, as the dominant cognitive and stylistic trope in the *Qur'an*. Showing that these two stylistic means are rooted in different perceptions of the world, I will indicate not only the dramatic Descent of the Revelation into the World, but also fateful sea changes in Tradition.

Notes

1 *Qur'an*, 36:69.
2 *Qur'an*, 36:69.
3 *Qur'an*, 69:40–43.
4 *Qur'an*, 39:23.
5 The word *mutashābihāt* receives different interpretations. Some understand it as a word denoting "vague parts", while others take it to denote similarity between certain parts in the Text.

6 *Qur'an*, 52:29.

7 The selection of the term prophet is well founded; being always in opposition to the poet-soothsayer, the word prophet does not imply the kind of "supernatural" mediation as the poet-soothsayer does. Hence the *Qur'an* states several times that the Prophet is a man like others. For example, "Say: In sooth I am only a man like you. It hath been revealed to me that your God is one only God" (*Qur'an*, 18:110).

Admittedly, the *Qur'an* holds the Prophet in great respect. The following ayah can illustrate this: "Verily, God and His Angels bless the Prophet! Bless ye him, O Believers, and salute him with salutations of Peace" (*Qur'an*, 33:56). However, such status of the Prophet is a result of the utmost respect for his mission, which can in no way influence the Text's statements that he is a common man in light of the fact that he does not create the Qur'anic Text, nor does he have any competence in this domain; the Revelation does not ascribe supernatural powers to the Prophet.

8 Non-Muslims frequently translate the word *al-nabiyy* (a prophet of God) as a diviner. Of course, this is not merely coincidental, because a diviner, from the Muslim perpsective, carries negative and pejorative connotations, thus positioning the whole religion of Islam in the sphere of frivolous divination. Besides, Islam treats divination (of future) as a major sin, since the future is considered to be known only to God.

The Arabic language has several words to denote a diviner (among which is also the term *kāhin*, whose negative connotations are explored in this text), while the word *al-nabiyy*, used with Muhammad's name, denotes only a prophet, a prophet of God – meaning the one who brings (reliable) news, not the one who conjectures and foretells.

9 See Irfan Shahid, *Early Islam and Poetry*, Ann Arbor, MI, University Microfilms International, 1976.

10 The word recite is given here because, originally, poetry was not written but delivered orally.

11 Thus, the noun cannot express processuality as the active participle can.

12 In the following text I will contrast the "positions" of the prophet and the poet one by one, and will number each item (Ad 1, etc.).

13 It should be noted that the *Qur'an* uses the verb *sha'ara* in the sense of know through feeling. For instance, "And say not of those who are slain on God's path that they are Dead; nay, they are Living! But ye understand not [do not feel it] [*wa lākin lā tash'urūn*]" (*Qur'an*, 2:154).

However, this knowledge is of a different quality than that expressed by the verb *'alima*. The verb *sha'ara* denotes knowledge acquired through feeling; it is inexact and non-rational, so that in translating this and other ayahs with the same verb, it would be more adequate to use the verb feel: … But you do not feel it.

14 It is possible to come across a wrong interpretation among Muslims that Muhammad is God's favourite prophet and suchlike. A specific sort of martyrdom and sanctification of one part of the Prophet's family can be found in Shi'ism. However, this has no grounds in the *Qur'an*, where God explicitly says that He makes no distinction among His prophets (cf. *Qur'an*, 2:285).

15 When the word text is applied to the poet-soothsayer, it implies not only his poetic work but also his act in general.

16 *Qur'an*, 26:224–227.

17 The two expressions with two different prepositions are quite indicative in this sense: *from* the valley and *in* the valley; the syntax of prepositions becomes very functional here.

18 *Qur'an*, 26:221–223.

19 At this point I must once more remember Plato, who permitted only hymnal poetry in his ideal state – therefore, poetry singing praises to the gods. With regard to the *Qur'an*, I can see no explicit attitude here: any work upholding the true belief is a sort of Islamic beneficence is poetry too; but poetry is not necessary for asserting the

Authority of the Revelation. The Revelation is considered to be sovereign and self-sufficient.

20 The fate of the mantle is unknown. According to some sources, the caliph Muawiyah (661–670) purchased the mantle from the poet's son and it was kept by the Abbasid caliphs, who wore it on Eid days. As alleged, it was kept in Baghdad until the sack by the Mongols in 1258, when Hulagu ordered that it be burned. Some sources, however, report that it is still kept in Istanbul.

21 *Qur'an*, 55:1–4.

22 The word *al-bayān* is often carelessly and inaccurately translated as speech, but it is more than just speech: as I have already mentioned, *al-bayān* is stylised expression in general (not necessarily in the form of speech), or stylistically refined expression.

23 More information on this topic may be found in my paper entitled "Stilske vrednote poglavlja al-Raḥmān" [Stylistic values of the surah al-Raḥmān], 2001 *Takvim*, Rijaset Islamske zajednice u Bosni i Hercegovini, Sarajevo, 2000, pp. 11–25.

24 The strength of such tradition is demonstrated by the fact that even much later prose genres in the Arabic literature – whether they developed under the influence of foreign literatures or represented their original literary adaptations – were always streaked with verse, or prose characterised by rhyme and rhythm. One should only think of the *Arabian Nights*, which is eminently a prose work, the Bulaq edition of which has several thousand verses and a vast profusion of passages in prose with rhyme and rhythm. In this tradition, even *waqfiyyahs*, as expressly legal documents, included long introductory parts written in prose marked by rhyme and rhythm, while the quality of such texts mainly corresponded to the waqif's reputation and ability to hire the most competent writer.

25 See Michael Zwettler, *The Oral Tradition of Classical Arabic Poetics*, Columbus, OH, Ohio State University Press, 1978.

26 *Qur'an*, 10:38.

27 *Qur'an*, 11:13.

28 The word reinterpretation with regard to the *Qur'an* should be taken conditionally only: certain aspects of the Text are susceptible to reinterpretation, while others, including some that are fundamental according to the Text itself, do not allow for reinterpretation.

29 Islamic tradition recorded three attempts at imitating the Qur'anic Text. See more in Issa J. Boullata, "Retorička interpretacija Qur'ana: I'jaz i srodne teme" [The rhetorical interpretation of the Qur'an: I'jāz and related topics], in Enes Karić (ed.), *Semantika Kur'ana*, BEMUST, Sarajevo, 1998, p. 493.

30 I use the term "educated believer" to refer to a person familiar with the history of Arabic-Islamic history and culture, which by no means implies that only those familiar with it are educated: this only involves the aspect of education serving a full understanding of 'i'jāz.

31 Arthur J. Arberry, *The Koran Interpreted*, Vol. 2, London, 1955.

32 The aspiration, or yearning even, to put an end to the single Arabic literary standard is not only present with Arabists but also with some orientalised Arabs whose authority was built by no one else but Orientalists. They can all be represented by the most famous negative hero of modern Arabic culture – Taha Hussein (Ṭāhā Ḥusayn, 1889–1973), who strove to completely erase the brightest poetic periods in Arabic history, strongly arguing even, in an Ataturkian fashion, that the Arabic script be abandoned in favour of the Latin alphabet.

33 The infinite semantics of the original often escapes even those reading the Text in Arabic, and when this semantics begins to unveil itself one is overcome by anxiety over his own reductionist reading of the Text. I will illustrate this with only one example. It is conventional to translate the Invocation (Bismillah), a commonplace in the Text, as: In the Name of God, the Compassionate, the Merciful. Even in modern Arabic, the original attributes *al-raḥmān* and *al-raḥīm* have semantically shifted

towards the meanings given in the translation, but it should not be forgotten that the text of the *Qur'an* is classical and always directs to its origin, to etymology and rich semantics at the same time. Thus, the semantic field of these words is actually fascinating: both attributes have the same root *rḥm* used to derive the noun womb (*raḥm*), which – should we really mention it – connotes childbirth as an act of giving life, ideal protection in the womb as the ultimate mercy and care (which a mother has for the foetus in her womb and then for the child being born out of the womb), etc. (A translator of the *Qur'an* into French, André Chouraqui, was aware of this and translated these adjectives into French as *matriciant*=of the womb and *matriciel*=motherly. Cf. André Chouraqui, *Deset zapovijedi danas* [*The Ten Commandments Today*], translated by Jadranka Brnčić i Kruno Pranjić, Konzor, Zagreb, 2005, p. 113.)

This richness of the most positive meanings within the same semantic field is truly impressive, particularly when these words are attributes of God's name, as the most frequent attributes; such cases wonderfully refresh the meaning of the Invocation often uttered automatically while making one helplessly wonder: Is there any end at all to the Text's semantic bountifulness?

34 *Qur'an*, 49:13.

35 I have mentioned some examples from astronomy, but examples can be found from other sciences too. There is rather extensive literature on this subject. For instance, see Maurice Bucaille, *The Bible, the Qur'an and Science: The Holy Scriptures Examined in the Light of Modern Knowledge*, Seghers, Paris, 1976. This work was translated into Bosnian as well: Maurice Bucaille, *Biblija Kur'an nauka, Starješinstvo Islamske zajednice u SR Bosni i Hercegovini*, 2nd edn, Sarajevo, 1979.

36 Rashad Khalifa, *Qur'an: Visual Presentation of the Miracle*, Islamic Productions, Tucson, AZ, 1982.

37 Esad Duraković and Lutvo Kurić, *Kur'an: stilsko i matematičko čudo* [*The Qur'an: Stylistic and Mathematical Miracle*], Svjetlostkomerc, Sarajevo, 2006.

I am informed that Lutvo Kurić has considerably advanced with his research of the mathematical and genetic miracle of the Qur'anic *'i'jāz* and it will soon be published.

38 The term *'i'jāz*, therefore, did not emerge together with the revelation of the Text, but only later, standing for human inability to imitate the Text or any of its parts, whether in content or form. (Cf. Issa J. Boullata, "The rhetorical interpretation of the Qur'an: I'jaz and related topics", in Enes Karić (ed.), *Semantics of the Qur'an*, BEMUST, Sarajevo, 1998, p. 494.)

39 It is quite striking that incorrect attitudes about the *Qur'an*, its *'i'jāz* and translation also persist among people whose lack of understanding of fundamental issues is incompatible with science and the offices they hold. Such is the case – worryingly as much as regrettably – with Jusuf Ramić, a professor at the Sarajevo Faculty of Islamic Studies, who has long been publishing texts about the *Qur'an* and its translation, proving – with amazing persistence only ignorance is capable of – that he does not understand the essence of *'i'jāz* and the translator's relationship to it.

In his latest book, *Kako prevoditi Kur'an* (*How to Translate the Qur'an*) (F. F. Bihać, 2007), just as in his previous works, Ramić starts from false premises that, as such, produce a vast number of scandalous conclusions. Namely, discussing the relationship between content and form with particular reference to the *Qur'an*, Ramić states the following: "we want to point out that, with regard to the conflict between content and form, priority should be given to content. Of course, the Qur'an was revealed because of the content and message, not the form and aesthetic experience" (p. 116).

The reader cannot but wonder how such a complex work as the *Qur'an* can be understood by a mind that – contrary to the whole experience of aesthetics – thinks that its content and form are in conflict, not in an unwavering aspiration towards ideal collaboration. In addition, the quoted statement denies even *'i'jāz* itself: *'i'jāz* of the *Qur'an* is not in its content, but in the revelation of this content in an inimitable form

– therefore, in their unity and ideal collaboration – where the form also has great aesthetic potential. What is even worse is that this mind has "educated" a number of generations of students. Essentially, it is unworthy of scientific discussion or any consideration in the main body of the text: such deviation deserves nothing more than the marginality and narrowness of a footnote.

40 An example of such a translation into Bosnian is the one by Pandža and Čaušević (first published in 1937).

41 The misconception of many people that a good knowledge of language is sufficient for translating works of high literary and aesthetic values requires a separate discussion.

42 The attitude of many Orientalists towards Arabic originals generally is rather interesting in negative terms. Most Arabists convey the brilliant form of the *Qur'an* through inarticulate theological and philological treatises. They treat the brilliant form of poetry in the same way, whether classical or modern. Their translations are alarmingly inadequate, or even degrading. It is incomprehensible that even many so-called leading Arabists should have no sense of responsibility towards the unity of form and content.

As a matter of fact, when being conveyed to the West, Arab-Islamic culture is handicapped by the fact that its aesthetic values have been "transmitted" by learned philologists who usually do not care for these values, though they deserve great credit for the philological discovery of Arab-Islamic classics. The aesthetic layer is yet to be conveyed.

In an ever so rich multiplication of forms around the pivotal Text, critical texts about translations of the *Qur'an* can be considered yet another category: it is also a particular form related to the Text, which branches into affirmative and negative reviews, or analyses of translations. These can be further categorised into authentic texts (regardless of whether they give positive or negative reviews) and non-creative texts, cultural pygmies and "outsiders" with respect to the cooperation established between the Original and its translation, etc.

The latter category includes, for instance, the intellectually chaotic texts Jusuf Ramić wrote about a good translation of the *Qur'an* made by Enes Karić; then, over two whole years, Mr Ramić assiduously wrote similar texts about my translation of the *Qur'an* in the *Glasnik* and *Preporod* periodicals published by the Riasat of the Islamic Community in Bosnia and Herzegovina. Such negativistic texts have two self-disqualifying characteristics. One is an arrogance typical of ignorance; the other maliciousness that, as another typical feature of ignorance, will not see anything positive in a paper. This travesty of form is unbecoming of the light of the Original and jubilation of the translator; such forms cannot survive at all due to their (ethical) rigidity and the author's lack of education.

4 The simile in Old Arabic poetry

A world at a distance

Prologue: the realism or "materialism" of Old Arabic poetry

Old Arabic poetry is dominated by the figure of simile. This feature has been observed by experts on Arabic literature, but they failed to deduce the poetic consequences of this fact.[1] Some scholars hold that the dominance of the simile and the relative semantic independence of the verse in a poem, closely related to the simile as a stylistic dominant, is a consequence of the inability of pre-Islamic Arabians to perceive a close relation between accidences and content transcended beyond the material world. This is why, according to this approach, the *al-Mu'allaqāt* – the most important corpus of Old Arabic poetry, which will be the basis of my discussion – is characterised by an absence of thematic unity, and even by an extraordinary thematic diversity.[2] In Arabic literature the stylistic dominant of old poetry has been interpreted, quite authoritatively, as "materialism" (*al-shi'r al-māddī*), which seems a rather inadequate term to me, and which I think should be replaced with the term *realistic poetry*, although the latter term requires explication as well.[3] It should be mentioned that, within such an approach, Arabic sources use the term *materialist poetry* as a negative value judgement with a number of negative connotations, regularly contrasting it from its positive opposite, the so-called *imaginative poetry* (*al-shi'r al-khayālī*) of the Western cultural community.[4] Such judgements are based on the dominance of simile in Old Arabic poetry but are methodologically inadequate and problematic in terms of value principles. Namely, they contrast corpora from different traditions, without valuating each corpus within its own literary tradition. This mechanical drawing of comparisons or contrasts in different experiences of traditions is non-immanent and inadequate as such, while the translation of conclusions about differentiation into a value qualification to the detriment of one tradition can be analysed within the Orientalist discourse that Edward Said describes as "Orientalizing the Orient".[5] It is methodologically wrong to identify differentiation as "artistic inferiority" given the different poetic evolution of corpora within isolated traditions – i.e. those of the Arab world and the West. Furthermore, among a number of misconceptions generated by such attitudes is the fact that there are comparisons – with the intention of translating differentiation into value categories – between pre-Islamic Arabian poetry and, for example, the poetry of European Romanticism, which was preceded by a wealth of literary experience in general.

Figures of description and the profusion of themes in poems

Old Arabic poetry – particularly the *al-Mu'allaqāt*, which is mainly the subject of my discussion as the exemplary corpus of this poetry – allows use of the term *realism*, considering the significant accumulation of similes or figures of description, but it is not the same as the (negatively connoted) term *materialism*, which has been imposed on it as its main value qualification. This poetry prefers descriptiveness, through which it introduces reality, time and space into a literary text in a very effective way, which in turn gives it a referential appearance. However, the pronounced *materialistic and referential nature* attributed to it is only an appearance, because the Old Arabic *qaṣīda* is essentially an *imaginary* journey, and an act of transposition has a powerful effect on its detachment from a factualist or documentarist description in favour of spatial figurativeness, or a description that makes it real in the reader's imagination through instruments of the artist's imagination.

The abundance of description figures is highly conducive to the rich thematic repertoire of the old *qaṣīda*. Brought to perfection, as was the case with the *al-Mu'allaqāt*, these figures necessitated the thematic enrichment of the poem; for their own perfection, they sought to master the horizon of the poet's/Bedouin's world, presenting it very realistically, which led to the development of a number of themes in the poem. Considering their strong inclination towards enriching the thematic repertoire, figures of description can hardly find a genre that would suit them better than the travelogue: it offers a multitude of landscapes, spatial sequences, nuances of reality giving themselves up to description figures for transposition. The perseverance and variety of description figures in the *al-Mu'allaqāt* thus create a documentarist and referential appearance that the aforementioned Arab authors negatively qualified as the materialist nature of the poetry.

Connected to the descriptiveness of old poetry is its thematic diversity. It is no accident that the old *qaṣīda* encompasses a number of themes held together only by the factors of form – a single metre and monorhyme. From a poetic perspective, there is an ideal realisation of cooperation between the stylistic dominant of the *qaṣīda* (predominance of the simile and description figures in general) and its thematic organisation into a whole "register" of themes representing the most important and captivating aspects of the Bedouin's *visible* world. The *qaṣīda*, in principle, first included the theme of the description of a place where the poet's beloved abided; then a description of the beloved; a journey through the desert, with a description of cold starlit nights; hot days; game hunting; the poet's weapons; a sudden storm, etc.

Arabic literary scholars usually treated this poetic diversity as a severe poetic deficiency that they interpreted in different ways, often as an expression of the Bedouin's supposed inability to perceive the relatedness of "segments of the world"; his poetry, according to these scholars, is the best proof, or expression, of his incapacity to make any synthesis of the episodes he moves through and the landscapes where he resides. (Islam was to disprove this most convincingly.) However, at a poetic level, an expansion of description figures steered old poetry into the form in which these figures could be most effectively acknowledged. From this aspect, the thematic diversity of the *qaṣīda* is not a deficiency, but a virtue.

Consequently, the travelogue is the most appropriate form for the diversity of themes. That is why the *qaṣīda* represents an imaginary journey on which the poet describes several themes. To illustrate this point, I will use the mu'allaqa of Imru' al-Qays, one of the more typical and best-known *qaṣīda* of Old Arabic literature. In verses 1–4 the poet describes the place where his beloved used to abide and where the traces of the encampment remind him of the days he spent with her in tender love. This reminds him of many a woman he visited at night, and he describes their physical qualities in detail (verses 4–42). In self-praising verses (43–51) the poet gives a detailed description of his daring on various occasions. A description of a horse and hunting on this horse (verses 52–69) is a new theme of Imru' al- Qays' mu'allaqa, which ends in an excellent description of a desert storm (verses 70–81).[6]

Other *qaṣīdas* occasionally introduce a new theme, but all of them are, in principle, a mosaic of various themes in the space the poet travels across and which he figures by descriptions. According to a rule that was seldom broken, a love lyrical prelude (*nasīb*), as the prologue of a *qaṣīda*, was also related to the journey: it was most frequently placed at the beginning of the *qaṣīda* and at the beginning of the journey as well.[7] Any departure from this traditional norm was regarded as a serious poetic excess. Therefore, the Old Arabic *qaṣīda* can be interpreted as the precursor of the travelogue, with, of course, considerable differences between the *qaṣīda* and the travelogue in contemporary literature. Notwithstanding, the idea and structure of the travelogue genre, as I have said, are very conducive to figures of description, or the figures are conducive to the travelogue, so that full cooperation between stylistic means of the *qaṣīda* and its poetics is established at this level as well. Bearing this in mind, we cannot agree with frequent Orientalist assertions that the *qaṣīda* is thematically chaotic, inconsistent and poetically quite deficient. On the contrary, the idea of the travelogue connects different themes within the *qaṣīda*, and the idea itself is, in turn, inseparable from figures of description, from the simile that dominates the style of Old Arabic poetry. The idea of the *journey* connects adventures, landscapes, scenery in general and events in it, giving an impression of a documentary-oriented reception of the poet/traveller. Moreover, it is inconceivable that a travelogue-based artefact should be saturated with one theme; this exclusivity would even be highly inappropriate to it. The travelogue is expected to offer not one but several landscapes, and several phenomena in each, since perception on the part of the poet/traveller cultivates the same kind of perception with the reader. The best means for conveying the traveller's observation is the means of description. A multi-thematic organisation becomes necessary in this case, because a journey (an imaginary poetic one) is not a journey if it is presented through one theme only.

Roland Barthes brilliantly observed that description is "a solitary note without meaning in a functional course of events".[8] This observation supports my interpretation of the poetics of Old Arabic poetry. Namely, since description, as one of the central means of composing a travelogue, is a dominant stylistic element of Old Arabic poetry, and since it stimulated the development of a wide thematic repertoire in the poem, it is evident that there is relative independence among themes/descriptions in this old poetry and that they do not participate in the functional course of events. On the contrary, the description seeks to be confined to one theme, to identify with it; a description develops as long as it represents a theme, but after this kind of saturation figures of description search for another theme, only to establish the same relationship with it, etc. Cumulativeness and digressiveness are important characteristics of description, enabling it to develop, in terms of composition, within a relatively wide space of the theme, with a number of juxtapositions and parallelisms – until reaching a limit at which it stops to necessarily allow for a new topic to suddenly open. This is why Orientalists have frequently talked about "voids" between themes in a poem, regarding this as its major poetic deficiency. I am going to quote only parts of a description of a camel to illustrate this cumulativeness and digressiveness, this successive addition that distinguishes description, noting that the description in the poem extends well beyond the following verses:

> She is very long in the neck, which is most erect when she raises it
> And is like the rudder of a boat going up the Tigris.
> She has a skull like an anvil; the two halves of it at the place
> Of their meeting join as upon the edge of a file.
> And a cheek like the paper of the Syrians in smoothness; and an upper lip
> Like leather of Yaman, the cutting of which is not crooked.
> And two eyes like two mirrors protecting themselves in the caverns of the eye-bones,
> Which are like a hard rock containing a pool frequented by the people.
> Constantly throwing away the dirt of impurities, so that you see them
> Like the antimonied eyes of the mother of a wild calf fearful of the hunter.
> And two ears true of hearing, and distinguishing the low sounds
> In the time of the night journey, the quiet whisper, or the high-raised voice.
> Two pricked ears by which you know the goodness of her breeding
> Like the ears of a wild cow alone at Howmall.[9]

Figures of description in this passage dominated by the simile illustrate the possibility of extension through successive addition until the theme is saturated. However, something else is important here in the sphere of poetics. Namely, in terms of composition, the successive addition establishes the principle of juxtaposition or relative independence of units of comparison and corresponding units of meaning. The segmentation of description is its essential quality: it can stop at any time, or can likewise be further added to; its sufficiency is relative. This poetic technique reveals the principle of arabesque structure at a very early period, or at the dawn of the Arabic literary tradition. Juxtaposition and segmentation are evident in the quoted verses. The digressiveness of description figures is functional in the arabesque structure of the poem. Almost none of the couplets in the passage are without a simile, which suggests that this figure is at the very core of Old Arabic poetry, so that a proper interpretation of the simile can best capture the essence of this poetics. Furthermore, such an interpretation will show a high degree of coherence in the poetics of Old Arabic poetry, and not its incoherence or some other deficiencies not infrequently attributed to it. Let us look at what the consequences of this are.

Since segmentation and digressiveness are typical of the simile, it is evident from the quoted passage (and from the entire poem as well) that the segments of description are in a state of parallel accumulation. Barthes's remark that "description is a solitary note" is well substantiated by these verses, in which the principle of segmentation and relative structural independence is so much furthered that, at the micro level, each verse can be an autonomous structural unit and at the same time an autonomous thematic unit within a broader theme – a description of a camel. The description of the camel is further "built into" the poem, which includes several themes, each of which has the same structure. This accumulation of figures of description is also characterised by the fact that verses/segments do not necessarily follow an unalterable sequence but can be rearranged quite imperceptibly owing to their parallelism and the fact that each verse is a self-sufficient structural and thematic whole; some verses can even be left out without structural consequences for the poem.[10] The poem thus has the form of concentric circles – it devises an arabesque structure.

The same applies to higher-level structures. Themes emerging in the poem are relatively independent. Their sequence in the poem is also not necessarily unalterable because it makes no difference to the structure of the poem whether the poet will first sing about his camel or a desert storm. Referring yet again to Barthes's remark made in a different context, I can say that these descriptions are "without meaning in a functional course of events". As a matter of fact, the poem brings no events as such, and the only event is the poet's imaginary *journey*, which integrates the segments of the poem.

This clearly points to the conclusion that Old Arabic poetry has optimal poetic coherence: its segmentation is consistently present at all the levels, which makes the simile, as a figure of description, dominant. The deficiencies attributed to the *qaṣīda* in terms of its structure are only a consequence of a superficial and non-poetic interpretation or of different reading habits and demands. An impressionist approach is inappropriate here, as well as an approach based solely on the present or on one's own tradition.

Among the poetic consequences of the dominant simile in Old Arabic poetry is the *obviousness* that characterises the world of the poem. Obviousness is the primary task of description figures. Unlike the metaphor, the simile is based on obviousness and transparency, whereas the metaphor, through its *transfer*, works on a different level – on one beyond obviousness. The success of a description depends on its being graphic, or the intensity of its obviousness and refinement in terms of nuances: the subject of description must be visible, transparent and in a way flat. Otherwise the following rhetorical question could be posed: What kind of a travelogue is this if it does not depict landscapes in their most vivid colours and with sharp contours – how can we see them then?! This is why one of the most important effects of description figures here is the *realism* of artefacts, which careless critics have called *materialism*. Within the simile, the relationship between its two correlates is such that the first one (the one being compared) is shown in its full obviousness by virtue of its being introduced into the comparison in the first place, by its being named, but this obviousness is *intensified* by introducing the other correlate (what the first is being compared to), which has the same quality to an even higher degree, so that both of them simultaneously work to highlight the quality of the first correlate. There is no metaphoric transfer between them; they are still absolutely separate due to grammatical markers of comparison (*like*, etc.). Therefore, while the metaphor effectively "*shifts* the reality" by transferring the meaning, the simile emphasises the reality by insisting on its obviousness.

Obviousness and transparency of the world and the necessity of distance

One of the key postulates of Old Arabic poetry is that distance is immanent in the categories of obviousness and transparency, and I will dwell on this in the discussion that follows. However, just as an illustration, let us first look at how Imru' al-Qays makes a desert storm obvious, transparent and realistic:

> Oh my companion, do you see the lightning, the glittering of which I am showing you;
> Like the flashing of the two hands in the thick collecting crowned clouds.
> Shines the glory of it, or, like the lamps of a monk,
> Who has "dipped" in the oil the well-twisted wicks.
> I sat down with my companions waiting for the rain between Zárij and 'Uzaib
> After regarding the lightning attentively.
> In looking for the rain, we guessed that the right of its downpour was over Qatan,
> While the left of it was upon Satár and beyond it upon Yazbul.
> The storm commenced pouring out its waters over Kuthaifah,
> Overturning upon their faces the big trees called Kanahbul.
> Then there passed over the hills of Qanán from the spray of it, that which was so very violent
> That it caused the wild goats to descend from every haunt in it.
> And at Taimáa it did not leave the trunk of a date tree standing,
> And not a building except those strengthened by hard stones.
> As if Thabeer at the first downfall of its rain was

A great one of the people, wrapped in a striped cloak.
As if in the morning the summit of the peak of Mujaimir
By reason of the flood and the debris round it, were the whirl of a spindle.
And the cloud poured out on the desert of Ghabeet its goods, and it resembled
The arrival of Yemani merchant with his trunks loaded with rich clothes.
As if in the morning the small birds of the valley Jiwáa
Had taken a morning draught of old, pure, spiced wine.
As if in the evening the wild beasts in it drowned in the furthest parts of it,
Were the root-bulbs of the wild onion.[11]

The storm rages across a vast space, which is evident from a number of toponyms the poet introduces, portraying the storm as a real deluge, while it is still transparent and obvious in its transparency. The precondition for all of this is the poet's distantness, since the visibility of the world depends on his perception and description. The poet, as the one presenting the world, is thus always outside of what he is describing – in order to make it obvious in transparency. Obviousness is an aspect of realism in the sense of presenting the material world. While the spiral of metaphoric transfer draws the recipient inside, the simile keeps them outside. Therefore, Old Arabic poetry can be called the *poetry of distance*.

Namely, the old poet is always a distant observer, outside the world in a way, not immersed in it and its processes. If this were not the case, his poem would not be woven of the simile: it is the dominance of simile that requires constant distantness in order to support figures of description. Distantness is necessary even with regard to the poet's own actions or impressions, since it gives the optimal transparency essential for the simile.

The poet's constant distancing is realised in two dimensions – the spatial and the temporal. In topography, as a figure of spatial description,[12] we can see the spatial distance, which is obvious in the quoted description of a storm. This sort of distance will be discussed later in the book. However, with regard to tenses, the poets of the *al-Mu'allaqāt*, including Imru' al-Qays, do not use the future tense or even the present tense proper but the narrative present – the poems of these pre-Islamic authors show a particular kind of perfectivity conducive to solid transparency and obviousness. Even when singing about love, for instance, the poet sings about it from the distance of the perfect: when the poet reminisces about it from the position of a desert bivouac, love is an episode that is over and is quite transparent in the past. His aspiration to cumulative description drives the poet so far that he is not content with the description of one (past) love but proceeds to describe a number of other bygone loves – or, better to say, of women he has delighted in, as there were many, presenting their physical charm – so that the category of distance is constantly developed, grading the perfect as one of the more important poetic elements.

It should be noted that this refers to the use of the perfect more as real time rather than a grammatical tense. At the same time, it pays to have in mind that the narrative present is in itself stylistically important in grading the past.

In lines 1–6 Imru' al-Qays remembers his beloved who rode off with her tribe and then, in *bayt* 7 already, imparts that, before her, he had enjoyed two more women; he also gives their names and toponyms where he lay with them, doing so in order to heighten the general impression of realism, only to sing the following from *bayt* 8:

> [...]
> Behold, how many pleasant days have you spent with them,
> And especially the day at Dárat-i-Juljul.
> [...]
> And the day, on which I entered the howdah, the howdah of 'Unaizah,
> And she said, "Woe to you, verily, you will cause me to travel on foot."
> She was saying, while the howdah was swaying with us,
> "You have galled my camel, oh Imra-ul-Qais; so dismount."
> So I said to her, "go on, and loosen his reins,
> And do not repel me from your repeatedly tasted fruit."
> For many a beautiful woman like you, oh 'Unaizah, I have visited at night and she was
> Pregnant or giving suck, and I have diverted her thoughts from her child one year old.
> When he the child cried behind her, she turned towards him with one-half,
> While her other half was under me, and was not turned away.
> One day on the back of a sandhill she made excuses to me for not fulfilling my desire
> And swore an oath to which she made no exception.[13]

Standing by the bivouacs, i.e. from a temporal distance, the poet describes his love for a woman who has gone somewhere, but the need to develop the description makes him describe other loves too, experienced before this one that, as it turns out, is only a motive for invoking a clear retrospective of others in his memory. The poet thus passes from one perfect to a "deeper" perfect and then to an even "deeper" one in order to grade the past time as his entire love past. However, as he goes deeper and deeper into the perfect, he suddenly distances himself from the *love* for the woman whose traces he is looking for in the sand, because he is not devoted to her alone: she is captured and distanced in a description of a few *bayts* in order for him to be able to "capture" other women in his *bayts* too. Something miraculous has happened. Namely, quite unexpectedly, the poet has distanced himself from love as an emotional state, or a quality, transposing it to its pure physical dimension, to its materiality. This brings about several important effects.

In the first place, the transposition of love to its physical dimension enhances the impression of realism, of almost factual accuracy. In addition to the fact that it mentions several women, such a procedure devised by the poet is further developed by introducing their names and a number of toponyms where he was with them. As if this were a biographical record. Three figures of description are particularly active here: chronography, or a description of temporal circumstances; topography, or a presentation of the place of events; prosopography – a figure describing shape, physical qualities, posture, etc.[14] All three figures, in interaction, yield excellent descriptive results.

The physical dimension is highly conducive to transparency and obviousness. "Inner" events are not as obvious as physical reality. A panoramic or retrospective presentation is the most appropriate form in such cases. That is why the poet mostly describes segments of his world from the "high ground" of his conviction that the visibility of the world depends on him and that the richness of this world also depends on his ability to describe it. Similarly, the poet uses retrospective or nuanced past in order to give a chronographic view of events.

Figures of description, and the simile in particular, represent the most appropriate means for all these forms of shaping the world of a poem. In consequence, it follows from this that these means successfully introduce reality into a literary text that, as I have already said, gives a distinct referential appearance.

Segmentation of textual space

It is interesting to see how textual space and time are positioned in such a poetics. The space is flat, as it must be transparent. It is almost factually identical with the poet's real world; the space is always obvious and description-yielding, but is not integrated into the whole without any "boundaries" or cracks. More precisely, this space is segmented on the same principle used by the poet to master it during his life: space is seen and presented in stages and landscapes the poet always travels across, with a certain similarity among them, and with cyclical repetition enabling the typification of space. The textual space is therefore not too rich in diversity, just as the world beyond the poem, according to the poet's experience: poems depict typical landscapes/segments of space that, due to such typification, strengthen the impression of transparency. For example, Imru' al-Qays opens his ode stopping on sand dunes that display the remains of an encampment (horizontal space!); the poet devotes a substantial part of the poem to descriptions of his loves, relating them to certain toponyms (horizontal space!); he describes stealing out to his beloved through underbrush and by the sentries (horizontal space!); his horse, so accurately described, is always active in horizontal space only; even the storm he is watching is placed in this space so that the poet is not watching it above himself but on his own level – from a distance, on the horizon, in a straight line. Thus, the entire space is *horizontal*, flat, straight and transparent. Only in this way can it be completely obvious and available for description. The journey is not characterised by either climbing or plunging, but by horizontal movement typical of *caravans*. Nothing in this world can express the horizontality of space better than a protracted caravan. Transparency is complete. Such space and journey are therefore transferred to the *qaṣīda* as a textual space and a textual journey. A consequence of this can be seen in the poet's/traveller's need for constant visualisation of the space. On a journey (the *qaṣīda* is an imaginary journey, whose connection with a real journey I have already explained), one is impressed by the world of phenomena, by the beauty of landscapes, perceiving the world around with almost no time for reflection in the perception of continuous horizontality; in such space and movement across it, the simile is imposed on the poet as closest to the state of his mind and of his world: reflection is a blood sister to the metaphor, not to the simile. The poet's/traveller's space is made of a number of sequences, since it is created by the journey. The Bedouin's real space – i.e. the space beyond the poem – is also made of a number of sequences, since he spends his entire life in nomadic journeys. However, he does not travel endlessly in the same direction, but circularly, which means that his spatial experience is formed on the principle of cyclicity, the repeatability of sequences or passages composing a particular spatial arabesque.

The same principle applies to the structure of textual space: it is not presented as an entirely compact whole developing *in continuo*, but as segmented and, as such, structured as the arabesque. The space is related to events taking place in it, which are presented through description; since these events are not mutually functionally related but are, on the contrary, isolated in description until its saturation, the space is then also segmented according to the events in it, or according to certain phenomena in this space. In other words, the relative independence of themes in the poem influences segmentation of the space, whose parts are relatively independent in the same way. Since the poet's task is to present the subject of description as well as possible using an intensified but, at the same time, digressive accumulation of descriptions through simile, he optimally directs his perception onto this portion of space, disregarding the wider space for a while, so that his descriptive concentration simply cuts this spatial segment out from the larger whole. Then, following the logic of the travelogue, he concentrates on a different portion of the space, etc. Therefore, space in the Old Arabic *qaṣīda* (which also applies to other genres created on the poetics of travelogue and descriptiveness) is made of sequences, as they completely yield to description figures. In addition, such space segmentation is utterly conducive to transparency – not the whole horizon can be transparent at the same time! – and to obviousness too, which the poet must optimally highlight to attract the recipient's attention. Furthermore, it again becomes evident how important it is to keep in mind that segmentation and obviousness require distantness. For, in order to successfully describe the *visible* portion of the space, the poet must keep a certain distance from it: the poet does not watch it from the inside but from the outside. This is why the simile includes twofold distantness. On the one hand, the correlate being compared must in a way be distanced in order to be perceived, and must then be specified and thus prepared for comparison. On the other hand, the other correlate, which the first is being compared with, must also be perceived and specified from a distance in order to be "brought" to the first correlate and engaged in an active relation of comparison.

Segmentation stresses the importance of space as such, though it may seem paradoxical at first considering the relative isolation of segments. Namely, segmentation stresses the importance of space in general by drawing attention to it through the act of segmentation: when, in a text or even in the real world, we have several spatial "segments" next to one another, and when they are depicted by majestic descriptions, we become more aware of the space than we are when it is taken as an integrated whole; segmented space simply warns about itself, so that we could call this a kind of semiotic stylistic relevance of space. To compare this with traditional stylistics: what is recognised as stylistic relevance at the level of some structures in the field of stylistics – for instance, different kinds of parallelisms, refrain, etc. – has a very similar effect in the semiotics of space as interpreted here: constant segmentation of space is stylistically relevant in semiotic stylistics. It is like a refrain. It can, actually, be treated as excellent semiotic syntactics of space. Space in one "piece" functions in an entirely different way: it is not poetically brought to be stylistically relevant.[15] Keeping in mind that the simile, or description figures, is at the basis of everything, we can see that the consequences of such a preferred position for the simile are profound and numerous: the simile is not a dominant stylistic element only in "traditional" stylistics, but in semiotic stylistics as well. Finally, it obviously follows that eminently descriptive genres promote space more than any other genre. The travelogue is exceptional in these terms, but it also represents the Old Arabic *qaṣīda* that, as I have already explained, is not a travelogue in the modern sense of the word, but can conditionally be included within a kind of lyrical travelogue genre.

The function of spatial segmentation is not exhausted here. It goes towards an important poetic goal. Namely, I have explained the general segmentation of the *qaṣīda*, which is poetically conditioned by the dominance of the simile as a "solitary note". We have seen that this principle is realised in the thematic completeness of couplets, in the relative independence of themes in the *qaṣīda* repertoire, etc., as well as that all of these are elements of arabesque structure. The principle of spatial segmentation, which is very functional, can now be added to these: it actively participates in the overall arabesque structure. The degree of poetic coherence of the *qaṣīda* is thus increased, once again showing the inadequacy of the approach treating the segmentation of the *qaṣīda* as a deficiency. Moreover, through such consistency, the *qaṣīda* is placed on the path of poetic perfection.

Let us see how Imru' al-Qays' segments are spaced.

The space in lines 1–4 is sand dunes located on certain toponyms where the encampment of his beloved was:

> Stop, oh my two friends, let us weep on account of the remembrance of my beloved,
> And her abode situated on the edge of a sandy desert between Dakhool and Howmal.
> And between Toozih and Maqrát, whose traces have not been obliterated,
> On account of what has blown and re-blown over them from the South wind and the North wind.
> You will see the dung of the white deer in the courtyards

And enclosures of it, as though they were seeds of pepper.
On the morning of separation, the day they parted it was as if I, standing near the acacia shrubs in the gardens of the tribe, were breaking the pods of the wild colocynth.[16]

The poet then suddenly "relocates" to another "place", to his memories of other women:

[...]
As was your experience with Ummul-Huwairith before her,
And her neighbour Ummul-Rabab in Māsal.
[...]
Behold, how many pleasant days have you spent with them,
And especially the day at Dárat-i-Juljul.[17]

The text contains semiotic signs of space: the poet is in a *howdah* with ‘Unaizah while the caravan *travels across the landscape* (verses 13–16); *sneaking* across the space *by the sentries* (verses 24–27); *crossing the enclosure of the tribe* and cuddling *on sand hills* (verses 28–41).

The poet's horse, for instance, displays his qualities in another space: he *charges*, *chases* game (verses 61–66), etc. A memorable storm *rages* in the space specified by *toponyms* (verses 70–81).

In short, the *qaṣīda* encompasses a vast space through semiotic signs and stylistic means, which actually makes it dedicated to the space where all the events take place. Seen in this light – for which there are valid poetic and structural arguments – Imru' al-Qays' mu‘allaqa promotes space as its hero, while everything else in it only has a walk-on role in episodes. Above this is only the poet, who makes the whole space obvious.

Nevertheless, it is always obvious that the space in the *qaṣīda* is segmented too. The poet swiftly moves from one segment to another, not because he cannot concentrate, but because his poetics requires him to do so. Segments do not appear linearly, or in one direction, but are set circularly – consistent with the poet's perception of the world around him.[18]

The space as we find it in the text is actually only a framework for the walk-on roles of themes. The desert environment (it is a desert environment in Imru' al-Qays' *qaṣīda*, but it can be a different one in another poem) is a framework for the love lyric strongly contrasted with it – like an unexpected lyrical gurgle amid the general sparseness. The space where the poet hunts for game is not specified topographically, but is "delimited" by the idea of how vast a game-hunting space can be; the entire horizon is the stage for the storm, etc. Each theme is adjusted to its space/environment, so that they promote each other through the development of themes in the spatial framework and through the spatial framing of the theme. Events or themes, as we have seen, are not mutually connected, as they take place or are perceived in a space also characterised by segmentation. Even the time in the text, whether as a grammatical or physical category, is not such as to be able to work towards overcoming general segmentation. On the contrary, time is segmented as well.

Gradation of textual time

In Old Arabic poetry, represented by the exemplary mu'allaqa by Imru' al-Qays, the world is described from the position of the narrative present. The past, as we have seen, is richly graded. There is no grammatical future; I should remind the reader that this involves constant gradation of real time, seldom of grammatical tense. The reasons behind such usage of time can be found in the poetics of old poetry, implying the poet's relationship to the space as well.

The poem opens with the grammatical imperative as a present mood:[19]

> Stop, oh my friends, let us pause to weep over the remembrance of my beloved.
> Here was her abode on the edge of the sandy desert between Dakhool and Howmal.

However, the poet is subsequently always in the past, whose boundaries he keeps extending, breaking the monolithic structure and monotony of the perfect. He first remembers a time with one woman (verses 1–6), then remembers a more distant past (*As was your experience with Ummul-Huwairith before her …*, verses 1–9), only to "recapture" his whole past with women (*Behold, how many pleasant days have you spent with them …*, verse 10).

The poet's great bravery is also demonstrated in the past (*Behold, many a bitter contender … I have turned him back …*, verse 43 and further). A remarkable description of a storm at the end of the poem (verses 70–81) is highly perfectivised in the poet's experience by means of a narrative intonation (*Oh my companion, do you see the lightning, the glittering of which I am showing you …*, verse 70). In fact, the sentence opening the description of the storm contains a very rare form of the future[20] which, in this stylisation of time, seems surprising because it is only a rhetorical, not a proper future: it is more related to the past, to the poet's experience, because the poet has already *seen* this storm, it has already *taken place*.[21] Even the horse, to whom the poet devotes several couplets (52–69), is described by the perfect and the narrative present by turns. For example:

> Attacking, fleeing, advancing, retiring, whichever I wish,
> […] like the boulder of a rock, which the torrent has hurled down from on high, […]
> Of a bay colour; he is such that he causes the numnah to slip off the middle of his back,
> As a smooth stone causes the falling rain to slip off.
> In spite of his thinness, he is very lively, and when the heat of his temperament boils over in him,

His snorting is as the boiling of a kettle.
At full gallop, at a time when the swift horses, on account of fatigue,
Raised up the dust on the rough ground beaten by their hoofs.
The light boy slips off his back,
And he throws away the garments of the heavy rough rider.

However, it is obvious that the horse's merits were proven in the past and that the use of this type of present only underlines its perfective function. The stylistic relevance of the narrative present is thus made optimal.

An analysis will show that the textual time is in the past. However, it should be said that this past is not a monolithic unit of time, nor a past time in continuity; it is expressed in the text in a specific way not obvious at first, though very functional in this poetics.[22] Namely, we have already seen how a particular gradation of the perfect is built that does not refer to grammatical categories. It may therefore be better to use the phrase *past time* than the grammatical term *perfect*: this phrase denotes nuanced textual time in the textual space, while the other term, in a narrow sense, denotes time as a grammatical category. This past time is introduced in the first couplet already and then, without grammatical means, situationally, shifted to a more distant past, almost to the limits of the poet's memory worthy of the reader's attention. The use of the (narrative) present, as I have already pointed out, also follows this unchangeable direction.

What are the poetic effects of such a structure in the textual time?

The main effect is in the fact that the past time, more strongly and in a different way than any other time, possesses transparency that – together with the simile – represents one of the postulates of this poetics. Namely, the present implies *immersion* that is incompatible with transparency. The past is seen more comprehensively, since it is over and defined and, as such, obvious and transparent. The present is a process that does not yield to descriptive transparency as much as the past. The future, however, is so non-obvious and non-transparent that it should not be mentioned here at all, nor do we find it in the poem. Keeping in mind the basic tenets of this work, which argues that obviousness and transparency are the most suitable for figures of description, with the simile the most dominant, it then becomes clear that the past time of the poem cooperates with these tenets in a poetically brilliant way: it is this time that enables optimal obviousness and transparency. Still, there is something else very important with regard to past time, which I am only going to indicate in passing here, and which is part of a rather different kind of research. Namely, the past is usually "coloured" by a particular kind of lyricism. The past strongly tends to present itself to us in "wistful lyricism" aspiring to completely turn itself into an idyll.[23] Imru' al-Qays' poem thus speaks in tones of lyric wistfulness, but it is also an expression of the poet's pride (like the heroes of other *qaṣīdas*), as the purest wellspring of pride is the described perception of the past.

In addition to ever so important transparency, the dominance of past time in the poem offers a precious distance already identified as very functional in the textual space of the *qaṣīda* as well. There is no need to explain in detail that a distance is immanent in the past and that, considering the aspect of completeness and distance, it is transparent and obvious in the most optimal way. Through this, the past meets the important criteria for yielding to lyrical descriptiveness. The future is also distanced, but it is non-obvious and its descriptions are hence fundamentally different from those of the past. The future cannot be presented as realistically as the time and space in the *qaṣīda* can. The simile in the *qaṣīda* is based in realism, since both of its correlates are taken from the world of the real and the obvious. The simile in future time cannot have the same quality, as one of its correlates is extra-experiential; in relation to our experience, it is transcendent and, as such, fluid, not fixed in realism implied by the simile based in the transparent and obvious past. Therefore, a negative relationship of criticism towards Imru' al-Qays' *qaṣīda*, and the other *qaṣīdas* it represents, is unfounded from a poetic perspective. The authors already mentioned in this context – as well as others sharing their value judgement – did not grasp the origins of realism in the *qaṣīda* they devalued from this perspective. They failed to understand the character of this type of realism and its coherent poetics.[24]

Grading the past time is also functional. First and foremost, the past time is distributed to different segments, thus participating in the general segmentation present at all levels in the poem except at the level of form, since the poem has a single metre and rhyme. The poem is thematically thoroughly segmented – until the thematic saturation of its couplet. It is also segmented in the domain of the semiotics of space, so that this consistency in segmentation of different levels of content applies to the textual time as well. The arabesque structure is always in play. The segmentation of time is realised in a special and, at the same time, a necessary way.

The singularity of the segmentation of time is reflected in the fact that grammatical tenses such as perfect–present–future, with all their variants, are not used; instead, the poem uses the past time in a gradation transcending its grammatical categories. All the segments of this past time are in a state of juxtaposition (which characterises the structural integration of elements), or of a very loose connection sometimes defined as mere associativeness. If we look at the love lyric part of the poem, for example, we will find this type of connection among time sequences: they are all in the past, with each being in a more distant past than the previous one, and are connected through a very loose principle of arabesque associativeness; owing to their juxtaposition, they can end even before the point where the poet decided to end them. Sequences are fixed in their self-sufficiency but, through the arabesque structure, they build their segmentation, their segments, into the meaning of the whole: on the basis of these segments we get a comprehensive picture/information about the poet's love life in general, and about the lyricism of his spirit. Moreover, this picture seems to be even more graphic because it is formed by means of the past time and its segmentation. If the poet used the present time alone, he would not be able to paint a picture of his love life of the same quality as the one richly nuanced by the forms of the past time.

On the other hand, such segmentation of time is necessary because, among other things, it prolongs the effect of the arabesque structure, thus strengthening the coherence of poetics. Moreover, we can observe the same effect here as those identified in relation to the semiotic stylisation of time. Namely, the poetics in question deliberately avoids the monolithism of the time perspective, thus also avoiding the effect of temporal monotony. Segmentation of the past time highlights the time as such, the passage of time and the awareness – unquestionable in Oriental peoples – that time/life is woven from a number of *sequences* that become mutually connected. It is exactly in the past that the time can best be seen in its segmentation. The episodic nature of time is essential to this awareness and to traditional poetics. Therefore, segmentation of the past time features as a sudden "stylistic technique" in the textual time. If the time in this text were presented linearly, i.e. as monolithic and non-segmented, it would also be monotonous; the sudden segmentation is stylistically relevant, even more so as it appears where least expected. Furthermore, segmentation contributes to the dynamics of description. Namely, since the poem is dominated by description, and description in turn by simile, the poem runs the danger – in proportion to its length – of becoming monotonous, which is exactly what it wants to avoid. Since the description is essentially segmented in an arabesque manner, it would make the poem in its relatively lengthy form, or even in its long love lyric prologue, turn into a monotonous accumulation of description figures. In order to prevent this, the poem resorts to specific "time cascades" (sequences/episodes, etc.) that make the description significantly more dynamic: description thus remains the dominant stylistic technique due to a number of important poetic tasks, but it also keeps being revitalised through extensive branching (segmentation), including the arabesque branching of time.

The segmentation of time in the past underlines its realistic dimension, which used to be recognised as the *materialism* of Old poetry. The repetition of "fragments" of past time and the positioning of (segmented) landscapes and situations into it emphasise the importance of these segments in their mutual relationships, so that the reality is transposed to a literary text so successfully and with so many nuances that an insufficiently competent reader gets the impression of a factual report or of the excessive materialism of the poem.

The same way and the same means are used to reinforce the impression of obviousness. Situations in the poem, landscapes, etc., become much more obvious and transparent when "separated" in terms of time and space. The function of distance is immanent in such a condition. Although it is always risky to compare works of different kinds of art, I can, conditionally only and from a poetic perspective, recall ornamental arabesque. Namely, when a recipient faces the arabesque, he can perceive its segments at very different levels of structure; he can perceive microstructures, he can perceptively fuse them into bigger wholes, etc. – until the phase when he can take in the whole arabesque from a receptive distance. This is nothing less than a feat of his perception. On the other hand, he can first perceive the whole arabesque, and then decrease the distance to study its structure and the underlying principle, and then return to the initial distance. In any case, the condition of distance, obviousness and transparency is very important to the reception of a work with such a structure. The reception of mu'allaqa involves a similar process.

Concentration on the flatness of the physical

Considering everything I have already said about the muʻallaqa, I should also explain why there is no description of character, or "states of pure spirituality", in it. Even where necessarily expected, such descriptions are not there. For instance, in a love lyric prologue the poet does not describe effervescent erotic feelings, does not present love as such, almost never dwells on the emotional world of his "beloved" (which is why I must now put her in inverted commas), nor even on his own feelings. This is the part of the muʻallaqa that critics of Old Arabic poetry take as the crucial evidence of its *materialistic nature*, for, according to them, the poet materialised beauty in general, and even love, reducing it to the superficial dimension of the physical. For example, Izz al-Din Ismail (ʻIzz al-Dīn Ismāʻīl) says:

> It is sufficient to notice that the poet does not dwell on any quality of beauty in spiritual/moral terms; all the qualities of his beloved that attract his attention are purely sensual. He dwells on her every part, from head to toe, offering us an ideal picture of each part of her body [...]. Thus the poet presents beauty in sensual terms.[25]

Another love lyric prelude of Imru' al-Qays' muʻallaqa offers a description of the poet's beloved preceded by such a flat description:

> Thin-waisted, white-skinned, not fat in the abdomen,
> Her breast-bones shining polished like a mirror.
> In complexion she is like the first egg of the ostrich – whiteness mixed with yellowness
> Pure water, unsullied by the descent of many people in it, has nourished her.
> She turns away, and shows me her smooth cheek, and is prohibiting me from caressing
> Her with a glancing eye, like that of a wild animal, with young, in the desert of Wajrah.
> And she shows a neck like the neck of a white deer,
> Which is neither disproportionate when she raises it, nor unornamented.
> And a perfect head of hair which, when loosened, adorns her back,
> Black, very dark-coloured, thick like a date-cluster on a heavily-laden date tree.
> Her curls creep upwards to the top of her head,
> And the plaits are lost in the twisted hair, and the hair falling loose.
> And she meets me with a slender waist, thin as the twisted leathern nose-rein of a camel,
> And a shank, like the stem of a palm tree bending over from the weight of its fruit.[26]

In only a few verses does Imru' al-Qays *suggest* a description of love, only in a verse or two, undeveloped and unspecified, so that realism still dominates the world of the poem. For instance, the following verses

Has anything deceived you about me, that your love is killing me,
And that verily as often as you order my heart, it will do what you order,
[...]
And your two eyes did not flow with tears, except to strike me
With your two arrows in my broken heart, conquered by love.[27]

indicate the poet's love distress, but this aspect is flat and insufficiently developed against the length of the poem, and confined to a comparatively small structural element. Compared with the first passage, where the poet describes his beloved in detail, the second passage is too short and undeveloped; it has a few figures of speech, but offers no usual extensive accumulations of simile, descriptive digressions, successive additions, etc. Comparing these two passages, the reader might ask this: Why does the poet find a physical description of a woman (he describes several women as his own!) so much more important than his feelings or her own? For the reader is led to the conclusion that the poet finds the first aspect more important than the second. Furthermore, the poem offers almost no description of character.

These passages from the poem, together with the observations I formulated as questions, are places that a number of scholars have used to draw conclusions about the poet's inability to transcend "materialist" descriptions, as well as about his supposed incapacity for "imaginative poetry". It is even suggested occasionally that Arabs are supposedly incapable (since this poem is representative) of imaginative achievements in general.[28] Of course, such conclusions are hasty and methodologically unfounded, because these same Arabs were to develop love lyrics later on, let alone the deep imaginativeness of Sufi poetry, etc. These are only vain efforts to disqualify, from the position of divergent poetics, the value of the differing poetics of pre-Islamic poetry that is – quite the contrary – characterised by optimum coherence. The two passages testify to this – always in accordance with the poetic postulates I have already discussed.

Namely, the longer description that Imru' al-Qays gives of a woman is luxurious, detailed, even meticulous. Perhaps nowhere in his poem is enormously accumulated simile as effective as in this place. Nonetheless, the description involves factual precision and realistic verse appearing – to paraphrase Imru' al-Qays' line – as a mirror, shining and polished: the verses reflect the physical appearance of a woman in full splendour. Why is it so? And why is the issue of the so-called *materialism* of old poetry so pointed and the most obvious precisely in a description of a woman and love? The answer to this may be found in a consequent discussion of poetics.

Since figures of description, the simile in particular, are dominant in this poetry, we have already seen that its poetic consequences are reflected in segmentation, accumulation, digressiveness, distance, obviousness and presence. In accordance with this, the woman is described as is only possible in this poetics. In her description, she is "*composed*" of a sequence of segments of beauty, and it is this segmentation in cumulative digressiveness that highlights her beauty: owing to the *enumeration* of her physical qualities, where an optimally effective simile is used with each, the woman is more than beautiful – she is dazzling, alluring, almost magical. It would produce quite a different effect if the poet described the woman in a different way, for example: *My beloved is prettier than any other, she has a lovely soul and passionate feelings* …, etc. Therefore, an abstract description and a description of a whole, without details, would have different effects. Owing to the fact that figures of description have a particular capability for segmentation – especially the simile, which can "develop" only in an arabesque, cumulative and digressive manner – this description achieves an ideal collaboration of all the key poetic postulates. The simile "has found its" most adequate object; it works brilliantly in the sphere of segmentation; the object on its part is very grateful because it is, owing to the inseparability of the simile and segmentation necessarily related to it, presented in full splendour, befitting a woman of the most distinguished Arabian poet and prince. Therefore, the woman is presented realistically, in an abundance of details that keep advancing the poet's main goal – to present her as something extraordinary. The ambience of realism is fostered, "from the background", by a number of tools only the simile can offer: breasts like a mirror (shining and polished) referring to the white skin in the previous line;[29] she is like an *egg of the ostrich* (again a virtue of a fair complexion!); she is nourished by pure and unsullied *water* (the most precious asset in the desert environment); *a wild animal*, with *young*; a neck like that of a *white deer* (fair complexion again!); *black, very dark-coloured* hair (in contrast with the fair complexion), thick like *a date-cluster*; a shank that looks like the *stem of a palm tree*, thin and slender, etc.[30] The poet introduces into the world of the poem a number of tools performing several functions. First, they have the function of comparison, but so as to strengthen the impression of realism, since they, as an aspect of reality, are summoned to reinforce the aspect of reality in the second constituent of a simile. On the other hand, it should be kept in mind that the poet introduces only *the best segments* of his real world as simile constituents – or as tools here, thus strengthening the impression of realism in the midst of which is the object of his simile – as the best "representative" of this reality.

The object of description is *at a distance*, like some beautiful landscape, which is necessary for a functional description in this poetics. At the same time, the woman described by the poet is clearly present in order to be described in this way. She is obvious. Moreover, the woman is so obvious as to yield herself to another description, with a number of details; these are all factors in a successful transposition of the world of reality into the world of the poem that, as such, also appears realistic. The description requires obviousness, and obviousness yields itself to the description. The tools of the simile must also be obvious in order to be introduced into the simile in their best quality. This is the reason why there is no description of character, or love as a feeling; this is, at the same time, quite compatible with the poetics in question.

Imru' al-Qays could lengthen his description of the woman in her static state – her obviousness and the simile enable him to do so – but as soon as he feels the need to sing about her character too, he realises how inadequate for this end is the descriptiveness he optimally developed in the description of the woman's physical appearance, the description of the storm or of his magnificent horse. He can sing about a character or love through suggestions only, as these two are not obvious, are not transparent and cannot be seen from a distance successfully. In the verses quoted stating that the poet *is killed by her love*, that *his heart will do anything she orders*, etc., these conditions are not obvious and are therefore not fit for description, so that the poet much more gladly and giftedly focuses on the obvious causes of these conditions. If he would want to depict the feelings of love more subtly, the character of his beloved or, say, the surges of her erotic passion, he could do it only from a perspective significantly different from the one through which he presents her bodily "landscapes". This would demand that the distance be abandoned – a reflection that this poetics does not allow as it is not immanent in it. Let us refer here to the introductory discussion stating that the simile dominates Old Arabic poetry, which is why the poet observes the world from a distance, in its full transparency; in a way he is always outside of what he describes, being related to it only through his "eyes". Character is neither obvious nor transparent and does not enable the same sort of distance to be established as in the description of physical qualities, etc.

In addition, the categories of space and time, in the meaning and functions discussed so far, do not facilitate the development of a description of character or love. They are, owing to their abstract nature, beyond space and time inasmuch as space and time contain physical realities. (The metaphor will later on establish sovereignty over this territory.) This is why the simile cannot be so successfully – i.e. so obviously – used for their possible description as in comparisons of the world of physical reality. This is also supported by the important fact that character and love cannot be segmented or parcelled, as the poet can do with other themes in the poem and with the past time within it. Owing to their inability to be segmented, a description of character and love cannot be included in the poetics of the arabesque segmentation structure, or in a coherent system built on a number of other factors. Since the simile is the most frequent figure of speech in this poetry, its tendency towards "seclusion" is incompatible with non-present and monolithic conditions. The degree of realism is thus optimally increased; the poet keeps emphasising his role of an observer, assuring the reader of his extraordinary gift for appreciating nuances among the manifestation of the world, and for establishing relations of comparison among them. The world is in great abundance before him, and such a world is only lucky to be rendered into the world of the poem by the poet.

The reader may or may not like the Old Arabic *qaṣīda*, and they can interpret it one way or another; however, an inflexible approach treating it exclusively from the present moment is inadequate, as well as any approach that fails to appreciate its poetic distinctiveness. Disregarding an impressionist approach, a meaningful analysis shows the exceptionally high degree of its poetic coherence. This is an argument justifying its permanent value.

Typicality before description

Subjects of description in the *qaṣīda* are typical. Each *qaṣīda* in the *al-Mu'allaqāt* corpus has a number of the same themes, the same objects of description, and they are all typical of the real world from which they are transferred into the literary text. Admittedly, they do not always follow the same order in the poems, nor is the length of description of an individual object always the same. It is possible to speak about the thematic distinctiveness of each mu'allaqa, although strictly conditionally: they mostly have the same themes, though a certain theme in a poem is accentuated to a degree not present in other poems. For instance, Imru' al-Qays' set of description instruments is best expressed in a love lyric prelude; Tarafa's (Ṭarafa, d. *c*.560) in an anatomical description of the camel; Zuhayr's in a magnificent presentation of wisdom and peace; Labid's (Labīd Ibn Rabī'a, d. *c*.669) in a subtle description of wilderness and nobleness; Ibn Kulthum's (Ibn Kulthūm, d. *c*.570) in exultant self-praise and pride; Antara's ('Antara Ibn Shaddād, d. *c*.615) in a description of true heroism; al-Harith's (al-Ḥārith Ibn Ḥilizza, d. 580) in the panegyric. The themes are typical because most of them are found in other poems as well, so that literary historians tend to speak about the tedious thematic monotony of Old Arabic poetry. This typicality can be illustrated in the example of Imru' al-Qays' mu'allaqa.

The poem has a typical prologue: stopping in the desert, by deserted bivouacs; a typical memory of beautiful days spent with a woman/women; then warrior skills and the ability to overcome adversity; a description of a horse; a description of a storm. In Old Arabic poetry typicality can simply not escape one's notice. The degree of its presence can be seen from the opening couplet of Antara's mu'allaqa: "Have the poets left in the garment a place for a patch to be patched by me;/And did you know the abode of your beloved after reflection?/[31] Therefore, Antara's poem is faced with the fact that (good) poets had already sung of everything, notwithstanding that his poem is at the very source of the Arabic literary tradition known to us (from the early seventh century). Despite this, he begins his poem, like other renowned authors, with a love prologue about "recognising the deserted abode of his beloved". Antara's example may be taken as the most convincing evidence of clichés in this poetry.

Where does this persistent typifying of the poem's thematic repertoire stem from?

Its causes can partly be explained by sociological methods, a general cultural milieu, etc., but I am going to interpret it here only through its poetic necessity.

The relationship between typicality and description is very positive for several reasons. In the first place, typicality creates a communicational situation with optimal cooperation between the poem and its recipient, because the poet aims at making the world visible precisely through a description of typical characters, scenes, etc., and at sharing even typical psychological motivation with the recipient (for example, fascination, delight, etc.). From this angle, typical situations and themes become privileged. In addition, typicality "conspicuously" offers itself to description, which is why we always try to describe it anew. Therefore, it is little wonder that Antara decided to sing (of typical situations as well) even if everything had already been sung about. Furthermore, the typicality of the visible world underlines the realism characterising the old *qaṣīda*. However, the poet's creativity is realised in his approach to typicality.

Namely, the poet proves his extraordinary skill in the best possible way – and this is the *creed* of this poetics – if he *describes* a typical scene or a privileged theme so well that they almost become visible, and if he succeeds in arousing in the reader feelings similar to those he had. Another poet will present and describe the same topic in a different way. Therefore, there is a standard repertoire of themes, which are typical as such, but originality lies in the diversity of their descriptive presentation.

For instance, the woman that Imru' al-Qays describes by means of the simile – more precisely, the situation he presents her in – is typical insofar as there undoubtedly are many such women in his real world (he even writes about several women); a situation in which a Bedouin establishes such a relationship with a woman/women is also typical; their separation is typical (she rode away with her tribe), etc. There is nothing special in Imru' al-Qays' relationship to the woman, nor in the woman herself, so that she should be unique in the given social and cultural environment in terms of her physical allure or her behaviour. If we go back to Imru' al-Qays' description of the woman, we can notice that he succeeds in raising her above typicality using the tools of the simile, so that the reader may feel excited at his success. Thus, the poet's success lies in an important breakthrough from subscribing to a typical theme (a description of the beloved) to its descriptive translation into non-typicality. This is an exploit of description. A consequent reflection can lead to a far-reaching conclusion.

Imru' al-Qays positively describes a number of women in the poem, giving the names of some and a description of others. By doing this, he adds plurality to the typical theme of woman in a poem, and it could even be said that he thus de-typifies the theme. Moreover, this description of a woman can be considered a description of Woman, since all the women he sings of belong to the most precious content of his world. Therefore, *typicality* acquires a *special* dimension here, which is an outstanding quality of his poem.

In order to make a comparison or contrast, let us look at Amr Ibn Kulthum's description of the same typical subject/situation:

> She will show you, when you enter in upon her privately,
> And she is safe from the eyes of her enemies,
> Two arms as fat and fleshy as those of a long-necked she-camel,
> White, young, pure white in colour, who has not been pregnant;
> And she will show you a bosom like a bowl of ivory, soft,
> Guarded from the hands of the touchers;
> And she will show you the waist of her supple body, which is tall and long,
> While her buttocks move with difficulty with what adjoins them;

And she will show you a big hip, for which the door is too narrow;
And a waist, at the sight of which I have become mad;
And two legs, white as ivory or marble,
The jingling of ornaments upon which makes a low noise.[32]

From a poetic perspective, this description is the same as Imru' al-Qays': the subject is obvious, transparent, distanced; it is temporally situated in the same way, its segmentation is obvious; the simile is dominant, etc. The linguistic syntax is different, but its poetic syntax is not.

Therefore, not only does the poet not shrink from typical subjects/situations, but he prefers them as themes made privileged through tradition. The proof of the poet's skill is his ability to use linguistic syntax, different words and similes, or description figures in general, in order to make his subject different. This poetic postulate – although poetics would change after the *Qur'an* – held very long even after the *al-Mu'allaqāt* epoch: the primary poetic goal was not to introduce new themes, but to make a different poetic presentation of common themes from the traditional reservoir.

"Selecting" typicality for his poem, the poet, through description figures he develops as much as possible, achieves something very important to him, to his reader and their shared world: he constantly strains to wrest typicality from commonness, automatism, monotony. His linguistic skill is crucial for this.

The Bedouin's world was very monotonous, woven from pausing, sequences, from typical landscapes very few in number. The nomad's life in this truly sparse world was almost entirely concentrated on this outer world he constantly circled. The monotony of his life and world was quite extreme. It should also be borne in mind that the supreme expression of their spirituality was precisely their poetry. This implies that, for the Bedouin, poetry is an important means of enriching typicality and monotony persistent to the point of being unbearable. The variation of typicalities in poetry, their enrichment through language and style, changeable rhythm, their incorporation into verses brought to technical perfection and captivating resonance through a single metre and monorhyme – all this amounted to a true struggle against harsh typicality. More precisely, such a poeticised relationship to the world represented a way of overcoming the sparseness of the world and its themes/contents. Everyone recognised their real world and its typicalities in the poem, identifying them as commonplaces in it, and rejoiced in the kind of shift or transposition of reality that poetry can make. Their goal was not to abandon reality or make it atypical and unrecognisable in the poem, but to poetically adorn this reality with description figures and to adapt this same reality to sound by means of a poetic form that was truly brilliant. The simile is actually the most adequate figure for such a purpose. However refined, this poem can never leave the real world and soar up into an imaginative arch as the metaphor can. Furthermore, since both correlates of the simile are present, and since both are from the world of reality, they promote reality, i.e. space and time, and enrich it through the relatively unexpected association of constituents. Naturally, the simile need not take both correlates from the world of physical reality, but the introduction of the second correlate from beyond this world substantially shifts the meaning of the whole figure and would establish a different relation to the world beyond the poem. For instance, if the poet said: *My beloved has arms white like my hope,/And hips that can hardly enter my consciousness,/And wrists round like a line of my poem*, such a series of similes would have an effect considerably different from the one produced by Imru' al-Qays' or Tarafa's description. Both types of description (the one from the *qaṣīda* and mine) are equal *formally*, or at the structural level, and can in this respect be subsumed under the same figure of speech. However, their second correlates (what the first are being compared to) are semantically quite different from the respective first correlates, as they are taken from two different worlds – the real and the abstract – which creates a great difference between them in the field of semantics. The descriptions of the two poets are formally and structurally typical, which is why their semantic achievements have quite defined ranges, limited by the world of reality. Unlike this, the similes I improvised for the purpose of this discussion suddenly create a high tension in the field of semantics, or even of stylistic importance, so that we feel they are about to transform into a metaphor at any moment: as soon as the linguistic barrier/particle (*like*) is removed, there is no obstacle to the metaphor, which would even be necessary in that case. On the other hand, the descriptions of Old Arabic poets ultimately remain typical, in a wide sense, even though they, at a certain level, succeed in transcending the typicality of the real world and traditional norms, which has already been discussed. They remain typical owing to a relatively limited selection of constituents: both constituents are selected from a sum of typical subjects, phenomena, etc. Unlike this, the similes I improvised largely escape this sort of typicality: in the field of semantics, they are much more innovative, with a higher degree of unpredictability.

Therefore, harsh though it may sound, it should be said that these old *qaṣīdas* shy away from the metaphor as their dominant stylistic element, and even from similes such as those I improvised, because these stylistic elements would considerably change the angle towards the world of reality and would substantially change the poetics. Similes like *My beloved has arms white like my hope*, or metaphor, do not express the obviousness and transparency of the world, its physical typicality and realism, and do not express the distance from which in a "standard" simile both correlates are taken, simply seen in specific interaction, etc. The world of the *qaṣīda*, as I have said, is a world at a distance, transparent and clear; it is truly real.

The simile is de-typified in these *qaṣīdas* by selecting *relatively* unexpected constituents, but normally taken from the world of high values. For instance, *Two arms as fat and fleshy as those of a long-necked she-camel … who has not been pregnant*: for the Bedouin, the camel was sometimes even more precious than a woman, because his survival depended on the camel; *A bosom like a bowl of ivory*: shiny and satiny (perhaps even firm), light coloured and precious like mother-of-pearl; *A big hip, for which the door is too narrow* (implicit simile): wide hips are basic to femininity, to the ability to give birth; in addition, for a nomad constantly travelling and living in a tent, the door as a semiotic sign may mean much more than to someone else – it means settling, security, etc.; *Two legs, white as ivory or marble*: ivory and marble are valuables, etc.

Constituents of the simile as architects of positivity

It is important to note that simile constituents have a high value in the Bedouin's reality owing to a generally positive attitude to the world, an attitude expressed in the poem to the extent that it can also be called an ode. However, this should be more thoroughly discussed on another occasion. It should be said here that both constituents of the simile are always taken from the real world. The correlates must be typical and must, as I have said, represent high values within this real world, while de-typifying is achieved by their selection from relatively distant spaces of the real world: woman – camel; bosom – mother-of-pearl; hips – door; legs – marble/ivory, etc. As can be seen, the "reality" of constituents is of the highest order. This re-emphasises the realism of the world of poem, while typicality is relatively de-typified. The de-typifying is necessary because, without it, typical subjects or phenomena would not be interesting to the reader; their factual quality, in its full meaning, is irrelevant and inappropriate for a poem in which typicalities are de-typified not only by stylistic means but also by means of the form. Typicality is, among other things, one of the important communicational requirements for the poem–reader relation, so that its de-typifying, though necessary, is limited by the frameworks of these communicational requirements.

The selection of the second simile correlate from the range of objects holding a high degree of importance in the Bedouin's real world has a particular poetic consequence. Namely, a selection of such values and the establishment of comparison between them creates exceptional positivity in the poem, but positivity realised from the poet's position. The poet and his position are always positive with regard to the outer world, even when the poet presents certain negative sides of this world, although such aspects are rarely introduced into the poem. The quotations I have given so far almost exclusively involve such positive correlates: the camel, gazelle, door, mother-of-pearl, and others. Since this poetry is dominated by the simile preferring positive subjects/situations in the real world, the world of the poem is very bright, airy, all but quivering in joy and transparency. This positivity is built from microstructures into the macrostructures composing the poem. The poet is as delighted at the appearance of his beloved as by the qualities of his horse, or at a storm temporarily changing the landscape. In other words, from the simile contained in a single line, or in a couplet, to the level at which these similes, through accumulation, present a subject until saturation – what is constantly promoted is the poet's main aspiration to have this inexhaustible positivity optimally shine upon the world of reality transposed to the world of the poem. However, the poet endeavours to emphasise his almost hymnal position not only by using positive simile constituents, but also by transforming essentially negative constituents and introducing them into a generally convivial atmosphere. This remarkable adroitness of the poet is actually a telling comment on his view of the world and is always marked by a joyfulness built by figures of description. I am going to use two examples to illustrate this.

Labid compares the speed of his riding camel to the speed of a wild cow running crazily after her young has been killed:

> Is the camel like that she-ass, or rather like a wild cow, whose young has been eaten by
> wild beasts,
> And who remained behind to look for her young, while she was the leader of the herd,
> and the director of it?
> A wild cow which lost her calf, and did not cease her moving
> Round the edge of the rugged tracts in a sandy desert, and her lowing.[33]

Sometimes in old *qaṣīdas*, the look of the beloved woman is compared to the look of a cow that has lost her young. Scholars interpreting this poetry state that this comparison is introduced because, in the given situation, the cow has a very sad look, which we cannot define as unhappy as an animal supposedly cannot be either happy or unhappy, but if her look was compared to a human look, then it would be very unhappy, considering the severity of the loss.[34] Therefore, this refers to a certain negative potential, in the sense of the negative events and reactions they cause. However, the poet transforms this markedly negative potential into a positive one, because the comparison conveys that the look of his beloved is infinitely tender, soft and even "big-eyed". Clearly, the poet very skilfully and effectively uses an unusual simile, with one negative constituent, in order to make *his position* positive. The outer world he always views through a "comparative lens" here highlights the lyric illumination of his position. Naturally, such an effect of the simile with the cow's look cannot be examined outside the general principle of the preciousness of constituents in the real world since, as I have said, the cow held a completely different value in the Bedouin's world from that in other cultures and other times.

We can use Kulthum's verses for the second example:

> But verily the tribes will not know that we have been shaken
> And become weak.
> Be careful, no one must act foolishly with us,
> Lest we should have to act foolishly with him above the folly of the foolish ones.[35]

Or Imru' al-Qays' verses about hostility as a negative potential:

> Behold, many a bitter contender, as it were, an adviser, reproaching me for my love
> For you, who was unfailing in his blame, I have turned him back from his reproaches.

And many a night like a wave of the sea has let down its curtains upon me,
With all kinds of griefs, that it might try me.[36]

The poet's life is not easy: he always has enemies wanting to execute him, and has other worries causing him sleepless nights. However, the poet is not depressed by it but is, owing to adversities, able to display all his virtues: rhetorical skill, perseverance, dignity, etc. In other words, even the negative sides of life cannot affect his invincible cheerfulness with regard to the world.[37] Negativity is always overcome by the positivity of the poet's position, from which he observes the world superiorly, presenting it through *his* descriptions. In these terms, it is possible to talk of a particular type of extroversion of this poetry. Namely, it clearly does not imply a Hegelian "descent of spirit into its subjective inwardness", but the Bedouin's entire spirituality is expressed by his coming out to an outer world presented to this spirituality as crystal clear, airy, transparent and susceptible to his descriptions, without too many whirlwinds that could stir the general brightness of the world. Submergence into his own spirituality would not result in such unconditionally bright and extroverted poetry, but would bring about a reflexive, even pessimistic, tone. Nevertheless, with the exception of two or three poets singing laments, the prevalent tone in Old Arabic poetry is the poet's joyful opening of his spirituality to the world within which he lives in full harmony and optimism, even when he is in battle, when his beloved has left him, etc. Figures of description, particularly the simile, are the most appropriate means for this type of poetry, as they can most adequately express the poet's bright attitude towards the world, as well as the brightness of the world itself. A "panoramic" "view" of the world, which we find in Old Arabic poetry, cannot have the same stylistic means, or poetics generally, as reflexive poetry, or poetry directed towards Hegelian "subjective inwardness". The presence of the world, left to descriptions, and the poet's extroversion result in a distinctly Oriental positive attitude towards the world and a gift for the kind of realism painted with the hues of the poet's inward brightness.

The simile and the travelogue airiness of the world

This general openness to the world, which the poet attempts to describe, affects at least two more important poetic aspects. In the first place, owing to the cordiality of his perception of the world and the creative joy of his transposition to the poem, the poet endeavours to discover the world by means of his expression. This implies that it does not satisfy him to present one landscape, subject or a situation, exhaustive as his description may be, but his relation to the world makes him set out on a (imaginary, poetic) journey to develop the lyric joy of discovering the world in harmony, as well as enrich his principal stylistic means – the simile. This is an important reason why the old *qaṣīda* has the form of a specific travelogue. Regardless of the old *qaṣīda* being a poem whose lines are developed to technical perfection, its essence as a travelogue manifests itself in the poet's mobility and the static quality of the landscape, the sequentiality of themes, and particularly in using the figures of description that characterise this genre.

On the other hand, and in relation to this, the old *qaṣīda* is essentially a narrative. This lies at the heart of the travelogue. Imru' al-Qays narrates of his loves. Even in a formal sense, narrativity is reflected in the fact that, at the beginning of the poem, he is travelling with two friends with whom he stops by deserted bivouacs and to whom he narrates stories of his loves. The function of past time, dominant in the old *qaṣīda* as I have already discussed, is very important for the narrative nature of the *qaṣīda*. The poet *develops a detailed narrative* of his love affairs, with extroversion and distantness being highlighted here. Namely, it does not behove his narrative manner to present the subtle nuances of his or the woman's *psychological states* – they are only indicated – but it rather behoves this manner to describe a sequence of *events*; the narrator persists in narrating events, regarding psychological nuances as marginal, since he is, first and foremost, open to the outer world. The poet then – in the same poem, of course – narrates his further journeys and encounters with adversities; he tells of his horse and narrates hunting on this exceptional horse – until the remarkable description of a storm, which he narrates with particular passion.

The narrative character of the *qaṣīda* is not as obvious as that of the genre of prose travelogue. Namely, the poem cannot be as extensive as the prose travelogue, but aspires towards a certain balance between narrative extensiveness and poetic intensity. Hence the *qaṣīda* has some ninety lines on average, which would be too much for a monothematic lyrical poem and too few for a prose travelogue. Owing to the special requirements of a poetic work, the travelogue and narrative character of the *qaṣīda* is somewhat modified, so that an insufficiently competent reader may not get an impression of narrative or the qualities it shares with a travelogue. Poetic syntax, rhyme requirements, rhythmic quality, accumulation of parallelisms as a main means of a poetic work, etc. – all of these cause a certain shift in the core of the travelogue and narrative character of the poem and, owing to its principle of intensification, lead to the accumulation of description figures, which are actually denser than in the prose travelogue. This, however, does not change the qualities it shares with a travelogue and the narrative essence of the *qaṣīda*.

Narrativity is certainly closely related to the transparency of landscapes, subjects or events, which in turn have distance immanent in them. The world of the *qaṣīda*, as well as the outer world for the *qaṣīda*, are completely visible and fascinate the poet. The world of *qaṣīda* is all but in a parallel relation established by a particular kind of lyrical rapture. It is narrated of, it is travelled across and it is best conjured up by comparing its (physical) realities and accidences.

This world of antique vigour and completeness had yet to see metaphoric raptures and whirlwinds. They would bring illumination and a bang in the history of culture, the extent of which have hardly ever been equalled in history.

Notes

1 Sulejman Grozdanić, for instance, rightly observes that the figure of simile is the most frequent figure in Old Arabic poetry, but fails to infer its ultimate poetic consequences. See Sulejman Grozdanić, *Na horizontima arapske književnosti* [*On the Horizons of Arabic Literature*], Svjetlost, Sarajevo, 1975, p. 29.

2 Cf. ibid., p. 39; Gustav von Grunebaum, *Kritik und Dichtkunst: Studien zur arabischen literaturgeschichte*, Wiesbaden, 1955, p. 2.

3 Two studies can be singled out from this body of literature. The first one is penned by ʻIzz al-Dīn Ismāʻīl and entitled *al-Usus al-jamāliyya fī al-naqd al-ʻarabī. ʻArḍ wa tafsīr wa muqārana* [*Aesthetic Basis of Arabic Criticism: Presentation, Interpretation and Comparison*], al-ṭabʻa al-thālitha, Dār al-fikr al-ʻarabī, Cairo, 1974. The other study is Abū al-Qāsim al-Shābbī, *al-Khayāl al-shiʻrī ʻinda al-ʻArab* [*Arabic Poetic Imagination*], al-Dār al-tūnisiyya, s. l., 1975.

4 Cf. Abū al-Qāsim al-Shābbī, op. cit., p. 122; ʻIzz al-Dīn Ismāʻīl, op. cit, p. 132. See also *Takhyīl: The Imaginary in Classical Arabic Poetics*, texts selected, translated and annotated by Geert van Gelder and Marlé Hammond, Oxbow, Oxford, 2008.

5 Edward W. Said, *Orientalism*, Penguin, London, 1978.

6 All the quotations from *The al-Muʻallaqāt* are taken from *The Seven Poems Suspended in the Temple at Mecca*, translated from Arabic by F. E. Johnson, Gorgias Press, Piscataway, NJ, 2002; further referred to as *The al-Muʻallaqāt*.

7 This is how Qays opens his muʻallaqa, stopping his two friends on their journey across the desert:

> Stop, oh my two friends, let us weep on account of the remembrance of my beloved,
> And her abode situated on the edge of a sandy desert between Dakhool and Howmal.
> And between Toozih and Maqrát, whose traces have not been obliterated,
> On account of what has blown and re-blown over them from the South wind and the North wind.
> You will see the dung of the white deer in the courtyards
> And enclosures of it, as though they were seeds of pepper.
> On the morning of separation, the day they parted it was as if I, standing near the acacia shrubs
> In the gardens of the tribe, were breaking the pods of the wild colocynth.
> [...]

8 Roland Barthes, "L'effet du réel", in *Le bruissement de la langue: Essais critiques IV*, Paris, 1984. Quoted from Živa Benčić and Dunja Fališevac (eds), *Tropi i figure* [*Tropes and Figures of Speech*], Zavod za znanost o književnosti, Zagreb, 1995, p. 432.

9 *The al-Muʻallaqāt*, pp. 41–43.

10 In fact, this was frequently the case. Namely, different editions of the *al-Muʻallaqāt* do not always have the same sequence of verses; in some editions certain lines are even left out. It should be noted that, in this poetry, the smallest semantic and structural unit is *bayt* (couplet), which often consists of two *half-bayts* (lines) written in horizontal parallel (we convey them in the form of a couplet). This is important because the segmentation is expressed at the level of *bayt*, as the highest level, which is conveyed as a couplet in translation.

11 *The al-Muʻallaqāt*, pp. 26–30.

12 For the basic figures, see Dean Duda, "Figure u opisu prostora" [Figures in spatial description], in Živa Benčić and Dunja Fališevac (eds), *Tropi i figure* [*Tropes and Figures*], Zavod za znanost o književnosti, Zagreb, 1995, p. 427.

13 *The al-Muʻallaqāt*, pp. 32–36.

14 See Duda, op. cit., pp. 431–432.

15 Such functioning of segmentation in the textual space of Old Arabic poetry strongly resembles film frames, or the poetics of film space.

16 *The al-Mu'allaqāt*, pp. 30–31.

The same verses were already given in a poetic translation. However, they are given in a philological translation here because the original is strongly linked to topography, or to the space whose intense segmentation is largely lost in poetic translation.

17 Ibid., p. 32.

18 It is possible to object here that Old Arabic poetry – pre-Islamic poetry in particular – is problematic in terms of authenticity. There is a vast body of literature about this issue and, in all probability, it is difficult to believe that this poetry existed exactly as we know it today. The first to point out the problem of the authenticity of pre-Islamic poetry was Ibn Sallām al-Jumaḥī (846) in his work entitled *Ṭabaqāt fuḥūl al-shu'arā'* [*Classes of Champion Poets*]. A lot attention in this regard was raised by a work written by Ṭāhā Ḥusayn in 1926, *Fī al-shi'r al-jāhilī* [*On Pre-Islamic Poetry*]. Ahlwardt also studied this issue (in *Bemerkungen über die Aechtheit der alten arabischen Gedichte*, Greifswald, 1872) as well as many others. Therefore, the reader might raise an objection that such conclusions should not be drawn, considering the great likelihood that some interventions in Qays' mu'allaqa were made by rhapsodists or those who wrote it down in the Islamic period. However, this is a problem for philologists: philological research into the authenticity of this poetry and philological analyses of its text do face great difficulties indeed, but it is irrelevant to my type of analysis: a stylistic and aesthetic analysis of the poem, or generally an analysis in terms of literary theory, starts from the fact that we have this poem, for example, as the final artefact, as a work fixed in the eigth century, and having been part of the tradition for many centuries in an unchanged form, and subjected to this type of analysis as a "done deal" too.

19 The present has four moods in Arabic: indicative, conjunctive, jussive and imperative.

20 *I shall show.*

21 It is interesting that the verb in question denotes both the present and the future in Arabic morphology (*al-muḍāri'*).

22 It would be interesting to analyse the grammatical tense in this exemplary poem along the lines of research done by Roman Jakobson in *Selected Writings, Vol. III: The Poetry of Grammar and the Grammar of Poetry*, ed. by Stephen Rudy, Mouton, The Hague, Paris, 1980.

23 This is observed not only in individuals but in very large communities: a sentimental relationship to the past is frequently built not only by individuals but also by whole peoples, or even whole cultures and civilisations.

24 The principle of contrariety in this case is a separate issue. A discussion of this complex issue requires a separate treatment and would be digressive in this chapter, but it should at least be indicated. A particular realism in Old Arabic poetry was traditionally cultivated by Arabs, who have an exceptionally "imaginative mentality", while the Western mentality, of a different quality, cultivates imaginative poetry more than they.

25 'Izz al-Dīn Ismā'īl, op. cit., p. 132.

26 *The al-Mu'allaqāt*, pp. 40–42.

27 Ibid., pp. 36–37.

28 Cf. Abū al-Qāsim al-Shābbī, op. cit., p. 122.

29 A fair complexion is held in high esteem, following the contrariness principle, in a world where it is rare; as its women mostly have dark complexions, they are "non-mirrorlike", exposed to the sun through labour, etc.

30 A commonplace of Old Arabic poetry is that slender shanks cause a particular kind of erotic excitement in the poet wondering, with ultimate erotic curiosity, how such shanks are capable of carrying the thighs and cheeks always like sand-hills.

31 *The al-Mu'allaqāt*, p. 194.
32 *The al-Mu'allaqāt*, pp. 161–163.
33 *The al-Mu'allaqāt*, pp. 131–132.
34 The cow is not chosen at random: in the Bedouin's world: it also represented a precious asset as it was relatively rare and was beneficial to man and his existence. This also testifies to the relativity or social determination of tropes and figures – in our current social environment, the least indication of any similarity between the woman and a cow seems extremely denigrating; in the world of the Bedouin at the time, the opposite was the case.
35 *The al-Mu'allaqāt*, p. 175.
36 Ibid., p. 44.
37 Tarafa will explicate this in the following lines: "By your life I swear that no intricate affair is perplexing to me during my day,/Nor does my night seem long to me on account of anxiety" (Ibid., p. 70).

5 The Qur'anic metaphor

The world within

Descent of the metaphor into the world and the metaphoric revolution

The Bedouin's world of antique vigour and completeness fell apart owing to the metaphor that the *Qur'an* brought into this world in an inimitable way. Everything suffered a radical change: the pre-Islamic poetics and figures of description in its poetry; the flatness of the world and man's distance from it; the principle of segmentation, which acquired a new meaning in its aspiration towards synthesis; the content–form relationship, which shifted in its emphasis, etc.[1]

The world had been transformed by abandoning the obviousness that the dominant simile expressed ever so brilliantly, always emphasising realism on the transparent horizon. Instead of obviousness there opened infinite worlds, with vague outlines, owing to the creativity of the metaphor that this world and the Arabic language in it rejoiced at, since Arabic has always been crucial for expressing Arab spirituality. A distanced description of the desert, which pre-Islamic poetry prided itself on, was replaced by an inside description of Jannah that began to gurgle with rivers and metaphors, elevating the souls of Arabians to undreamed-of heights. From the visible horizon, presented through the simile, the focus shifted onto the invisible beyond that presented through the metaphor. The world had, therefore, completely changed owing to the metaphor that transformed it, demonstrating in an unpredictable and ever so flamboyant style to what extent reality depends on language, or on what language creates. For, speaking about these changes, I am speaking about one and the same people – about Arabians – who, owing to the Qur'anic Text, completely and almost in a historic instant changed their attitude towards the world, and then changed this very world as well: they made a rapid advance beyond the physical, visible world, with strength born of the newly discovered metaphoric world.

At this fateful historic moment – at which, according to the *Qur'an*, the Metaphor descended to the World in order to refine it and impart to it something about a different world – it became clear how much language and revolutionising the world were connected. At this energy spot in history, whose impact is constantly felt, there "descends" the Text that maintains a permanent relationship between its two aspects. The first aspect is linguistic and literary, since the

Text, as one of its greatest qualities, emphasises the linguistic and literary-aesthetic value that has amazed the world since this distant descent till this day. The second aspect is ideological: the Text caused a permanent turnabout in the faith of the Bedouins, and then of a great portion of humanity as well. Therefore, the turnabout was complete – the world of Bedouins, who lived happily in their simple worldview immersed in transparency, changed suddenly and thoroughly, so that the entire literary tradition suffered something of a shock. It is a notable fact, and must never be disregarded as such, that the Text closely linked its cultural and even civilisational turnabout with language and with its own literary and aesthetic values. Moreover, the Text presented its language as well as its literary and aesthetic exceptionality as an important argument for the ideological turnabout, for history recorded that this had a strong impact on spreading the faith of Islam: there is evidence confirming that people converted to Islam owing to miraculous achievements of the Text in the field of language and style – they took these arguments as the indisputable supernaturalism of the Text. Poets fell silent because they realised how mute their poetry seemed before the eloquence and aesthetic architectonics of the Text.

It is true, though, that other heavenly revelations convey that "first there was the Word", but the literary and aesthetic importance of the Word is particularly prominent in the *Qur'an*, since this importance is explicated in it through ayahs about the supernaturalism of the Text, and is also expressed through its literary and aesthetic structure. It is always very important to bear in mind that, unlike other texts-revelations, the Text has kept its authenticity down to every single letter.

In a number of places the *Qur'an* refers to the exceptionality of its language and style raised to the level of supernaturalism. It is the Text's commonplace, and quotes illustrating it would be redundant here. It is sufficient to refer to the previously mentioned surah 55, which explicitly and implicitly testifies to the miraculous language and style in the Text, as well as to the exertions of such language and style to convey ever so rich layers of content.

Linguists and scientists studying the philosophy of language should bear in mind the establishment of this correlation between the World and Language at the dawn of the distant seventh century. It is important to know that the Text does not underline that, as the highest token of His grace, God gave Man not only the power of speech in general, but also the power of articulate, stylised expression, thus distinguishing him above all beings. This promotion of language and rhetoric/stylistics represented, at the same time, the gilding of tradition mostly affirmed in the field of language; through this Text, language was raised to a higher level, transcending poetry *as an art*. Namely, language became connected with Faith, since language was conceived as a gift rendering man capable not only of artistic refinement of the world but also of supreme religious cognisance.

In the flatness of the Bedouin's world, religion was suitable to this general worldview. The Kaaba was full of more or less skilfully made artefacts representing Arabian deities, and this collection was completely in line with the

Arabian belief about the overall obviousness of the world, whose containment was in the simile I explained earlier. Everything in that world was present and transparent, so that the deities were under man's hand as well, rather in order to strengthen the Bedouin's position, which I have defined as central, and from which he viewed the world with superiority, embodying his own deities as well. Precisely these deities could, as such, yield themselves to figures of description, could be comparatively graded, and could be addressed directly – directly in terms of physical transparency and presence, and even of a direct visual contact frustrating transcendence. In this conception – the world is complete, flat, non-processual, and in such a world gods are (definitively) wrought, arrayed and transparent in the Shrine.

However, the Text brought an end to such an ordering of the world. Beyond the described world – as the Text reveals – is a different and *more beauteous* world, and beside those present and static deities is a God that is unceasingly active and present, except, in part, in the results of His actions. This God is *incomparable* and *indescribable*. Figures of description – therefore, the simile as well – are helpless here. The turnabout is complete and dramatic.

It follows from this that the means of language and style, which had previously dominated tradition, were not able to express this new awareness and a new, fundamentally different attitude towards the world. Since Allah is invisible, unequalled, incomparable and indescribable, it means that He can partly (as He is transcendent) be conceived of only through Language, and only through the greatest linguistic exertions. God cannot be described by the simile that was previously dominant in language, because the world cannot offer correlates of sufficient quality that could enter the relation of comparison in order to present Him. Similarly, the Other World cannot be completely described by means of the simile or other (travelogue) figures of description. Everything is on the other side of senses and experience. The Bedouin's world suddenly proved to have been imperfect, transient, almost momentary. Description is too "mirror-like" – to paraphrase Imru' al-Qays – to even begin presenting the "shading" of the Other World, and God is utterly indescribable.[2] The form of the poem the Bedouin tirelessly polished and prided himself on, on the one hand, appears as insufficient because the poem is semantically inconsistent and, on the other hand, all the linguistic and stylistic means of the poem seem to be superseded (dominant description figures, in the first place) and incompetent before new conceptions of God and the World. At the same time, there were no other means (nor do we have them today) for conceiving of and presenting God and the New World except language, which was then believed to have reached, in tradition, the ultimate limit of its expressive potential. Language had to surpass itself; it had to make a huge step that would be up to the task, or be in keeping with the unprecedented revolution in conceptions of the World and Thinking, and in order to be at the level of the fourth ayah of surah 55, forging an unbreakable relation of the *Qur'an* and Man with the divine gift of *articulate expression*.

Thus, without exaggeration, the Metaphor entered this World, *descended* into this World in order to master it and to save it. It is the highest quality of *al-bayān* (stylised expression, referred to in ayah 4 of surah 55) and language. Namely, everything I have just said about the indescribability of God and non-transparency of the Other World suggests that God and the Other World, in their transcendence (and non-presence), are "reachable" only through metaphor: only metaphor is equal to the miraculousness and supernaturalism of all the worlds, and only the metaphor can itself perform miracles in this world. When something must be conceived of, presented, or in a way reached in its remoteness – as is the case here – it can only be done through metaphor. Its function is essentially cognitive. Admittedly, the "knowledge" that a metaphor offers us about something differs from the knowledge offered by a simile, or by some other figure of description, but it is the only possible knowledge where positive, rational cognition is helpless: such knowledge has vague outlines; unlike the edges of the experiential world, such knowledge is made subjective to a degree and is, as such, fluid and elliptical to a certain extent – that is, relatively dependent on an individual conception of meaning, but still remaining an irreplaceable cognisance reached only through metaphor. The Qur'anic metaphor speaks, on the one hand, of the inviability of (this) world only to underline, in metaphoric outlines, the permanent completeness of the Other World. For, speaking of the miracles the Qur'anic metaphor performs in the world, it should be kept in mind that it does not only represent a stylistic means, even though I will mostly speak of it as a trope. Namely, the metaphor in this case transcends its effects in the field of stylistics – it belongs to the fields of religion and philosophy; it is a form of the special relationship between man and the world. Unlike other tropes, only the metaphor can express very complex ideas, branching indefinitely, without even resembling the kind of accumulation we have seen with the simile. Nietzsche was right to say that the drive towards the formation of the metaphor is man's fundamental drive. Bearing all this in mind, it is evident why the Text operates through its language and style with so much self-confidence.

The *Qur'an* descends into the world as a metaphor: it is not only a work whose text abounds in metaphors but, in many aspects, the form and way in which it was delivered to man can be considered a metaphor.[3] Namely, according to Islam, the *Qur'an*, as humankind knows it, is a specific transcript, an excerpt, perhaps even a transfer from the *Tablet Well-Preserved* with God (Lawḥ Maḥfūẓ). Following this, it was adapted to the human language and mind from the Original whose unchangeability is suggested by the *Tablet* – therefore, by something that is, as a semantic sign, in human experience both transparent and permanent at the same time – just as it is suggested by the *Careful Preservation* in the World Beyond and in divine reliability. This actually concerns a complex metaphor. On the one hand, the copy of the Text we are familiar with is a metaphor enabling man to understand the divine *authenticity* of the Text. Since one of the conditions for the realisation of a metaphor is a context (Ar. *al-qarīna*) preventing a literal interpretation of figurative meaning, it cannot be literally interpreted in this case that Someone saw Some Text in the World Beyond, copied it and conveyed it to people in the vertical. Therefore, a copy of the Text from the *Tablet Well-Preserved* is a metaphor for its authenticity, unchangeability and its divine origin. At the same time, another aspect of the metaphor should be kept in mind in this case. One of its constituents is elided in order to optimally strengthen the tensions between them. The other elided constituent displays the shared quality to a greater degree, which means that the *Qur'an* is, actually, a specially adapted expression of the Original non-comprehensible in its absolute originality. It may be like a translation of the original that mankind received in the Arabic language. This understanding is strongly suggested by the *Tablet Well-Preserved.*

On the other hand, owing to its unique capacities, the *Tablet* metaphor enables the Tablet to be interpreted as something prominent and visible considering its importance, or considering the importance of what is written on the Tablet; the Tablet means steadiness; it can be approached and written on only by someone representing an authority (the Absolute Authority in this case), who has the knowledge matching the right of access to the Tablet, etc. Therefore, the Tablet is a metaphor for a number of values of the highest order, so that the text of the *Qur'an*, as an exceptional value, is "copied" from this Tablet. It is naive to think that Somewhere, in an unknown space and time, there literally exists a tablet on which the Text is written, for the tablet and the text belong to our world and experience, so that their meaning and sense are transformed into something resembling them in values alone, and by no means literally and in the way expressed by the simile, which rather dwells on the "surface" layer of the resemblance, without intense interaction between the correlates.

Hence, the very origin of the text is defined metaphorically, as there is no other way to present its source to man in its full originality. There are many people who take the statement about the Text originating from the Tablet literally, but this understanding need not be discussed here because it belongs to a mind not prepared for great epistemological achievements offered by the metaphoric approach. In ideological, religious terms, such understanding is effective, as it does not question the belief itself, but is substantially impoverished in terms of understanding the complexity of the world and the majestic relations created by the metaphor.

The advance of metaphor irreversibly put an end to the form of realism of the world known to the ancient Bedouin and expressed in his poetry. Beyond reality there was "revealed" a "new world" of immense importance, which, through metaphoric mediation, is comprehended more or less in contours, or in a "relief" that is not as fixed as this reality, because, being mediated by the metaphor, that world is in unceasing processuality. Owing to this, of course, this reality too receives an entirely different meaning, since it is always understood in relation to the "reality" of the Other World: they cannot be separated any more and cannot be interpreted completely separately. Furthermore, this reality is strongly influenced by the future "reality" still reachable only through the capacities of metaphor, as this world is accepted and modelled from a perspective of the future (of the future world), so that the realism of this world is substantially qualitatively changed with respect to pre-Islamic Bedouin realism. The turnabout is complete and powerful. But, considering this epoch-making change in awareness of *the world* that the Text transforms into an awareness of inextricably related *worlds*, it is difficult to describe how glorious the opportunities given the metaphor in terms of comprehending and mediating these worlds. Cognisance of the world/worlds and the expansion of Islam depended on the capacities of metaphor, as well as the entire – both this-worldly and other-worldly – faith of a man who had completely transformed his life in keeping with a radically new reality. It is therefore no accident that the Text names this faith *Islam*: *Islam* means complete submission. Language and its metaphor, which I have already defined as something more than just a stylistic means, have taken upon themselves a huge task: they are entrusted with mediating the worlds for man to cognise them through language and metaphor – that is, inexactly – and were, at the same time, charged with kindling the redeeming flame in man's spirit and soul that keeps at bay the cold futility of existence, the flame called *faith* as it defies ultimate rationalisation. Only man and his language were able to carry so great a burden of the Text.[4] This dual and simultaneous operation of language and its metaphor is the main element of the effect of the *Qur'an* that cannot be explained and accepted through reason alone, since the metaphor itself cannot be rationalised. It is true that, within its arguments, the *Qur'an* often refers to reason, as it considerably relies – not separating faith from the overall life – on the instrument of reason and arguments available to it; but the *Qur'an* also insists on imagination that actually represents the powerful wings of metaphor able to attain levels of elation that reason is not.

Hence the *Qur'an* is a true miracle *in language*. Furthermore, even after these fourteen-and-a-half centuries since the Text was revealed, language seems not to have become fully aware of all the potentials brought into it by the Text reproduced from the Tablet. Similarly, linguistic stylistics has not yet fully elucidated all the stylistic potentials of the Text and their epistemological range, as the Text is only a "hollow echo", adapted to man, of the inconceivably rich original on the Tablet. If read as a semiotic sign, the transparency of the Tablet is of quite a different kind from the transparency of the Bedouin's tablet: the former is, metaphorically, as transparent as "possible" and "necessary" to God; the "language" that it is written in and that can be encompassed only through knowledge of metaphor is inconceivable as it is a language of Perfection, of Perfect Infinity, a language of divine communication with all the worlds. Therefore, we have an excellent metaphor here: the language (on the Tablet) is actually a metaphor in this case; the Tablet (to be written on in language) is also a metaphor; "writing on" is a metaphor – and all of them together make an extremely big semantic field of the Metaphor.

The Text unveiled in language and stylistics

With this in mind, it is no wonder that, ever since it *descended* (I also use this metaphor for the vertical order of the Universe and for subordination within it), the Text has been explored and interpreted with undiminished intensity. This should not be read as an attitude resulting from a religious devotion and from, some would say, partiality; rather, it is explored and always unveiled anew, unveiled to linguistics as a scientific discipline, as well as to stylistics: none of them is a theological discipline so as to be qualified as being partial, as having an a priori approach, etc. The reason for the banking up of linguistic and stylistic potential lies in the fact that language and stylistics are charged with the enormously important task of mediating the worlds, of expressing what cannot be fully expressed by anything else.

The linguistic and stylistic unveiling of the Text is closely related to the unveiling of its sublime content. The purely linguistic aspect of the *Qur'an* is not self-sufficient for research as this aspect, of necessity, always refers to the stylistic aspect as a complement and a meaningful explication. Linguistic and stylistics are here remarkably mutually conditioned, complement each other, and interpret each other. This is caused, again, by the obvious and extremely high poetic function of language in the Text. However, its pregnantness with meaning affects a relative instability of linguistic and stylistic "findings" and openness to reinterpretations, and affects their temporariness. Namely, since the Text places Content/Meaning at the forefront, regarding the form merely as a necessary though important manifestation of a "sensory emanation of the Idea", linguistic and stylistic "frames" keep spreading through reinterpretation in order to carry the meaning stored inside them. They are almost "elastic". In other words, language and style are, as I have said, tasked with mediation, with conveying (re) cognition of transcended superabundance, and must therefore use special means to "portray" the hardly portrayable – this is a figurative language in which the metaphor is absolutely privileged.

Metaphors in such important, monumental texts are never definitive. They can "die down" (*table leg* is widely known in this regard), but can also be revived, reincarnated, only to shine again with a new meaning. In texts such as the Qur'anic one, this potential of the metaphor is enormous owing to the standing ellipsis of the Text, with which the metaphor cooperates brilliantly, considering the importance, as I have said, for the metaphor to eschew sharp edges and to express processuality. In a consequent analysis this means that, in line with our discovery of the Text's potentials – which are enormous, since the Text insists on them in the first place – we shift our interpretations of figurative language, relativise them, develop them further, etc. This is the main reason for incomplete interpretations and scientific relativisations. However, this is always accompanied by the aesthetic layer of the Text. It is also important to keep in mind one fact to which I will often have to return: the Text does not define itself as art, but always clearly distances itself from art. The Text's ultimate goal is not the amalgamation of content and form, as is the case in art; its goal, rather, is behind this – in presenting arguments. This fact must be kept in mind because the Text, intentionally, does not transpose reality in order to culminate in the aesthetic but, through and behind the aesthetic, it *presents the very reality*. This leads to far-reaching consequences.

There are many examples of the openness of the metaphor in the Text, as well as of its cognitive achievements, which is one of the sources of the Text's constant openness to reinterpretation. In these terms, the first ayah in the *Qur'an* can serve as an example: *Praise be to God, Lord of the worlds*. The noun worlds (*al-'ālamīn*) is offered as a metaphor, but can also be read as a noun without a metaphoric transfer. Namely, at the time this ayah was revealed (in the seventh century) the Bedouin, who knew only a limited and monotonous horizon, found the statement about the Lord of the worlds truly remarkable, impressive, polysemous, etc. The *worlds* from this ayah could not have been understood then in the same ways as they are today. From a Bedouin perspective, they could have represented worlds of reality beyond the reality he was familiar with; they could have implied this world in unconquered distances; positive and negative forms of the Other World; they could have stood for separate worlds of humans, jinns, angels, etc. It is not easy to fathom what meanings this could have had for the Bedouin, despite the texts of renowned exegetes. However, modern man, owing to the expansion of his horizons through science, can arrive at different interpretations of the word *worlds*. For example, this word can denote (modern interpreters love such interpretations) the worlds of humans and animals, each of which in turn has its own separate world; finally, it can denote modern man's hope that there are many worlds in the Universe.

In any case, the word *worlds* functions as a metaphor with different epistemological ranges – depending on the level of education and scientific degree of its recipient. Finally, it can at once cease to be a metaphor and prove to be a scientific fact: presuming that science should discover the existence of other civilisations in the Universe, the noun *worlds* would be reduced to a "regular" noun, without any connotative meanings.

Be that as it may, it is probably difficult to even imagine what a revelation the divine statement about the worlds represented for the seventh-century Bedouin – this proud man of antiquity that so masterfully ruled his world, the one and only, transparent and yielding; the world encompassed by his description and completely in alignment with his great art of comparison.

In another example I will present here, connotation, or metaphorical meaning, is already eliminated owing to scientific progress.

In the first five ayahs of surah 96 – these are the first ayahs revealed in chronological succession – there is an important noun that has seen all sorts of interpretations depending on the interpretative skill of the exegete. The beginning of this surah reads: *Read in the name of thy Lord who created;/Created man from a small hook*. The noun *'alaq* (small hook) was translated as the interpreter understood it, waiting in its originality for adequate understanding and translation. *'Alaq* is among those words of the Text that have always kindled great interest; it was mostly believed to belong to the sphere of science (biology and medicine), but it was not known what exactly it represented in science.[5] Its basic etymological meaning is *to hang*; *to hook*. During past centuries, before science clearly elucidated all the phases of man's conception and birth, the word *'alaq* could have had a number of connotative meanings. It could even have been a metaphor for a rather vague phase of man's genesis. However, when we watch the phase of (artificial) insemination on TV today, owing to the progress of science and technology, we can see that, at its earliest stage, a spermatozoid is indeed *hooked (on)to* an ovum, and that a fertilised ovum is *hooked onto* the uterine wall; in an attempt to move this small hook using medical instruments, it firmly clings, it will not budge. It follows that the *hook*, owing to science, has lost its original connotations, ceasing to be a metaphor and becoming a medical term and a biological fact. Something unusual has happened: in time, a metaphor has turned into *mu'jiza* (miracle); a metaphor crossed over to obviousness, to exact verifiability, and Muslims now use it to prove the divine origin of the *Qur'an*, because it is said that the prophet Muhammad, to whom non-Muslims ascribe the authorship of the *Qur'an*, could by no means have known this biological phenomenon of the genesis of man. In line with this transformation of a metaphor into a scientific fact, of which there are a number of examples in the *Qur'an*, Muslims maintain that some other semantic "areas" of the metaphor, such as resurrection and the Other World, will once also become facts, though they can now be grasped only through the arch of metaphor.

In any case, a large portion of the Text is metaphorical. Some entire chapters are metaphors; extremely complex metaphors are developed in certain places, such as Jannah and Jahannam, with a number of smaller metaphors, or, for instance, the Scales for "weighing" good and bad deeds, etc. Admittedly, it should be said straight away that many people, believers in particular, do not consider this superabundant language of the metaphor to be metaphorical at all, being groundlessly fearful that the assertion about a considerable portion of the Text being metaphorical in a way falsifies the Text's meaning and eschatological future, and that it tries to deprive them of everything they believe is waiting for them. To such people, the metaphor is too deceptive, unreliable, fluid and blurred, which is why they prefer to take these subtle representations of the Other World literally: to them, they are convincing, realistic and, most importantly, correspond to their experience of this world. I can still remember how violently certain theologians reacted to my essay on the Qur'anic metaphor of *Jannah*.[6] They find the interpretation of Jannah as a metaphor to be blasphemous. Of course, from a religious point of view, I must repeat this, it is not crucially important whether someone takes these metaphors as such or reduces them to descriptions, i.e. it is not important whether someone believes in their literal meaning, because the primary aim is for their captivation to have a positive effect on faith, but such people should not concern themselves with whether someone else takes parts of the Text as metaphors.

Reduction of these metaphors to literal meanings brings them back to the state of pre-Islamic Bedouin description discussed with regard to the simile; such an approach greatly impoverishes the literary values of the Text, as well as the vast sums of good (or evil) it portrays through the language of metaphor. Moreover, the reduction in question unjustifiably brings the Text back to the state of pre-Islamic description, or to the phase of tradition realised in the brilliant poetics of description and distance epitomised by the *al-Mu'allaqāt*. Consenting to such reduction, the Text's values are brought down to its rhythmic and melodious qualities alone, depriving it of its rich tropes, and leaving it even beneath the level of those figures of description found in the *al-Mu'allaqāt*. Namely, we have seen that figures of description, particularly the simile, are very rich and cumulative in the *al-Mu'allaqāt*. Since one of the metaphor's constituents is never formally present/visible, then a literal understanding of the metaphor does not even possess the quality present in the simile, but translates the metaphor to the poorest type of description, or of representation deprived of picturesqueness. In that case, the simile is at a much higher stylistic level. Out of a number of examples, I will offer two typical representations of woman – one from Tarafa's mu'allaqa and the other from the *Qur'an*.

This is how the *Qur'an* speaks about women of the Other World:

> In each [Jannah], the fair, the beauteous ones [...]
> Houris kept close in their pavilions.[7]

Or:

> And we have made them ever virgins,
> Dear to their spouses, of equal age with them.[8]

Then:

> And damsels with swelling breasts, their peers in age.[9]

This is how Tarafa describes his beloved:

> And in the tribe there is one like a young gazelle, with deep-coloured lips, shaking
> The Arák tree to obtain its fruit, but wearing double strings of pearls and emeralds;
> A doe, who has left her young, and is grazing with the herd in a dense grove,
> Eating the edges of the fruit of the Arák tree, and clothing herself with its leaves;
> And she is smiling with her deep red lips, and shows teeth like a jessamine
> Blossoming in a damp sand-hill, situated in the midst of a plain of pure sand;
> The rays of the sun have watered her teeth all but her gums, which are smeared with
> Collyrium, while she does not eat anything against the collyrium so as to affect its color. And she smiles with a face, as if the sun had thrown his mantle
> Of brightness upon it, pure of colour, which is not wrinkled.[10]

If Qur'anic metaphors are taken in their literal sense, then Tarafa's descriptions are incomparably superior to these two. His description is rich owing to a number of similes constructed by means of objects or phenomena of the highest value and brought to comparison so as to highlight the exquisiteness of the first correlate of the simile. Description as such is a commonplace in Old Arabic poetry; woman as a theme is also a typical "object" of description, but the poet makes all of it special by comparing the woman with the most valuable details of his whole world: a young gazelle; strings of pearls and emeralds; a gazelle in a dense grove; a neck clothed with leaves; a smile as a flower blossoming in a sand-hill; teeth shining white in the sun, with contrasting dark gums; a face bright as the sun himself, and unwrinkled, on top of it, etc.

Therefore, in only a few couplets the poet brings all the beauty of his world, all its splendour, so that, owing to the beauty of the world brought into the simile, the poet's beloved becomes an ornament to the world itself. She is described very abundantly and extensively.

The woman in the passage from the Qur'anic Text is represented very modestly in comparison with Tarafa's "picture". A Jannah beauty (houris as the *Qur'an* calls them) is actually not described but only denoted; her presence is shown, but not her physical splendour. Except for the etymology of this noun (actually, it is morphologically an adjective: *big-eyed woman*), there are no details with regard to description of the woman in the *Qur'an* like those in the poet's description; there are only modest representations beyond her physicality such as, for example, bracelets, armlets and anklets, silk robes, etc.

This opens the question why the *Qur'an* is so restrained in description compared to poetry. It is the same with descriptions of other landscapes and rewarding features of the Other World: gardens with over-branching trees and fountains flowing through them, soft green cushions and beautiful carpets, etc.[11] Having this in mind, it is not clear why the *Qur'an* is generally considered vastly superior in terms of style, as well as how some people – who take everything in the *Qur'an* in its literal sense – can explain the "fact" that the woman, as one of the greatest rewards in the Other World, is depicted so modestly, without graded and accumulated descriptions. Judging by these descriptions, the Qur'anic representation of woman is much poorer than the poet's. Finally, and paradoxically, why is it that, despite modest representation, the houri should become a metaphor for a supremely beautiful woman in *this* world: a woman of exceptional qualities is often said to be a true houri.

The analysis of the two quoted excerpts (one from the *Qur'an* and the other from the old poetry), as well as the issues this analysis raises, is neither arbitrary nor digressive. I have given only two examples, which are representative, in order to suggest the very essence of the pre-Islamic tradition and Qur'anic poetics, a different usage of stylistic means and poetic methods, as well as their different attitude towards the world(s) and their values. Therefore, in the discussion to follow, I will contrast the fundamental postulates of these two poetics, which are not issues pertaining solely to literary theory but ones that can be quite revealing about their conceptions of the world and man's position in it. I will necessarily have to refer to certain things I have already said about the simile in Old Arabic poetry.

Among a number of these postulates are the poet's attitude towards reality and his distance from it. Experts on Arabic literature are here faced with the problem of the "materialism" of old poetry that could be represented by Imru' al-Qays' or Tarafa's description of the woman. The poetic positions of the pre-Islamic poem and Qur'anic Text must therefore be presented from this perspective as well.

Realism of the simile and transfer of the metaphor: poet's belle and houris in Jannah

Pre-Islamic poetry is characterised by realism. The poet is open towards the world he perceives in its outward manifestation, in an abundance of real qualities. The best stylistic means for expressing such a relationship to the world and for transposing such a world to a poem is the figure of simile. We have already seen that the simile dominated the old poetry that many researchers negatively qualified as "materialistic". A remarkable testimony to this realism, as a deeply rooted poetic dominant, can be found in the quotation from Tarafa's poem, a quotation that could easily be replaced with many other poetically identical quotations. The poet's beloved simply radiates, so much so that one cannot *look* away, because the emphasis is on her radiance indeed: the description holds only to what is visible on her, just as it holds to correlates of the simile as they are "the best vistas" of the poet's world and, as such, promote her impressive beauty. At one stage of reading, the poem may appear to indicate a possibility of departing from the world of reality. For, the woman is described through an abundance of similes whose correlates, in terms of their values, are sometimes above the woman's physical qualities (such as sunshine, for instance) so that, owing to the accumulation of relatively diverse comparisons, there rises a sort of "descriptive tension" that, at a certain moment, gives the reader an impression it will elevate them beyond the physical world, beyond reality, and that the elevating description of the woman will outweigh her physical qualities. Although this never happens, in stylistic terms it is still valuable to keep even the mere tension that the poet creates for the reader through masterful and rich similes. The simile never succeeds in soaring above the physical because its correlates are all from the real, physical world, and because such correlates are quite explicit, without substitution that might suggest a metaphoric arch. Look at the "status" of the second correlate of the simile in the real world: a gazelle, strings of pearls, a dense grove, fruits, jessamine, sunlight... All these are tools belonging to the most obvious reality, to a *physical dimension* of the highest order. There is nothing abstract, not even an indication of it. Of course, since we have a simile at work here, these "physical tools" are represented as the physical qualities of the woman, so that she herself – in a world where she is always in a state of comparability – is simply reified: owing to this nature of description, she has no chance of soaring up beyond physical appearance in any direction whatsoever – towards universalisation (the beauty of a woman as the Woman) or towards unveiling spirituality. Tarafa's woman is not universalised; he does not sing about the Woman, but about a specific woman who is made physically very particular. This is very much in line with the poet's worldview: he sees the world in sequences, in segments, in an abundance of details, and establishes among them only the type of relations established by the simile: these relations are external, mechanical, without interaction. For the simile is a particular kind of deception: it does not realise the actual, true similarity but always stops at a distance *as if* that can never form the arch of interaction the metaphor can. The correlates of the simile are essentially isolated much more than they are interactive.

The "picture" of woman that Tarafa left is really a relief, richly nuanced and adorned through the simile, but contained in the external physical splendour: it wholly belongs to the sheer reality, regardless of its (physical) beauty; it matches the real world in which it is passively present.

Tarafa's description also offers something else interesting and important for the poetics of old *qaṣīda* and which I will later contrast with the "description" of woman in the Qur'anic Text. Namely, the quoted passage offers a number of erotic indications. The second couplet is already a suggestion of the erotic, with the woman putting double strings of pearls and emeralds on her bare neck. A woman's bare neck is erotic and this eroticism is increased by the bracelets on it, which almost appear as a coital symbol, or a signal. The woman intensifies this symbolism/signalisation by *stretching* her neck, like a gazelle in brushwood stretching her neck to obtain fruit. In a further interpretation, stretching the neck suggests erotic activity. The bare and not accidentally long neck represents an excellent erotonym, and the stretching of the neck for *fruit* works in the same direction, because the fruit the bare neck wants to reach may, in the first place, represent the stretching of the neck for the erotic quality of the opposite sex, as the need for erotic gratification.[12] Deep red lips are an erotonym that needs no explanation, except that it is here enriched with multiplied comparative correlates: a flower, warmth, a sand-hill, all of which are cooperative erotonyms, particularly the sand-hill, an extremely frequent erotic symbol in Old Arabic poetry, owing to its being ideally rounded and soft at the same time.[13] Finally, the greatest erotic age of a woman is indicated in the first and last couplets of this quotation: the woman is like a *young gazelle*; her face does not display either a childlike grimace or wrinkles as heralds of old age and erotic withering.[14] Light and its effects are then introduced into the simile: brightness, warmth, a smile, the sun, pear-like teeth typical of youth, etc.[15] Therefore, everything in this description testifies to the most favourably highlighted "erotic capacities" of a woman. However, there is something interesting with regard to this eroticism that I find worthy of further elaboration so as to explain a general atmosphere of realism devotedly created by old poetry, which I will contrast with the Qur'anic Text in a discussion to follow.

Despite an abundance of erotonyms, the eroticism of Tarafa's description remains in indications only, merely hinting at what these erotonyms should open like a gateway. In the first place, it is remarkable how distant the poet remains from this woman – at both a physical and erotic distance – to describe her in such detail. What is particularly interesting is that this erotic distancing is achieved by describing the woman's physical details: almost everything in this section of Tarafa's poem belongs to an erotic description, but persistent attention to visible erotic symbols screens the essence of eroticism that, as I have said, remains only a suggestion. The poet is delighted at the *appearance* of his beloved, but is restrained with regard to the "content" of her eroticism – with regard to love. A deep sigh is unknown to old poetry. The poet could write about any woman like this, since two important aspects of particularising their relationship are nowhere to be "seen": there are no indications of the poet's romantic (spiritual) involvement with the described woman; the woman is static, despite the action of stretching her eroticised neck, etc. There are no spiritual developments in the poem, no erotic sparkling. Its static nature is further underlined by a sequence of descriptions with simile correlates from the real physical world: it is this superabundant, almost unstoppable amassment of physical realities – both that of the woman herself and the correlates to the woman's physical qualities – that underlines the realism of the image to such an extent that the woman, as an *object* of description, not as the subject of an action, looks like a magnificent statue. This is why this poetry has been accused of "materialism". Its woman is objectified, reified. The use of erotonyms – which suggest eroticism and which could end up in passion – in the poem, as well as their remaining at the physical level, have created a particular tension with the reader, but with everything still remaining on the surface, in the realm of physical reality: despite the words *light*, *warmth*, *whiteness*, etc. – everything is just a cold shine of the *external world*, even of the poet's steadfastly "externalising" relationship to the woman. Moreover, it would be wise to exclude the term *relationship* here, as there actually is none – everything is placed in a panorama of physical reality, yielding to observation and comparative description, without interaction, without personalisation. This characterises the Bedouin's attitude to the world in general, including a *beautiful* world.

The description of woman in the *Qur'an* is considerably more modest than descriptions we can find in pre-Qur'anic poets, including those writing after the revelation of the *Qur'an*. In addition to this, it is important to keep in mind two facts that appear to be contradictory. Namely, the analysis of Tarafa's description of a woman, representative of Old Arabic poetry, raises an important issue: How can we explain the fact that the Qur'anic Text depicts the woman quite modestly while, at the same time, a majority of believers consider her one of the most, if not the most valuable gift of the Other World; is it not reasonable to expect this gift, as a first-class one in the Other World, to be depicted in much more captivating terms?! I find the second issue to be paradoxical as well: Since the houri as a Jannah woman is modestly portrayed, how can it be that in Bosnian, and in many other languages too, this noun has won the status of a metaphor: recall that an extraordinarily beautiful woman is said to be a *real houri*!

Before offering an analysis of this apparent paradox, which results from an inadequate understanding of the Text, I will give several quotations related to this topic. In fact, I have already quoted these passages in an abbreviated form, and I will now give them integrally so as, paradoxically, to get a better view of their meagreness. I will offer several of them to demonstrate that the woman-houri is mentioned in relatively few places in the Text, as well as that her description is relatively scanty.

Surah 55 imparts that in the Other World there will be

> Two other gardens of dark green (ayahs 62–64)

further stating that

> In each, the fair, the beauteous ones/Which then of the bounties of your Lord will ye twain deny?!/With large dark eyeballs, kept close in their pavilions/Which then of the bounties of your Lord will ye twain deny?!/Whom man hath never touched, nor any djinn.[16]

The same surah, in ayah 56, indicates the bashfulness and chastity of houris:

> Therein shall be the damsels with retiring glances, whom nor man nor jinn hath touched before them.

Surah 56 reads:

> Of a rare creation have we created the Houris,/And we have made them ever virgins,/Dear to their spouses, of equal age with them.[17]

Surah 78 brings an ayah saying there will also be

> Damsels with swelling breasts, their peers in age.[18]

Other places in the Text, which are also very few, convey that women and (men) in Jannah

> decked shall they be therein with bracelets of gold, and green robes of silk and rich brocade shall they wear.[19]

Beside these, similar quotations could hardly be found – in any case, they are few and scanty in relation to their merit as a reward in Jannah.

These descriptions can, in the first place, illustrate several characteristics in terms of women's physical appearance, if it is indeed at all possible to talk about physical appearance in the Qur'anic description; this questionability is my point.

Houris are named for their markedly big eyes (a feature of Oriental female beauty); they could be called *big-eyed* in translation. This is the first indication of their physical qualities. We further find some physical qualities that are quite unspecified in relation to the poet's: *the fair, the beauteous ones*; *virgins*; [women] *of equal age*; *peers in age*, with only one erotic phrase – *damsels with swelling breasts, their peers in age*.

However, these ayahs offer many more strong indications of spirituality, unlike the pre-Islamic *al-Mu'allaqāt:* they are *beauteous ones* but are also *soft-hearted*; they are *dear*; they have *retiring glances*, etc. Thus, while on the one hand the Qur'anic ayahs forestall eroticisation and restraint in relation to descriptions in pre-Islamic poetry, on the other hand there is a new quality introduced at the same time – *soft hearth, dearness, retiring glances*. All these are attributes that even emphasise non-eroticism in their direct meaning; they refer to the *softness of the female soul* (unlike *physicality* in poetry) which is non-erotically complemented by explicative terms *virgin, retiring glance*, etc. Even the phrase *damsels with swelling breasts* does not seem erotically heaving in this semantic context. Therefore, it is obvious that the *Qur'an* avoids eroticising the houri by emphasising her spiritual and, in particular, *moral* qualities; these attributes are also supported by an ayah repeated several times: *whom nor man nor jinn hath touched before them*.

A non-erotic representation is also achieved through frequent introduction of covers, which is mostly absent from the poet's description of woman, or is very rare. Thus, in several places the *Qur'an* says that women, among the triumphant inhabitants of Jannah, will also be clothed in *silk robes, rich brocade*, etc.[20] Beside the intended non-eroticism, these implements (silk, bracelets, etc.) should be understood as sub-metaphors of the grandiose metaphor of Jannah: garments and jewellery metaphorically represent values women attach great importance to.

Any close comparison of a typical description in Tarafa's poem and the Qur'anic one will lead to a conclusion about their contrariness in terms of the realism of scenes/objects. Apart from the information about houris' big eyes and a very general suggestion of swelling breasts, there are no other (erotic) physical details; houris are fluid, their beauty is rather unspecified (*beauteous ones*) and general – the reader does not actually have as subtle a notion of their physical appearance as he does of the woman in the poem. While the poet's woman can be seen as if painted and in full allure, and yet only physical in a physical dimension, the appearance of a houri is only suggested alongside dominant information about her moral and spiritual qualities. While the first type of woman provokes primarily a sexual urge, the houri elicits affection, closeness, a particular kind of fondness that does not exclude sexuality but that comes as a result of the first *feeling*, not of *perception*.

The difference between these two descriptions is fundamental in terms of a relationship to the woman, whose spirituality and chastity are, according to Qur'anic descriptions, of primary importance, while in the poem the situation is just the opposite. This is a consequence of the vast, epochally revolutionising changes in the conception of the world as expressed by pre-Islamic poetry and that expressed by the Qur'an. This change could be made obvious in any aspect by citing other examples, including those explicitly governing relationships between sexes, but my topic directs me toward analysis by stylistic means in the texts.

It is almost unnecessary to analyse the realism of the poet's description: the woman in the poem is presented extremely realistically, ever so contained in her physical appearance – like a most picturesque synthesis of an oasis and a sandy desert landscape waved with curves of sand dunes, bathing in light and comfortably warm from the sun. The woman in the *Qur'an* is beauteous indeed, but she is not as real-life and reified as the one in the poem: the houri's *moral oasis* is her virginity and meekness, her warmth is the softness of her heart, her curves are in her gentleness. The contrast is too obvious. Nevertheless, this does not exhaust an analysis of stylistic means in the texts: it will keep revealing fundamental differences between the two texts and their "understanding" of the world.

The poem is dominated by figures of description or, more precisely, by the simile that I have established as especially functional in realistic presentation. There is no simile in the Qur'anic "description" at all: houris, as everything else in the quoted passages, are represented by means of their names, without comparative gradations, without comparisons with values of any of the worlds. The absence of simile is a stylistic fact of crucial importance for further analysis, before which attention must be drawn to differences in nuances of description.

The poet's description is exceptionally rich – always in the realm of the physical! – while the Qur'anic description is not so rich and is not primarily in the realm of the physical. A reader accustomed to "realism" or factuality in reading will favour the poet's description owing to a wealth of description figures that conjure up a described object more vividly. Transferring such a reading habit to the Qur'anic "description" as well, the reader will be surprised. However, this involves two quite different stylistic means and their different ranges.

The houri is not described in the real but eschatological world, and that world is completely on the other side of the Bedouin's horizon and of our experience. That world is quite unknown to us, beyond our reach and, as such, incomparable. What can we compare the houri with, what values of this world – or, what values of that world when we have no experiential knowledge of them?! One symbol of beauty in this world – a stunningly beautiful woman – is transposed, as a supreme value, to the Other World which cannot be said to represent a reality of the type this world represents. Therefore, these are distinctly different contexts, or ambiences, where, considering the indescribable differences between them, the "same object" cannot be represented by the same means and in terms of the same qualities. Furthermore, keeping in mind the profound differences between the two worlds, not even the "object" itself can be the same. The Text could have described the houri adding much more piquant details, but it does not insist on them because with such an approach, or description, it would have achieved the same that the poet had already achieved, perhaps even more than that: it would have offered a quite realistic and eroticised representation of the woman, while neither is its aim. Let us imagine the houri described as a glorious beauty, with white teeth and dark gums, with the maximally eroticised neck – all but radiating sexuality! It would be highly inappropriate to the sacredness of the Text, no matter how much men will project their sexual desire to the Other World. That is why the enjoyment with women in the Other World is but a vain projection of this lust.

Woman as an extraordinary symbol of beauty and merit in this world is transferred *as a metaphor* for one of the greatest rewards and merits of the Other World. *Houri* is a metaphor, not a reality. She is, as the highest ornament of this reality, transferred to a world that, if real, is certainly not real in the way familiar to us here. The concept of ideal woman and everything she stands for is *transferred* to the metaphor of *houri* representing the sum of the greatest pleasure that God will bestow on true believers and those submitted to Him. The Text could have said, for example, that a true believer will be given a *reward* in Jannah that will *make him happy like the most beautiful woman in this world*. This would be a simile with different effects than those of the metaphor, as it would be unambiguous, unelliptical: it would be known immediately and it would be known to everyone that it is not a woman after all but something completely different, and this knowledge would "impoverish" the expectations of those reading the Text literally. The *houri* is not represented by figures of description – which is why the simile is absent either – because it is a metaphor: a metaphor is a transcended simile, and there is no possibility for the metaphor, or one of its constituents (as only one is visible indeed) to be brought back to the simile; it is stylistically impossible and even illogical. For instance, when we say of the stars on a clear night sky: *They are pearls*, there is no possibility to proceed to a simile then, as a simile is already contained in this metaphor, but is also subsequently transcended. The beginning of the metaphoric arch is the real woman, as the poet described her and as we know her in a most positive experience, while the other end of the arch is the *houri* that *implies* all the qualities of the woman from the beginning of the arch, or in our reality; a simile is not possible here as it has become redundant. But, the other end of the metaphoric arch (*the houri*) is, in a metaphor, never the same as its first constituent; rather, their similarity with regard to a certain quality is highlighted in a particular way. The first simile correlate is elided, it is not visible, but its qualities are transferred – never literally, as the context will not allow it – to the second constituent of a metaphor, while the first correlate itself remains "visible" in terms of these qualities. Saying of the night stars that they are pearls, we have transferred the name of the first constituent (*pearls*) to the second constituent (*the stars*) whose name is absent, but the context (watching the sky and possibly pointing at it) makes it clear that our reference is not to pearls in the literal sense. Therefore, the metaphor has the ability to "curve" reality in a particular way, to shift it powerfully, expressing our relation to what we denote by the metaphor.

The houri is, therefore, the same as pearls in the abovementioned metaphor. It is a sign for something the name of which cannot be seen, is not stated; what can be seen is only the first constituent – a gorgeously beautiful big-eyed woman – whose qualities signify something that is *not a woman*. Reality is here even more "curved" and shifted as the arch is much bigger than the one in the metaphor of night pearls: an experiential distance between this world and the Other is infinitely larger than that in the case of someone watching the night sky and its stars. It is this experiential distance, or the essential difference between this and the Other World, that represents the *context* that will not allow for the houri to be taken literally as a woman. It is unthinkable that the afterlife will simply repeat this world: it is too simplified to believe that, in the Other World, people will play on swings, with fruits within arm's reach, surrounded with beautiful women. It would be really tedious, considering the Eternity.

This metaphor, like others working on the same principle, has a high aesthetic value, but this value is not its ultimate goal: being aesthetic, it performs its cognitive function as well. Its task is to present something that cannot be represented in any other language. Rewards of the Other World are transcended, they are beyond our perception and knowledge, on the other side of our entire experience, and since they must be presented to believers in their great allure, then there is no other way to express them except by means of the metaphor. Science is helpless here because it strives towards exactness, precision, while the human mind cannot exactly and precisely grasp the immeasurable sum of goods in the Other World. Thus the metaphor emerges as the only cognitive means that portrays "its object" in vague outlines, but with undoubtedly great value potential that is impossible to measure exactly.

As I have said, the woman represents an ideal pleasure to the man, so she is, as a *value*, transferred to the concept of houri as an unknown but exceptionally high value of the Other World. She is not a reality and is hence quite "different" from the one in the poet's verses. Therefore, the metaphor emerged as the dominant stylistic means in the *Qur'an*, replacing the stylistic means dominant in old poetry. While this poetry was tightly linked to the reality of its world, it preferred and favoured figures of description of this world, but the *Qur'an* radically changed Bedouin views of the world and life, enriching them with completely new qualities that, for the purpose of presentation, required new means of expression as well. For the Bedouin poet realism was the highest achievement, but for the Qur'anic Text the ultimate goal and range is the non-realistic Other World impossible to describe definitively (in terms of a travelogue), only to be imagined on the basis of the type of knowledge offered by the language of metaphor. Clearly, as much as the Text came to save the true faith, so the abundance of its metaphors came to save the World from shutting itself in realism, and to save the Awareness of values beyond the horizon of this reality.

Nevertheless, whatever is behind the horizon of the Bedouin's or of this reality belongs to another time and space. Completeness of the Bedouin's world, as represented in poetry, is completely surpassed, as well as the use of the past in gradations; in fact, the Qur'anic Text imparts the incompleteness of the world, surpassing its ancient transparency and, in particular, imparts the Future as the ultimate meaning of the past and the present. At the same time, the poetic postulates of distance and transparency are questioned. All this imposes an important task of using language and poetics to express the state of processuality.

Past time of the simile and processuality of the metaphor

The metaphor is generally not characterised by a positioning in time. In fact, it can be temporally positioned by means of certain grammatical categories outside the metaphor itself – or, by means of certain syntactic tools or of the context, the metaphor is structurally situated in a certain time, while the very essence of the metaphor, beyond the scope of linguistic means, is characterised by processuality that can be positioned in any time.

I will give an example from surah 55, which abounds in metaphor:

> And beside these [shall be] two other *gardens* –
> Which then of the bounties of your Lord will ye twain deny?! –
> *Of a dark green* –
> Which then of the bounties of your Lord will ye twain deny?! –
> With *gushing fountains* in each –
> Which then of the bounties of your Lord will ye twain deny?! –
> In each [are] *fruits* and the *palm* and *the pomegranate* –
> Which then of the bounties of your Lord will ye twain deny?! –
> In each [shall be] *the fair, the beauteous ones* –
> Which then of the bounties of your Lord will ye twain deny?! –
> With *large dark eyeballs*, kept close in their *pavilions*.[21]

In the original, in the quoted passage, there is no verb expressing the future time and it has to be deduced from the general context established by a relatively distant ayah 31 of the same surah, containing a morphological future tense appearing for the first time here: *We will find leisure to judge you* (*sanafruġ lakum*). However, if we focus on metaphors only, we can observe they express non-temporality: two other gardens/of a dark green/two gushing fountains/fruits and the palm and the pomegranate/the fair, the beauteous ones/pavilions and houris kept in them.

Apart from the morphological future in ayah 31, the widest context situates these metaphors within the unknown future of the Other World, but the metaphor as such can be placed in any time whatsoever. This marked indifference of the metaphor towards temporality is a result of its processuality as one of its central features. In a poetic contrast with old poetry, the relation of the metaphor to the category of time has far-reaching consequences.

Old Arabic poetry, as we have seen, is poetically focused on a past time that is relatively richly graded. Even the use of the morphological present is transformed into the narrative present. The reason behind this is that the Bedouin's world is completed, shaped, so that the travelogue and narrative character of the *qaṣīda* focuses on this completeness of the world optimally expressed by the past time. Closely related to this is the category of distance and transparency. This was thoroughly discussed in relation to the simile as the most important stylistic means for expressing the pre-Islamic Arabian's attitude towards the world.

However, since the metaphor is a stylistic dominant of the *Qur'an*, it expresses a different attitude towards the world. As a matter of fact, no stylistic means can underline processuality – which means the incompleteness of the world – as the metaphor can. It expresses tension as a kind of particularly active state which is not fixed, which is changeable in accordance with the changeability of our relationship to constituents of the metaphor and to the meaning it conveys. For, I have already said that the "knowledge" the metaphor offers about something is different from the knowledge offered by reason and positive science – it is fluid in a way, with changeable outlines, and somewhat dependent on the recipient's ability to reach a very wide range of its meanings. Someone will ruin the metaphor, for example, through the interpretation that those rewarded in the Other World will frequent pavilions with houris chosen for them, while someone will understand pavilions and houris as a metaphor for the highest good.

Therefore, it is very important to understand the metaphor as processuality expressing the incompleteness of everything it tries to present through its powers. A work such as the *Qur'an* – enormously rich in metaphors, from "monolithic" ones (*pavilions* or *the houri*) to grandiose metaphors such as *Jannah* with plenty of "sub-metaphors", or even the entire *Other World* – in essence and in its major part expresses this very processuality as a key feature of the world, which is why the metaphor is its dominant.

At the level of ideology, the *Qur'an* made a historic turnabout by translating the pre-Islamic pagan worldview from its ancient simplicity, transparency and completeness into an essentially different quality – into the awareness of and faith in the incompleteness of the world and its transience,[22] which is, in relation to the Eternity, reduced to the momentary, even to illusiveness in relation to the quality of Eternity. The turnabout is complete.

Considering such a relation between this and the Other World, between the momentary and Eternity, it is obvious that much more importance is attached to what is "beyond the horizon" and beyond experience of this world, which further implies increasing the distance from the transparency of the Bedouin's horizon towards something that cannot be seen and can only be conceived of through metaphor. In other words, the *Qur'an* optimally highlighted processuality as a radical transcendence of the Bedouin's view of a perfectivised world. Considering the undoubted revolutionising of the world by the Text, this turnabout clearly could not have stayed with the same poetics, with the same stylistic means, not even with the same language in the field of its semantics or even syntax: the Text reversed the poetics – it turned inductive poetics into deductive poetics; it altered stylistics, releasing the dominant simile into the past and promoting the metaphor as its stylistic dominant; it enriched language in the field of semantics, with the metaphor deserving great credit for it. The world represented by the *Qur'an* – both the transient and the forthcoming one (ever-present processuality!) – cannot be expressed, it is now obvious, by the simile, but by other stylistic means, among which the metaphor is the most privileged.

By preferring the metaphor, the Qur'anic Text enriched semantics enormously, which is not typical of pre-Islamic poetry. For the metaphor – apart from its epistemological potentials, but also because of them – is quite prone to and quite capable of undreamed-of semantic innovations and expansions of meaning. This ability is largely a consequence of the metaphor not being bound to time but to processuality, to expressing a certain state and tension in "similitude". It is always dynamic, intensified in the aspiration to express a state that is much more than the similitude of simile correlates, so that operating in its own particular way in the domain of epistemology, it simultaneously operates in semantic terms as well. It follows from this that the metaphor is "warmer" and more immediate; it is non-distanced.

There are many examples illustrating this, but I will stay with those that I have mostly used so far and that are commonplaces in the Text.

The meaning of *houri* – a big-eyed woman generally – is considerably enriched with the metaphoric processuality. We have seen that this word became a metaphor for an extraordinary value of the Other World, which is one level of its enrichment: the *houri* is no longer a big-eyed woman, but much more than this. However, in the return arch of the metaphor, the optimally enriched word *houri*, when used as a metaphor for an exquisite woman of this world, denotes a woman that does not have the same qualities as the other-worldly *houri*, but the ideality built in this metaphor remains, as the very heart of the metaphor, because the metaphor always strives to express the optimum, so that this-worldly *houri* is a successful "semantic echo" of the *houri* as the other-worldly metaphor. In this discussion, two things should be kept in mind.

First, in the metaphoric arch stretching from this-worldly *houri* to the other-worldly metaphor and back, we can observe an important change in semantics: this-worldly *houri* is not only a big-eyed woman any more, she was not so in the first place, but when a woman is said to be a *houri*, then the whole sum of her qualities is implied – from a number of physical qualities to a pleasant disposition, yielding nature but, at the same time, to faithfulness, loyalty, etc. The quality of being big-eyed remains confined to etymology, while the noun *houri* itself has "picked up" all the best qualities of both worlds on its long and never-ending metaphoric journey and, precisely owing to the metaphor, has thus turned what before was merely a big-eyed woman (which is only one of its attributes) into something hardly describable by a number of attributes. Semantics is thus enormously enriched.

Second, it is interesting to observe which direction implies greater enrichment in meaning with this type of metaphor. In the language we use to describe this world, a *houri* is a woman with only one attribute: big-eyed (Ar. *ḥawrā'*, pl. *ḥūr*=big-eyed woman). Through its transfer into a metaphor for woman, or for the good of the highest order in the Other World, this attribute is enriched so much so that it turns into an ideal, perhaps even into the Idea-of-Beautiful-as-Good. After this meaning expansion, following its return arch, the metaphor must of necessity leave something behind, but it does convey its tension, its lasting need to always convey an optimum of specified content in the process, in the transfer of meaning.

The same example applies to Jannah, for instance, and generally to metaphors of a markedly "sacred" nature. Metaphors of the other type – those that are not "markedly sacred" – do not achieve such extreme enrichment, but also harbour the metaphoric drive for semantic field expansion. For example, the *pavilion* metaphor in the quoted passage is enriched, through a transfer of meaning, with ideal isolation, rest, intimacy, etc. The same applies to *mansions* promised to the rightly guided.[23]

The simile cannot accomplish such complex tasks. In terms of semantic innovation, it is helpless, as it were, even indifferent, since relations between the correlates in a simile remain formal and artificial: the distance between them is prominent and insurmountable, with the *as if* component being always emphasised – which means that *it is not, after all*, and despite elements of similitude, a difference between the correlates is always underlined by the presence, or even obviousness, of both correlates, as they express the awareness of presence and transparency. In addition to underlining distance, the simile is clearly non-processual owing to the aforementioned formalisation in comparability, and to the distance of the correlates, which does not generate tension as the metaphor does. Simile correlates are static, separate and do not express identification of the kind we find in metaphor. This is an essential difference between them. For instance, Tarafa's simile *One like a young gazelle* does not establish an active relationship of identification between the correlates; this relation is of a formal nature; the distance between the correlates is virtually insurmountable, and much larger differences than similarities are actually *visible to the naked eye*. There is no process of closeness, identification or emphasis. The metaphor, in contrast, implies all this.

Owing to these specific features of the figure of simile and the trope of metaphor, there are significant differences in their perception as well. The simile can never be understood literally: its correlates, as can be seen, are too distant and too different for identification to be possible, or for qualities of one correlate to be fully transferred to the other until the level at which one correlate can withdraw in favour of the other, and when there arises a possibility of literal understanding *as well*. Not even the formal structure of the simile can allow this.

In the metaphor, however, there happens exactly what is impossible in the simile. In a formal structure, one constituent withdraws in favour of the other, so that, to an insufficiently sensitive and insufficiently responsive recipient of literary values, the metaphor can also have a literal meaning. Only the context can save the metaphor from literal understanding, and if its recipient is not sufficiently sensitised to recognising this context the metaphor is lost. Since elision of one constituent in the metaphor makes room for an enormous closeness of meaning – or since transfer in the metaphor is all but total (it is only simulated in the simile, in a very obvious way), the metaphor strongly suggests the "overlooking" of a very important metaphoric context – or it attempts to optimally relativise this context, to "dilute" its outlines, as the success of a metaphor greatly depends on it, but the context has to stay – nevertheless the effect of such "dilution" of the metaphoric context on some recipients is that they cannot see it at all. Therefore, the fact that the metaphor can be understood literally (which is never the case with the simile!) indicates to what degree it expresses processuality and closeness with the recipient's awareness. Thus, it is frequently the case – it seems particularly among Arabs, but among other Muslims too – that many Qur'anic metaphors pertaining to eschatology are taken in their literal meaning.

It may be an advantage of the metaphoric language of the *Qur'an*. Namely, as I have said, the *Qur'an*'s ultimate goal is to offer arguments, not to pursue aestheticism, implying that what it finds most important is to inspire and keep alive faith in people, whether through the literal or metaphorical allure of the Other World. If someone takes it literally, so much the better, but such understanding is not necessary for believing. The Qur'anic metaphor works on both levels, which need not be mutually conditioned.

For example, the *houri* is not a beautiful big-eyed woman who will serve to please male sensuality in the Other World. In a higher sphere of understanding, the context that discourages such understanding of the *houri* is, simply, the Other World. I cannot imagine it as a repeat of this existence, be it even a greatly improved version of This World, because the Eternity and Infinite-God's-Grace are incompatible with playing on swings, with diverse fruits always (O tedium!) within arm's reach, sensual pleasure with women, etc. The context of Eternity and the all-embracing divergence of the two worlds prevents the *houri* (I use her as one pleasant example among many examples) from being understood literally. And what about the pavilions where the *houris* are kept? I cannot possibly imagine the Other World with tents!

Nevertheless, sacred metaphors are specific, owing to their specific context I am discussing here. They offer the recipient an opportunity to create a context, opening even the meaning of literacy to them. The specificity of context lies in its non-obviousness, in fluidity and, consequently, in its relativity, or subjectivity, unlike non-sacred metaphors.

For example, when I am looking at the clear night sky with someone and say: *What wonderful pearls these are!* the context is so salient that it cannot be overlooked and the metaphor cannot be understood literally. However, no metaphor for the Other World has an obvious and experientially familiar context that would conserve it as a metaphor for everyone and at all times. This is why some people – owing to the context being undefined – *create* this context themselves: they believe in a repeat of physical existence (food, drink, clothes, sensuality, etc.) and, in a context thus created, they deal not with metaphors but with description.

In consequence, such understanding of metaphor in sacred texts, or its interpretation in a literal sense, deprives it of its cognitive or epistemological function. As long as we understand it as a metaphor, it offers us a kind of precious knowledge of specific and momentous values. However, as soon as it is understood in its literal meaning, the metaphor ceases to perform its epistemological function and translates into a description: in this case Jannah, for instance, is described as future reality; it is simply portrayed, we know everything about it, or a major portion of its most important amenities, and I have already defined this as impoverishment of the unimaginable good.

Reduced to a description, the metaphor loses some other important functions, in addition to its epistemological one. It loses processuality as its most important quality: a description is static, it "portrays" an environment as such, not as it could be; on the other hand, metaphor makes ceaseless and exciting "cognitive vibrations", because the recipient of the metaphor imagines, following its instructions, the environment and states that which cannot be described but only metaphorically discerned. In this regard, the metaphor represents a precious *process*, while description a *perfective state*.

Another essential quality the metaphor loses through literal understanding is its precious non-realism of a particular kind. Namely, owing to its relative openness to subjective metaphorical "perception", the meanings of a metaphor cannot be firmly reified, unchangeable. Description, on the other hand, is based on the opposite: it describes de facto, and always strives to obstruct subjective "curving" made by the metaphor. Description implies a distance, while the metaphor "*internal*" whirling. Should momentous Qur'anic metaphors be translated into description, the Other World is then quite impoverished – in its positive and negative aspects, so that the style the Text is so proud of is also unjustly impoverished to an extreme degree. Finally, in that case the stylistic supernaturalism of the Text would be made relative to the previous and following traditions, which is baseless, after all.

However, there is yet another important argument concerning the predominance of metaphor in the Text – predominance related to surpassing tradition characterised by the flat transparency of the world, best expressed by figures of description, particularly the simile.

Transparency of the world in the simile and the metaphoric vertical world order

A condition for the simile is the transparency of its correlates and of the relation the simile is realised in. In a travelogue-description simile of the old *qaṣīda*, transparency is complete. Moreover, success of the simile is proportionate to the obviousness of the correlates and their comparability in a certain aspect. Since the simile is predominant in this poetry's expression of a worldview, it means that the world of the pre-Islamic Arabian is completely transparent and, as such, flat, "horizontal". Owing to this, the ancient unity of man and the world is achieved. The *Seven Golden Odes* express such optimum unity within which the world is spread before man in its entirety; as a corpus, they are also within reach of epic totality, which later Arabic literature never managed to come so close to.

The Qur'anic Text made a turnabout by means of the language of metaphor. I have already said that it highlighted the incompleteness of the world, its transience as a central quality. Totality was taken away from the world. Considering this transience, the quality of the relationship between man and the world changed considerably, because man could no longer see the possibility for achieving totality in his unity with this but with the Other World. Man's fulfilment in this world is but a short stage in Eternity. At the same time, the "borderlines" of this world, which the pre-Islamic Arabian saw as the whole world left to his description, and the borderlines of his life transformed into the *gates* for a triumphal entry into the Other World and its Eternity. At this moment description became helpless; the metaphor became necessary.

Namely, the Other World with all its content was identified as a priority, as a value that draws all the attention and that can be strived towards through cognisance. At the same time, that world is non-transparent and unreachable by any powers of description. Nevertheless, it should be noted that, owing to the turn-about, there was also a turn of the perspective expressed, on the one hand, by the simile and, on the other, by the metaphor.

While the world of the *Seven Golden Odes* was organised flatly, horizontally, as this made it most transparent, the Qur'anic Text organises the world vertically, as the Vertical provides a superior point of departure and a refuge, and as the Vertical is, at the same time, not transparent, not obvious and as such not yielding itself to description and similes of the realistic type. Of course, I do not refer to the physical dimension under the term *Vertical* – i.e. in a literal sense, as something literally above our heads – but I use the *Vertical* as a metaphor for the Primeval Origin, Absolute Superiority, Sublime Meaning, Value of the highest possible order, Divine Authority, etc. Simultaneously, and in accordance with the aforementioned, the Vertical represents the "dimension" that promotes metaphor in the best possible way. Namely, since contents in the Vertical are non-transparent and non-obvious, only the metaphor can soar towards them, as a specific and actually the only means of cognisance.

It is no accident that, for its communication with the world, the *Qur'an* insists on the verb *nazala*, which basically always means *to descend*: descent is the only adequate way of the Text's arrival to the World, and also the best way to promote the Vertical as the organisational principle of the World, according to which God and the Origin of the Text are at the absolute top of values. The same principle applies to the path to Eternity: souls *ascend* to God, angels *ascend* to Him, etc. (Generally, man instinctively turns his gaze to *verticality* in moments when he wants to "communicate" with God affectively, in ecstasy, despair, etc.) Therefore, the descent of the Text, or the ascent of the soul, angels, etc. should not be understood literally, but as very successful metaphors whose possible meanings I have already mentioned. Since, as I have said, the metaphor expresses a specific understanding of the world, in this case it also means that an abundance of Qur'anic metaphors, including the *descent/getting down*, expresses a (re)ordering of the world in which its flatness and transparency end and are replaced with an infinite Vertical whose great meaning is in ethical rearrangement of the world. For, we have seen that the pre-Islamic transparency of the world implies that virtually everything is transparent; even the deities could have been taken in by a single look in the Kaaba, in a *narrow* space and in an inappropriate potter's clay *materialism*. With such an attitude towards the world, its ethic arrangement and quality cannot be essentially different: it remains superficial, "two-dimensional". This is the realm of poetry indeed. Unlike this, only the Vertical can ensure the highest Authority – it is not possible in a flat dimension of the world; it is inexpressible in "horizontal" communication. Verticality and Authority are in a certain proportion. Even when Adam and his wife Eve, having sinned against God's command, were expelled from Jannah to Earth, God's decision was not communicated to them as *move*; *go to the other side, to the other world*, etc. In this motif recurring in the Text several times, as the most dramatic moment in the divine history of the world, a verb expressing the verticality principle is most frequently used:

> And we said, "O Adam, dwell thou and thy wife in the Garden, and eat ye plentifully there from wherever ye list; but to this tree come not nigh, lest ye become of the transgressors." But Satan made them slip from it, and caused their banishment from the place in which they were. And we said, "Get ye down! The one of you an enemy to the other: and there shall be for you in the earth a dwelling place, and a provision for a time."[24]

The key word in this context is *Get down!* (*'Ihbiṭū!*). It implies the Vertical as a metaphor. As a matter of fact, the verb *get down* is itself a metaphor imparting quite a lot about the genesis of the World and its arrangement, certainly from the viewpoint of this sacred Text. It is not necessary to further explain the inadequacy of its literal interpretation: Wherefrom the first man could not have *got down* to the Earth at all if we know that the Earth is round, and that there is no *up* and *down* in the Universe in physical terms. This concerns an ethical universe, and the verb *Get down* has a metaphorical meaning only. The Earth too can have an ethical meaning in this context: the descent to the Earth is a metaphor for degradation, for demotion to a world of hardship and temporariness, quite distant from the sum of blessings at the Top of the Vertical.[25]

Therefore, it becomes obvious to a careful reader of the Text that the world was completely transformed from a flat to a vertical arrangement. The unity of man and the world is not destroyed but only organised in a different way. These two principles of world organisation can by no means be expressed in texts with identical poetics: the pre-Islamic Arabian poetics is inductive and normative, while the poetics of the Qur'anic Text is deductive and indifferent to any kind of normativeness. In line with this, their dominant stylistic means are also different: the pre-Islamic poetics prefers the simile due to its inherent transparency and presence, while the Qur'anic poetics is represented by the metaphor, considering its unique ability to express the importance of the world's non-transparency and vertical order.

It seems that the predominance of metaphor in the *Qur'an* implies yet another feature expressed at the level of form. Pre-Islamic poetry developed its form to technical perfection. The homophonous monorhyme and single metre in the poem could not be disrupted. Several reasons lie behind this strict insistence on the precision (and monotony!) of form, and I will discuss some of them elsewhere. In this context, I will offer only one conclusion.

Since the simile, considering its predominance in old poetry, is not able to express an important kind of closeness between the correlates, or in a relation towards the recipient, this is then compensated for through the powerful effects of the form. On the other hand, the metaphor – particularly if it is a stylistic dominant, as it is in the *Qur'an* – has enormous potential for this closeness, even emphasis and ecstasy, so that it does not need such strong support for the form's technicality. One could even claim that bringing the form to the forefront, as was the case with old poetry, caused rivalry and distraction with respect to the priority epistemological efforts of metaphor and generally to the stylistic effects it produced so confidently and self-sufficiently. Hence the *Qur'an* is indeed in prose characterised by rhyme and rhythm, but its Text is not metrically organised, and can even deviate from its rhyme in order to make it relative and wrest it from automatism. The elements of form in old poetry were the only cohesive agents in a general segmentation of structure, whereas the *Qur'an* does need such cohesive agents, since the metaphor can achieve cohesion on its own.

The simile undertaking segmentation and centripetal forces of the metaphor

The simile in Old Arabic poetry generated poem segmentation. One couplet (*bayt*), sometimes even a single line, was confined to one simile; another couplet opened another simile, etc., with each couplet usually representing an independent semantic unit. A number of such units, making the poem, were simply threaded on a single metre and the monorhyme of the poem, which kept them – these semantic units – together like a necklace.[26]

The metaphor also has the possibility of segmentation. Each metaphor, or sub-metaphor, I quoted from the abundance of Jannah metaphors (I could have done the same with Jahannam metaphors, but Jannah ones are airy and pleasant) can be self-sufficient inasmuch as an element of the arabesque is self-sufficient. The level of self-sufficiency is important for preservation of the general principle of arabesque structure. However, each metaphor also has the power with which it strives to surpass segmentation. For instance, the Jannah *houri* is a powerful metaphor and, as such, can be interpreted in relative self-sufficiency. The same applies to Jannah *mansions*, *pavilions*, etc. However, to be understood as metaphors in their full capacity, which indeed is their intention, they need to be mutually connected in order to establish strong interaction at the same time.

If we go back to Tarafa's description of the woman, we can easily see the independence of the simile at the level of structural elements: *his beloved like a young gazelle*, *like a jessamine*, etc. These similes are in a mechanical relation and accumulation; they are hence relatively independent, truly segmented, because one simile does not require the other, nor does the second simile necessarily result from the first. Furthermore, their parallelism and mutual independence are underlined precisely by this sort of cumulativeness. The situation with Qur'anic metaphors, however, is quite different. When the *houri* metaphor is used, it requires its metaphoric and semantic complementation – *retiring glances*; this searches for its complementation in her *virginity*; then complementation is required in terms of a general environment: *various fruits*, *deep shade*, *pavilion*, etc. These metaphors thread in necessary complementation until they reach a synthesis in the grandiose metaphor of *Jannah*. Thus, there is also an "accumulation" with regard to the metaphor, but a completely different one from that related to the simile: sub-metaphors are rather active in their metaphoric and semantic environment where they keep creating meanings. Owing to the exceptional dynamics of re-creativity, to the drive for establishing strong connections, metaphors essentially *create* the world in a special way. While the simile forever remains in description as a record and account of a state *as found*, metaphors (or sub-metaphors) firmly connect a world that they thereby re-create as well. This is one of the reasons I find the metaphor mediates an incomplete world, or even mediates its incompleteness.

If we stay with the complex metaphor of Jannah and consider the formative effects the sub-metaphors produce within it, we will feel the powerful effect of the centripetal force of this grandiose metaphor. Namely, it firmly holds together all its sub-metaphors by means of a powerful centripetal force of Meaning. This brilliantly reveals a huge difference between the metaphor and the simile. While an artefact dominated by the simile implies no centripetal force that would hold together a number of segmented meanings, except a *thread* (I use this word to emphasise the form/formality!) in the form of a single metre and rhyme, the World and the Text created by metaphors are connected by Meaning as an outstanding centripetal force.

Naturally, such effects of the metaphor are conducive to its constant enrichment and expansion – until the point when sub-metaphors create the Universe of Metaphor. For, the metaphor of *Jahannam* is structurally the same; it is inconceivable without *Jannah*, which means that the "gravitational field" keeps expanding. *The Day of Judgement*, with a number of sub-metaphors it keeps together, requires a necessary complementation by *Jannah* and *Jahannam*, etc. – until the Metaphor-Universe called the Other World (*Ākhirah*)[27] that holds together all of the other, extremely graded, metaphors. From this perspective, from this ultimate achievement of the metaphor, this world looks different as well, since an extremely strong gravitational field of the Text and the Other World as the ultimate Meaning and Recourse affects this world as well. As a matter of fact, these forces affect the understanding of this world, affect the awareness of it, not permitting it to "break free", to "get off the hook" and lose itself in the depths of futility.

The metaphor is called upon to uniquely save the World.

Nevertheless, a glowing face of this World is a Tradition that finds literature extremely important, testified to by the fact that the *Qur'an* uses the metaphor so magnificently that it had a fateful influence on the establishment of poetics after its descent into the World, or an influence on the development of entirely new experiences of Tradition.

Notes

1 I am aware of the possible objection that, at certain places in my interpretation, the trope metaphor can be replaced with allegory: certain developed metaphors in the Text can indeed be taken as allegories as well. Acknowledging such a possible objection, I support a number of authorities who believe that the metaphor is the queen of tropes, and that all other tropes can be seen alongside metaphor.

2 The *Qur'an* says that to Allah belong *the most beautiful names* and, according to tradition, there are ninety-nine names of Allah. This statement deserves a separate interpretation. It should only be said here that this actually refers to the same number of His attributes (only *Allah* is His personal noun) always "describing" him in terms of abstract, not physical, qualities. Even the figure *ninety-nine* is, I believe, symbolic: it suggests the practical and absolute indescribability of *Allah*.
3 Of course, a large portion of the Text is not metaphorical – particularly the one governing relations among people, the legal aspect of the community, etc.
4 The *Qur'an* expresses the immense weight of the Text and the responsibility for carrying it in an excellent metaphor: "Had we sent down this Qur'an on some mountain, thou wouldst certainly have seen it humbling itself and cleaving asunder for the fear of God" (*Qur'an*, 59:21).
5 The word *'alaq* was translated as *embryo*, most frequently as *blood clot*, *coagulated blood*, etc.
6 "Kur'anska metafora *Džennet*" [Qur'anic metaphor of Jannah], 2000 *Takvim*, Rijaset Islamske zajednice u Bosni i Hercegovini, Sarajevo, 1999, pp. 11–20.
7 *Qur'an*, 55:70, 72.
8 *Qur'an*, 56:36–37.
9 *Qur'an*, 78:33.
10 *The al-Mu'allaqāt*, pp. 61–63.
11 *Qur'an*, 55:76.
12 Eroticisation of the female body has been present with Arabs from their earliest times to this day. Just as women put beautiful necklaces on their bare necks, sending erotic signals, it is also common for them to put bracelets around their wrists and even anklets around their ankles. This erotic *threading/insetting* of a delicate wrist into a ring not only visualised an erotic act, but anklets around female ankles also jingled as they walked, which powerfully added to the intended visual effect and signal.
13 Old poets often used to compare female curves with sand-hills, particularly the bottom part of the female body that the thighs can "hardly support"; this is a commonplace of old poetry. In Tarafa's description, this figure is successfully innovated by a complex simile where a smile on the deep red lips is like a flower blossoming in a warm sand-hill.
14 Poets most frequently sang of women whose ideal erotic age was at the turn from the age of a girl to that of a mature woman. Thus, Qays says:

> In the evening she brightens the darkness, as if she were the light tower of a monk, A recluse, which is lighted in the evening to guide travelers; Towards one like her, the wise man gazes incessantly, lovingly, when she is well proportioned in height between the wearer of a long dress and the wearer of a short frock.
>
> (*The al-Mu'allaqāt*, p. 44)

15 We can learn from some other poems that women of that time used to darken their gums using special preparations in order to sharpen the contrast with white teeth. This can be seen in the following couplet by Tarafa: "The rays of the sun have watered her teeth all but her gums, which are smeared with Collyrium, While she does not eat anything against the collyrium so as to affect its colour" (*The al-Mu'allaqāt*, p. 62).
16 *Qur'an*, 55:70–74.
17 *Qur'an*, 56:35–37.
18 *Qur'an*, 78:33.
19 *Qur'an*, 18:31.
20 I will give only two examples: (1) "[...] this is the great merit:/Into the gardens of Eden shall they enter, with bracelets of gold and pearl shall they be decked therein, and therein shall their raiment be of silk" (*Qur'an*, 35:32–33); (2) "Their clothing green silk robes and rich brocade: with silver bracelets shall they be adorned, and drink of a pure beverage shall their Lord give them" (*Qur'an*, 76:21).

21 *Qur'an*, 55:62–72. Grammatical categories expressing temporality are isolated in square brackets, as the Original does not actually have them, but they are necessary in translation in order for the text to be read at all and are indicated by the broad context.

22 *The Qur'an* explicates it in the following way as well: "All on the earth shall pass away, but the face of thy Lord shall abide resplendent with majesty and glory" (*Qur'an*, 55:26–27).

23 *Mansions* as a metaphor for a great reward are mentioned several times in the *Qur'an*. For instance: "But for those who fear their Lord are lofty mansions beneath which shall the rivers flow: it is the promise of God, and God will not fail in his promise" (*Qur'an*, 39:20).

The interesting example of the *pavilion* also deserves a short digression. Its specific "metaphoric meaning" is completely reified in some parts of the Arab world. In fact, it implies a particular symbiosis of the metaphorical and the symbolic on the one hand and of the practical on the other. For example, for decades we watched on TV Libyan President Gaddafi (al-Qadhdhāfī) receiving international statesmen in his *tent*. His loyalty to tradition and a sort of eccentricity, rather peculiar creativity in a diplomatic (con)text, have turned the *tent* in Gaddafi's action into a symbol and a metaphor, but a practical working space as well. In proportion to the change of its functions, the *tent* has, as can be seen on TV, extremely enriched its size and comfort, actually retaining only the *idea of a tent*.

24 *Qur'an*, 2:35–36.

25 For the banishment of shaytan, the Text uses the verb *get out* (*ukhruj*); the positions of shaytan and Man are not the same from the moment of their creation to their positioning in Eternity (see *Qur'an*, 7:18). The verb *habaṭa* is most often translated as *get down*, but its semantics includes several meanings that can even be given priority and that express forcefulness and an "optimum incline": *fall down, plunge, tumble down, precipitate*. It would be worthwhile to try to incorporate one of these dramatic meanings into translations, as they are more appropriate to the context and semantics.

26 The metaphor of *necklace* that, long after the Prophet Muhammad, was used in literature for a poem or a literary work generally, does not only express the value of a work, but also indicates its structure. One of the names for the *Seven Mu'allaqāt* corpus is *al-Sumūṭ*, which means Necklaces, in this sense exactly.

27 The Arabic terms for what we call This World and the Other World are quite interesting. We use several different terms (mostly not translations of Arabic terms): *this world, (this) earthly life, the other world, the next world, the afterlife, the hereafter*, etc. However, the Arabic term *Dunya* (*al-Dunyā*) means *the one that is near, that is here, immediate*, etc., while *Akhirah* means *the endmost one, the ultimate*.

6 Maturation of post-Qur'anic poetics and literary tradition

The departure of poetry from the Truth in ideological, primarily religious terms which the *Qur'an* inevitably forced permanently affected the poetics of Old Arabic literature. Faced with the forcefulness of the Text and its uncompromising content, tradition came to a standstill for a short while (mainly during the Prophet's life), impressed and in a way frustrated with the Text's unattainable merit. Yet this tradition was too vital, too precious to the Arabian world, even to the Text itself, to just disappear. Such a wasteland was inconceivable, since poetry was almost the only and a very successful form of Arabian artistic creativity. It would have been inconceivable for the Text itself in the world it descended into, because it firmly established itself precisely among other textual forms, first and foremost among different poetic forms. Nevertheless, this point of origin of Arabic literature, located in the pre-Islamic period, was authentic and there are at least two aspects to be underlined in this respect.

First, pre-Islamic poetry – as far as scholarship is aware – was quite genuine, authentically Arabian, without any foreign influence, which is one of the important reasons why tradition has remained proud of it, until the point when a basis for traditionalism is created. Although it is generally known that other cultures, particularly in their "childhood", also established a supernatural, socially and ideologically privileged status for poetry and poets, this aspect of Arabian poetic tradition was quite original.

Second, pre-Islamic tradition had also engendered a very original poetics that, even hundreds of years later, has not been completely surpassed. Namely, while the *Qur'an* did rearrange its poetics in the field of (religious) content, other important elements of this poetics survived in tradition, through which tradition kept alive the precious memory of its point of origin, adhering to continuity perhaps even too rigidly. All the merits of this form of poetry should be mentioned among these surviving elements: the couplet (*bayt*) structure, identical poetic metre, the principle of arabesque structure, etc. Even the simile as a stylistic dominant was not completely surpassed after the Text's descent: the simile still remained frequent in poetry, but the metaphor remained the stylistic dominant of the sacred Text.

The essence of the entire Arabic-Islamic tradition lies in the fact that, by virtue of its fundamental "formal and structural" characteristics, such pre-Islamic poetics continued to reign even long after the *Qur'an* was revealed. It follows from this that tradition was actually very resourceful: not only did it refuse to completely give way to the Text, but also brought some of its elements forward to the new age, though it was forced to make concessions at the ideological level. Nevertheless, this also established a measure of traditionalism, which I will discuss separately. Traditionalism will actually serve as a red thread throughout my discussion of the poetics of this literature, since traditionalism became its backbone, until its modern poetic turnabouts.

Pre-Islamic poetry, therefore, is like a fresh wellspring: a whole tradition sprang from it and created new beds – though not too deep and with cliffs – but its originality remained forever recognisable. Considering this, we can question the validity of the term *pre-Islamic poetry*. As a matter of fact, one of the fundamental issues of Arabic literature generally is its periodisation, as well as the periodisation of some other great ancient literatures, such as the literature of the European Middle Ages.[1] Keeping in mind the importance of this issue in terms of literary history and theory, I will give a brief overview of it here.

Normative poetics and the difficulty of literature periodisation

All histories of Arabic literature – Oriental and Orientalist – subject it to historical and political periodisation (*pre-Islamic*, *Umayyad*, *Abbasid*, etc.). The problem with such periodisation is much bigger when it is done according to political dynasties in the history of Arab-Islamic caliphate. Such periodisation is non-immanent; it is external, as it reveals nothing of the development of *literature* or its vicissitudes. Historical and political periodisation does not indicate any immanent system of values derived by marking the course of literary development, by comparing and contrasting, poetic directions, stylistic epochs, etc. Hence such periodisation cannot belong to literature that, among other things, must identify value relations among epochs (stylistic and others) and among epochal poets. Periodisation is not a mechanical or arbitrary segmentation of literary history: an adequate methodological approach and evaluation of an ever-living system as literary tradition must yield a periodisation of literary history, not the other way round. Namely, the periodisation of Arabic literary history, of the kind I have already mentioned, is imposed from outside, from a different kind of history, and can therefore not be considered a valid history of *literature*. Nevertheless, such periodisation still survives I think for two reasons, although they cannot justify the absence of *literary* periodisation, which I believe will once be reasonably proposed and thoroughly expounded.

One reason is the extremely strong traditionalism in the history of Arabic literature – a phenomenon that will be permanently present in my discussion in various aspects, with important poetic elements from the entire corpus of old literature at work. Traditionalism was concerned with its own continuity and represented a formidable barrier to changes. However, this is not a reason that can justify the established periodisation since, already at the level of terminology, it clearly shows its own inadequacy (*Umayyad* literature, for example) or even the incompetence of the literary history approach. Even though the main poetic genres (panegyric, lampoon and others) remained predominant until the modern age – throughout all political epochs – there were certain poetic "meanderings" from the pre-Islamic point of origin, such as the flourishing of love lyrics in one period, or the flourishing of bacchius wine poetry in another period, etc. Therefore, the possibility for adequate periodisation should be considered with regard to these lyric and genre innovations in tradition. But, even if they are not powerful enough to characterise an epoch, or to represent a radical renewal of tradition, a periodisation should use terms immanent in scholarly studies of literature and literary production, such as *classicism*, *neoclassicism*, or others corresponding to poetic, not political epochs.

The other reason the aforementioned periodisation survives lies in a methodological approach to literary history. This approach is – occasionally and ephemerally – an impressionistic approach that, as such, is not capable of establishing literature as a *system*, the same literature that, at the same time, exists and functions in history and in the present. Nevertheless, the dominant approach to Arabic literature has always been positivist, regardless of the fact that, in European literary scholarship, positivism has long been gathering dust. This means that the study of Arabic literature is mostly focused on biographic and bibliographic inventorying in history, without establishing the subtlest associations, as formed by art, among different works, particularly among epochs. A meaningful literary history must explain even traditionalism by identifying and presenting the means through which tradition turns into traditionalism. Brockelmann's *History of Arab Literature* – though valuable at certain periods and for certain purposes – has remained a paragon for Arabists. Still, this work is only an excellent, singular *catalogue* presentation of Arabic literature, but not its history, despite its title, because it is not built on value judgements realised only through explaining *relationships* among works and epochs. Brockelmann's *History* is a triumph of positivism and has almost endless merits, but they cannot be the ultimate end of the matter.

As a matter of fact, the history of Arabic literature is handicapped in a particular way and can hardly be expected to be revised soon. Its handicap results from the fact that philology is the doom of Arabic literary history. This literature was a subject of study of Arabic authoritative philology from the early Islamic period throughout the Middle Ages, and then became a subject – until our age – of not only authoritative philology, but Orientalist philology, which used its systematic approach to impose itself as a true science. In the overall new-age Saidian "Orientalist orientalisation of Orient", the philological method imposed itself as unsurpassable on Arab researchers as well and, since the philological method has been predominant in Arab history too, it was only natural that a sort of positivist cooperation and mutual support of authorities should develop between them. Presuming the reader is familiar with the essence of the philological method, I will not give its detailed presentation here, but it should be noted that the results of its research – with emphasis on the German philological school

– were of extreme importance for plucking from obscurity into light and the world of scholarship a vast body of Arabic literature that had been compiled over many centuries.[2] Oriental philology has made an enormous contribution, meticulously and thoroughly studying old texts and establishing their authenticity, as well as publishing whole libraries of critical editions, their philological commentaries and bio-bibliographies. However, this method left a large part of the body of literature in a state of factual presentation, in biographical and bibliographical transparency. It was the best possible preparation for situating this body in terms of literary history, its evaluation, and even periodisation. Nothing more could have been expected from philology as a science. Finally, it should be noted, Oriental philologists – being absolutely committed to their method, in which they were competent – mostly did not care for the diverse theoretical approaches to literature that had meanwhile developed, and thus could not capture their subject matter from the aspects of literary history and poetics. On the other hand, Oriental researchers were themselves fascinated with the authority of Orientalist philology, so that theoretical approaches remained beyond their grasp, even beyond their interest.

Arabic literary tradition generally is characterised by the absence of theoretical consideration. Such consideration is important nonetheless as an expression of self-awareness articulating values in tradition, and at the same time exerting a certain influence on the direction of artistic production. The extent to which this absence is typical of Old Arabic literature can best be seen from the fact that it was in no way influenced by Aristotle's *Poetics* and *Rhetoric*, although Aristotle's philosophical work influenced the development of Arabic-Islamic philosophy so much that it named Aristotle the *First Teacher*. It is interesting that even the contemporary Arab world, having rather diverse and intense relationships with the literature of Western literary circles, displays no substantial influence from a whole range of theoretical consideration in literature. I believe the Arabic term for *poetics* can clearly illustrate this, since it appears to be the only term in the Arabic language.

The Arabic term for *poetics* is *fann al-shi'r* or *al-shi'riyya*. It is doubly inadequate. First, the word *fann* is originally not *art* in the sense defining art in the Western culture: *fann* is craft, téchnē, but this term for art has survived throughout the history of Arabic literature and, as such, it is quite telling of the poetics of this literature, focused on technique and generally on the formal side of poetry.[3] Second, the word *shi'r* is *poetry*, exclusively poetry. As a constituent of the phrase conveying the concept of *poetics*, it also tells quite a lot about the Arabic literary tradition, with poetry reigning supreme over it, even today, although the modern age has seen the development of prose genres. Therefore, *fann al-shi'r* is the *technique of poetry*, not *poetics* in Aristotle's meaning or in the sense of Aristotelian tradition.

In addition to the valuable indications this term provides with regard to characteristics of the traditions from which it originated, it is particularly revealing – which is important in the context of this discussion – about the absence of151theoretical thought in a literary tradition; furthermore, it testifies to the non-understanding of the very essence of theory and the theoretical consideration of literature.[4]

In any case, Arabic literary history is still waiting for its own Curtius, someone who will treat it as a value system of literary history and who will properly name the elements of this living system, such that these names will express the very essence of literature. An analysis of its poetic postulates is a very important step on the path towards achieving this goal.

I will illustrate this problem using the names for the first period in the history of Arabic literature.

The first period in this vast tradition is called *pre-Islamic literature*. This label does not reveal anything about the nature of the literature – neither about its characteristics or values within a specified period nor about its relationship with other periods, even though it is a very dynamic relationship. The label is neutral even with respect to the adjective *pre-Islamic*, although I have already explained – discussing the effect of the Qur'anic Text on the tradition of the time and the tradition that reorganised itself after the Text – that "pre-Islamic" poetry underwent a poetic redirection and intense re-evaluation, and adjusted its whole tradition to the Text. Therefore, this term is a historical or philological one, inappropriate for the literary and aesthetic position of this literature in history and its "poetic constitution".

Arabic literature uses the purely ideological term *pagan literature* (*al-adab al-jāhilī*), defining it completely negatively with respect to Islamic enlightenment. It is often disregarded that, even after the spread of Islam, many pre-Islamic poetic postulates, even entire poetic genres, were carefully cultivated and popular. Would it not mean then – ideological classifiers should ask themselves – that even in the period of Islam, poetry was ruled by effective "pagan" elements of "pagan literature"?!

Having in mind the extraordinary position of "pre-Islamic" poetry in the history of Arabic literature, the fact that it was at a very high level of development, and that it greatly influenced literary production throughout subsequent centuries, I believe the proper term for it would be *Arabic ancient literature*: this name situates the literature not only in a time frame but also in terms of its values; it defines the position of this literature towards later periods, as the ancient period of a culture actually represents its point of origin and its childhood. In poetic terms, "pre-Islamic" literature is a literature of the heroic age of Arabic and even Arabic-Islamic literary history.[5]

A similar analysis should be done in terms of other dominants in this long literary history, which would certainly result in a different periodisation.

It might be useful to suggest possible guidelines for literary history "marking" and naming the following period in Arabic literary history as well – that following the short poetic silence in the time of the Prophet Muhammad and the first four caliphs, which is termed the *Umayyad period*. Even if it may seem digressive in my discussion, I will mention this period since I believe this might be suggestive in terms of a proper periodisation of Arabic literature employing immanent methods.

Despite the fact that the poetic authority of ancient *qaṣīda* (which is how I will refer to the "pre-Islamic" period, though this is not established in literature) survived even after the spread of Islam, the following period is marked by changes additionally developing poetics, even though it remembers its origins in the ancient *qaṣīda*.

Namely, the love lyric prelude of ancient *qaṣīda* (*nasīb*) "brought forth" a separate poetic form known as *ghazal* – love lyric poetry. There were other poetic genres that developed from thematic segments of the ancient *qaṣīda* as well (panegyric, lampoon, descriptive poetry, etc.), but a whole epoch was marked by the flourishing of two subtypes of love poetry: *urban hedonist* and *desert Udhri*. The first type – also known as *Umarite* poetry, named after its best representative Umar Ibn Abi Rabi'ah ('Umar Ibn Abī Rabī'a, 644–711) – as well as the second, known by the chivalrous love poetry of its best representative Majnun Layla (Qays Ibn al-Mulawwaḥ, d. *c.*689), marked the most brilliant period of Arabic love lyricism in the entire history of Arabic literature. Certainly, love poetry was composed before and, particularly, after this, but never had a territory or a period been so effectively marked by love poetry as was the case with the Hijaz territory in the period of Umar and Umarite poets. It represented a poetic *dominant*. However, inadequate periodisation concealed its importance, as it was placed within the so-called *Umayyad* period (named after the Umayyad dynasty, 661–750) not revealing anything about it; furthermore, the Umayyad dynasty did not encourage this kind of poetry but patronised genres – panegyric and lampoon – and did not consciously affect its development. This is another reason not to call love poetry *Umayyad*. In terms of literary history, the marking direction is rather the opposite: the Umayyad socio-political epoch is marked by *ghazal*. I am not aware that another culture, or literary tradition, was so strongly characterised by a poetic form, so it seems to me that, within the periodisation, no successful analogies can be drawn with periods in other literary traditions.

From the perspective of a poetological analysis of Old Arabic literature, the period in question could be called the *love poetry period*; the *ghazal period*; perhaps even the *epoch of lyricism*.

The Qur'anic text as a generator of changes in tradition

The *Qur'an*'s influence on the birth of this lyric poetry was significant, though it may not appear to have been a direct one at first. Namely, when the *Qur'an* deprived poetry of the right of expressing the highest religious content, poetry took to expressing the kind of spirituality known as the love lyric. Since tradition had already had great poetic experience and since the Arabian spirit could not renounce a constant and essential need for poetry, in the creation of a new universe of values tradition "devised" a new poetic form that optimally expressed spirituality, demonstrated the technical poetic experience of tradition and, at the same time, did nothing to "revise" the "agreement" reached with the great Text. Taking its position within the tradition of that time, the Text generated *ghazal* (love poetry), which marked the whole epoch; the entire tradition could not suddenly vanish, regardless of the innovative poetic authority of the Text that suddenly appeared in it, and regardless of the Text's uncompromising attitude. Great texts do not obliterate all others, but act as the most creative part of tradition: they cause "tectonic" movements within it and shape a new "relief", or create a state of optimum value tensions and bring the seeds of new precious forms. Let us imagine a completely hypothetical situation in which there would be no Text, or in which it would come several centuries later. In that case the situation would be completely different. This huge empire would not have been created, and there would have been no Umayyad dynasty, which is certainly of importance for literary history as well. However, what is particularly important here is the poetic aspect of the hypothetical and actual events. If there had been no Qur'anic ideology of exclusiveness in terms of the poet's ambitions, love poetry would not have been so rampant; however, it blossomed because it was distinctly non-ideological and because tradition was too vital, not suicidal, turning to a different kind of expression. There is another fact that testifies to all this.

Namely, Umarite lyricism is neither righteous nor chaste at all. It is even considerably hedonist, and it is quite interesting that – being such – it developed in the Prophet's native area and next to the Holy Shrine. Umar's and Umarite courtship of respected women is not a pure lyrical transposition or fiction but, according to testimonies of many relevant sources, it was real and represented a subject of poetic and lyrical attention. There is certainly no need to explain that it was quite improper from the position of Islamic morality, but the fact that it was done nevertheless tells something about the nature of compromise between Tradition and the great Text: poetry had to renounce direct and magic communion with God, or with gods, it had to step down as an instrument of Cognition and as a Revelation, but was then allowed "lyrical transgressions" that, compared with its aspirations in the period before, were purely human and worthy of forgiveness. For, as the Text says, every human sin hopes for forgiveness, except associating other gods with Allah, which the former poetry did not hesitate to do.

In other words, the Text made tradition a particular favour, as without the Text's intervention there would have been no new developments such as Umarite lyric poetry. This poetry is an important genre invigoration of tradition and, at the same time, a poetic innovation, since this sort of lyric poetry – as well as other poetic forms that developed later – does not convey the Truth in a religious sense; lyric poetry is not cognitive in these terms but conveys the subtlest human spirituality. Poetic inversion is thorough and it is hard to imagine something better happening to tradition than the flourishing of love poetry caused by the Text's intervention. This released pure and vibrant spirituality extroverted in its most brilliant manifestations and expressions. It is difficult to enumerate all the consequences of such a position of lyric poetry with regard to the Text and its implicit and explicit requirements.

Oriental-Islamic lyric poetry is generally characterised by spirituality going out into the external world and its joyful and comprehensive intertwining with the world around a subject. The poet does not ponder his own spirituality but opens to the world he lives with in full harmony and in its most beautiful manifestations. Arabic literary tradition, and even the Arabic-Islamic tradition generally, is hence dominantly lyric in this sense. It is utterly non-pessimistic poetry, non-introverted and mostly not even reflexive. Admittedly, together with Umarite joyful lyricism, so-called Udhri poetry was also cultivated, representing an antipode to Umarite poetry with respect to understanding the concept of love and its realisation. However, Udhri lyricism is more of "transpositive" nature than is Umarite; it is "oppositionary" in a very specific way but is *not pessimistic* even then, because the lyric suffering of Oriental people carries a special lightness that does not lead to gloomy moods. Even suffering is in such cases in harmony with the world outside the subject.

In short, uncompromisingly condemning the soothsaying and religious poetry the ancient period was proud of, the great Text forced tradition to search for new forms, to re-create itself, and it "found its way around" in a manner befitting its experience and determination to survive.

I am not aware that researchers of Arabic literature have observed this connection between the Text and poetic dominants of later periods. Furthermore, many are inclined to claim that there was no influence of the Text on poetry in the Islamic age, stating that, generally, the Arabic-Islamic culture knew no "religious" poetry in the form and to the degree known to the literature of the European Middle Ages. This statement is only partly true, but poses certain methodological problems.

Namely, it is true inasmuch as there really was no religious poetry as in the European tradition, except Sufi poetry that, in turn, is not religious in the same way as European poetry. However, the statement is not true where it "establishes" the absence of any influence of the Text on poetry that emerged after it. In methodological terms, it is incorrect to deny *any* influence, unless it was directly manifest, or to establish the absence of influence in terms of the fact that poetry did not accept or treat religious themes, for instance, that it did not affect the promotion of Islam, etc. For, in this case, there was another kind of influence that escaped the notice of comparatist habits. The effect of the *Qur'an* was different from the effect of other momentous works in various cultures, different even from the effect of momentous works in the Arabic-Islamic culture itself. In principle, works of great importance in a culture represent its landmarks, factors of emulation and commensurability, poetic paragons and exemplars, etc. The *Qur'an* had a different effect in every respect. Unlike everything else, it a priori rejected any possibility of its imitation, poetically defined itself as absolutely unique and inimitable, and in this regard denied the possibility for the entire subsequent production to emulate it in any way, for anything to be comparable to it. It is curious in this vein that the *Qur'an*, as well as the entire tradition, admits that it uses the highest achievements of literary experience. Therefore, the *Qur'an* affected tradition is such a way as to force it to search for different poetic postulates. On the one hand, it decisively put an end to the poetry of its time in its ideological dimension and, on the other, offered new prospects to tradition in its search for new poetic genres. The great Text is a divide after whose cut into tradition nothing could remain the same any more and, at the same time, nothing could be similar to it. More precisely, everything is different from it and distinct – by its own decision, poetic power and ideological uniqueness – and this is the kind of specific influence remaining unobserved in, for instance, the literary newness of the Umayyad or any other historical period. Positioning itself in the epicentre of Tradition, the great Text created the universe of a culture defining all its forms in relation to the Text, in terms of certain elements of similitude, but much more through crucial elements of differentiation.

Elements of similitude can be found in the use of the same language, in using principally the same literary means, etc., for – from the literary perspective – the entire tradition certainly has much in common with the Text; without this, they would be incommunicable to the point of utter incomprehension. However, at the selfsame level, there are considerable differences between them, since the poetics and stylistics of the *Qur'an* are superior and – as believed by those to whom the Text arrived – are even supernatural, so that tradition abandoned any attempt at mirroring. By and large, similitude is mostly identified as influence, but influence also consists of the differentiation forced by the Text. Moreover, it follows that differentiation is more precious than similitude, and I do not think the *Qur'an* generated this by accident. For, the principle of persistent similitude generates most serious candidates for sterile epigonism and traditionalism, while the principle of creative differentiation is a fundamental requirement of avant-garde breakthroughs. The *Qur'an* is thus at least doubly momentous within literary tradition. On the one hand it is, in its own right, a novelty of the highest order throughout the entirety of Arabic-Islamic literary history. (I am not discussing the theological aspect of the Text here, since I am interested in its literary, its poetic merit.) On the other hand, it is momentous because – being different from all momentous works – it initiated and created literary and cultural differentiation as richness that had been unimaginable before and that would initiate the rapid creation of a vast – also previously unimaginable – Oriental-Islamic *cultural* empire that was the largest in the world at the time, but always with the Text at its centre. The differentiation inevitably created by the Text's uniqueness and inimitableness is its decisive and most creative power.

The Text could produce such effects only owing to its constant and argument-supported refusal to be reduced to the level of art. Had the Text been received as a work of art and not as the real, non-transpositional and non-fictional Word of God, all the aspects and achievements we identify in this culture, as well as the development of this civilisation generally, would undoubtedly have failed to come. For the Text mobilised all the potentials of Arabians and subsequently of other peoples not because it is a literary work of art, but because it was understood as the Word-of-God-about-Truth, so that these peoples first thoroughly changed themselves with respect to the Text, only to subsequently change a large portion of the world. Therefore, without the Text there would have been no Arab-Islamic caliphate. Similarly, and at the same time, without the Text there would have been no differential Umarite poetry (nor other important literary forms), there would not have been very advanced philosophy, nor would have ancient Greek philosophy and art been conveyed to Europe, etc. The world would be quite different if there had been no Text. What could have been reasonably expected at most, had the Text been received as art, is its imitation until utter epigonism.

Only when seen from this perspective does the Text's distance from poetry appear as fateful for history, or the fact that it defined as the greatest heresy the claim that it was a work of the "possessed poet" (*shā'ir majnūn*). At the same time, when the Text was revealed, it was not possible to imagine what we can see today, and this seems to be rather unique in history. Namely, it turns out that the explicit and implicit *differentiation* of the Text can simultaneously operate as both a disjunctive and a cohesive factor: on the one hand, it almost forcefully and necessarily generates new forms of culture and, on the other hand and at the same time, it keeps them in its orbit, in the universe it created.

Even after the ideological and literary triumph of the Text, poetry was created following the principle of differentiation from the Text, although every textbook on Arabic stylistics – from the earliest times to this day – have been full of its stylistic achievements. I will discuss this poetic differentiation of literary creation in the section that follows, but before that it should be mentioned how the Text, through its supreme authority, established a new way of studying tradition. Namely, the philology that I have already mentioned as the doom of Old Arabic poetry deserves special attention – as a science devoted to tradition, but which acquired its great, albeit indirect, impetus from the Text.

Philology as impetus and a trap

The main direction from which the *Qur'an* influenced poetry is philology that developed after the revelation of the *Qur'an* and that provided a framework for philological criticism having actually represented the only form of literary criticism for centuries. Therefore, the *Qur'an* indirectly affected literary tradition also by encouraging the preservation of the existing poetry production in order to use this poetic material in the first place, and then the poetry technique as well, to study the language and authority of the Qur'anic Text, by comparing or contrasting it with the existing production.

Much of the ancient poetry would probably have been lost without the philological initiative to record it, to transfer it from an oral tradition onto paper so that its linguistic material could illuminate the *'i'jāz* of the *Qur'an*. Therefore, the selfsame poetry that the *Qur'an* had dealt with in ideological terms was saved through the Text's mediated request that it be preserved, although poetry was very likely "de-paganised" while being recorded, in the sense that everything expressing or merely being associative of the pre-Islamic belief was very likely eliminated from it. There are strong indications to that effect. Theses about the de-paganisation of ancient Arabian poetry seriously question the authenticity of this corpus as we know it today; they also multiply the influence of the *Qur'an* on poetry. Namely, there is no doubt that the primary need for a linguistic interpretation of the *Qur'an* initiated the development of philology and the recording of pre-Islamic poetry, but a possible *Islamic* intervention in the recording stage is a particular example of the Text's influence, once more demonstrating its powerful effect not only on the future but also, "retroactively", on the past. Owing to the need for a stratified exegesis of the *Qur'an*, ancient poetry was, thus, preserved, regardless of the degree of its authenticity. Even if during its philological processing and recording this poetry was revised with regard to the position of the Text, it could undoubtedly have affected only its ideological layer, by dint of which the poetics of this poetry was reduced in one of its aspects.

First and foremost, the development of philology, as an important exegetic discipline, was in a causal relationship with the preservation of ancient poetry, as philologists' starting point and their point of reference. Paradoxical as it may seem at first, it follows that the Text, in a very important aspect, is the Text of continuity. Namely, although it dramatically confronted poetry, which I discussed in detail, the Text unexpectedly emphasised the importance of Tradition as *Continuity*: the Text's intervention in tradition was radical and fateful, but it was not of such an order as to completely erase everything that had existed before the Text. On the contrary, the intervening nature of the Text arose for tradition to be saved as such. This is exactly what very developed philology testifies to, as well as precious poetic heritage preserved under the Text's wing. This is why everything always points to the conclusion that the Text is a work of continuity and context.

Among other consequences of the Text's relationship to philology and ancient poetry is the fact that the authority of ancient poetry was also built owing to the authority of philologists. This also points at an apparent paradox, and there is no end to paradoxes when it comes to the Text's effect. Namely, it is curious and seemingly contradictory that, in all the historical periods of Islam, ancient poetry had the status of indisputableness and of an exemplar, even though the Text assumed a position of severe criticism towards it at the time of the descent. It also seems paradoxical that philology – though being initiated by the *Qur'an* – situated poetry as an exemplary corpus in the entire tradition.

This perspective leads to an inescapable conclusion about the philological "de-paganisation" of ancient poetry. Namely, being certainly ideologised to a degree at the time of a general Islamic enthusiasm, philology would not have so devoutly preserved and cherished as an authority poetry that, in its authenticity, was still defiant of the Qur'anic dogmas. Such hypocrisy of tradition is inconceivable. Poetic heritage could not have survived in that form. But, there is also a historic fact that we do have, for instance, the *al-Mu'allaqāt* corpus from the ancient period, regardless of the degree of its authenticity, as well as the fact that this corpus kept its status of an undisputed authority.

It follows that the de-paganisation of heritage imposed a "subsequent will" of the Text, emphasising the importance of continuity as a prerequisite for cultural communicability, but this gives rise to one poetically long-term consequence.

Namely, philology could possibly intervene in ancient poetry only in the sphere of its (ideological) content. The form of poetry was irrelevant to the

Qur'an, and there was no need to intervene in this field. Nevertheless, an intervention in any sphere of poetry constitutes interference with its poetics. The depaganisation seems likely to me, regardless of the absence of material facts proving it, since there are facts arising from a consequent consideration: the poetry at the time is one of the markedly negative themes in the *Qur'an* – at the ideological level, there was no compromising with it, but it was preserved by philology born under the wing of the *Qur'an*, suggesting that poetry could itself find a place under this wing provided that it "subsequently renounced" its ideological positions and preferences. Therefore, there were three authorities collaborating here: the *Qur'an*–philology–ancient poetry. The *Qur'an* and philology provided ancient poetry with its authority, particularly the *al-Mu'allaqāt* as its exemplary corpus. A requirement for this authority was a poetic intervention in the poetry of that time. Hence, the *Qur'an* rearranged poetry which thus "became authorised" to promote the Text's values; what seems more important than anything else is that poetically revised ancient poetry had a crucial influence on subsequent poetry during several centuries. These are also far-reaching and comprehensive influences of the *Qur'an* on literary tradition.

Arabic philology certainly deserves great credit for this early period. I believe it can be discerned precisely in the discussed relationship to ancient poetry and its poetic importance for the entire literary tradition. However, this early philology – as well as modern Orientalist philology discussed previously – had serious limitations, the interpretation of which I will frequently have to go back to, considering the fact that philology, as both a science and criticism, dominated the Arabic tradition until the modern age. For, it was not only committed to studying old texts but also directed the existing and future literary production with unexpected might.

In the nature of things, philology is a discipline that conserves. Since it dealt with old texts as valuables, it was not satisfied with value-neutral philological descriptions, philological textual expertise, etc.; instead, Arabic philology has always wholeheartedly been committed to value judgements. Thus, in its excessive enthusiasm, behind the scientific horizon, it consecrated its field and dealt with past works as with genuine antiquities – in terms of time and value. The history of Old Arabic literature, or the history of its poetics, is hence a history of traditionalism, or a history of an unequal struggle between conserving and dominant philology and philological criticism, on the one hand, and the essentially irresistible urge of great literary authors, on the other. Only having this in mind – and we must if we want to study Arabic literature properly – can we assess the poetic importance and artistic achievement of the tradition in, for example, Umarite and Udhri love poetry. Or, in the following, Abbasid political period (750–1258), a poetological story about the most important poet of the epoch, Abu Nuwas (Abū Nuwās, 757–814), may be the best illustration of the fierce struggle between the traditionalist and the avant-garde, philological conservation and authentic creation. The story is a commonplace and seems like an anecdote, but it is, in fact, very informative, optimally relevant in terms of literary history and poetically dramatic.

When this greatest poet of the classical epoch of Arabic literature asked an authoritative philologist, Khalaf al-Ahmar (Khalaf al-Aḥmar, d. 796), how to become a good poet, the philologist's answer was in perfect conformity with the norms of the time – that he first had to memorise a thousand *qaṣīdas* of Old Arabic poets. When after a time that certainly could not have been short, diligent Abu Nuwas came to the philologist again, informing him that he had accomplished the task, the philologist told him: "If you want to start writing yourself, you must now forget those verses."

The story sounds too rigorous but, whether authentic or not, it illustrates the general mood of the time. As a matter of fact, the story is somewhat optimistic as well, since it still opens up a possibility of renewal, however marked by tradition it may be. Other philologists were not so generous because their requirements left no possibility for the verses to be forgotten at all: they recommended that they be imitated, and many poets who submitted to such authority remained epigones only.

Nevertheless, Abu Nuwas' quest for the "golden fleece" offers another epochal moral. Namely, the poet – perhaps as no other poet of the classical period – refreshed tradition with a language that defied archaisms, and enriched it with new poetic forms that his tradition would pride itself on for centuries to come. His experience with tradition and philologists, and his innovative poetry are an eloquent testimony to a great struggle of a philological authority and a creative urge. Even so, Abu Nuwas' opus offers enough on the traditional side, since his epoch so required, while al-Ahmar's recommendation can also be understood as a request to master poetic technique through knowledge of traditional poetry. There are many indications supporting this interpretation, since the téchnē was a fundamental requirement of the time, and I will discuss it separately.

It seems necessary to add to this context the opinions of two more great authorities, Ibn Khaldun and Ibn Rashiq (Ibn Rashīq, d. 1063), on how essential for every poet – in order for him to become one – it is to thoroughly master traditional versification, primarily the language and technique of traditional poetry.

Eminent Ibn Khaldun says:

> We say: It should be known that the production of poetry and the laws governing the poetical craft are subject to a number of conditions. The first condition is to have an expert knowledge of its genus – that is, the genus of Arabic poetry. This is the thing that eventually creates a habit in the soul upon which, as on a loom, the poet is able to weave. [...] The poetry of poets who have no expert knowledge of the old poetical material is inferior and bad.[6]

Ibn Rashiq instructs poets to concentrate on the oral poetic tradition, to memorise poetry and thus acquire poetic education. He also refers to the authority of al-Asma'i (al-Asma'ī, 740–828), quoting him: "One cannot become a true poet until one has become a rhapsodist of Arabic poetry."[7]

Ibn Tabataba (Ibn Ṭabāṭabā al-'Alawī, d. 934) proclaimed that it was necessary for every poet to be educated in the literary values of his time, particularly those pertaining to the language and specific features of Arabic poetry.[8]

Many other philologists set more or less the same requirements. A poet had to be highly educated, which did not include theoretical knowledge, as there was no literary theory at all. A poet received his education through memorising poetic production, thus mastering the traditional poetics, much more in terms of its form rather than its content. Memorising old poetry also contributed to mastering the archaic lexis that philological criticism rated extremely highly, while a detailed knowledge of the metrical system was *sine qua non* for every poet.[9] It is also well known that poets from metropolises of the time, such as Baghdad, had to spend some time specialising with Bedouins. The alleged reason behind this was the need for poets to master the so-called pure Arabic language, uncontaminated with the foreign influence it was exposed to in cities. However, behind this relatively reasonable request there hid another end that philology had never abandoned. Namely, in the nature of things, the Bedouin environment was rather isolated, and conservative in its isolation, so that the Arabic language among Bedouins was much more archaic than that in big and crowded urban centres. It was this aspect that philology aimed at and, considering the fact that poetry was more popular than any other form of art, and that poetry was universal as it were, not elitist or popular, it also contributed to linguistic and poetic conservation. Philology was triumphant.

Since philology and the "reading" audience (poems were mostly recited, much more than they were read) required a poet to fully master traditional poetry – by memorising it, which defines the attitude towards tradition – it was only natural to expect that most poets would not be able to resist the influence of this obligatory and memorised exemplary poetic abundance, and that they would imitate it more or less successfully, even more so as the authoritative philology and tradition-adhering wide audience expected them to do so.

As a matter of fact, the Arabic literary tradition saw only a few authentic philological critics whose works set out guidelines for the entire philological criticism: for hundreds of years other critics were engaged in epigonic imitation or in rewriting the opinions of these greatest philological critics.[10] Among the authentic ones, the following names should be mentioned: Abū 'Amr Ibn al-'Alā (689–770),[11] Abū 'Ubayda (728–825),[12] Abū 'Amr Ibn al-'Alā al-Asma'ī (740–825),[13] Ibn Sallām al-Jumaḥī (758–846),[14] Ibn Qutaybah (828–889).[15]

Al-Asma'ī believed that great poets were only those from the pre-Islamic epoch or those from the Prophet's period at best. He even went so far as to claim that three notable poets of the Umayyad epoch (Jarīr [653–732], al-Farazdaq [641–731] and al-Akhṭal [640–710]) would have been good poets had they been pre-Islamic ones.[16]

As unusual or even illogical as this judgement may seem, it is authentic and predominant in philological literary criticism. A great authority of philological criticism, Ibn Qutaybah, positively regarded so-called new poetry as well; he was one of the few brave enough to do so. However, even in such rare cases antiquity was always given priority: it was crucial to every judgement. Philological critics, or the greatest among them, were clearly aware that certain innovations in tradition were necessary and that it was not wise to a priori dismiss them, but ancient poetry still remained an undisputed poetic authority in their system of values. Hence Ibn Qutaybah also positively valued new poets but, paradoxically, valued them according to how close they were to ancient poets in terms of theme and form. Their poetic ideal was the "three-part" ancient *qaṣīda* (stopping by deserted bivouacs on an imaginary journey typical of the *al-Mu'allaqāt*; love poetry – *ghazal*; continuation of the journey). "A well versed poet", writes Ibn Qutaybah,

> is one who, following this path, sustains a balance among different parts of the poem, not letting any of them develop too much lest it should bore the listener and, in parallel, not shortening one or another part as long as the souls desire them to last.[17]

The thematic composition of *qaṣīda* specified by Ibn Qutaybah is typical of the *al-Mu'allaqāt*, representing the best poems of the ancient Arabian period. Although this type of poem had already become stratified in Ibn Qutaybah's time and some of its themes had developed into independent and self-sufficient poetic forms, it is interesting that Ibn Qutaybah highly regarded the thematic diversity of a poem. The theme of (an imaginary) journey was also expressly and predominantly ancient, but philological criticism also imposed it on poets who were its contemporaries. A "balance" among thematic units of the poem was clearly one of the major concerns of both poets and critics, while the measure of success of these units was the requirement for them not to be either too long or too short, but completely adapted to the listener's/reader's desire. Such requests obviously reinforced ancient poetics. If we remember that philologists, as I have said, also requested the so-called pure Arabic language that mostly implied an archaic language, it then becomes even clearer how philological criticism tried to immortalise ancient poetics.

Certainly, in this short but meaningful critical attitude of Ibn Qutaybah a particular importance is on the phrase *a well versed poet*, at the beginning of his critical statement – something that defines the whole statement. The term *well versed* does not necessarily imply the critics' qualifier *good* in the sense of literary art; *good* and *well versed* are not identical in meaning. A well versed poet is one carrying/having the experience of tradition. Therefore, precisely in line with the attitudes of Ibn Qutaybah and other philologists, a poet had to fully master tradition and its poetics in order to be a poet in his own right. This is a particular kind of experience where tradition is fully realised in a poet on the one hand and, on the other, a poet is realised in tradition. Their mutual experiences – the experience of one about the other and of one in the other – are so complete as to be mutually conditioned. When, in addition, preference is given to the point of origin of tradition in its ancient period (as is the case with the attitude of Ibn Qutaybah and others), then the whole tradition is actually directed towards traditionalism, which must be explored separately.

The term *well versed* (poet) has yet another important poetic aspect. In addition to conveying that a poet must have the experience of tradition, this term mostly expresses the experientially *technical* aspect of poetry. Namely, a poet gains experience, on the one hand, through knowledge of the poetic experience of his predecessors, as well as through constant work, practice, refining his technique, etc. It becomes evident how these two crucial factors work together and are dependent on each other. A poet gains or broadens experience on his knowledge of tradition. However, knowledge of tradition is precious at all times and opuses, but only in order for the poet to become realised in an *individual* poetic feat.[18] Ibn Qutaybah's representative statement leaves no room for individual talent and creative steps forward from the "platform" of tradition already mastered, since the pre-Islamic ancient *qaṣīda* is set as a model to be emulated, while the poet's talent is replaced with experience that implies, first and foremost, that versification technique be successfully mastered. This leads to an ideal environment for traditionalism as a non-creative part of tradition. Writing technique is brought to the forefront, and hence it also deserves to be discussed separately.[19]

Ibn Qutaybah's views had an enormous influence over the development of Arabic poetry throughout the Middle Ages. He was essentially a classicist, although he did not ignore "new poetry", recognising its "right" to aesthetic values even beyond philological norms.[20] Despite this, his classicist influence remained unsurpassed. It is no wonder, then, that even the poets considered to be "poets of innovation" composed traditional poetic forms and cultivated an archaic language in them. For instance, Bassar Ibn Burd (Bashshār Ibn Burd, 714–748) and Abu Nuwas (757–814) introduced new forms into poetic tradition, in which they used their contemporary language known to a wide audience, but at the same time also wrote traditional forms requiring the archaic language. According to a judgement of the epoch, no poet could command the greatest respect unless he had proved his mastery of traditional poetic genres. Poets were not required to undermine tradition but to refine it. Across a considerable time span – practically throughout the Middle Ages and generally after the revelation of the *Qur'an* – poetry largely represented a number of recurrent themes, commonplaces and topoi. The concept of originality at the time was substantially different from that of our age. An authentic poet was a poet who successfully mastered tradition and used the poetic achievements of others. Even the concept of criticism (*naqd*) must be interpreted in and explained in this context.

Philology: text's authenticity and author's originality

The Arabic literary history has never developed literary criticism in the same sense and function as it is known to European literature. Originally, as a lexeme and a concept belonging to literary theory, *naqd* stands for examination of poetic work authenticity: since plagiarism was widely spread, the task of criticism was to distinguish plagiarisms from authentic works.[21] Therefore, what is important in this context is that the Arabic term for criticism, *naqd* (still the only term), is eminently philological. Criticism did not primarily deal with establishing authenticity in terms of a work's individuality – its artistic individuality – but in terms of its philological authenticity. The work as an artistic value was not the focus of this criticism, but the work as a philological rarity. Terms can never be separated from the science using them, and it seems particularly true of terms in Arabic culture.

Therefore, the originality philology was interested in was of a scholarly nature: a profusion of forged tradition had to be "sifted through", among which works that were not plagiarisms were accordingly identified; this concept of originality is different from the one defining originality as individuality, or as an original *artistic* value in terms of authorship. However, it would be incorrect to claim that philology completely excluded value judgements from its field of interest. We can see from the philological views paraphrased or quoted earlier that their authors preferred certain poetic postulates and traditional experience, and recommended for literary production to be directed towards ancient poetic exemplars. They did not shy away from discussing which poetry was *better*, which poet was *better*, implying actually that they presented a value system, the specific nature of which should be explained.

Their system of values did not develop, *primarily*, from poetology or from the interpretation of literature as a system of artistic values, but the system of philological criticism developed from philology as such. This first and foremost implies a philological textual analysis, as well as biographic and bibliographic expertise establishing the authorship and authenticity of a work, which subsequently yields a value judgement that can clearly not be radically separated from the philological method and aims of philology. As a matter of fact, there is quite an unusual process taking place here.

Since the authenticity of authorship is the main goal of philology, its subsequent evaluation – in philological criticism – became deformed because two fundamental concepts got confused: authenticity of authorship (non-apocryphalness) and artistic originality. Authorship authenticity was substituted for artistic originality. In other words, authenticity is presented as a value, which is quite in compliance with the method and aims of philology, but not with requirements of artistic criticism: authenticity is not equal to artistic originality as a value. This confusion of two distinct values created (philological) criticism that, on the one hand, presented itself as quite competent, even scientific, while being on the other hand incompetent in a particular field that rendered its value judgements inadequate. Proof of this can be offered in the following way.

First, pursuing its main goal – defined as the exploration of literary past, as far back as possible – philology penetrated deeper and deeper into the past until it stopped by ancient exemplars it then proclaimed as the highest values. Dealing with literary and linguistic heritage, philology preferred the past as such, implying that the "logic of the past", or the "principle of historicism", was the principle that governed the very being of philology: philology could not resist a kind of (philological) inertia establishing the past, or even antiquity, as the criterion for identifying values. Any different approach would not be inherent in philology; philology could not be constituted in a different way. This is the main reason why philology favoured the past so zealously. There is also something else to be added to this reason.

Searching for authorship authenticity also has its own direction of inertia. Recreating the inertial path philology committed itself to in establishing authenticity of authorship can lead to such a conclusion. First there was a search for authenticity (under which I imply non-apocryphal, non-forged poetry, i.e. that whose authorship is certain) of works nearest to the time of a researcher-philologist. However, as the purport of tradition lies in continuity expressed through different forms of imitation and a specific understanding of originality, philologists searched for the authenticity of motifs, themes, poetic treatment of individual themes, etc., in the depths of their continuity, further and further back into the past, as their authenticity criteria became stricter in time. Inertia was now in action: the depths of literary past become more and more captivating and "valuable" as they revealed the undreamed-of potentials of their authentic value. Considering such a direction of philological inertia, it is no wonder it led to assigning ancient poetry the highest value. However, there happened yet another "shift" of methodological levels here. Namely, the search for authorship authenticity in the strictest philological sense was, perhaps unwittingly, confused with poetic authenticity. For, a work can be authentic in terms of its authorship, but not necessarily authentic in poetical terms, when it can even be epigonic. These are quite distinct levels. When authorship authenticity is mistaken for poetical authenticity, or when the two are not differentiated, most of the Arabic tradition is then identified as unoriginal, inauthentic, since its works developed within a poetics having been constituted long before these works. This is the only way that could have led to ancient poetry as the highest value: poetically, it is at the very source of this tradition so that philology favoured its poets over all others. The priority of antiquity is made absolute.

The second proof in arriving at my attitude to classical Arabic philology can be found in the following. Non-philological criticism has a different attitude to tradition. In an Eliotic manner, it acknowledges tradition as the only space where a literary work is realised as a value, but the essence is precisely in a reversed "evaluative direction". Through the dictates of authorship authenticity, philological criticism, inevitably and with each step more elaborately, points towards authenticity as the highest value, whereas the other type of criticism points towards crossing the horizon of values established through tradition. Authentic literary criticism, non-philological, requires an authentic work to be comparatively different from all previous works, but also to be based on the experience of tradition, which is the absolute condition for communicability. Therefore, according to authentic criticism, originality is equal to a particular kind of avant-garde – always forward and always *plus ultra* – whereas the philological concept of originality means a backward movement – *non plus ultra*. In these terms I have already said that classical Arabic philology understood poetic "creativity" as something that refined, not undermined, tradition, using linguistic archaisms and poetic discipline to introduce this "refinement". The "refinement" is actually of a "technicist" nature and could, through wordplay, be translated as an "ossification" of tradition, in the sense of its non-innovativeness. Authentic criticism refines tradition but in quite a different way, actually in an authentic way. Favouring originality as a breakthrough at the very horizon of tradition and as a fundamental principle of evaluation, this criticism – or literary works it regards very highly – refines tradition essentially and in a different direction: this is a way to keep expanding its horizon through new experiences and innovations, not through imitations; tradition remains recognisable and authentic; there is no discontinuity but the border has been creatively pushed forward and the experience of tradition substantially enriched. Authenticity is omnipresent, as it were – principled and consistent.

There is a significant parable mentioned by al-Ghazali (al-Ġazālī, 1058–1111), which could have at least two meanings. Namely, story has it that a powerful emperor ordered that an exquisite room be built for him. Among others, Chinese and Muslim masters got to work. The Chinese masters diligently painted the most beautiful frescos on the walls while, on the opposite side of the room, the Muslim masters tirelessly polished the walls. When the emperor, after the works were done, entered the part of the room painted by the Chinese masters, he was enchanted with their work. Then the room divide was removed and the Chinese masterwork made an astonishingly beautiful reflection on the walls perfectly polished by the Muslim masters. The story further has it that the emperor began to quiver at the moment when he saw the reflection.[22]

The parable is polyvalent. Eva de Vitray-Meyerovitch puts in a context of interpretation of the "poetics of Islam" according to which the reflection is more beautiful than reality. Although this interpretation cannot, I believe, be refuted (it should not be identified with the Aristotelian theory of *mimesis*), it can also wholly relate to the Arabic-Islamic concept of tradition I am discussing here. To "polish" tradition is a way to refine it; new poets are new because their works reflect the old that is reflected differently in every epoch. This reopens the issue of the relationship between tradition and traditionalism in Arabic literature. In any case, al-Ghazali's parable uniquely speaks about the poetics of this tradition.

Far-reaching deformations of tradition discussed here resulted from the incompetence of philology, which approached its subject too pretentiously, also covering certain aspects of tradition that escaped its methods and goals, and acting, at the same time, as an authority not only examining the past but also decisively influencing the literary future.

However, philology cannot deal with poetics successfully because it cannot understand poetics sufficiently or adequately, wrongly positioning even those aspects of poetics it can understand as a norm that should not be deviated from, for as we have seen philology, searching for authenticity, reaches as far back into the past as it can, where it identifies exemplary poetic postulates, establishing them as a norm. It is no wonder then that philology presented ancient poetry as the highest traditional value, even though philology should not deal with poetic postulates or literary works as artistic values. It is precisely Arabic literary tradition that shows the negative achievements of this wrong direction. For, this orientation of philology and the fact that it had been the strongest influence in the field of literature for hundreds of years had two negative effects.

First, dealing with poetics and literary artistic values, philology (or, more precisely, philological criticism) necessarily took over the competence for establishing poetic norms. It was fascinated with antiquity, in which philology identified the initial poetic postulates, proclaiming them as norms. The consequences of this are manifold and negative. A normative poetics is inappropriate to authentic art that, at its very soul, has the urge to resist norms. This normativeness prevents the most important aspects of art: originality and individuality, creative assimilation of tradition and Eliotic individual talent, etc. Admittedly, works of art are created within the framework of a certain poetics, or of some of them – which form a system by their nature, not within anarchies – but non-normative poetics has a very broad basis: in the form of literary experience and of our experience of it, an experience on whose horizon a new work of art becomes realised. A poetics understood in this way is incompatible with, for example, Ibn Qutaybah's norm according to which the "three-part *qaṣīda*" is the best because it is ancient. Ibn Qutaybah does not only say that this *qaṣīda* was the best in the epoch it was created in, but that it is the best from the position of his time as well: he recommends it as a paragon to his contemporaries and successors. His relationship to the *qaṣīda* does not imply only the "philological expertise" in studying certain works in their past, but also an explanation of values projected as a value norm from the past into the present. This is a trap philology walked into: instead of dealing with the authenticity of texts, issues of authorship, etc., it became committed to poetic norms and value judgements as well, failing to differentiate them from its principal methodological focus on antiquities.

Second, apart from normativeness, but closely related to it, the poetics within the explorations of such philology is conceived as inductive. The poetic production existing at the time, the one at the source of poetic tradition, was proclaimed as the best part of this tradition, and its poetics became the norm. This means that the poetics was arrived at inductively – by establishing certain rules of poetic creation in the existing exemplary production. (This perspective shows more clearly why, even today, Arabic literature uses an inadequate term for poetics, *the technique of poetry – fann al-shi'r/al-shi'riyya.*) The inductive character of poetics strongly underlines normativeness: from a certain literary corpus in literary history there derived poetic postulates set up into a system, implying that the selfsame corpus and laws of artistic creation in it were established as the norm. Traditionalism gets new strength and verification. A deductive poetics would have an opposite effect to that of traditionalism. By means of deduction, it establishes general and rather broad rules of artistic literary creation, in which the authenticity of artistic value should be realised; since it is identified as the broadest experience of literature, deductive poetics is not familiar with the normativeness of inductive poetics: no corpus, nor any individual work, regardless of its value, can be established as a norm within deductive poetics but, on the contrary, following its nature, deductive poetics establishes it as a precious and authentic literary experience showing that not only is it possible to deflect from the so-called exemplar, but that it is also a requirement for a work to become realised as an authentic literary value. This is a profound difference. The former poetics generates traditionalism and epigonism, while the former generates avant-gardism.[23]

Inductive poetics gives birth to its criticism – just like the Arabic philological criticism – dealing with almost exact identification of the degree to which poetic norms were realised in a "new" work. Hence, such criticism is not authentic either, and can therefore not deal with authentic values – it does not recognise them as such.

Deductive poetics, however, cultivates criticism that, as the previous discussion indicates, promotes deflection from the norms as originality, within the broadest literary experience. Thus anti-traditionalist *plus ultra* appears as the *creed* of the second type of criticism. Understandably, it is inconceivable for Ibn Qutaybah and his followers to endorse such an opposite view, since their destiny was philology that had cultivated its own literary criticism.

Considering the described position of philology (and its criticism), it is easy to understand why poets were so hesitant to step out of the normative poetics framework. They were, actually, forced to compromise so that, as I stated above, they introduced certain innovations into traditional poetic genres based on the archaic language.

The authority of philology and *Shu'ubiyyah*

The authority of philology was additionally encouraged by a great antagonism between *Arabism* (*'urūba*) and the *Shu'ubiyyah* (*shu'ūbiyya*) movement that was particularly active in the ninth century – more precisely, it grew very strong in the middle of the ninth century as a rival confrontation for dominance in the culture and politics of the Arabic element and Arabised peoples, Persians in particular. Invoking the ayah stating that God does not favour one people over another but ranks them according to their fear of God,[24] Persians contested the conviction of Arabs of their supremacy and desire to impose elements of their culture, which was indeed at a very high level for those times. Arabs used classicist philology as a very powerful means in their reaction to Shu'ubiyyah.[25]

As can be seen from the previous discussion, it was philology that constructed the belief of the "exceptionality" of Arabs, expressed precisely in exceptional Arabic poetry, *in the language of the Qur'an*. Philological classicism was the foundation of Arabism as a cultural dominant in an important period of the Arab-Islamic caliphate.

I believe this can be related to a significant literary-historical fact. Before – but also after – the spread of Islam, Arabic literary tradition was markedly poetic. This fact promoted philology that, on its part, favoured Arabic poetry. Prose forms appeared relatively late, under the influence of the Persian literary heritage, or even under the influence of some works from ancient India (in Sanskrit), but again through Persian culture. This phenomenon is very interesting from the perspective of poetics because, among other things, it reveals the poetic sources of certain literary forms in (Arabic-)Islamic literature. However, the phenomenon can explain yet another feature of Arabic poetic and philological classicism.

Defending the "supremacy" of Arabic poetry as an important argument of Arabic nationalism, philology led old and classical Arabic poetry along the described path to a complete traditional isolation. It gave this tradition an overdose of self-sufficiency and self-confidence, cutting off its ways towards other traditions. This is the best means of conservation. It is no wonder, then, the Arabic poetic tradition remained completely beyond Aristotle's influence, even though Arabic-Islamic philosophy was considerably obliged and indebted to his influence; poetry also remained beyond the influence of all other poetic traditions, as well as of theoretical consideration. Philology does deserve due credit for the idea of Arabism, but the cost of it was very high – traditional isolation. This stands in complete contrast to all other creative and scientific fields developing during the Arab-Islamic caliphate. It should be kept in mind that Arabs *were* a people that, as very few others in history, were open to others, ready to infinitely learn from other cultures usually more developed than their own science and culture. This is the primary reason behind their meteoric cultural and civilisational rise in universal terms: as long as they remained open to other people's values, to which they had an attitude of "creative melting" rather than of mere consumption, there was no end to their rise. But, like a miracle – only their poetry remained isolated, narcissistic and hence creatively overclouded for too long. Philology was triumphant, and the future of its subject was, more or less, sacrificed.

I have mentioned that the Arabic tradition is characterised by the absence of theoretical consideration, and that it failed to develop aestheticism and literary theory in general. The importance of this fact becomes evident in the context of this discussion. Namely, the poetic issues philology dealt with were within the competence of literary theory and, certainly, aestheticism. Had they developed, they would certainly have established different relations to tradition and originality and, we can assume, the faith of Arabic literature would have been different. As it happened, philology took up the free space, acting outside its competence as well. Its initial virtue – commitment to the task of recording and preserving precious poetic heritage – became "corrupt" in time, as virtues will. Namely, philology turned the heritage it preserved into a norm against which the entire tradition was measured. It was a repressive demand on poets devoted to technicism and sorting through well-known and previously explored poetic motifs.

Tradition as a reservoir of motifs and poetic technique

Authoritative Arabic philologists had a more or less identical interpretation of the form–content relation in poetry. Identifying this relation was one of the fundamental aesthetic criteria in their approach to poetry; more precisely – it was of crucial importance for forming a value judgement from the position of *philological* criticism I represented so far, not of aestheticism that, as I said, was not developed. Establishing the form–content relation is certainly a fundamental poetic issue, so that the representation of the relation, in philological interpretation, was of huge importance for evaluating the current literary production – i.e. not only that of the past, but also strongly influencing future poetic production. The significance of this poetic issue requires a further discussion of it, summing up the views of several of the most important philologists that, at the same time, were (philological) literary critics of such authority that most other philologists were their epigones.

To begin with, it is necessary to give at least an outline reflecting the same problem in European literary theory and aestheticism. Although a commonplace, it should still be pointed out in order to contrast it with the classical Arabic interpretation of the form–content relationship. It will reveal a considerable difference in this regard, but the reader should keep in mind that it is not methodologically correct to unconditionally adhere to contrasting results, even though they may be useful since, as I explained, there was no mutual influence between the two traditions being contrasted; the contrariness is especially not surprising considering that it involves two very distant periods in two very different traditions. Nevertheless, I believe that contrasting still has its purpose since we refer to (deductive) poetics as a general literary experience and as a need for the general, common experience of it. The modern European literary-theory thought and poetics are not similar to European Renaissance poetics either: the former is, however, closer to Arabic classical poetics. I primarily refer to a relatively close conception of originality and the attitude towards ancient paragons of European and Arabic literatures. European Renaissance poetics and Arabic classical poetics set their ancient paragons as exemplars to be only emulated, without emphasising its own originality with respect to them in terms of the meaning of originality in the post-Romanticist period. In both cultural circles, this relates to their landmark or even revolutionary epochs that can be approached through the methods of comparison or contrasting, but I believe it mostly concerns a peripheral and almost momentary contact between the two circles: there is no intense blending of their respective experiences, but each culture remains within its own circle; their contact in a single point is more like a traditional excess than actual interpenetration. Such contact highlights the "roundedness" and self-sufficiency of each circle rather than their mutual "inflow". This certainly relates to the literary traditions of the two cultural circles, while the situation with their respective sciences, particularly philosophy, was completely different: the openness and "melting" method gave excellent results in this field.

For example, since scholars have long been disposed towards the method of comparison – which is frequently and incautiously equated with (direct) influences, there have been attempts to identify a direct link/influence between some fundamental works of the two cultural circles. Thus, there is a search for the influence of al-Ma'arri's (al-Maʻarrī, 973–1057) *The Epistle of Forgiveness* on Dante's *Divine Comedy*, the influence of Ibn Tufail's (Ibn Ṭufayl, d. *c.*1185)

Alive, Son of Awake on Daniel Defoe's *Robinson Crusoe*, etc. There is a vast body of literature about it – particularly about the links between al-Ma'arri's and Dante's works – claiming that Dante could certainly have had an insight into al-Ma'arris's work. Nevertheless, not even this is sufficient to support the conclusion about the interpenetration of their respective poetics: the literary *systems* remained unknown to each other.[26] A powerful and sparkling contact of the two circles happened on the periphery of Arabic-Islamic literary tradition so mightily filled by Arabic-Islamic literature in Spain, in Andalusia. The contact was so powerful that it opened a serious possibility of breaking the traditionalist isolationism, but from our distance, we know today that Arabic literary tradition resisted this temptation as well. Namely, two hybrid poetic forms did form in Andalusia – *muwashshah* and *zajal* – but they still remained, globally speaking, on the margins of the literary tradition. Despite their contemporary popularity, these two forms had not managed to permanently and generally change the ruling poetics in a vast literary empire and production, remaining at the level of a memorable poetic "incident".

However, returning to the dominance of the content–form dichotomy, the approach of Wellek and Warren immediately comes to mind, according to which the differentiation between the "form as the factor aesthetically active and a content aesthetically indifferent" encounters insurmountable difficulties.[27] The following discussion will show that the literary work in Arabic (philological) tradition was dichotomised in precisely this way. Insisting on "form" and "content", state Wellek and Warren,

> encourages the illusion that the analysis of any element of an artefact, whether of content or of technique, must be equally useful, and thus absolves us from the obligation to see the work in its totality. [...] A modern analysis of the work of art has to begin with more complex questions: its mode of existence, its system of strata.[28]

The philological analysis in Arabic tradition mostly treated the form and content of an artefact as distinct categories, analysing each of them separately and, even when it established a connection between them, upon an "expertise", the already established dichotomy could not be overcome, so much so that the form and content were evaluated differently – the form was favoured over the content, even though only together could they appear as a value. In addition, owing to its nature, philology paid special attention to language as an important, perhaps even crucial part of the form. It is also important here to keep in mind that philology was oriented towards archaic language as a value. We will see whether philologists succeeded in differentiating between words in themselves – i.e. aesthetically indifferent words – and the way they are organised into certain structures, aesthetically effective, or how philologists see the relationship between the aesthetic function of language and its "philological value".

Similarly, there is the issue of whether the preference of archaic language and traditional poetic forms is in some relation with the selection of poetic themes.

In other words, is archaic language, or modern language, appropriate for every theme and every poetic form?

When the *Qur'an* confronted poetry at the ideological level, poetry faced the problem of themes, at the highest possible level. For, the Text deprived poetry of the right to treat religious themes in the way it had done before the Text's descent. We have seen that the intervention in this domain had a shocking effect on tradition, which still agreed to the Text's terms of its survival. However, this opened the issue of themes that were recommended, or of the themes that were allowed, as well as that of the relationship to themes that were "already sung of". This context evokes Antara's "topical" couplet opening his mu'allaqa: "Have the poets left in the garment a place for a patch to be patched by me;/And did you know the abode of your beloved after reflection?" This couplet is at the beginning of not only Antara's mu'allaqa but also of the Arabic literary tradition, in a corpus that philology situated as an exemplary value. This means that the issue of poetic themes opened at the very wellspring of tradition, and that it represented one of the key and primeval poetic issues. However, the *Qur'an*'s intervention in the field of poetic themes was extremely serious, fateful, because poetry was denied the right to treat the most important religious themes. It can even be said to have been more than just a theme, as Antara's theme of love, for instance, is not at the same poetic level as the ancient poets' theme of pre-Islamic pagan deities. Antara's theme – just as a theme of some other poet – is not *differentia specifica* of a poetic epoch, not even of his poem, in the same sense as singing about deities and their communication with the poet-medium in authentic poetry of the pre-Islamic epoch. The theme in this epoch defined the character of poetry, its reception, the highest ideological and social status and function of poetry, just as its theme was much more than a theme: it represented a spiritual universe of Arabians and, at the same time, the subtlest expression of culture and sociality. This was the reason behind the sacred Text's determination to put an end to this theme as the very soul of poetry of the time, and was also the cause of the mayhem generated in tradition.

Certainly, poets had a myriad of themes at their disposal, apart from ideological pre-Islamic ones, and they turned to these themes after the Text's descent – from the lampoon and panegyric to love poetry. However, the Text's intervention with regard to the central ideological theme of poetry of the time was so forceful and significant that tradition was left with the issue of Theme as such in poetry. In other words, after the Text's decision, the issue was not whether there were themes to sing about but what themes these were, etc. – something like this is too ordinary and banal; it is neither a theoretical nor a poetical problem. The issue of theme was thus raised to the highest poetical level, and could be interpreted in the following way.

What is generally the importance of theme as such for poetry (and, certainly, what is its relationship to form)? Can its previous and supreme importance be retained by marginalising its significance, which was forced by the Text? What will happen with the social position of poetry by obliterating the importance of its themes dealt with in the literary past and of the same themes in the current production? This raises an important issue of epigonism and originality, technical virtuosity, etc. In short, the Text's intervention was positive in this domain because it turned the relatively banal issue of the selection of poetic themes – from one poet to another and outside the system – into a poetic issue of the highest order. It had to be resolved within tradition as a system.

The Qur'anic turnabout was complete and far-reaching because, for hundreds of years following it, poetry was developed on postulates making the issue of the poetic theme quite relative. Philologists-critics went so far as to claim that poetry had no ambitions with regard to the truth and truthfulness, which resembled the affirmation of Sidney, according to whom "the poet is the least liar; he nothing affirms and therefore never lieth".[29] This inaugurated an indifference to the truth in Arabic literature in ideological terms, as well as to truthfulness in terms of any social engagement of literature – until the twentieth century, when the term *artistic truthfulness* (*al-ṣidq al-fannī*), as the key poetic issue, was established by the *Mahjar* and *Apollo* poets, building a new and quite belated poetic turnabout in the long history of Arabic literature.

Poetic theme not necessarily sublime

Very few works in Arabic literature have had such a profound influence on philological criticism and literary production as the work entitled *Criticism of Poetry* (*Naqd al-shi'r*) by Qudama Ibn Ja'far (Qudāma Ibn Ja'far, 888–948). Qudama claimed that a motif per se had no value in a literary work; a motif per se had no poetic value.[30] Explaining this attitude, Qudama states that certain contents can be "ugly" in themselves, but it is the duty of the poet to shape them into a pleasing form. A sublime theme is not a prerequisite for a sublime poem.[31] One can hardly believe that such a turnabout was actually made in a literary tradition – from the demand imposed on pre-Islamic poetry to communicate the Truth to completely ignoring the importance of poetic theme! Of course, Qudama's attitude – as well as the attitudes of other philologists-critics, as we will see – was an essential prerequisite for promoting the technical values of poetry, for the exquisite mastery achieved by mastering tradition imposing itself precisely through philotechnical values. It further follows that the poetic polishing of a motif in terms of, for instance, its psychological correlation with the subject, in terms of its wrenching itself from the bizarre owing to the artist's gift to perceive it in particularities, in invisible, so-called ordinary people, etc. – all this is of no concern to Qudama; his only concern is for the motif to be clad in the robe of form and language.

Deriving other consequences from Qudama's attitude, one could rightly conclude that poetic mastery, demonstrated through "creating" a brilliant form, is all the more proven if the poet takes up a banal theme in order to successfully clad it in form; his success (and the value of his work) is proportionate to his ability to dress an "ugly" motif in as beautiful a form as possible.

Such derivation of ultimate consequences may seem far-fetched and malicious, but it is, undoubtedly, poetically immanent in Qudama's attitude. The dichotomy is poetically and aesthetically fatal. Admittedly, there is yet another nuance in Qudama's statement to be pointed out, but not even this nuance can change the basic tone and sense of the statement. Quite the contrary. Qudama says that a certain motif *in itself* has no value in a literary work. The paradox is precisely in the fact that the motif of an artefact cannot be discussed as a motif *in itself*, beyond the artefact: as soon as any motif is separated from the work of art, a living, pulsating "organism" is destroyed whose parts/elements, when separated, are not what they are in the organic whole. They are absolutely inseparable, which is why Wellek and Warren rightly say that a work of art must be analysed as "a *system* of strata" (my italics). None of these "layers of a system", in itself, has an aesthetic value; not even language that philologists pay considerable attention to has a literary or a poetic value beyond a literary work: all of them are aesthetically active when operating simultaneously in an artefact, and only then does a work have an *artistic* value. Dividing a work into its content (motif) and form can never interpret and present an artefact as a living, aesthetic value. Similarly, and for the same reason, the form cannot be given so much preference in presenting the essence of an artefact, just as the same preference cannot be given to the motif/content either, because they simply live, without giving preference to either of them, in a Crocean identity of intuition and expression. Nevertheless, Qudama's attitude, as I said, developed "technical arguments" for an unprecedented historical outburst of poetic technicism.

The described form–motif relationship in "post-Qur'anic" poetry is a consequence of a redefined importance of theme in a poetic text. In fact, the *Qur'an* correctly positioned the importance and meaning of a poetic motif, but the reason why poetry carried the form–content dichotomisation to an extreme is quite a different matter. Namely, by its own example, the *Qur'an* demonstrates an absolute unity of form and content, even emphasising – contrary to philologists' attitudes – that it is the content that aspires and succeeds to "assume" an appropriate form; the content is of primary importance in its poetics, but it is unimaginable for it to be separated from the form it is revealed in: the aesthetic values of the Text promote the revealed Idea, so that they are inseparable from each other. Therefore, the poetic importance of motifs in the *Qur'an* is enormous. At the same time, its polarity to post-Qur'anic poetry is also reflected in the fact that the *Qur'an* insists on the Truth as on the Beautiful and as on a condition of its survival, whereas poetry, deprived of the right of this quality of Truth, makes it quite relative by claiming that the poetic theme is irrelevant, that it can, "as such", even be ugly, etc., while the form is of crucial importance. Such contrasting must take into account the fact – and it is always very important! – that the *Qur'an* is not a work of art. This means, first of all, that it does not operate on the principle of artistic transposition, but proclaims and explains Reality and the Truth. This essential difference between the Text and poetry yields a number of further poetic differences. Nevertheless, taking a position on the importance/truthfulness of the motif or content, the *Qur'an* initiated the poetics of traditional poetry towards a direction in which poetics of literary art should actually develop. The poetics it initiated is in fact very modern, and is still current today, but philology led it astray for too long. Namely, the Text convincingly demonstrated that the Truth was not a condition for poetry's survival. This is an excellent anticipation of Sidney and many other modern theoreticians. For, according to the poetic implications of the *Qur'an*, poetry deals with transpositions that build worlds of fiction, so that the Truth should not be expected from it. Poetry can choose among a myriad of themes, instead of presenting the Truth in religious terms, so that the *Qur'an*'s implied attitude makes poetry actually privileged: it has no responsibility to the Truth and the World in terms of their authentic or factually truthful presentation, it is only supposed to express them in a number of artistic ways. Al-Ghazali's parable about a reflection on polished walls is constantly re-topicalised. It was only modern Arabic literature that raised the issue of art's responsibility to reality.

The poet's lack of obligation towards motifs, or his duty to prove himself only with regard to mastering poetic forms, is explicated in the next part of Qudama's discussion. He says: If a poet describes something as beautiful in one poem, and then describes it as ugly in another, the contradiction cannot be held against him, provided that he has managed to realise a beautiful form in both cases. Moreover, it shows him to be a true master.

There is hardly a better way to express the relativised importance of motifs. For, not only is the poet not bound by the selection of a motif and the perception of its singularity, which I have already pointed out, but he is recommended – in consequent consideration – to prove that he is able to clad even extremely "ugly" motifs in a beautiful form, or that he is such a virtuoso in the domain of form that he can present the same motif in two different, even opposite ways. Of course, the quotation clearly shows that the reference here is not to perceiving a particularity of the motif not perceived by other people, but to dressing the motif in a different form. From this position, Qudama can speak about the conditions for a good poem: it must consist of three parts, its parts must be mutually proportionate and related to the listener's/reader's desire, etc. One cannot but remember here the *Qur'an*'s attitude about the poets' "character" ("they rove distraught in every valley"), which indicates their "hypocrisy" in relation to the Truth.

There is yet another far-reaching aspect of such poetic constitution to be emphasised here. Namely, a complete relativisation of motifs, extremely explicated in Qudama's attitude quoted above, resulted in the fact that poetry did not deal with themes requiring the poet to have a stable and a high ethical position – expressed poetically, of course – because the outlined poetics of the Qudama type would not allow it. Not only the relativisation of motifs, but also the aforementioned stimulation to demonstrate the poet's "hypocritical" abilities preclude the possibility of a poetic treatment of *important* and *stable* themes – such as religious poetry with a wide range of "sub-themes", ethical poetry, etc. I have already said that Arabic old or classical poetry had no religious dimension such as poetry in Christian Europe, and one of the main reasons behind it becomes evident here. Sufi poetry is not a feature of this tradition, since it points to other sources.

Old Arabic poetry is not remembered as being didactic either, for the same reason. It was the utmost pleasure, completely extroverted, committed to its "external charms", ever so adorned with jingling rhyme and metre; it was, in Kantian terms, purposeless or disinterested.

In this regard, it is interesting to mention the literary-history constitution of the term *adab*, denoting literary art today. A brief discussion of this topic may seem digressive, but it essentially is not: it can indicate an earlier origin of the post-Qur'anic poetic purposelessness, its ethical and didactic disburdenment, and its thematic unboundedness as well.

In a long and historically significant period, the term *adab* did not denote *literature*. In the Prophet's time it denoted *moral upbringing*. In the transitional period and during the Umayyad dynasty (661–750) in addition to *moral upbringing*, *adab* also denoted *tutoring* (*ta'līm*); thus, engaged in *adab* were people who educated children of caliphs and taught them poetry, history, rhetoric and the like. In the caliphate Golden Age – during the Abbasid dynasty (750–1258) – *adab* denoted all the disciplines of science, human and natural, which cultivated man towards the social and the cultural.

Therefore, in a crucial, long period of tradition development, *adab* did not include poetry and did not even denote literature in its contemporary meaning. Poetry was autonomous and sovereign – in terms of its terminology, concept and genre. *Adab* was not compatible with poetry (*shi'r*) in terms of its concept or terminology. I have just shown that poetry was not bound by thematic choice, that it had no ambition to teach and morally educate, so that its nature was incompatible with the nature of *adab*, and it remained outside it. In the caliphate Golden Age, *adab* incorporated several prose forms mainly originating from outside the Arabic tradition (Persia, India, Greece), among which were, for instance, the works of Ibn al-Muqaffa' (Ibn al-Muqaffaʿ, d. 759), al-Jahiz (al-Jāḥiẓ, 775–868) and others. The primary goal of these prose works was to teach and morally educate caliphs and the general public, which is why they were subsumed under *adab* (education, moral upbringing). *Adab* included poetry only inasmuch as it dealt with it as a form of artistic creation, which every person pretending to be educated and cultivated had to know about. Poetry was part of a general education system, while it did not itself deal with teaching, education, etc.

I find this fact extremely important in terms of literary history and poetics. It testifies – factually, not speculatively – to three things.

First, poetry in the original Arabic tradition did not belong to the field of *adab* (*literature* in the meaning established in the Abbasid time) until a later period, when it was included under *adab* owing to the development of other literary forms coming from other traditions. It should be kept in mind that it had always remained mainly outside foreign influences – originally Arabic, even Arabian.

Second, poetry did not belong to the field of *adab*, either conceptually or terminologically, because it did not provide education in religious or extra-religious disciplines. It was the ultimate individual and collective expression of pleasure, a game with language and form with only aesthetic commitments. Owing to the decision of the *Qur'an* to deprive it of ideological prerogatives, poetry could thereupon become quite airy.

Third, poetry expressed the awareness of its own unboundedness through a complete relativisation of poetic motifs or themes. After the *Qur'an*, poetry did not consent to provide education or teaching, but directed full attention to its "corporality", to the form for the sake of purely aesthetic enjoyment, not for the sake of epistemological rise or educational achievements. It actually became "pure poetry" and, as such, dominated the Arab-Islamic empire for hundreds of years, an empire that, at its peak, encompassed a major part of the civilised world. It was, no doubt, a truly poetical empire, a long-lasting poetic empire.

This perspective re-illuminates the rootedness of the term used for poetics – *technique of poetry* (*fann al-sh'ir*). Considering all of this, *poetics* could not possibly have found an Arabic equivalent in the (non-existent) term *fann al-adab*. Retaining the term *technique of poetry* for *poetics*, this tradition preserved the memory of the described status of poetry with respect to literary history and poetics, indirectly suggesting that it was included in the concept of *adab* through force of circumstance, and implying that it has been dominant in the tradition that it still marks with crucial terms.

Reducing aesthetics to the content–form relationship, medieval philological critics underlined that contents/motifs were in the nature of all people, those illiterate and unskilled as well as those educated and skilled. The whole point was, they believed, to present these universal motifs through a masterfully developed form and optimally chosen, adequate words. Only outstanding persons – poets – could do it.[32] Ibn Rashiq in his famous work *al-'Umda...* states that poetic mastery is not being proved through the singularity of contents or motifs, since there actually are no such contents and motifs, but through forms resulting from content.[33] The given context reveals the importance of a branch of Arabic classical stylistics *al-ma'ānī*, which I have mentioned as a stylistic discipline concerned with "rules according to which speech is adapted to a certain speech situation". Other distinguished philologists also expressed similar views on motifs. By offering an optimal summary of their positions on this issue I run the risk of increasing the redundancy of my text, but I will do so anyway in order to demonstrate how redundant this huge philological production actually was. Its persistence was quite remarkable and it is interesting that reiteration of more-or-less the same attitudes was of little or no detriment to the authority of their authors.

Al-Askari (Abū Hilāl al-'Askarī, d. 1005) also states that content is common to all reasonable people: a plebeian, a so-called common man and a black man, can have good content, but people are distinguished from one another by their word arrangement, composition, versification.[34]

Ibn Tabataba is among those who believed that all motifs were exhausted rather early and that new poets may borrow them, provided that they embellish and tirelessly refine them. Accepting a frequently used comparison between a poet and a jeweller, Ibn Tabataba concludes that many beautiful motifs were ruined by form, and conversely many ugly motifs were promoted in beautiful attire.[35]

This analogous image of the jeweller's craft is worthy of mention in the section discussing the technique of poetry as a dominant criterion of literary value. The image is quite frequent in classical philological criticism, just as the one Qudama Ibn Ja'far gives of a tree and the carpenter's craft. We will see how far Abdul-Qahir al-Jurjani ('Abd al-Qāhir al-Jurjānī, d. 1078) went in developing this image.

Following the demands of their field, medieval philologists arrived at a conviction that all motifs had been exhausted prior to the ninth century, so that poets composing poetry after had no selection of new motifs but had to compose variations on "old" motifs. Centuries before these philologists, at the dawn of ancient Arabic poetics, Antara Ibn Shaddad lamented precisely the tradition's saturation with motifs: it seemed to him that the poet had nothing to sing about any more.

If the importance and nature of motifs are seen from the perspective of medieval philologists, it is only natural that it will lead to their archetypes in the antique, just as it is natural for these (proto)motifs to be proclaimed (proto) paragons.[36]

The origin of poetic motifs in Arabic antiquity

Not understanding the poetic status of motifs properly, medieval philologists searched for the origin of motifs, or for the first appearance of a given motif in tradition. Since philologists' main task was to differentiate authentic poetry from that which was forged or plagiarised, they also applied the principle of authenticity to the philological "valuation" of motifs. Their "authenticity" or primariness was to be established, which, at the same time, meant that the relation of all other poets to the same motif was also something to be identified. The authenticity of a motif in deductive poetics is of no concern because a motif is always authentic, but primariness did matter in philological poetics, since classical poetics was steadily directed towards the past – always towards authenticity! – then defining the authentic period of tradition as exemplary, by means of the opposite direction of induction. Normativeness is inevitable on such a path.

From the temporal and "value" position of these philologists, the entire past represented a reservoir of motifs, making it impossible for new motifs to be found, or for them to participate in the originality of a poetic work. Originality was, actually, something unfamiliar. Motifs were drawn from the patterns of the ancient and, possibly, early Islamic epochs. Since the chronological criterion was very important to this philology, it was exactly this authenticity pattern that was valued as the highest. It is no wonder then that distinguished philologists judged pre-Islamic poetry as the best type of poetry and that, for example, al-Asmai said that the famous Umayyad triad – Jarir, al-Farazdaq and al-Akhtal – would have been good had they been pre-Islamic poets. This "judgement" is not a rhetorical figure or poetic nonsense, but an inevitable result of the constitution of inductive philological poetics.

A model-paragon from these early periods was compared with a different pattern of the same motif, with a certain deviation from the original pattern allowed, but without tolerance for a poetic "shaping" of the same pattern in the same form as presented by an earlier poet; it had to be given new robes of language, rhyme, metre. Therefore, the mastery of form was crucial. A motif already treated previously in tradition was denoted by the root *sbq* (previous), by which criticism emphasised that someone else had "found" the motif, and that this person had absolute primacy in its hierarchy of values. The term *innovative* (derived from the root *bd'*) denoted a motif containing an idea of novelty, or a rare originality contained in the author's ability to master motifs "created by God". The poet never creates: he only discovers, whether motifs created by God or motifs of his predecessors. We are yet again in front of al-Ghazali's polished wall. In fact, Arabic tradition saw a transformation of motifs only.

One of the main forms of motif transformation was amplification – i.e. branching out, or expanding the main motif identified in the poetic heritage.[37] For example, the motif of charity was identified in the ancient *qaṣīda* in one of its main thematic parts. Namely, one of the major goals of the *qaṣīda* was often to praise the charity of a notable in order for this notable to give a patronage gift to the poet. This is one of the dominant motifs of ancient, pre-Islamic poetry. The motif was built in the multi-thematic structure of the *qaṣīda* in such a way that it remained insufficiently developed, not independent in terms of genre. Other poets of the ancient epoch also included this motif in their poems. The motif had become a collective one. Of course, poets also expressed it in different words in poems that had a different metric organisation. Moreover, one and the same set of motifs was conscientiously and competitively treated in the ancient *qaṣīda*, so it is no wonder that, even several centuries later, the repetitiveness of motifs held such an important position in poetics. Poets often used even the same figures of speech to praise a patron's charity: a patron is like sea waves, like bountiful rain, like sunlight, etc.[38] In later epochs, actually as early as the Umayyad epoch, the motif of charity branched out into an independent poetic form – into panegyric, a genre every poet cultivated within his opus, particularly poets at court, or those close to powerful persons, for which there were two reasons: poetry was rather lucrative so that panegyric was an excellent source of income and, at the same time, it was a proof of an important adherence to tradition. If a poet had not transformed the motif of charity in terms of its branching out, he was obligated to at least cloak it in a different form.

Let us take another characteristic example. The motif of love was compulsory in the pre-Islamic *qaṣīda*, in the position of its prologue – as a love lyric prelude. The motif was made stereotypical not only in terms of its position within the *qaṣīda*, but also in terms of a number of other details. Namely, as a rule, poets – on an imaginary, poetic journey – stopped (usually with two friends) by a deserted bivouac where the poet's beloved had her abode before riding off with her tribe into the sun-drenched immenseness. Stopping by the bivouac, the poet sings love verses, still making his motif typical: situations in which his love developed are more-or-less also typical – stealing love between soft sand dunes with female curves, preceded by the poet's penetration to his beloved through her tribe, etc.[39]

The poet did not dare compose a poem without such a lyric prologue because, without it, his poem would not have been accepted. The greater persistence of a motif can hardly be imagined. Moreover, when the motif of lavishness, for example, became an independent form in panegyric poetry, poets began even their panegyrics to caliphs with a love lyric prologue.

In the Umayyad epoch the motif of love was transformed into *ghazal* as a poetic form – therefore, into love poetry that further developed into two subtypes – into Umarite and Udhri love poetry. The motif kept transforming, but even as an independent poetic form it preserved the memory of its origin – not only in terms of ambience (the desert, dunes, long caravans and riding animals, various obstacles and hardships), but also in terms of form and style, because not infrequently did poets use the same figures of speech to present the motif of love. Nevertheless, there was always the condition to do so in a different metre and different rhyme. Thus the motif branched out into a number of "motif sequences" that were mildly and very gradually "enriched", as traditionalism had become too strong to be confronted with originality.

It is important to give a clear presentation of poets' relation to the motif, since it is one of the foundations of old poetics, both the old and the entirety of medieval Arabic literature. I will therefore illustrate the adherence to classical motifs through Bashar Ibn Burd's relation to them. My choice of the poet is not random, but is based on two reasons. First, he appeared long after the structure of the ancient *qaṣīda* and the motif of love in it had been established. Second, tradition pronounced Bashar Ibn Burda a *poet of renewal*, revealing a lot about the concept of renewal at the time. Before the reader pays attention to the figures from Bashar I will offer, they should know the poet was blind: the figures he uses singing about the traditional motif are also traditional – other poets used the same figures as well, but they used different metres and rhymes.

Bashar's lyric heroine is somewhere between a gorgeous Bedouin woman and a harem beauty (the novelty compared to the pre-Islamic period consists of the "*harem* beauty", since harems were a legacy of the new age); her waist is like a palm branch; her thighs are round and heavy like a sand-hill; when her veil is removed, she shines like the sun or the moon (the Arabic ideal of female beauty ever since Imru' al-Qays is a fair complexion suggesting non-exposure to the sun, protection, etc.); she is like a desert mirage (the ultimate typicality).[40] Her skin is white; her complexion is always fair; her teeth are a string of pearls; when walking, she resembles a snake lured by bushes; her hair, when loose, falls heavy like vine clusters.[41]

Poets treated other motifs in a similar way as well: the camel, desert heat, wine, etc. Evidently, and with reference to the previous discussion, a thorough knowledge of tradition was crucial. The poetic variation of traditional motifs was recommended, and poets did not shy away even from using the same figures of speech. Truthfulness and sincerity, in terms of a poet's truthful perception of reality, became quite insignificant and even turned into their opposites, which Bashar's variation of motifs only testifies to, even more so as he was proclaimed one of the best representatives of the so-called Abbasid epoch. Namely, Bashar's contemporaries were not bothered by the fact they were all aware of – that the poet was blind and that the figures and motifs were not from his world, as he could not physically perceive them; the motifs and figures in his world were rather an echo of traditionalism. In different "poetic conditions", a blind poet could be expected to sing about *his* perception of a woman, not based on his sense of sight, and such a poem would probably be different from all other love poems, as it would "result" from a different kind of (sensory) perception. But, the point is that the poem was not to be *completely* different, since tradition and the ruling traditional poetics did not allow it. The audience found such poetics and its demonstration in artistic production more important than originality, than truthfulness and sincerity. Bashar's poetry, being representative, testifies to the authority of a traditional motif more than any originality. For, had Bashar written poetry following his senses and their particular sensations – as an experience of a woman and love in the world of a *blind* poet of such great and "peculiar" sensibility that he was able to mark the most important epoch in the history of Arabic literature – it would have raised a possibility, a danger actually, for the motif to be transformed into something poetically unrecognisable, or even for a new motif to be discovered, for example, the motif of pain for not being able to enjoy the physical allure of a woman through "eyesight". But the infinite loyalty to the tradition of motifs would thus have been betrayed, and it is most clearly and most confidently recognised precisely in motifs. The audience was interested in it more than in anything else, while originality in the new-age or Romanticist meaning of the term was faithless and, as such, unwelcome. Bashar's poetics and poetic "valour" could – paradoxically – gain strength exactly from this paradoxicality: though blind, the poet brilliantly mastered the tradition whose poetic and stylistic dominants he optimally promoted, for which, perhaps first and foremost, he deserved to be praised.

Bashar's high poetic status in his time suggests these conclusions. They may seem too strict, perhaps even speculative, as someone may say that my reconstruction is inauthentic, or that one can hardly believe the audience had such a way of thinking. Nonetheless, such doubts have no basis. We have enough reliable sources testifying to the fact that Bashar was held in high esteem by his contemporaries. This fact and his love lyricism lead to such conclusions. Seen from the distance of today's panoramic transparency, there is no doubt that the poetics of the time was such indeed and that Bashar continuously promoted it through his love poetry. The poet composed in other poetic forms as well, but what I am interested in here is the position of the dominant motif (of love) in his poetry.

There is yet another important aspect of this motif to be highlighted here, an aspect taken over from the reservoir of tradition, or, more precisely, from its wellspring in the heroic period of Arabic literature.

While discussing the simile in Arabic ancient literature, I gave a detailed interpretation of the so-called materialism of this poetry, expressed in images of sensory perception and stylistically represented by the dominant figure of simile, as well as the observable absence of metaphoric transfer. It is now brilliantly, and retrospectively, reflected in Bashar ibn Burd's figures. His love poetry not only conveys the motif of love from the ancient *qaṣīda* prologue, with an abundance of ancient "sub-motives", but it also contains their "stylistic treatment" of the same kind. Ancient poets are today often reproached for being focused only on the sensory perception of the woman, but it is overlooked that their poetic experience and stylistic means were taken over even in the most brilliant period of Arabic literature, such as in the poetry of Bashar Ibn Burd. His poetry confirms that post-Qur'anic epochs saw the branching out of not only motifs but also the same stylistic means used to represent them. The "materialism" of Ibn Burd's *ghazal* is obvious, but it is also extreme considering the fact that it is not a result of the poet's sensory perception but of a poetic dictate. In addition, the simile, as a stylistic means, is dominant, or even exclusive; its nuances or branching out, just like the branching out of motifs, can only conditionally be treated as an innovation, although it is non-innovative in poetic terms; moreover, the old poetics demonstrates the enormous strength of its normativeness here. For, the motif is *taken over* as an ancient pattern, its "materialistic treatment" is *taken over* and the dominant figure of simile is *taken over*.

As most other philologists, al-Asmai thus claims that everyone pretending to be a good poet must have a thorough knowledge of the themes, or motifs, of old poets. He understands the motif (*ma'nā*) not only as a thematic element that, in practice, can correspond to a number of specific individual instances, the author's realisations, or varieties.[42] It follows from this that poetry is based on a set system of motifs poetically promoted in tradition. Transformation and innovation of motifs appear to be quite limited.

Motifs as commonplaces or topoi

Among the far-reaching consequences of philological criticism and the poetics it cultivated is an abundance of commonplaces in Arabic literature. In this regard, it is similar to the literature of Latin medievalism in Europe. It seems that a methodological encouragement can be found in the work entitled *European Literature and the Latin Middle Ages* by E. R. Curtius, who identified a number of topoi in European literature of this period. Similarly, Arabic literature can also be successfully presented through studying and identifying its topoi that basically represent a large part of this literary history. The motifs of love and charity, which I analysed as examples of the position of motifs in tradition, are actually commonplaces in Old Arabic literature, with more or less developed variations in the works of individual poets. In other words, defining the "traditional sum" of motifs, poetics turned them into topoi that, owing to their superabundance, made the concept of artistic originality quite relative. I am convinced that this method of researching the history of Arabic literature will offer an extremely interesting and authentic "topographic picture" of Old Arabic literature. The topoi are not only the motifs of charity and love (with their branches), but also other motifs that were given the same status in tradition – that of paragons or patterns. An indecisive and insufficient innovation of these motifs in works of subsequent poets does not in the least affect their nature as topoi, because tradition makes them immortal. Moreover, a constant repetition of the same motif paragons, albeit only for a poet to demonstrate his mastery of tradition and poetic technique, underlines their poetic function as commonplaces time and time again. Thus, tradition as a reservoir of motifs is, actually, defined as a specific relief of topoi.

In the history of Arabic literature there is a fact strengthening the status of motifs as topoi in addition to the one I presented as the poet's duty to adhere to traditional or, better, old motifs having already been attempted by poetic pens.

Namely, the motif of love always held the position of the prologue in the structure of the ancient poem; the motif of panegyric came at the end of the poem, having the function of a particular colophon; other motifs were arranged between these two. I have already mentioned that, even deep into the Islamic epoch, panegyric, for instance, opened with a love lyric prelude. This means that their relatively settled positions in the poem's structure appeared as a commonplace factor: they were on the border of structural schematisation. Furthermore, in these cases one can even speak about a particular accumulation of topoi. Namely, since the motif of charity and the motif of panegyric "conditioning" it are already topoi in old literature, it is quite unexpected for another motif/topos to be placed in their introductory part – a love-lyrical prologue confirming by its positioning not only its nature of topos, but by the accumulation principle, association with other topoi, underlining the functionality of topoi in this literature in general.

Finally, in addition to this, there is also the fact that philological criticism attached the highest value precisely to such structure of themes/motifs, therefore considering ancient Arabic poetry exemplary. Philology and its criticism clearly found their ideal in literary topoi. For, discerning the authentic in terms of authorship authenticity (which is different from authorship originality) from the inauthentic, philology and its criticism aspired to achieve their two main goals through the same research procedure. One goal was to identify the chronological authenticity of certain motifs, while the other, concurrent goal was to establish the repetitiveness of motifs in tradition and their possible variations. Thus, registering the repetitiveness of motifs and recommending an endless poetic exploitation of the same motifs, philology defined these motifs as topoi. We have already seen that the philological path to the source of motifs led to the consecration of ancient Arabic literature, which had generated a majority of these motifs.

It is interesting to see how the distinguished philologist al-Qadi al-Jurjani (al-Qāḍī al-Jurjānī, d. 1003) classifies motifs in Arabic poetry. The first category includes *common motifs* (*mushtarak*). These are motifs we have discussed so far, and they are dominant in Arabic poetry. Common motifs are the most frequent, as a "common good" on which literary tradition is based. The second category consists of *hackneyed* or *banalised motifs* (*mubtadhal*) resulting from banalising common motifs (pre-motifs) through their poetic reintroduction. The Arabic term for banalised motifs, *mubtadhal*, actually suggests motifs having become hackneyed through frequent use, as the basic meaning of the word *mubtadhal* is *worn-out*, *hackneyed*. However, if we bear in mind the general, dominant attitude of philology that a motif in itself cannot be unworthy of a poem, or that the use of pre-motifs is desirable provided they are put in a different form, then the *hackneyed status* of motifs results from the inadequate form in which they are clad, rather than from their repetition. The motif of charity or the motif of (desert) rain, as well as a number of other motifs, are pre-motifs, motifs-paragons, used in poetry as topoi for hundreds of years, but are not judged as hackneyed if re-dressed in an adequate language and form. Finally, al-Jurjani offers the third category of motifs: *independent motifs* (*mukhtaṣṣ*) that are an author's individual, special and specific motifs. Such motifs are relatively rare and are, in time, transformed into common motifs, thus becoming part of the reservoir of motifs.[43]

Even the conventional form of *qaṣīda* from the Arabic ancient period represents a topos, if such a complex structure can be called a topos at all. Namely, I have just said that the old *qaṣīda* was composed of a number of obligatory motifs, which more clearly separated and branched out and which, in time, tradition translated into topoi. However, the positions of certain themes within the poem's structure were mostly fixed, with rare exceptions that tradition judged as excesses, so that the entire (thematic) structure of the poem appeared as a particular topos, or as a commonplace in tradition that, only in the Umayyad epoch, saw motifs separate and develop into independent poetic forms. When a poet, for instance, composed a *qaṣīda* without the love lyric prologue, it was considered a poetic excess.

In the Umayyad epoch the motif of love lyricism developed into *ghazal* as an independent and self-sufficient poetic form that represented the literary dominant of the whole epoch. However, other motifs of the complex ancient *qaṣīda* also developed into independent poetic forms: panegyric (*madaḥ*) and lampoon (*hijā'*) were the main, popular and profitable patronage genres in all the Islamic epochs – until the last great panegyrist, an Egyptian poet Ahmad Shawqi (Aḥmad Shawqī, 1868–1932), who became very wealthy through his masterly panegyrics.[44] The epoch of classicism (corresponding to the Abbasid period and the period of decadence, according to the usual classification) saw the appearance of several independent poetic forms – wine poems (*khahmriyyāt*), ascetic poems (*zuhdiyyāt*), hunt poems (*ṭardiyyāt*), descriptive poetry (*waṣf*), etc. Although literary histories often define these poetic forms as radical innovations in tradition, as completely new poetic forms, still, it is not so. Namely, each of these thematic-genre forms had existed as a pre-motif in the ancient *qaṣīda* but, in time, the motifs branched out through amplification into independent thematic-genre forms. The unexpectedness of these forms in literary history and their allegedly absolute originality can appear as such to those interpreters of Arabic literary history who fail to discern the fundamental principles of its poetics or the philological nature of poetics and its poetry. Nevertheless, bearing in mind that uncompromising philology defined tradition as a repository of motifs whose origin it identified in the ancient *qaṣīda*, and that it encouraged the branching out of these motifs as – from its perspective – an ideal way to refine tradition, it then follows that these poetic forms were not created outside the identified reservoir of motifs but as the highest achievement of their refinement. What is more, these forms can – through the consequent consideration that poetics require – be defined as the genuine triumph of the simultaneous influence of philology, philological poetics and philological criticism.

Triumph of philological poetics: spreading across the entire Islamic cultural community

The previous discussion leads to an important conclusion that an abundance of topoi prevents the originality of an individual talent. All its poetic endeavours are subordinated to exploits of tradition. The ultimate consequence of this, which is not surprising in the context of the previous discussion, is that tradition is the only true "protagonist" of poetics and literary history; it is only tradition that is inherently valorous and creative, although its creativity should be understood rather conditionally as it is based on normative inductive poetics. Creativity of tradition is realised in a closed system of values set as norms. This kind of creativity has a limited range of achievements since poetics introduced the content–form dichotomy, giving preference to the form and reducing content to a sum of motifs already known from poetic variations. In other words, individual creation can only be realised *within a framework of norms* that, as such, not only impose no commitment but even prevent revolutionary creative breakthroughs on the edges of traditional experience. Tradition thus strictly controls the potential of an individual talent, directing them to the greatest extent possible towards the technical side of poetry that – in this technique – reflects traditional motifs time and again. At the same time, it controls an individual talent by requiring it, without any exception, to fully master tradition, or even to memorise traditional poetry to an extreme degree – in order for a "new" poet to become completely aware of the indisputability of traditional poetry. This created a general atmosphere of poetic traditionalism, having always been known for building impenetrable borders as a condition of its survival, as well as for finding the true meaning in self-isolation that, in turn, necessarily leads to decadence. Breaking these stranglehold borders and healing tradition from the illness called decadence can only be done by huge vortices in cultural history that appear ever so rarely and that we name the renaissance of a culture. Minor breakthroughs are of no avail here because traditionalism subdues them to its own laws – even if such breakthroughs are like those Abbasid poetic forms that I have defined as not being even close to poetic innovation, let alone renaissance, even though some literary historians consider them to be poetic forms of reformative importance.

Philological poetics had tremendous achievements. Peoples who entered the circle of Arabic-Islamic culture, and the Arabic-Islamic civilisation generally, could not significantly affect Arabic poetic creativity. Persian poetry (and culture generally) seems to have been the strongest among those that entered the field of Arabic tradition and that very confidently sought their place in this culture, or literature. There is no doubt that some giants, like Hafez (fourteenth century), gave new impulses to the so-called Islamic tradition they still deeply marked by their opuses. However, two things should be kept in mind with regard to this.

First, the Persian tradition introduced significant innovations into the Arabic-Islamic culture by bringing literary forms unknown to Arabs. There are various prose literary forms among them. I have already said that poetry was traditionally and distinctly Arabic and that a discussion about the poetics of Old Arabic literature is, in fact, a discussion of the poetics of poetic artistic creation. This literary-history fact should always be kept in mind.

Second, a beneficial effect of Persian poets was nevertheless from a different language, from Persian, which Hafez wrote in as well, and it only emphasises the fact about the isolation and autonomy, even self-centredness of the Arabic poetic tradition. Therefore, Hafez and other great poets of the Persian language do not belong to Arabic literature but to a wider system comprising Arabic literature as well; I will offer more details about this system further in my discussion. I here refer to a poetics that aspired to convey its postulates – actually its poetic system – onto other authors of the *Islamic aesthetic circle* as well, regardless of the fact they wrote in different languages.

A similar situation occurred when Turkish culture entered this great Islamic circle, though with significant differences, as Ottoman culture prior to Islamisation was not as developed as Persian culture. The development of a culture will greatly affect its ability to refine another culture through "grafting". Turkish and Persian cultures were not equal in these terms before entering the circle of Islamic culture. Still, the Turks provided a number of important poets later on, though in the Turkish language. However, Arabic poetic tradition was not too willing to accept the poetic influences of Islamised peoples. It rather strived to impose its own poetic principles on them and did it rather successfully. It had the strategic support, inter alia, of two significant factors.

The first factor is language with its several "assistants". It is well known that Arabic is the language of Islam, which made it privileged because Persians and Turks had to be well familiar with it – as with the language of the *Qur'an* and worship. It is also important to bear in mind that it is the same Arabic language in which Arabic poetry was composed. In other words, the *Qur'an* did not impose language alone on Persians and Turks – although it would have sufficed for exerting an influence; it also used its ideal model of this language to constantly keep a number of *stylistic means* as supernatural stylistic patterns alive in the minds of educated Persians and Turks. When I speak about imposing the Arabic language on Persians and Turks, I refer to the degree of knowledge they had to have of it as the language of the *Qur'an* and worship. Nonetheless, even though the Persian and Turkish languages kept on, they took over many things from Arabic precisely owing to Islam, or to the *Qur'an*. Every book on Arabic stylistics abounds in stylistic examples from the *Qur'an*, as well as from Arabic poetic production. It follows from this that the Arabic poetic tradition very inventively and unexpectedly "sneaked" by the *Qur'an* into the literary experience of even those peoples belonging to other major languages. It is also generally known that both Persians and Turks adopted the Arabic script, which is also important in the context of the aforementioned influence.

The other factor is unavoidable philology. Since Arabic philology was in a way also a theological, exegetic discipline, generated to promote the *Qur'an*, it inevitably conveyed experiences of (and about) literature to Islamised peoples as well, because the exegesis of the *Qur'an* is inconceivable without an interpretation of its linguistic and, generally, literary and aesthetic layer. Consequently, this "installed" philological poetics into the literatures of Islamised peoples, supported by the authority of the *Qur'an*'s literary values. Owing to the *Qur'an* and its language, with all the other effects the *Qur'an* generated in terms of culture and civilisation, a huge circle was created that considerably surpassed the boundaries of the Arabic world, including other major peoples and their traditions. The circle was importantly marked by Islam, which is why it can only be called an Islamic circle, and its culture and civilisation Islamic culture and civilisation.

Islam is more than a religion in the sense that the term is applied to other religions. Leaving aside its regulating the economic, legal and all other aspects of individual and community life, it should be noted that it has its particular aesthetics, on which a vast body of literature has been written. However, little attention is paid to the important fact that is not very obvious but is quite complex and effective indeed. Namely, the whole previous discussion shows that Islam had a powerful influence on literature as well. This influence was, first and foremost, evident in the *Qur'an*'s attitude towards poetry, then in the very high literary and aesthetic values and language of this sacred Text, and also in the development of the philology it initiated and directed. This clearly led to a very complex system for influencing literature as well.

The expansion of the Islamic circle in terms of its culture and civilisation entailed the expansion of a specific influence of Islam on poetics that had important elements common to the artistic production of all the Islamised peoples, regardless of the fact that literature was also produced in other languages as well, not only in Arabic. This generated literature that was promoted as a supranational system. However, this was not a specific quality of literature produced by non-Arabs in the Arabic language either. The Latin language in medieval Europe, for example, had the same position. The Turkish language – once the Ottoman Empire was established – was the language of very successful production by non-Turkish nations, including Bosniaks. It is characteristic of Arabic literature to have affected the literatures of non-Arabic speaking Islamic peoples as well. In other words, there are many reasons to speak about *Islamic literature* as a vast system, even though its works were produced in several languages, not only in Arabic.

The term *Islamic literature* is a less than ideal solution because it is, quite incorrectly, associative of a religious dimension of literature, suggesting a literature that promotes the theological values of Islam, suggesting some religious literature, etc. Quite the contrary – the term *Islamic literature* does not imply a theological literature, but a vast abundance of literary works that, through the mediation and described influence of Islam, poetically became a part of a special cultural circle, of a supranational and, paradoxically, non-monolingual system inheriting and generating common poetic postulates throughout the Islamic world. In the following discussion I will illustrate this community of postulates on the example of shared motifs and topoi.

In chronological terms: ancient Arabic poetry – the *Qur'an* – philology – philological poetics are factors that Islam conveyed to other traditions, affecting not the "religiousness" of literature but only the universalism of a poetics.

On the other hand, the term *Islamic literature* – especially today, in the age when the Islamic and Judeo-Christian cultures and civilisations are in confrontation – connotes the political idea of (pan-)Islamism that the West immediately identifies as ideologically aggressive. Of course, this literature, or the term I use in want of a better solution, has nothing to do with it.

The other possible term – *literature/literatures of Islamic peoples* – is, I believe, also inadequate because the phrase fails to express the unity of literatures of different peoples; it fails to point at what is important indeed – rather than the system in which it was created, it emphasises a mechanical correlation instead.

The fundamental constituent element of a poetics that had created a supranational or even supra-linguistic system consisted of the motifs we have discussed so far. Presenting tradition as a repository of motifs that were only to be refined, philology used its great authority to impose the same poetic *credo* on other nations entering into the Islamic circle as into the firmest "framework" into which all other cultural and civilisation experiences had melted. Motifs kept being taken over so that they branched out into other languages as well. One example will serve as a sufficient illustration.

The love lyric prelude, as a motif, developed from the ancient Arabian *qaṣīda* into an independent poetic form, into *ghazal*, which had two main branches – Umarite and Udhri *ghazal*. Through the method of amplification, the Udhri *ghazal* saw the rise of the everlasting epic of Majnun and Layla, which became a love poetry commonplace and which continued to multiply. However, the *Majnun–Layla* motif was conveyed from Arabic literature to literature in the Turkish language, where it also won the status of a commonplace. There is a myriad of such motifs. The poetics of the cultural circle was such as to encourage the stability and repetition of motifs in tradition. Moreover, peoples joining the Islamic circle felt, through the charm of novelty, a creative curiosity towards motifs having already been established in a tradition brimming with self-confidence, so that they refreshed these motifs with their own stylistic interpretations and assimilation into their experiences of literature. Turkish *Majnun and Layla* are not quite the same as Arabic but are not so different either as to not observe the same motif behind it.

Expanding diachronically and synchronically, motifs established as commonplaces further strengthened their character as topoi. Namely, branching out in history and space, motifs became reinforced as commonplaces, and since they were transferred to literatures in other languages marked by the broadest symbols of Islam, they became the topoi of the highest order. On the other hand, topoi concurrently proved to be the strongest cohesive element ensuring a certain poetic community of literature as a huge system.

There is something I find very interesting, even unique in relation to this system. Namely, *Islamic literature*, in the described sense, as a system, is not composed of a single language, since it has been produced in several languages; what makes it a system is precisely the system of motifs-topoi. I therefore believe that a study of the three major literatures (Arabic–Persian–Turkish), systematised in their classical periods, would give excellent results if the system of topoi all three abound in is researched. It would show that they have common poetic grounds and that such an approach is very fruitful in terms of scientific research. I am not aware that the classical period of the Islamic cultural circle literary production has been researched in this way as yet. These literatures are studied as three separate bodies. The basis for such an approach is found in the fact that they were produced in three different languages even though, as I have already mentioned, the factor of Islam generated many elements of similarity and influence among the languages in question: from their scripts, lexis and figures of speech, to complexes of topoi, etc. This type of similarity and influence has been closely studied on a linguistic level, but – since its effects did not stop at a linguistic level, it would be very interesting – and I believe this will be done – to examine the linguistic aspect at the poetic level.

Studying these three literatures separately – of course, I here refer to their classical periods, and later on I will show why I stress *classical periods* – is not unjustified, but is not sufficient either, because it fails to reach important results for two reasons.

First, what I have termed *Islamic literature*, as a supranational and supralinguistic system, testifies to the fact that the linguistic criterion is not self-sufficient, that it cannot be the only constituent of literature and poetics *as a system*, because it fails to grasp many other important constituents, among which topoi appear particularly strong. The absence of authorship originality in its modern sense, or a complete poetic and critical legalisation of topoi – typical of the classical period – made relative the importance of language to a much higher degree than is the case today. I believe *Islamic literature* to be unique in this regard.

Second, their completely separate research is an expression of the "attitude of the present" to a different past. For, if these three literatures are studied separately today, which is reasonable, it is methodologically wrong not to notice that, in their classical periods, they were not made specific in the same way and with the same quality. The *exclusiveness* of the "attitude of the present" has never been methodologically appropriate in its relationship to the past. Three Oriental Studies departments in Yugoslavia study Arabic, Turkish and Persian literatures separately. Since they are studied within the same department, they are actually brought into a relationship of (mechanical) parallelism, instead of an interactive one. I am not aware of anywhere else in the world where they are studied according to an essentially different methodology. Certainly, this concerns a vast body of material that must be segmented for practical purposes, but I believe that a study of Oriental philology should include an approach/course that would apply a comparative method to these three literatures – in order to explain their shared commonplaces and shared initial poetics.

The terms for certain poetic forms in *Islamic literature*[45] are closely related. These terms, in most cases, originate from Old Arabic literature and are domestic in all three "components" of *Islamic literature*. Such terms, for instance, *ghazal*, *madaḥ*, *hijā'*, *rithā'*, etc., are taken over by Persian and Turkish literatures.[46] This is not a sheer terminological resemblance, or coincidence, but a literary historical fact suggesting the common source of the genres, leading all the way to the ancient Arabian *qaṣīda*. At the same time, having in mind that the genres had developed from pre-motifs in the *qaṣīda* and that they were named after a motif/theme, it follows that the terms also testify to the level and depth of the community of *Islamic literature*.

The current situations of these three modern literatures are different from their classical periods. Today, they cannot be studied within the same system in which their past should be studied. The reasons behind this differentiation lie in their renaissance turnabouts. The explanation of the differentiation can also serve as an explanation of the importance of motifs in old philological poetics, and of their maturation into topoi within a huge traditional system.

Namely, modern literature in the three languages separated into three distinct systems by abandoning traditionalism and through maximally intense interpenetration with completely different literary traditions. Anti-traditionalist new-age rebellions had a renaissance importance and range. Let us remember, for example, the openness of modern Arabic literature towards the poetics and artistic production of the Anglo-American literary community, or the openness of Turkish literature towards French literature. The influence of philology has been marginalised in poetics and literary theory, and philology directed towards the subject that methodologically belongs to it, so that it has not actually been "euthanised" but only appropriately reoriented. This was a precondition for constituting a different poetics whose substance is in a qualitatively different relation with tradition. Wrested from philology in a poetical sense, literature can now reach values beyond the horizon of traditionalism and open undreamed-of possibilities of fruitful interpenetration with other traditions; instead of being mesmerised by the past and gazing into it, literature tirelessly and industriously hastens towards the future, always resting, with newly gained self-confidence, on the principle of avant-gardism.

The crucial "moment" took place within the act of abandoning the classicist topos system. Not only were commonplaces abandoned in the new works, but the idea of topos was itself devalued – the idea having reigned for hundreds of years – as a poetic category. This opened horizons to the author's originality and to the traditional avant-garde as well. The turnabout was complete. It led to the dissolution of a system, but it introduced literature into the realm of another system. Namely, abandoning the set motif principle, literature decided to step out of a "set" system, or out of tradition having become sclerotised in time precisely owing to its commitment to predefined motifs. This is the principle of poetic inductivity and normativeness. At the same time, abandoning the predefinition of motifs that had generated a plethora of literary topoi, literature pushed away the fundamental factor having marked it as a system even when it was produced in different languages. For, had Arabic–Persian–Turkish literature, quite hypothetically, been produced in a single language, it would have had a powerful argument for constituting a single system. However, being produced in different languages, by losing topoi it irreversibly headed in the direction of mutual differentiation.[47]

On the other hand, abandoning the classicist topos system enabled these three literatures to enter a system quite different from the one composed of old and medieval Arabic as well as Islamic literature. This system is outside inductive poetics and normativeness. Within this system literature is so broadly based that it is not understood alone and above all as past experience in literature, with the predominant experience of motifs within it, but also as its experience of (and about) the future. Only on the basis of this did it become possible to communicate with other traditions and poetics. Traditionalism was given a proper burial. The centuries-old relief of topoi was finally outgrown and overcome. Tradition is no longer adjusted to values in itself, but becomes open and adjusted to world traditions.

Form as a technique or philotechnic poetry

A discussion of tradition as a reservoir of motifs, and the emergence of these motifs as topoi in the frame of Islamic literature, opens a number of other issues of poetics in Old Arabic literature, first and foremost, and in Islamic literature generally. Closely related to the motif/theme/content in any discussion of a poetic work as an artefact is the issue of form. This, however, opens the issue of artistic originality, the issue of literary borrowings or thefts and, in Arabic literature, the particularly sensitive issue of so-called artistic sincerity, or of literature and "lies", etc. This constitutes a whole vortex of issues and their interactions. They cannot be analysed separately, since each represents a constitutive and vital part of the system we call poetics. Still, it should also be pointed out that, owing to their inseparability, every researcher that wishes to explain the constitutive function of one of these elements must frequently go back to other constituent(s) as well, regardless of their having already been explained: they explain one another, complement one another, condition one another, etc., thus building a system. Therefore, occasional revisits to certain issues or constituents in a new context should not be understood as a lack of research focus but as a compulsion imposed by the system being researched.

The previous discussion gives an explanation – I hope it is a detailed one – of the issue of poetic content, within an analysis of the poetic position of motifs and topoi in this literature. In the obvious form–content dichotomy, supported by the poetics I discuss here, the content is marginalised as an aesthetic factor of the artefact, while the form has the status of its only aesthetic factor. It is now time to closely analyse this prevalence of form, which philological criticism insisted on and with which authors also complied.

It is not certain whether the prevalence of form had always existed in Arabic literature. The uncertainty results from the fact that ancient Arabic poetry is of uncertain authenticity. Namely, its literary corpus, the record of which we have today, was established and forwarded to history by philology which, as I said, had strong reasons to intervene with the content of pre-Islamic poetry while recording it – due to the *Qur'an*'s attitude towards it. A consequence of this hypothetical intervention – as is also possible – was that the poetic form was brought to the forefront and that the poetic content was declared irrelevant, or marginal. Owing to the lack of material facts, the issue of the authenticity of this poetry remains in the sphere of speculation, but there are undeniable literary-historical facts about the quite far-reaching, even crucial influences of recorded ancient poetry on the centuries-old poetics and literary production that subsequently developed. If this hypothesis is correct, and it very likely is, it then proves that the *Qur'an* affected literary tradition in a way probably unmatched by any text in history. The Qur'anic Text retroactively subsequently corrected the poetic tradition that had existed before it, and then, initiating and directing philology, it fatefully influenced the entire subsequent literary history. This reflects the surprising ability of the Text to act in both directions from a single position in history – towards the past and the future.

The issue of the Text's possible interventionism with regard to the "de-paganisation" of ancient poetry is of extreme importance for discussing the content–form relationship. For ancient poetry as we know it was thematically schematised, diverse and unsaturated, but was quite opposite in formal terms: a single metre and a single rhyme of the poem were completely contrary to the thematic diversity; the appreciation of language (as part of the form) was also extremely cultivated. Therefore, the form of the ancient *qaṣīda* was almost perfect, so that those researching this literature have always wondered how Arabians, at a relatively low level of social development, could have poetry in such a perfected form, though its earlier development, in more distant history, is unknown and must have preceded such impressive poetic experience. This section of history, though important, is quire blurred. Nevertheless, there remains the fact that ancient Arabian poetry known to us preferred the form, among other things, by imposing no simple request on the poet to compose a *qaṣīda* of some hundred couplets encompassing several themes ("thematic indiscipline") and having a single rhyme and a single metre (quantitative metrics: i.e. requiring that each line should have a defined number of open and closed syllables composing metrical units that, in turn, compose the metre). This is extraordinary discipline of form.

The *Qur'an* is highly likely to have intervened in the sphere of ideology with poetry at the time, which was thoroughly discussed in the previous text. Nonetheless, the verifiability of this serious hypothesis is not crucial for studying the poetics of Old Arabic literature: this poetics may have been different but reached us in the state as it did, and we now have it as a literary-historical fact. The entire history of this literature can actually be divided into the period of the pre-Qur'anic attitude of poetry towards the form and the post-Qur'anic period of the prevalence of form. Nevertheless, this seems not to be a specific trait of Arabic literature, because literary history generally knows two kinds of poets. One kind, as Wellek and Warren correctly observe, implies the "half-crazed" poet, whom pre-Islamic tradition called the *majnun* (*poet possessed*), and was the poet-soothsayer whose soothsaying function was terminated by the *Qur'an*. The other kind is the poet "creator", or a well-trained poet, a master of his craft, extremely diligent as he keeps refining his skill, learning it from his ancestors and perfecting it.[48] The *Qur'an* was a "watershed" for the two different concepts of poets. The modern age has no such sharp division, as it is believed there is no poet without exceptional inspiration and imagination, and without the art of presenting their quite specific view of life and the world in a form or a way deserving of this specificity. However, let us go back to the old concept of artistic form in Arabic tradition.

Most old, philological critics held that the motif or the theme of a literary work was of ephemeral importance, and that the value of a work should not be assessed in terms of its thematic choice but in terms of the skill with which the theme was presented in a literary work. I will offer the attitudes of several of the most distinguished Old Arabic philologists and critics. I must point out that most used the simile or metaphor for a literary work of art as a jeweller's, shoemaker's or weaver's product.

Abd al-Qahir al-Jurjani, neglecting the importance of poetic theme and stressing the importance of assessing a work by the form in which the theme is put, resorts to such an image, also used by other critics:

> If one ring is valued more than another on account of the quality of its silver, it does nor represent a valuation of the ring then; the poetic quality of a verse is not valued only by its content either.[49]

In fact, says al-Jurjani, a ring is not valued by the quality of its gold but by its masterly workmanship.[50] Referring to language in this context, this author says that words do have their (semantic) content but, despite their meaning, they have no value in themselves, they are not sufficient to constitute the value of a literary work; their value is rather realised through the way they are organised into the form.[51] Valuing a ring by the quality of its silver or gold would not represent valuing of the ring as such, concludes al-Jurjani.[52]

Ibn Qutaybah also saw poetic creativity as a sort of jeweller's work, though he did not deny the value of the poet's talent.[53]

The term for the form, or poetic jeweller's work, used by al-Jurjani and other philological critics, deserves a brief discussion as it truly belongs to the sphere of crafts, or of art beyond the realm of literature in which it subsequently became established. The basis of this term is *ṣwġ*=*ṣiyāġa*, which means *goldsmith's craft, casting into a specific mould/form*; the active participle of the same root (*ṣāiġ*) is *jeweller*. Contemporary Arabic dictionaries of literary terms undoubtedly recognise the etymology of the term *ṣiyāġa*, which even builds phrases, thus branching out terminologically. Since the term *ṣiyāġa* is quite frequent and important in Old Arabic criticism and the poetics of Old Arabic literature, it eloquently informs us of the predominance of form in this literature and poetics. Namely, according to this analogy, the motif is "gold"; it can be available to anyone, but most do not know what to do with it. It will remain worthless, used inadequately, etc., unless it gets into the hands of a master. Moreover – in accordance with Ibn Tabataba's statement that many a good content was ruined by poor form – an unskilled master can completely ruin the motif/gold through inappropriate treatment, or by "casting" it into an inadequate form. This makes the issue of motif/gold quite relative. However, someone could contest my statement, saying that it still refers to gold, not just any metal (I will have to continue using this metaphoric terminology). In other words, the semantics of the word *gold* might suggest that philologists nevertheless prefer certain motifs, or that it matters which motif is introduced into poetry. I believe, however, that this semantics is deceiving because it does not have this meaning in the given context after all; it is rather the context that has made a huge shift in the semantics of *gold*, thereby making the entire figure quite unusual.

We should dwell a little on the analysis of the *motif/gold–form* relationship and *jeweller's work* in the given poetological context. It is interesting that the poet's work was *compared* to a jeweller's, but in time – acquiring the status of a literary term – it actually grew into a metaphor. The metaphorical character of the term *ṣiyāġa* (*jeweller's casting*; *casting gold into a mould*) is evident, and its momentousness is enormous considering that *ṣiyāġa* is one of the key poetic terms and, at the same time, one of the fundamental elements of critical value judgement. I am not aware of a similar term in other cultures – i.e. as a term highlighting the concept of craft and mastery. Literary science readily borrows terms from other sciences – especially from so-called natural ones whose exactness it has always unsuccessfully aspired to – but this seems to me a singular case in which Arabic philology expresses its aspiration towards exactness through a term that is distinctly technical and essentially concerned with craft.[54]

Therefore, gold as a metaphor for a poetic motif does not aim at expressing the particularity of the motif, but represents semantic preparation for highlighting the other constituent of the metaphor: gold is a "precondition" for speaking about the *goldsmith's art*, about the jeweller's craft. The ultimate effect of the term/metaphor is – and which is indeed the aim of the author of the term – in the jeweller's craft, in the technique of work, not in the "material" itself. In other words, this metaphoric term displays a brilliant value inversion supported by classical Arabic philology: gold has a purpose if it is masterfully moulded, if it is cast in a unique form – the more unusual, the more valued. The same principle applies to diamond cutting today: a diamond has no particular value in terms of its composition, but its value enormously increases in proportion to the unusualness of its cut. Certainly, the metaphor would not be successful if its other constituent were a different metal instead of gold: other metals are treated by, for example, blacksmiths, but gold is treated by jewellers.

Quite simplified, but not incorrect – this metaphor implies that gold serves the promotion of masterful moulding, rather than implying a reversed "direction of purposefulness". This underlines the important motif of moulding as immanent in the jeweller's craft as is the form in Old Arabic poetry. Philological critics did not shy away from speaking openly and positively about the motif of the mould, or about its value function in Old Arabic poetry. The mould implies elements of poetic form, first and foremost the metric system that was not only unavoidable in appreciating the value of an artefact, but was also a key element of the self-same appreciation. Understandably, language was also an important element and, owing to philology, as I already said, it preferred archaism. However, since metrics is not an unlimited system but rather finite, poets were thus required to present a certain motif, already treated by another poet, in a different metre lest it be considered sheer plagiarism. Of course, the motif had to be presented with a different rhyme, which is also an important instrument of the form. Under these conditions a critical comparison of forms could be made, where the motif was irrelevant in a way – being universal and generally accessible – and the crucial aspect was mastery in finding an adequate, or a different, metre and rhyme. Developing the metaphor of this philologist, I can say that the value of an artefact is proportionate to its jeweller's uniqueness.[55] In post-classicist, modern poetics, such "authority of the mould" is inconceivable. It is, in fact, quite inappropriate to art in production, poetic or aesthetic categories, but this was not so in Old Arabic literature or in other old literature. Any competent literary history must take these facts into account.

Prevalence of artistic form and the servility of criticism

The consequences of these demands of philology discussed above – for the "jeweller's aspect" of poetry, or its form, to be taken as the criterion for valuation – manifested themselves in the nature of a criticism that is impossible to discuss in the modern sense of this term. Criticism was not independent and was undeveloped. It fell within the "competence" of the same philologists who established the philological and poetic principles. In fact, precisely speaking, these two disciplines could not be completely distinguished as it was hard to tell where one ended and the other began. Criticism had its inventory of poetic metres and rhymes, against which it assessed the "behaviour" of poetic motifs. One way or another, each motif had to yield itself to metres while, according to its philological nature, criticism compared it to the relationship of the same instruments of form with the same motifs in history. It always reached to the depth of the past as a fundamental value. Criticism thus almost achieved the ideal of exactitude, in which philology had prided itself, because the Arabic metric rules were exact indeed, and it was obvious and simple to identify the motif and metric "feats" of a poem, as well as its breaches of metric rules. On the other hand, it was also obvious that such criticism was servile and uninventive. Its servility manifested itself in relation to philological science, and its non-inventiveness, its non-authenticity proven in relation to art. Philological criticism was unable to understand the principle of artistic originality. Since it was itself non-authentic and non-creative, it could not grasp the meaning and virtue of artistic literary authenticity. Of course, a poetics of a "jeweller's nature" is not capable of this: no matter how unusual, unique or deceptive in their unusualness they may be, *moulds* are unbefitting of an infinite and, in essence, positively inappropriate spirituality. The difficulty with comparisons – particularly with those aspiring to interpret a "great meaning" – is that they underline differences much more than similarities. The comparison between the jeweller's craft and poetry could not even be saved by its metaphoric ambition.

The concept of form in Old Arabic poetics was reduced to three elements: metre, rhyme and language. The number of metres was limited (sixteen) and there could be no essential innovations in this aspect of poetry. The possibility of enriching the form through rhyme was also limited, as the key element of rhyme in Arabic poetry is always one consonant (*dhū rawiyy wāḥid*); it knows no "male" or "female" rhyme, etc. In other words, the number of rhymes is restricted by the number of consonants in the alphabet. Language, however, offered the greatest possibilities for the author's creativity, although philology, as we saw, strongly directed it towards archaism. In any case, giving strong preference to the poetic form and concurrent decisive suppression of the importance of poetic content became the main source of normativeness in Old Arabic poetics. The poet's creative freedom and curiosity were restricted in an optimal and dual way. On the one hand, poetics gave strong preference to the poetic treatment of motifs already established in poetry, which was certainly a limiting factor. On the other hand, the insistence on the form as the principal aesthetic factor, where the form was reduced to everything involving the concept of mould, was another important limiting factor in poetic production. Normativeness had thus reached the highest degree. It reigned over Arabic poetry for hundreds of years: monorhyme and metrically impeccable *qaṣīdas* became the absolute condition for poetic knowledge and promotion within this tradition. It may seem incredible but it is true that only in 1948 did Arabic literature see poems written in so-called free verse. At the time, two Iraqi poets – Nazik al-Malaika (Nāzik al-Malā'ika, b. 1923) and Abdul-Wahab al-Bayati – caused real mayhem in Arabic literature by their poems in free verse, which traditionalists received as true blasphemy. The emergence of new poetics faced the problem of redefining the concept of *poetic form* – and of overcoming the content–form dichotomy by implication – since the new poetry was freed of metre and rhyme, which constituted the poem in classicism. It was important to decide on what grounds new, "freed" poems could be considered works of art. However, this belongs to the sphere of post-classicist poetics interpretation, which is not the subject of this discussion.[56]

According to classical philologists, a critic must analyse each element of the form in detail in order to pass a judgement about a work. Generalised judgements are not considered valid and sufficiently explained. There is yet another interesting image/analogy here: the poem is like a silk fabric. In this regard Abdul-Qahir al-Jurjani requests the following:

> The art of words wants more than establishing a criterion and giving a terse description [...]; on the contrary, you will learn nothing about it until you

> analyse and study it, until you touch its particularities building a story, and until you list them one by one, and name them gradually. Your knowledge will thus be like the knowledge of a true master who knows each silk thread in brocade, who knows each fragment in a gateway made of parts, each brick in a fascinating structure.[57]

Abdul-Qahir's insistence on the form and on its comparison with a silk fibre or brocade – which is the principle underlined by other major philologists as well – belongs to the kind of criticism analysing a literary work to the tiniest elements of its form. Yet its problem is that it cannot go from this direction back towards a synthesis. Even if it succeeds in reconstructing the formation of the "brocade fibre", this criticism sees the fibre as a pure form: it can even be beautiful but it is not alive in the way a work of art lives. In fact, philological comparisons of art works with fibres and gold rings brilliantly indicate the fateful limitations of this criticism, as well as the unoriginality of a work made following its "recipe". An analysis of form – no matter how meticulous and no matter how beautiful the form may be – still remains with the form alone, while the "soul" clad in the form (to use their metaphor) is beyond critical interest. It is quite reckless to split one "being" into these two segments. Moreover, the "soul" (which is the work's content in this case) should be given poetic and critical preference, because it searches for a form or the forms it dresses itself in. Their separation resembles the euthanasia of an art work. Finally, the selfsame philological comparisons highlight their mechanical attitude towards works of art.

Nonetheless, in the wake of the same poetics, other philologists liked to "outspread" the same "poetic fabric" as well. Thus, al-Asmai states that Labid's poetry is like Taberias fabric, meaning well-made but not beautiful.[58]

Ibn al-Athir (Ibn al-Athīr, 1162–1239) offered an illustrative event from literary history. When Sayf al-Dawla, the patron of one of the greatest Arabic poets in general, al-Mutanabbi (al-Mutanabbī, 915–965), criticised his two couplets for resembling verses of Imru' al-Qays, claiming that Imru' al-Qays was also wrong with regard to the two couplets, al-Mutanabbi replied:

> If whoever emended Imru' al-Qays' poem, he would have been more knowledgeable in poetry than Imru' al-Qays. Should this be the case, both Imru' al-Qays and I made a mistake. But your majesty knows that tailors know garments better than cloth merchants. Cloth merchants know general things, but tailors know both general and specific things, because they are the ones who make cloth into garments.[59]

Ibn Rashiq made a similar claim: "He who recites poetry can discern it as a merchant discerning a fabric that he has not woven."[60] Certainly, Ibn Rashiq's belief is utterly problematic, as it implies a well-known mistake that proper criticism can only be written by poets, and vice versa – only poets can be good critics. However, Ibn Rashiq may have expressed this thought in the context of the unusual popularity of poetry in the Arabic world, where everyone, from a ruler to a sentry, loved poetry, recited it and valued it in accordance with their level of education.

In addition to the term *ṣiyāġa*, in Old Arabic literature, and in its literary criticism and philology as well, another frequent term was *ṣan'a*, also suggesting the poetic prevalence of form. The word *ṣan'a* has several meanings, with the following ones being the most basic and mutually related ones: *production, mastery, professional work*. Semantic links among these meanings are evident in the fact that each conveys that *someone produces something masterfully within their profession*. The noun *ṣinā'a* (*craft*) is derived from the same root. Philologists and critics claimed that poetry was *ṣan'a*. It primarily emphasised that poetry was the peculiar work of a master, involving the aspect of its craft in terms of the highest achievements. Thus, the term *ṣan'a* is poetically close to *ṣiyāġa*, with the former having a somewhat diversified meaning.

In all interpretations of old philologists, *ṣan'a* is based on *artful–masterly–"production"* of poetry, despite the certain nuances the term includes. Let us see how Ibn Tabataba defines it in his work *'Iyār al-shi'r* (*Standards of Poetry*). Poetry writing is, to Ibn Tabataba, a volitional, rational act taking place in several stages. (This again shows the inability of old poetics to present an act of creation, or a work of art, as the "identity of intuition and expression", realised in simultaneity.) First, Tabataba believes, ideas and their motifs appear in the poet's mind. The motifs are then expressed in words through which the poet chooses a particular poetic metre, where the poetic expressions still do not form the structure of the poem, and are not aligned into the sequence present in the final version of the poem, i.e. the lines are not yet connected. In the third stage, the lines become connected so as to be able to take one another's position. The third stage also implies reading through the words and checking them against motifs/meanings that have appeared in the poet's mind, taking account of preserving the harmony between these meanings and rhymes. Ibn Tabataba calls the last stage of poem composition *ṣan'a* and *tathqīf*, i.e. *masterly work* and *cultivation*.[61]

Such a model for the generation of a poem was supported not only by Ibn Tabataba but also by most philologists and critics. In this heterogeneous process, the following aspects should be underlined. First, writing poetry is a rationalised act. Second, the technical aspect of poetry is optimally emphasised. Third, lines are independent semantic units, which I have already discussed in detail, so that their positioning is only possible in the final version of the poem, but – according to the same principle, owing to the semantic independence of lines, as well as to the monorhyme and monometric organisation of the poem – the lines can be repositioned even after the author has determined their "final" position, or they can even be omitted. In a poem bringing the content to the forefront and requiring a thematic saturation, something like this is not possible. In short, to Ibn Tabataba, *ṣan'a* is the last and markedly technical stage of poem formation. This author also gives the conditions for the ability of the poet to compose: maximum discipline, excellent education and the memorisation of poetry in the oral, rhapsodic tradition.[62]

Al-Qadi al-Jurjani sees the term *ṣan'a* as underlining the necessity for a poet to be well familiar with poetry in tradition, both old and recent, as well as to be ideally disciplined, since being talented is itself not sufficient for writing poetry. But, adds this author, mere mastery of technique, or creative experience, is not sufficient without talent either, as these two factors strengthen each other.[63]

Ibn Sallām al-Jumaḥī wrote one of the most influential works in the history of Arabic literature and philology, entitled *Ṭabaqāt fuḥūl al-shu'arā'* (*Classes of Champion Poets*), in the ninth century when it was popular to systematise poets according to epochs and the power of talent. In this work, al-Jumahi wrote that poetry was *ṣinā'a* and *thaqāfa* (poetic mastery and cultivation), or mastered only by learned persons, like all other types of knowledge and skill.[64]

Qudama Ibn Ja'far attached high importance to the factor of rationality (*al-'aql*) in composition, insisting on the pillars of poetry (*'amūd al-shi'r* – "the art of versification") traditionally consisting of the poetic metre, rhyme and style. Consequently, he also promoted the principle of the poet's talent (*maṭbū'*) and diligence (*mutakallif*) established by Ibn Qutaybah in his work *al-Shi'r wa al-shu'arā'* (*Poetry and Poets*).[65]

Relying on the attitudes of many philologists, al-Amidi (al-Āmidī, d. 987) held it was not difficult and it was necessary to establish so-called objective criticism, as well as that a critic must have the daring to apply it.[66] Of course, this kind of criticism could be established since it dealt with the exact verifiability of form realised in individual works. As pointless as it may seem today to argue for objective criticism in the sense of reliable verifiability, philology achieved this ideal rather early by bringing the form to the forefront of its value system – the form significantly reduced compared to the new-age concept of the literary art form.

Ancient poetry mentioned in the *Qur'an* could have developed into philosophic poetry but, through the careful and centuries-long cultivation of the form, it developed into philo-technic poetry. Philological criticism went so far in this direction that the term annual odes (*ḥawliyyāt*) became very important: these are poems that were composed and refined, following Ibn Tabataba's model, over the period of one year (*ḥawl*=year).[67] Critics refer to an ancient poet, Zuhayr, recommending his practice of tireless poem refinement, which they held in high esteem.

In his work *al-Shi'r wa al-shu'arā'*, Ibn Qutaybah writes about poetic diligence, concluding that the best poet is one who keeps polishing his poetry, like Zuhayr and al-Atia (al-'Aṭīa).[68]

Considering the nature of poetics having established a relative stability of motifs in tradition and the necessity for them to always keep being re-dressed in special forms resulting from thoroughly mastering the experience of tradition, a particularly competitive relationship developed among poets, which was manifest in the sphere of form as well. This is why critics of the time highly valued the method of a special kind of comparison – Ar. *al-muwāzana*. This term originally means *striking a balance*, *evenness*, *balancing*, etc., with the emphasis being rather on the material quality/qualities of what is being balanced. The reason for pointing this out is my intention to underline yet again that the method of criticism of the time, and the term assigned to it, indicates the prevalence of form and the spirit of competition among poets. Comparison among poets was performed by "balancing" the elements of form, which was the basis for passing a value judgement.[69] It is interesting that this sort of comparison strikes a value "balance" between two poets who composed the same poetic form in the same metre. As an example we can use comparisons between Jarir and al-Farazdaq, each meeting the other with rebuttals (*naqā'iḍ*). Modern Arabic literary scholarship could not have adopted such a term due to its non-inclusiveness, as it focused on one poetic form or on two poets. On the other hand, focusing a comparison on the technical aspect of poetry made the term inappropriate for comparative literature in its modern sense, in the sense of the term we first knew as *world literature*, which was subsequently replaced with the term *comparative literature*. Arabic literature today uses the term *al-adab al-muqāran* to denote comparative literature.

Poetic inspiration and technique

The tireless polishing of form opens the issue of inspiration. I have already cited the opinions of some philologists on the importance of talent. Defining the role of talent in composition, they made implicit statements about the importance of inspiration as well.

I believe that the aforementioned description of the poem-generation "process" penned by Ibn Tabataba testifies to the priority of rationalisation in the whole process. Ibn Tabataba, like other philologists and critics, does not deny the value of talent, but gives definite preference to rationalised mastery in the technical shaping of the poem. What could possibly be called inspiration is found in an imprecise statement about the "appearance" of ideas and motifs in the poet's mind. Strictly speaking, it is not poetic inspiration, for which the Arabic language does have appropriate terms. Ibn Tabataba explicitly minimised the importance of inspiration.[70] I have already said that Ibn Qutaybah preferred exemplary *annual odes*, while Ibn Rashiq (1063) also held that poetry was a volitional and rational process, and highly valued verses testifying to long-lasting and careful polishing; verses relying on spontaneity could not compare.[71]

The value and poetic position of inspiration in the ancient poetry that the *Qur'an* confronted was completely different. Since the idea had priority and primacy in this poetics, it attaches an extreme importance to inspiration; inspiration is crucial because the entire poem is composed because of it and is devoted to it. The poet proved his exceptional status precisely through inspiration that represented a testimony to his privileged position and his particularity as supernaturalism. Understandably, the poet had to be a master of words, a follower of the form that was important in "poetic and magic" reception, but in no case was the form a priority and it always appeared as secondary, as derivative. Such a poet was much more a "crazed one" than a creator.

The situation was quite the opposite in poetry of the Islamic epoch, or of the Islamic epochs. Since the motif/idea/theme was situated in poetics in such a way that, no matter what kind it may belong to, it is in no way exceptional, meaning also that inspiration is insignificant as an extraordinary mental and imaginative exertion in which the idea "pops up", vigorously searching for an expression, for its form. The technique insisted on is not compatible with inspirational restlessness but requires two other important things. On the one hand, the technique requires utter steadiness and discipline, like that required by feats of craft. On the other hand – as we have seen so far – the technical competence demands a thorough knowledge of poetic tradition, in whose experience the poet is educated. Such a poet belongs to the "creators", but his "creation" is drastically reduced to mastery, albeit a supreme one. Of course, it would be wrong to conclude form the previous discussion that poets wrote without even being aware of inspiration. Some were more aware, some less, but they still relied on inspiration. There were even some, although they were exceptions, who claimed they had inspirational contacts with jinns or shaytans, in accordance with pre-Islamic postulates regarding inspiration. Jarir, for instance, was one of these. Or, for example, literary-historical sources say that Abu Nuwas wrote/recited his Bacchus poems in moments of direct inspiration from court celebrations, bacchius seances, etc. Nevertheless, even such poets paid careful attention to the technique of the poem, which always fascinated listeners more than its inspirational unusualness or its idea. The poem had to be philotechnical, whereas it need not have been original. Finally, this is a discussion about the situation of one poetics – explicit and implicit – while the occasional visits of exceptional poets to its edges confirm the nature and "reign of terror" of this poetics rather than describe its serious violations.

Universalism of philological poetics: tradition as inspiration

Considering the extremely high degree of poetic normativeness in Old Arabic literature, quite an unusual form of inspiration dominated this tradition. Namely, poets – generally and traditionally – were not so much inspired by ideas as they were by tradition itself. Furthermore, since the form was exaggerated, we can speak of drawing inspiration from the form. Let us remember the recommendation to poetically "treat" motifs of predecessors, but in a different form (different metre and rhyme), implying that a "new" poet drew inspiration from already existing poetic achievements that he competed with at the level of form, i.e. a technical treatment of the same motif. Evidently, inspiration is tradition, not a motif itself. The volitional element and rationalisation, as well as poetic education in such understanding of the poetic act, are crucial factors, not inspiration as an irrational, imaginative act.

Since I have already established that this poetics was promoted within a universal system (I termed it Islamic poetics) that could not be undermined even by the fact that its literature was produced in different languages, it means that tradition was promoted at the highest level in this sense as well – in the framework of *Islamic literature*. Owing to the poetic constituted in such a way, tradition as such kept growing bulkier, spreading both diachronically and synchronically, being refined to an undreamed-of degree. Its aspiration towards spreading and its normative strictness made it a sort of imperial poetics that ruled over the literary production of the entire culture and civilisation of this circle – literature in the Arabic, Persian and Turkish languages.

Refinement of tradition through the poetics of philotechnic poetry led the tradition to a state of being concerned with itself, with a narcissism I am unaware of existing in other traditions. Thus it produced "poems about poems", a special form of "meta-poems" that were so cultivated and so frequent that they caused the development of entire poetic forms in which poems remarkably communicated with one another in distinctly poetical terms. It was technically a quite weighty, overripe tradition. It is sufficient to remember two poets of the Umayyad epoch – Jarir and al-Farazdaq, who created so-called *rebuttals/naqā'iḍ* – poems referring "to" one another, or poetic "squabbles" where the opposing poet immediately had to compose a poem in reply to his adversary's, but using the metre and rhyme of the poem referring "to him". However, in poetic terms, this is not an innovation, as the technique/form has the function of the key aesthetic factor in this case as well.

Jarir and al-Farazdaq appeared relatively early in this literary tradition – relatively because the following examples will illustrate that the tradition was refined for hundreds of years in this direction even in spaces very distant from the homeland of the two poets. I will refer to two poetic forms created in the Turkish language, remotely in history after Jarir and al-Farazdaq, even in Bosnia, in opuses of Bosniak poets writing in Turkish. These forms are *takhmīs* and *naẓīra*. I will also give an example of *naẓīra* of two famous Bosniak poets writing in Turkish.

Instead of offering examples from Arabic literature, which are many, I have chosen the following ones to demonstrate the imperial power of poetics that would not be impeded by centuries or regions, not even by different languages. For, it is evident that these poems in Turkish, i.e. the two poetic forms, testify to the same poetic source, the same poetic principles, in other words – to the irrelevance of motifs for value judgements, or for a judgement about authorship originality, about the importance of tradition and about the priority of the technical virtuosity of the poet in terms of value judgement.

The first form is *takhmīs*. It is a poetic form with stanzas consisting of *five* lines.[72] In composing it, the poet introduced into a stanza two lines of another poet whom he poetically communicated with, then adding three lines of his own. Certainly, the five lines had to compose a neat stanza structure. This is why all the lines had to have the same metre and the same rhyme. Philological philotechnic poetics was triumphant here. The form play was truly brilliant and brought to the ultimate level of technicism. Only from this position of "poetic exhibitionism" and a temporal distance from *takhmīs* to the philologists I discussed previously can we see the overall importance of the previously explained poetic postulates *ṣiyāġa* and *ṣan'a*. For, in *takhmīs* the meta-poem has its defined mould in the proto-poem:[73] it implies a set theme/motif and a set form. This reduces the possibilities of the meta-poem in a certain sense, because it does not create either the motif or the form.[74] However, its aim is to show its appreciation and thorough knowledge of tradition and its poetics, as well as to compete with the authority of the tradition that it actually refines. The meta-poem has the possibility to create in the sphere of language and style – it can, and in fact should, show that it is able to sing of the same motif in the same form but by using a richer language and different figures of speech. Without it, the meta-poem would have no purpose whatever. The "meta-poet" is therefore inspired by the "proto-poet", or by tradition as such. Consequently, and quite correctly, he is inspired by the technique itself, and such inspiration can hardly be called inspiration in the usual meaning of the word. In this case the poet has strictly set *norms* that he must realise on the basis of his poetic erudition and virtuousness, masterly or craftily, rationally and competitively, and not in the state of imaginative inspiration and creative *restlessness* in which the experience of tradition is only implied. Normativeness is optimal in the case of *takhmīs*, and tradition basically represents only a huge area with fixed boundaries. *Takhmīs* also offers a good confirmation of other images of old poetics, images that are much more than just a simile. Namely, *takhmīs* is an excellent illustration of what philologists spoke about as brocade, silk fibres, jeweller's skill, etc. The poetics of *takhmīs* condenses, as the true quintessence, poetics having been confirmed in its fundamental premises throughout tradition. At the same time, *takhmīs* can be studied as an example of commonplaces in Islamic literature that – paradoxical as it may sound considering the nature of *commonplaces* – were also modulated, so that tradition yielded a sort of poetic miracle that appeared as such only at first sight, whereas it was a logical and reasonable consequence of such poetics. Namely, a commonplace lies in the fact that, in time, the poetic technique became a poetic motif; it was exactly the poetic form that became a motif. At the early and mature stages of this poetics, motifs were poetic themes, or poetic content – therefore, the aspect of poetry separated from the artefact's form. I referred to it as the motif of charity, panegyric, love lyric prologue, and there were, of course, a number of other motifs as well. Poetics separated this from the form that was, as we saw, a crucial factor and the cornerstone of the value judgement. The form was stimulated enormously. From the inertia of this stimulation, the epoch of overripe classicism of Islamic literature saw the form itself becoming a motif; the technique became a purpose. Admittedly, *takhmīs* still had motifs/themes as before, but the form became the meta-theme; the original meaning of motif was completely marginalised and was only apparent because the suppression of theme was done through a brilliant play of technicism, brought to its utter limit. This poetry is absolutely philotechnical.

Such "achievement" of the poetics in question is neither surprising nor paradoxical, though it may appear as such (the form itself became a motif and a meta-theme!), because its two main features stimulated its development in this direction. One feature lies in the insurmountable normativeness of poetics, and the other – related to it – in its philotechnic orientation.

A similar poetic position is held by yet another poetic form from the epoch of overripe classicism. The form, *naẓīra*, was also cultivated in Turkish divan literature, and was recorded as a characteristic poetic form even with Bosniak authors writing in Turkish in Mostar.[75]

Two famous Bosniak poets in Mostar each composed a poem on the same theme, using the same metre and the same rhyme. I will give the integral text of both poems as I believe they eloquently express the poetic achievement discussed here. I will also give their originals, which clearly show the metric organisation of the poems, even their rhyme, as well as some typical stylistic means, although their poetic translation can also serve the purpose: it shows how the poems communicate poetically, how side by side they entice comparison of their "poetic stature" and their rustling "silk robes". I find this outsinging impressive, but – renouncing any pathetic local patriotism inappropriate for scientific research – I would like to point out yet another aspect of this impressiveness. The poems were composed in Mostar at the turn of the seventeenth century, which testifies to the literary and poetic competence or even exclusivity of Bosniak authors of the great epoch in a hardly visible "literary empire". However, what is more important for this discussion is that the poems testify to the limits the poetics achieved – undreamed-of limits in history and space, as well as its own great poetic endeavours. Its basis – its purely poetic basis – can be reliably traced from ancient Arabian poetry to Mostar *naẓīras*, as sudden as it may seem. It all actually began in the cultural "bang" of the sacred Text in whose Islamic poetic and literary orbit this amazing literary tradition developed. But, let us hear the voice of these two Bosniak coryphaei:

This is how Dervish Pasha Bajezidagić (d. 1603) sings to Mostar:[76]

There is no describing the incomparable beauty of Mostar
Can you blame me, oh my heart, for loving Mostar?
Except perhaps in Firdaws lofty, this world knows no
Mild air and water clear to match those of Mostar.
He who once sees it a new life will his soul feel
And no power will ever turn his gaze from Mostar.
In waters and fruits abounding, Damascus another,
Like the Heaven has borrowed its gardens to Mostar.
Guarded by two towers, its bridge standing proud
As if the belt of zodiac passed there through Mostar.
Not even a heavenly rainbow is a match to it,
'Tis but a pale copy of the mighty bridge of Mostar.
Even if you travelled searching across the globe whole,
Nowhere would you find people so able as in Mostar.
Both the sword and the pen in their hands do fit,
Equally honourable and learned are those in Mostar.
Even Indian birds can do no justice to it,
Oh Dervish, be the nightingale to sing to Mostar.[77]

Inspired by the poem by Bajezidagić, Dervish effendi Mostarac composed a *naẓīra* – a parallel or counterpart poem to that of Bajezidagić. Mostar is the theme of both poems, and the theme includes a series of segmented motifs. The meta-poem encompasses almost the same motifs as the proto-poem, but the same motifs are poetically realised by a different language usage and different figures of speech. Admittedly, the second poet introduces a new motif here and there, but it does not change the general poetic ambience. It is generally known that no repetition in a literary structure – not even in the same poem – has an identical meaning, because it always changes in a new context. It can certainly not be said that the entire poems have identical meanings in a strict sense. Their aim is not to express identity at all; they aspire to express the diverseness of the same. But, this poetic game is majestic, as if there is no end to it: the diverseness of the same is realised in the identity of poetics, and is even realised in order to promote the identity of poetics – to show that the diverseness of individuality can be realised in a general framework of identity. This is why *naẓīra*, like *takhmīs*, is an expression of poetics' commitment to itself and poetry's commitment to its corporality in the form.

Let us finally allow Dervish effendi Mostarac to testify to it poetically:

> Every corner do beauteous lasses hide in Mostar
> No wonder many a lad finds his love in Mostar.
> Air sweet, waters straight from the Heaven flow
> Mounts and meadows a fresh life give in Mostar.
> Nothing similar is found elsewhere in the world
> A new experience awaits everywhere in Mostar.
> He who comes here once never will he leave
> Gardens of Eden does his soul enjoy in Mostar.
> Its beautiful mighty river next to Safa does run
> Bestowing peace on every soul in Mostar.
> Not a drop of water less than in Damascus great
> Even souls can feed of ripe fruits in Mostar.
> The span of two towers standing elegant like Taq-i Kisra,
> Only the Heavenly arch matches the bridge of Mostar.
> If ever there was a spring of truthfulness and knowledge,
> It poured many a learned and honest man into Mostar.
> Oh, my sire, Hajji Dervish dear, you are not alone,
> Those known and unknown sing praises to Mostar.[78]

These poems are illustrative in more than one way. They bear testimony to the ultimate achievements of a tradition and poetics – to its borderline achievements in the sense of space and time, to the reach of philotechnic poetics. Certainly, they are a testament to the reception of poetry at the time. The popularity of *naẓīra* was so great that it was recorded as a significant literary phenomenon. Its high valuation was not in the hands of philologists any more, but the poetics philologists had established and promoted for hundreds of years had cultivated the taste of the audience according to its norms.

These silvery poems testify to yet another source of importance. Namely, they are the fruit of an overripe poetics that could not continue in the same direction any more, but had to cave in, or to save itself through renaissance ferment. Since

– juxtaposed as they are – these poems have beautiful attire (and sound) indeed, they resemble the purple evening light: there is hardly anything that can compare to this overripeness of day, which is precisely why it is inevitably approaching its end and must give way to the dawn of a new day.

A reservoir of motifs and the legalisation of "literary theft"

Limiting poetic motifs in the experience of tradition to a specific reservoir imposed the issue of literary borrowings, which was studied in depth by medieval Arabic philologists, critics and, certainly, authors. This has already been discussed previously – to an extent necessary to show how the limitation of motifs affected the degree of authorship originality. Nevertheless, I will here specify the issue of literary borrowings from the perspective of medieval philologists and literary critics. This first requires certain terminological clarifications.

Old philologists used the term *al-sariqa* to denote a special kind of literary theft I will discuss here. *The Dictionary of Arabic Literary and Linguistic Terms* by Magdi Wahba (Majdī Wahba) gives a rather reduced explanation of the term *al-sariqa al-adabiyya*: it is partly true but not precisely contextualised in poetological terms – in the broad context of Old Arabic poetics and classical philology.[79] The *Dictionary* uses two terms that explain each other, and equates the two: *al-sariqa* and *al-iḥtiyāl*. However, differences between them do exist.

Old philological criticism used the term *al-sariqa* meaning *theft*. It was sometimes euphemised by the word *akhdh*, meaning *taking*, *taking over*. The word *al-iḥtiyāl* (plagiarism) was used relatively seldom as a literary term in Old Arabic literature: the dominant term was *al-sariqa*. Modern Arabic literature does not use *al-sariqa* as a term for plagiarism. The reason for this lies in the fact that modern Arabic poetics and poetology are constituted in a different way, which makes it only natural for them to express it in different terms. Today *al-sariqa* is an "ordinary" lexeme, not a literary term. However, modern Arabic literature uses the term *al-iḥtiyāl* for plagiarism. More frequently still, it uses the term *al-intiḥāl* to denote plagiarism. This word means *to use stratagem/guile against someone*, *to deceive*; the word is therefore quite appropriate for expressing the essence of plagiarism. Thus, a plagiarist in the sense of the Arabic word *al-iḥtiyāl* is a person using a stratagem or deception to present as their own a part of or a whole work belonging to someone else. The semantic epicentre of the term/lexeme *al-iḥtiyāl* is *deception*, *delusion*. Modern poetics has a quite different conception of artistic value from that of Old Arabic literature, meaning that modern poetics, unlike the old, does not accept literary *thefts* or *borrowings* in the traditional sense of the word. Anything resembling this procedure is thus qualified as a *deception* and *delusion* aimed at presenting something stolen as original. Although we have already become familiar with the concept of originality in Old Arabic literature, I will have to continue explaining it as a term significantly affecting the understanding of plagiarism, or literary borrowings, the utilisation of old motifs, and forms, etc. I have just demonstrated with the example of *naẓīra* (though there are other examples) that the concept of originality in Old Arabic literature and mature Islamic classicism was made relative, different from what we know today. Therefore, the poet in the classical period did not have to practise deception in order to use the same poetic means employed by his predecessors or contemporaries. Furthermore, to complete the difference between the classical and the modern, the poet publicly and proudly took elements of other persons' works (motifs, first and foremost, but as we saw in the example of *naẓīra* or *naqā'iḍ* certain elements of form as well). There is no trace of stratagem as a dishonest deed or intention here. One of the main goals of such a poet is to take over the *other person's* elements so as to enrich them with *his own*, not to steal and present them as his own. He thereby promotes both the other person's and his own work in an amazing synthesis of community, as tradition was regarded at the time.[80]

In the conditions of the poetics of Old Arabic literature and that of modern Arabic literature, the difference between literary borrowings and plagiarism is perceived as radical, with far-reaching consequences. Considering the distinction I have just pointed out, it follows that what appears to be *stratagem* in plagiarism (in the concept of modern poetics) seems to represent *experience* in literary borrowings. Such value and ethical dimensions, quite contrasting ones, are assigned by different poetics.

Namely, the modern age does not allow parts of another author's works to be taken over because it prevents the main goal of originality. An author nevertheless that takes something over from others must therefore disguise it in different ways. This makes their act doubly unethical and, importantly, non-creative: therefore, its detrimental effects are multiplied, as it is unethical towards others, towards the audience and towards the tradition expecting creative originality from the author; it is also faithless to the poetics whose postulates it undermines, etc. All the negative effects and potential consequences of the author's act can hardly be numbered, which is why even the term *plagiarism* may represent a somewhat inadequate charge.

What such poetics defines as plagiarism, or a deceptive and dishonourable stratagem, is revaluated as *experience* in old poetics. Namely, the classicist poet had to be well familiar with tradition. Without a vast knowledge of tradition, and without great experience gained within this tradition, he could not even pretend to being a distinguished poet. One of the main tasks set by philologists and philological critics was for a poet to be familiar with so-called *riwāyat*, or to be familiar with poetic lore, so that his poems were expected to be relatively proportionate to his mastery of traditional poetry: he had to know poetic motifs in tradition, poetic genres, had to have a perfect command of metrics and, generally, had to know quite a lot about the traditional form as a poetic category, and about its individual realisations as well – all of this he had to have thoroughly mastered. The poet was required to have an appropriate literary education, much more than talent itself. These issues have already been discussed at length here. It may also be beneficial to mention an important aspect of *oral* tradition in the given context. Namely, oral tradition and learning a vast amount of verse by heart were widely practised, and not only for practical purposes as books were only handwritten and difficult to copy. Learning vast quantities of verses by heart establishes a different relationship to them than that established by reading: through memorisation, verses more deeply and permanently "sink into" the recipient's consciousness, longer and more actively stay in his experience, more persistently and definitively cultivate his taste, more firmly attach him to the tradition they memorise, etc. In addition, the fact that poets (and other recipients) memorised thousands of verses only enhanced all of these effects. The story of Abu Nuwas and the philologist telling the poet, who had memorised thousands of verses, that he was to forget them all, should not be understood superficially or literally. It was already a done deal: even if he would have, Abu Nuwas could not "suddenly" forget the huge body of verses – they had already so shaped his literary experience that he would never be able to completely erase them, nor would he try to do so, since it was not required by the poetics or criticism of his time.

Unlike the case of plagiarists in modern poetics, such huge and necessary experience on the part of the old poet did not remain only an "invisible thread" of his production. On the contrary – which is precisely the point in terms of making a distinction between new plagiarisms and old literary borrowings – it turned out that, in the classicist period, the poet was obliged to publicly and proudly demonstrate his experience by consciously taking over elements from other artefacts or tradition as a whole in order to create a "masterly poetic play", and to compete with tradition as well. The public nature of his act is general and promoted, on the one hand, through the poetics within whose system he creates and, on the other, by a general acknowledgement of the audience. Admittedly, there are certain rules for taking over from tradition, as well as a certain extent beyond which a new work turns into a surrogate. I indicated these rules while discussing poetic motifs, but I will return to them now, presenting them in relation to a new element of the poetic system.

The word *al-sariqa* has a negative meaning (theft), but it differs from the word *intiḥāl/iḥtiyāl* inasmuch as its ultimate goal is not for something stolen to be *publicly presented* as not stolen, or to use such presentation for promoting the subject and "its" work, thus gaining *public appreciation*. In principle, a theft does not aspire towards public promotion as its main goal, though it is done to achieve a specific interest. Moreover, the essential purpose of theft is contained in its secretiveness. It is interesting that the semantic field of this Arabic word – very close to its centre – also includes the meaning connoting a *hoarse voice* (which is quite indicative, even metaphorical with respect to "literary borrowings"), or a state of being *overtaken by sleep*. However, literary history made relative even this meaning, semantically "displacing" it to the sphere of positivity. I will offer the views on literary thefts held by a few philological authorities, who always elaborated their views with respect to poetic motifs.

Al-Askari holds that every poet is entitled to use motifs (*ma'ānī*) that were used by his predecessors, but must give them a new form, must "clad them in new words".[81] Following this view, al-Amidi explains that the selection of motifs is limited by the same milieu poets live in, so they necessarily use the same motifs. This necessity results, on the one hand, from the relatively similar conditions poets live in and, on the other, from what is a commonplace in classical philology – motifs get exhausted in time and it is difficult to always find new ones. Therefore, believes al-Amidi, it is necessary to use the same motifs, with individuality being displayed in an "individual" form, i.e. a form different from the one in which the given motif originally appeared. The theft happens, continued al-Amidi, only in the field of the originally stylistic expression and form: the poet's duty is to display this originality in this sphere, not in the domain of motifs, since they were common to all people and were perceived as quite usual in the widest community. Motifs are made unusual through form, style and language, which is the competence of the poet, and not of so-called ordinary people.[82] The concept of theft becomes relative in such cases, even turning into a positive value and being replaced with a synonymic term *akhdh* (taking). Ibn Qutaybah confirms this view, stating that something an educated and talented poet is capable of can be added to the motif taken over. It is exactly this addition, concludes Ibn Qutaybah, that makes the "new" work valuable. He also gives the example of Abu Nuwas and al-A'sha.[83] The parallel between these two poets is not accidental. They are temporally very distant from each other,[84] but their effective poetic communication, until the "take-over", testifies to the inviolable continuity of tradition. On the other hand, the goal of the example, implicit as it may be, is to demonstrate that even the poet considered the most innovative in classical Arabic Literature, Abu Nuwas, did not hesitate to use borrowings.

Ibn Tabataba belongs to a group of philologists who conceived the alleged necessity of taking motifs over so as to ultimately define it as a virtue. As noted earlier, Ibn Tabataba believed that all the motifs had been exhausted until the ninth century and that new poets had to borrow them, provided that they "adorned" them. In this context the author resorts to the famous image of a "jeweller melting previously cast gold and silver items to recast them into a better form than before". The new form is a proof of the poet's mastery, which is something that gives value to his creative work.[85]

Following this direction, Ibn al-Athir established in theory as many as eleven types of commended literary thefts.[86]

Abd al-Qahir al-Jurjani also discussed the topical issue of literary thefts, distinguishing two kinds of motifs in this context. The first category includes general or "rational" motifs (*ma'nā 'aqlī*) that are a common reality to all the people of one region and one culture. The other kind are "imaginative" motifs (*ma'nā takhyīlī*). The latter are innovative, original motifs that cannot be taken over, unlike motifs of the first type, the taking over of which is allowed.[87] Naturally, the second kind of motif changes its status in time: they become a "common good" in tradition, so that the relation to them also changes, permitting their borrowing.

In Arabic literary history there is yet another image of the content–form relationship, an image essentially like that of the jeweller's work, as described by Ibn Tabataba. It concerns a famous comparison penned by Qudama Ibn Ja'far, which was later used by critics for hundreds of years. Namely, Qudama compares an artistic literary work with wood as its material and the carpenter's mastery. Wood per se, says Qudama, has no value; rather, the value is in carpentry, in the masterful processing of the wood into a certain form.[88]

In developing these theories regarding motifs and literary thefts, it can be observed that a majority of philologists held that the permission to take motifs over so as to present them in a new form and to "add something" to them (as Ibn Qutaybah said) represented a specific transformation of motifs, their constant refinement and branching out, as discussed earlier. It is in this sense that Ibn al-Mu'tazz (861–908) says that a "borrowing" implies *interpretation* of traditional motifs, not their literal take-over.[89] A true theft, in the full capacity of its negative meaning, consisted in taking over both poetic content and poetic form: such procedure was deemed unforgivable and disqualifying as it opposed the fundamental principles of the given poetics.

"Literary thefts" were legalised through the introduction of certain rules that made them possible. The rules were rather broadly based at the level of the poetic relationship to the content and form of the work new authors communicate with; the rules were then illustrated at a lower level, by offering examples of either their violation or their observance. Some of these examples can be dubious, but the principle of legalising poetic thefts by establishing certain rules is not. The point is that the very fact of establishing rules implies the public nature of their application, whether they are applied positively or negatively; the public application of these rules implies a certain responsibility to them, which constitutes the act of legalisation.

There are issues relating to an apparent paradox of the expression *legalisation of theft*. Namely, how can theft be legalised? Moreover, how can theft be not only legalised but also encouraged, and spoken of as commendable thefts in the sphere of literature? Finally, to make the paradox complete: How can (literary) theft be so encouraged as to make it a dominant of tradition, protected and legalised by the system? This opens other important issues as well, such as the issue of theft being ethically in opposition to the general attitude of Islam towards theft, according to which hands are cut off for theft.

Searching for answers to these complex issues, it should first be noted that the previous discussion clearly shows that the meaning of the word *al-sariqa* (theft) is here semantically shifted so much that it is not theft in its usual sense. Poetics and its criticism defined the described attitude towards the works of earlier poets in such a way that it was not possible to speak about literary thefts any more, but only of the transformation of motifs whose main goal was to refine tradition. Such a procedure is therefore commendable and the meaning of *theft* completely "displaced" semantically. Its semantic content thus comes close to what I mentioned as *being overtaken by sleep* (one is "taken over" by sleep for a short while, deceived for a moment), which by no means connotes negative meanings. Theft in this sense is a sort of transformation of the existing reality (existing artefact) so as to use it as a basis for another reality (another artefact), as another quality or another experience based on the previous one. Finally, the word *al-sariqa* in this context is much closer to the word *borrowing* (*akhdh*), which is often used as a synonym. The meaning and use of the concept of *theft* in the poetics I present here is sufficiently explained with regard to existing poetic motifs, poetic form, the concept of originality, etc., but there is yet another aspect of its use to be discussed here.

Namely, I began explaining the poetics of Old Arabic literature by interpreting the relationship between poetry and the *Qur'an* as the Great Sacred Text fatefully influencing the constitution of poetics and artistic literary production. This omnipresent relationship certainly did not fail to affect the genesis and interpretation of the concept of *theft*. For its proper poetological interpretation we must remember the momentous confrontation of the *Qur'an* and poetry.

The confrontation of the *Qur'an* with poetry took place at the level of a great though unequal duel for establishing and defining their relationship on the lines of truth–untruth, authenticity–theft, etc. The *Qur'an* easily and permanently won the right to the Truth, while poetry was left with what was on the other side of the Truth. This is not necessarily defined as untruth, or even as a lie; it suffices to say that poetry does not represent and does not present the Truth in the sense and the way the sacred Text does. This, inter alia, means that poetry belongs to the world of transformations and transpositions; I already discussed it as a sort of purposeless play of imagination and words; it is an art and artistry, not the Truth itself. The ideological concept of Truth was taken away from poetry in the sense in which poetry had claimed the right to the Truth before the Text's descent. This outcome fundamentally changed the relation towards the truth in general, so that it was possible to determine in the newly constituted poetics, as we have seen, that the Truth was required from the prophet (of God), not from the poet, as well as that the poet did not maintain he told the truth and could not be held accountable in this regard, and that it could not be involved in the valuation of his work. The poet was absolved from the responsibility for the truth. This opened completely new possibilities to poetry as *art*: it became so-called pure art, unburdened with the relationship to the *Qur'an* and its competencies, but impressed with its exemplary stylistic values. However, there was a trap here that Old Arabic literature failed to avoid. Namely, through the force of inertia that pushed poetry away from the Truth, it became too dedicated to technicism, neglecting content entirely and not only the Truth, which it completely pushed into the background in order to refine form. Moreover, poetry ceased to be interested in any social engagement: it was mainly indifferent to so-called religious or moral poetry and to social developments generally.

In fact, to avoid misunderstandings, it should be noted that poetry did have a special sort of engagement. Owing to its widespread popularity, many patrons used poetry for achieving their (usually political) goals, so that poetry was rather manipulative in this sense. Two genres played main roles: panegyric and lampoon. However, poetry was not engaged beyond this – as autonomous, independent, in terms of the engagement of modern poetry, in accordance with its own "beliefs", not with patrons' commissions. In other words, the poetry of the time was not poetically directed towards engagement involving responsibility to the truth, or even to truthfulness. This is why it was only in the first half of the twentieth century that Arabic literary schools established *artistic truthfulness* (*al-ṣidq al-fannī*) as a key poetic term, which implied the need for poetry to finally wrest itself from technicism and assume responsibility towards its own reality. Therefore, the sacred Text did not explicitly declare every kind of poetry a lie (except the poetry existing at the time), but it did direct poetry towards various expressions of non-Truth: towards play, purposelessness, form and technicism, transposition, even – as we saw – towards specific "thefts" typical of art in the defined sense. It is literary thefts that represent a powerful differentiation of poetry from the sacred Text, and I thus believe that the word *theft* was not groundlessly introduced into the poetics of the time.

At the ideological level, theft is one of the gravest sins. Hence the sacred Text condemned it utterly strictly, uncompromisingly. Theft is opposed to the sacred Text in every aspect: it is, among other things, the opposition to its Absolute Authenticity; at the same time, the Authenticity is the absolute Truth, while theft is opposed to the Truth, etc. Therefore, the Text so forcefully disqualified poetry from the perspective of its ideologically privileged position that it defined poetry, in several aspects, as a sphere not only incompetent in the domain of Truth, but as also consciously being at the other end: as irresponsibility towards the truth, as a sort of play finding its purpose only in thefts. A more efficient way than that of the Text of the specific ideological positioning of poetry could hardly have been imagined.

Adopting the term *theft*, poetics optimally distanced itself from the religious and generally ethical prerogatives of the Text. Such identification looks like a sort of overly repentant attitude on the part of poetry with respect to what it represented before Islam, as well as marked servility in later poetry towards the Text's ideological values. For, since theft had become such an important postulate of poetics and since it was widely practised, poetry became identified as a kind of spiritual activity that was prominently unethical, in the sense that ethics was beyond its sphere of interest, and not in the sense of authenticity. Hence, a difference should be pointed out between the disinterest in lies and ethical values on the one hand and the promotion of lies, theft and unethical values generally on the other. Poetry at the time of Islam simply did not care for them. In Old Arabic literature theft had such important poetical status – as we saw – that, in the described meaning, theft could ultimately be said to be defined as the existential purpose of this literature, which irrevocably differentiated it from the sacred Text, although it remained in the universe the Text created. Refining tradition by the method of sustained literary thefts/borrowings and a strong inclination towards the creative technique steadily promoted the Text's Absolute Authenticity – following the principle of utterly sharpened contrariness. The Text feels inviolably superior in this domain.

Theft also differentiates the Text in the following way. Its established inimitability has been sufficiently discussed. However, it should be added in the given context that the postulate of literary theft and the Text's inimitability are at quite opposite poles with regard to authenticity as the highest value. Tradition legalised literary thefts and, accordingly, the imitative principle was promoted as a fundamental principle of poetics and literary production, regardless of imitativeness being governed by certain rules and almost insignificant restrictions. The point, anyhow, is in the promotion of the principle: imitativeness is possible, even desirable as a way of refining tradition as human work. The situation is just the opposite with the sacred Text: it is unimitating and inimitable; its essence is in absolute authenticity, in both ways: it does not imitate anything from the past, and it is inimitable in the present and future. Any theft is inappropriate to it. Such relationship of tradition and the Text is a measure of differentiation between God's and human work. Cultural history has not recorded pilferage of the *Qur'an*, in terms of it being plagiarised or imitated, except two or three unsuccessful attempts that, precisely by the power and logic of their failure, re-affirmed the Text's inimitability. It should be underlined that differentiation between the Text and tradition was made not only through legalising literary thefts but also through the selection of terms denoting them. I have explained that the word *theft* shifted its meaning towards positivity owing to legalisation and the poetic system, yet this word was selected, remaining acutely distinguished with regard to the Text's authenticity. The Text is undoubtedly the active and central factor of this whole universe. The meaning of its effect is expressed in the notion of originality as well.

Originality was made quite relative in old poetics. It was also largely collectivised. The "individual talent" was required to refine the works of his predecessors and contemporaries. Borrowing common motifs and using metre and rhyme, a common heritage, the poet consciously clipped the wings of his creativity, or his originality. By recognising or even highly valuing literary thefts – regardless of their very broad historical scope – originality was prevented, or very reduced at best, not only through narrowing the creative space but also through a relatively low value attached to originality. In fact, originality was collectivised precisely through literary thefts: originality was not the virtue of an "individual talent", but was realised in tradition refined through the exertions of submissive poets. What else can commonplaces or topoi represent if not the servility of individuals towards rigid norms?!

The sacred Text again takes the opposite position. Through the contrast with tradition, it emphasised its originality and individuality to the highest degree. There is almost no need to explain that the Text is original, not only in terms of its explications (claims of singularity, of its being from God, etc.), but also with respect to the fact that no such text had been revealed before it, and no such text, even in parts, was written after it. Moreover, it undertook to settle accounts with poetry of the time essentially to prove originality and establish the highest degree of authenticity. Clearly, it was completely opposite to the notion at the time of originality in literature. At the same time, the *Qur'an*'s individuality is emphasised through the principle of contrariness as well: it is in no way realised in collectivism, except in reception. In the given context/contrast, this means that it does not lend itself (let alone allow pilfering) to other literary works, not even to other sacred texts in relation to which it steadfastly professes its authenticity. Similarly, it does not borrow from other literary works or sacred texts.

Among the consequences of such a position of the sacred Text and constitution of poetics in tradition, there is one that appears to be the Text's constant. Namely, distinguishing between the Text and literary production and poetry, the *Qur'an* underlines again that *it is not a work of art* even though it uses a plethora of literary means. This is the essence of the *Qur'an*, which it explicated textually a number of times and emphasised through this attitude towards literary art. In short, it follows that the entire literary *artistic* tradition is based on relativising originality and authenticity, which does not apply to the Text, as its originality and authenticity are absolute, they are with God. Furthermore, this shows theft as typical of *artistic* literature, or even as its virtue, which is absolutely improper for the Text since it is not *art*. It is as its differentiation, by which it keeps confirming its status and affects all the texts in its universe, extends to infinity. I will mention yet another consequence of this distancing.

The beautiful in Old Arabic poetry arises from its form, with language, style and metre as its main elements. Since poetry was indifferent to the religious and ethical (prose was engaged in this sense!), it was quite distant from the Platonic concept of the Beautiful – as revelation of the Idea in an appropriate form. Admittedly, as is well known, Plato did not value art very highly exactly on account of its attitude towards the Idea, so that, in this sense, one could conditionally speak about the coincidence between Plato's attitude to art and that of Arabic poetry to the Truth, since it consciously minimised the importance of the Idea in poetry. In fact, Arabic poetry went much further, but I will not sharpen this contrast here as the contact between Plato's aesthetics and Old Arabic poetry has not been established; what should be contrasted rather is the relation of poetry to the *Qur'an*, which involves very dynamic relationships.

The artistically beautiful and literary theft: contrasting the sacred text and poetry

Raising the category of so-called literary thefts to the very high level of a constituent, Old Arabic poetics formed a close connection between *the beautiful* and *theft*. The previous discussion, informed on facts pertaining to literary history, confirms that Old Arabic poetry was art that proved its beauty by taking over poetical motifs and dressing them in a new form, but it should also be kept in mind that elements of the form are limited, as heritage or general literary experience. Therefore, these elements were themselves essentially taken over. In other words, the poetic beautiful in this aesthetics that was not theoretically articulated was achieved on the principle of artefact resemblance, even of conscious partial identification based on legalised literary thefts. (Certainly, *theft* sounds too harsh in this context; it is imprecise in the context and is much closer to the term literary borrowings.) Ethics and religion are excluded through theft as possible subject matters of poetry. Theft in such art is basically purposeless, public and poetically explained, and only with regard to this can it be beautiful – because it is only an exceptional play. In different circumstances *the beautiful* and *theft* cannot be brought in a relationship of synergy. In Old Arabic poetics literary theft is beyond reality, i.e. it happens in the sphere of the fictional, where poetry resides and cannot be sinful as such. In this poetics, theft is committed for the Beautiful that justifies and specifies its purpose. The essence of the whole "play" is in art as play and in the transposition of reality.

The *Qur'an* is distinguished here as well. It is not artistic play, nor fiction; it is not artistic transposition. Quite the contrary: the *Qur'an* defines itself as the Truth, as sublime reality, and as the highest possible level of truth(fulness). Considering such self-determination (also accepted by a significant portion of humanity), any form of theft is absolutely unbecoming of it, even in the shifted sense of the word resulting from literary tradition. The differentiation between them can have the following focus as well.

The ultimate aim of poetry is the artistically beautiful. This is the sphere where it ends. To achieve this aim, poetry is entitled to the technique of taking over the priority from the Idea, entitled to theft as specific art play, or even entitled to a special type of "lie", in the sense of artistic transposition and reshaping. Certainly, the word "lie" is used very conditionally here – in relation to the Qur'anic truth and its related explications. This status of "lie" must be discussed here. Let us remember that the *Qur'an* condemned poets because "they say that which they do not", "they rove distraught in every valley", etc. In the context of this severe condemnation, the *Qur'an* speaks of the mendacity and sinfulness of those on whom shaytans "descend", which refers to poets.[90] Nonetheless, its main argument for condemning poets in relation to the Truth – hence, for the lie as well – is in the fact that they inadequately treated religious truths. This is the purpose of condemning poets for lies. In other words, the *Qur'an* in a way initiated tradition to take a stand, poetically, on the "lie" in poetry. Like the notion of *theft*, *lie* also shifted its basic meaning in poetry. Poets' abandonment of the same Truth the *Qur'an* is entitled to did not imply their automatic consent to the lie: concepts do not necessarily exhaust their meanings in oppositions. Finally, the *Qur'an* is ethically based in such a way that it is absolutely unbecoming of it to encourage theft or lies in their basic meanings. This is a sufficient indicator that special meanings of these words should be searched for.

Retreating before the *Qur'an* and being forced to constitute a new poetics, poetry did not deal with the issue of truthfulness or mendacity, as the new poetics implied that a poetic work was a separate reality that could not be properly valued by criteria and realia beyond it. There were poets and critics who discussed the lie in poetry, but they always assigned a special meaning to this concept. Since the poem is a play of imagination and language, the criterion of truthfulness or sincerity is inappropriate to it. Al-Qartajanni rightly observed that a correct opinion of poetry did not start from the truth or falsehood of what it represented. This does not make it poetry. A proper attitude takes into account whether a poem is sufficiently imaginative and coherent.[91] Al-Qartajanni's notion of imaginativeness (*takhayyul*) is a key and representative one among medieval critics. Owing to this concept, the establishment of its sincerity or mendacity became irrelevant for poetry. Moreover, the concept of poetic imagination implies transposition and a particular kind of distancing from sincerity, or truthfulness as a faithful representation of the Truth in the sense in which it is presented by the *Qur'an*. Al-Marzuqi said the best poetry was poetry that was the most mendacious.[92] However, this is not a statement to be taken literally but should be understood to mean that the best poetry is that which is "most imaginative", which has the best command of imagination and the *beauty of expression* (*ḥusn al-kalām*), which is also an important element of poetry valuation. Thus, both *theft* and *lie* are justified by the fact that poetry ends in the sphere of the aesthetic, making the two categories (*theft* and *lie*) ethically irrelevant, provided they submitted to the system of old poetics.

However, the *Qur'an* uses the aesthetic as only one of the "means" for achieving its goal lying in everything opposed to the means by which art reaches its goal. Its sublime aim is the Idea, not the technique, not the lie but the Truth, Authenticity not judgement; its ultimate goal is the highest Seriousness, not Play. These grounds lead to a conclusion arising in interpretations of all the aspects of old poetics and its relationship to the sacred Text: the Text always assumes an opposing position towards all forms of art, primarily towards poetry dominant in the given cultural context. Considering the Text's power and wisdom, it appears that poetics could not have been constituted apart from it and its fundamental claim of its not being a work of art. The Text's influence on old poetics – and its literary production, of course – took two seemingly opposite directions. On the one hand, it defined, directly or indirectly, literary poetics on the principle of divine contrast to all the elements I have discussed so far. On the other hand, the Text held all other texts within the reach of its influence by not letting them "float out" of its universe. It would have excluded them from the *system*, putting them outside our sharpened theoretical horizon and beyond literary experience. They would not have been worthy of mention.

The beautiful in old literature was based on similarities, on borrowings and parallels – as there has always been, to a lesser or greater degree, an impulse to compete among artists – so that this aesthetics can, in principle, be considered the *aesthetics of identity*.[93] Resemblance has the power to delight, as it matches human habits and abilities to observe. Thus resemblance(s) in very different fields fascinate us, particularly when unexpected. How many times have we exclaimed at a sudden similarity?! This is magnificently attested to by the entirety of old and classical Arabic poetry – it had done so until historical fatigue, when it had to resort to a different kind of surprise and delight. The simile has an aesthetic task as well – to emphasise the beautiful through the principle of resemblance. It is little wonder that the simile is so dominant in Arabic literary tradition, in parallel with the poetic postulate of resemblance derived from borrowing motifs or from legalised literary thefts.

However, difference is mesmerising as well, even more so as it eludes similarities until it begins to emphasise uniqueness. This is the aesthetics of opposition affirming the Beautiful in a unique way. The simile implies difference rather than similarity, but this differentiation is self-effacing, it withdraws in favour of similarity. However, an opposition brings differences to the forefront, while similarities become self-effacing, for contrast includes them as well: there must be a common basis that the entire contrasting process rests on. What is common to the sacred Text and artistic literature are the literary means they employ; I have said several times that the Text very efficiently employs literary means, which is also a point of their great differentiation in a number of aspects. The literary means the *Qur'an* uses represent, in the context of this meaning, a preparation for contrast. Its utilisation of (common) stylistic means is supreme, and most researchers stay within such an interpretation. However, this is only a minor part of differentiation visible to the "naked eye" in the framework of something they have in common. Only from these positions is their contrasting powerfully heightened – not only in the sphere of stylistics, but also in that of poetics as a system making sense of all their layers and procedures. The purpose and ultimate meaning of the sacred Text is identified in its differentiation from everything – until the powerful contrast presenting it as God's Revelation, absolutely unique, different from everything else. While centuries-old literary tradition built the *aesthetic of resemblance*, encouraging the principle of taking over or even "pilfering", the sacred Text promoted the contrasting principle at the highest level. Yet the contrasting is not an end in itself or some "poetic spite", but arises as a result of the fact that the Text, which is a literary one as well, is not artistic. In other words – I again refer to the Text's position – art is created by establishing a special relation to reality. It is, conditionally speaking, a sort of "play" in which all poetic means are permitted, among which even theft, forsaking the idea, being unbound by the truth and reality, etc. However, God does not play but creates authentically, so that His Text is not art or a purposeless "aesthetic play" but pure reality: God's Word is, just like the Truth and the Revelation, absolutely unique. Therefore, in a way the Text needs literary tradition as a background for additional and powerful contrast. Researching this literature as a system – in whatever direction – is thus always related to researching the singularity of the sacred Text. Overlooking this extremely important fact can possibly testify only to the researcher's incompetence, to their inability to identify and define relationships between the great Text and other texts created within its culture and civilisation's context. The information just presented regarding it is not the result of a speculative approach, but of a comparative and contrastive analysis of two huge poetic systems being contrasted "on the background" or on the basis of what we call literature. On the other hand, literature needs the Text because, as we saw, it was poetically determined in contrast to the Text. The Text's superiority did not stand in literature's way, nor did the fact that the Text defined itself as a non-artistic work. Quite the contrary. Emphasising that aesthetics, that the Beautiful, is not its ultimate aim, while the Truth-as-Beautiful is, through the principle of contrariness the Text retained the Beautiful as a means of reaching *not the artistic truth*, but the Truth itself, non-transposed and authentic. Through the same principle, it surrendered the *artistically beautiful* to poetry; through this principle the Text, in fact, enabled poetry/literature to create its own and sovereign realm of art. Poetry defended its sovereignty and self-sufficiency so staunchly that it pushed away even Aristotle's *Poetics* and the experience of ancient Greek literature.

Isolation of tradition: the lack of influence of Aristotle's poetics

Interestingly enough, Aristotle's *Poetics* left no trace on Arabic literature generally – on its poetic shaping or its literary artistic production. This fact is important for at least two reasons.

First, Aristotle's opus was well known to Arabic-Islamic culture, in which Aristotle bore the honorary title of *the First Teacher*, suggesting that he was a great authority acting as a teacher: his opus was well received in Arabic-Islamic culture, leaving an indelible trace, as first teachers do. However, this refers to philosophy. In literature, Aristotle's work had no influence. His *Poetics* was familiar in Arabic-Islamic culture, though there are indications it was introduced relatively late, in almost sporadic attempts. There is the question why Aristotle's philosophy had such powerful influence, while the *Poetics* did not. There have been attempts at answering this question, and I will consider their justification in the discussion that follows.

Second, Aristotle's *Poetics* is the literary-historical and poetic basis of Western culture's conception of literature. Probably no work in the history of this culture has had such prolonged and strong influence as Aristotle's *Poetics*. This leads to the conclusion about the extraordinary competence and "acceptability" of Aristotle's *Poetics*, as well as a conclusion related to Western culture which opens an important issue: why did the *Poetics*, though known to Arabs, fail to influence Arabic literature at all – whether by raising awareness of the need to develop literature at this theoretical level (I have already said that the absence of theory is typical of the Arabic-Islamic tradition), whether by (re) directing literary artistic production. It would all be much simpler if Aristotle's *Poetics* could be claimed not to have been known to Arabs. However, given the evidence that it was, we must face the issue why it remained completely outside their tradition and their poetic system. This is not a rhetorical question or a false dilemma, but is related to the very essence of Arabic poetics and its value system. In other words, I do not wish to open the issue on account of Aristotle himself but because of the Arabic literary tradition, which ignored him so powerfully. No doubt it had its own reasons, which we now search for from a huge distance. All the answers remain speculative, without facts, since Arabic tradition did not properly try even to explain the reasons for ignoring it. Admittedly, there are rather sporadic attempts to explain this surprising literary-historical fact, but they seem to me not to result from a coherent system and consequent deduction. Regardless of the fact that no answer can escape speculation, it should be informed by literary-historical facts that must be introduced into a coherent system.

Why do I attach such importance to the absence of Aristotle's *Poetics* within a discussion of Old Arabic literature? The easiest solution seems to be to state that there was no influence and let the matter rest. However, closing the previous section, I said that the nature of a matter or a problem could often be more clearly presented in sharpened contrasting than in the parallelism of resemblance. Following this, I believe that, by interpreting the absence of influence of such a momentous work, one that marked an entire culture, I also interpret the nature of Arabic tradition, or its poetics for having ignored this momentous work. Before I do this, I will offer a sketch of the periods and authors related to the presentation of Aristotle's *Poetics* to the Arabic world.

Aristotle's *Poetics* first appeared in an *abridged form* (the abridgement is indicative) by Ya'qub al-Kindi (Ya'qūb al-Kindī, d. *c*.870).[94] The *Poetics* was actually first translated by Ishak ibn Hunayn (Isḥāq Ibn Ḥunayn, d. 910), and then by Matta ibn Yunus (Abū Bishr Mattā Ibn Yūnus, d. 939).[95] Ibn al-Nadim (Ibn al-Nadīm, d. 995) stated that Yahya Ibn Adi (Yaḥyā Ibn 'Adī, d. 939) rendered it from Syriac into Arabic.[96] Interestingly, besides the philosopher al-Kindi, it was also translated by one of the greatest Arabic-Islamic philosophers – Ibn Rushd.

Many Arabic authors expressed their regret, wonder and perplexity at the fact that *Poetics* was not met with a positive response in Arabic literature. One of them was 'Abd al-Rahman Badawi ('Abd al-Raḥmān Badawī), who said:

> Reading the summaries of al-Farabi, Ibn Sina and Ibn Rushd, one cannot but feel a terrible loss that Arabs had no use of this book as did Europe in the renaissance period, or as they themselves made use of other Aristotle's books.[97]

The most effort spent on the promotion of Aristotle's *Poetics* was by al-Qartajanni. In *Minhāj al-bulaġā'* … (*Path of the Eloquent* …), he discusses a number of poetic issues, remaining clearly influenced by Aristotle. For example, he holds that imaginativeness (*takhayyul*) is the key instrument of poetic creativity. To be fair, imagination was not unknown to traditional Arabic poetics, but was not a poetic dominant even upon al-Qartajanni's explication of its importance. No doubt that traditional Arabic poetics attached much more importance to a poet's education on tradition, and knowledge of the metric system; generally it preferred technique. As a result, as we said, the volitional or rational element was more important than inspiration and the sphere of the imaginative, while the idea of "mould" and "casting gold" was truly dominant. Yet, despite most philologists and despite their authority, al-Qartajanni neglected the postulates of traditional poetics, claiming that poetics rested on "imagining" (his term *takhayyul* means *imagining, achieving through imagination*, etc.), and that poetry was *kalām mukhayyal*, i.e. *speech "trimmed by imagination"*, while rhetoric relied on persuasion. It is interesting that, in this context, al-Qartajanni states that both poetry and rhetoric incline to a sort of a lie, but it is precisely through their deception that they attract the listener's attention. The imitation theory, as one of the fundamental premises of Aristotle's *Poetics*, is also unknown in Arabic poetics, while al-Qartajanni states, in an Aristotelian manner, that poetry is imitation that, actually, beautifies nature, or reality.[98] The best poetry is poetry most successful in imitation, maintains al-Qartajanni, and poetry that seems sincere while hiding its mendacity. The worst poetry is poetry that poorly imitates, clearly displaying its mendacity.[99] Since poetry rests on imitation and beautification of the natural, the simile is its most important figure of speech: the simile beautifies and is strongly related to imaginativeness (*takhayyul*).[100]

Such an interpretation of imaginativeness, or even of mimesis theory, is inappropriate to the Arabic experience of literature, which establishes a different relationship to reality, persisting, quite the contrary, on the so-called realism factor, not on imaginativeness. Even al-Qartajanni will admit it indirectly, which I will explain later in the text.

Among al-Qartajanni's other Aristotelian postulates, the so-called *organic unity of the poem* (*al-waḥda al-'uḍwiyya*) should certainly be singled out as its exceptional quality, or a condition without which the poem cannot be a valuable work of art. This is the essence of Aristotle's *Poetics*. However, in Old Arabic poetry, as well as in the classicist epoch, the organic unity of the poem did not pose a problem at all. It was distinctly non-unified in this regard since, as we saw, it encompassed several themes that were not connected except through the element of form: the multi-thematic Old Arabic *qaṣīda* was "kept together" only by the single metre and monorhyme. Moreover, the couplet (*bayt*) mostly represented an independent semantic unit. Organic unity of the artefact in Aristotelian terms cannot even be mentioned in this poetry: its *distinction* is the non-unity of content in the unity of form. This was already discussed earlier in the book. Only in the twentieth century, owing to a true openness to other traditions, did Arabic writers raise the issue of "organic" (non-)unity of the poem to the highest level, as the fundamental requirement for overcoming classicism.[101] Finally, the poetics of the arabesque, being the basis of all Arabic arts, does not recognise the Aristotelian principle that a literary work must have a beginning, middle and end. Aristotle valued drama much more than other forms because, inter alia, no literary form or genre stresses "organic" connection as much as drama, thus emphasising a beginning, middle and an end. On the other hand, Arabic literature had no drama at all. Perhaps there is nothing else that speaks so convincingly of the distinction between these two poetics as this difference. After all, let me remind the reader of an important fact: modern Arabic dictionaries of literary terms still incorrectly translate the term *poetics* (just like Aristotle's title *Poetics*) as the "technique of poetry" (*fann al-shi'r*).

Al-Qartajanni undoubtedly devoted a great deal of effort to promote Aristotle's *Poetics*, but the effort yielded no results. With regard to the absence of Aristotle's influence, al-Qartajanni expressed a thought suggesting the futility of his effort to transfer it to the Arabic tradition, where it was to rearrange poetics and production, but this thought of al-Qartajanni's also indicates that, most likely, this author failed to understand the heart of the matter.

Namely, al-Qartajanni expressed great regret – to interpret his thought – that Aristotle had not known other literary traditions, referring primarily to the Arabic tradition. This is followed by his really bold and very important conclusion: Had Aristotle been familiar with other literary traditions – including the Arabic tradition as a huge literary tradition – he would have certainly been able to enrich all his rules, or even modify them to a certain degree.[102]

This thought deserves special attention.

Aristotle's *Poetics* is based on his experience of literature. These two facts stand in an unchangeable relation. Old Arabic poetics is quite different from Aristotle's. This means it would be naive – and methodologically incoherent – to believe that Aristotle would have corrected his *Poetics* had he known Arabic literary tradition. The *Poetics* is a system resting on coherence – without coherence the system collapses. Therefore, in a coherent system that needs consequent consideration and conclusion in order to survive, it is absolutely impossible to exclude some of its elements and include others from quite a different system. Whoever thinks this is possible is not familiar with the very nature of poetics or does not realise the principles of proper theoretical consideration that cannot survive without coherence. Arabic poetics and literary production, on the one hand, and Aristotle's *Poetics* and ancient Greek literature, on the other, represent two self-determining and self-reliant systems that simply could not enter into synthesis as neither would have survived. This means that Old Arabic poetics was wiser than those who, carried away by the discovery of Aristotle's *Poetics*, regretted or failed to understand why *Poetics* did not influence Arabic literature or why Aristotle never became familiar with Arabic literature so as to "enrich" his *Poetics*. In order to make this exclusion clearer, I will give some pivotal yet divergent points on the two poetics.

At the centre of Aristotle's *Poetics* are drama and epic. Without these two literary forms, his *Poetics* is inconceivable, just as is ancient Greek literature. At the same time, Arabic literature knows neither drama nor epic. As if it were a trifle to be neglected by a poetics that encompasses artistic literature generally and that could be constituted as some "mixed poetics". Or, the line in Arabic literature is, traditionally, raised to the level of an independent semantic unit linked to other such units in the poem only by the same metre and rhyme. There can be no mention of "organic unity" in such a poem, which is also a pillar of Aristotle's *Poetics*. What about the absence of the Aristotelian *beginning–middle–end* poetic principle, which is not found in Arabic poetry at all, and whose tradition, as I said, had neither drama nor epic?! The Arabic *qaṣīda* has an arabesque structure: most themes it includes can be reshuffled without any consequences for the structure, and even the lines in a poem can change place. This is something quite inappropriate for a poetics/work insisting on "organic unity" and the *beginning–middle–end* principle. All these are essential issues that prevented the two traditions and poetics from mixing and influencing each other. This is why al-Qartajanni's regret over the lack of influence of Aristotle's *Poetics* is pointless; it is completely baseless, so much so that it is not possible to speak even about a hypothetical influence, just as his effort to introduce Aristotle's *Poetics* proved futile. The same applies to his judgement about the great loss because – as quoted from Badawi – "Arabs had no use of this book ..."

Other Arabic researchers who I am aware of also wander searching for the reason behind the absence of Aristotle's *Poetics*, and that of ancient Greek literature generally. I will give two more related examples.

Dawud Sallum wonders why Arabs kept silent about the possible influence of Greek literature and Aristotle. He then offers three possible reasons, only the third of which is founded and certain, and I will dwell on it later. The reason may have been, hesitates Sallum, Arabs' desire to keep their authenticity and fame in literature, or perhaps a result of the struggle between Arabs and Shu'ubiyyah.[103]

The dilemma is posed so that both its parts are baseless. There is no need to analyse such thinking in detail as it does not see the problem from within, following immanence laws, but deserves a sentence or two for being representative: many Arabic authors think in this way.

Whether "someone else's" poetics or literary tradition will influence another poetics is not a matter of consensus or goodwill of a nation or its culture. They have no say in it, nor does their wish to preserve their authenticity and fame have any influence. Poetics and tradition are self-reliant and have their own laws, independent of the nation's rational judgement, Arabs' in this case. The struggle between Shu'ubiyyah and Arab nationalists could not have had a crucial influence on the absence of Aristotle's *Poetics* either. Proof of this can be found in the fact that Persians (Shu'ubiyyah protagonists) introduced many novelties into tradition and that owing to them artistic prose was introduced into tradition. Moreover, following Shu'ubiyyah's logic of antagonism, Persians may have been expected to support Aristotle's *Poetics* to weaken Arabic domination. Nothing of it – the cause lies in the incompatibility of poetic systems.

The third possibility Sallum offers is the fact that linguistic, criticism and rhetoric studies served the interpretation of the *Qur'an*'s perfection, which recognition of foreign influences would only desecrate.[104] Sallum's presumption is founded except in its last part, which is incongruent with the first. Namely, receiving foreign influences as desecration reflects the attitude of a part of the elite or the nation deciding on it. This is again non-immanent logic: had there been influences, they would have shown themselves and Arabs would not have been able to hide them, nor could Arabs make a *decision* to resist influences for whatever reason. The causes lie in the poetics themselves and, since Old Arabic poetics was shaped by philology (which includes linguistics and stylistics), it provides a strong foothold for Sallum's presumption.

Taha Hussein states the main reason of the stagnation of Old Arabic literature is the fact that Arabs neither knew the literatures of other peoples, including Greek literature, nor cared for them. This is the extraordinary strength of traditionalism.[105] Taha Hussein's statement is actually correct but it does not answer the question or solve the problem. For, traditionalism in Arabic literature is very prominent and should certainly be related to the absence of Aristotle's influence and of other experiences of literature. The real question is: Whence the powerful traditionalism and why was it so unbending, impervious to different experience? Answers to many other questions depend on the answer to this one. Before I offer an answer, I will give several important arguments relating to the lack of proper understanding of Aristotle's *Poetics* in the Arabic world, even in the works of those who translated or rendered it into Arabic, hoping it would have certain influences. Al-Qartajanni is not alone in this. In fact, in addition to the *Poetics* not being understood, the attitude of Arabic authors shows that any other poetics would meet the same reception – poetics as such. Even the great minds translating/rendering the *Poetics*, the renowned Ibn Rushd among them, could not overpower the almost incredible strength of Arabic tradition (its poetics and artistic production as well) and impose on it another system represented by Aristotle's poetics, i.e. open it to the influences of a different literature such as that of ancient Greece. What I will presently say shows how strong and self-reliant this tradition was even in the minds of those who were open to the fruitful influences of Greek philosophy.

First of all, it is obvious that Aristotle's *Poetics* was transferred into Arabic culture in two inadequate forms. Thus, al-Kindi conveyed it in an abridged version. The compendium tradition was well developed in Arabic-Islamic culture and compendia mostly served for teaching, as textbooks. However, developing compendia requires prior knowledge of the integral text. The presentation of Aristotle's *Poetics* in an abridged form, in a compendium, indicates the attitude to it: it was probably not taken so seriously as to be presented right away and in several integral *translations*. It was reasonable to expect the contrary. Namely, considering the epochal importance of the *Poetics*, albeit in a different culture, an integral text translation could have been expected to be accompanied by a number of commentaries, such as those accompanying other works judged to be of extreme importance. Nevertheless, even when they appeared, translations of *Poetics* were all too modified, following Arabic tradition.

Arabic authors agree that translations of Aristotle's *Poetics* are actually rewritings and adaptations to Old Arabic literature. For example, an enormous figure in philosophy, Ibn Rushd, rendered the key Aristotelian poetic terms and genre distinctions *tragedy* and *comedy* as Arabic "equivalents" *madaḥ* (*panegyric*) and *hijā'* (*lampoon*).[106] Many other terms are also questionable, but it will suffice to remain with these key ones to illustrate a complete failure in transferring Aristotle's *Poetics* into Arabic culture. Its effect on this culture was prevented owing to its "translators" as well, which resulted from the absolute self-sufficiency of Old Arabic poetics. Al-Qartajanni, who wholeheartedly promoted Aristotle's *Poetics*, also rendered these terms into the same Arabic "equivalents".[107] What conclusions can be drawn from this incompetent and inadequate substitution of basic terms?

It is difficult to say from this distance what cultural conditions and what factors led to such a clumsy adaptation of the *Poetics*, which raised high expectations. Actually, it can probably be said that expectations of the *Poetics* were high only if seen from our angle, from the perspective of our time and experience, while the same expectations probably did not exist at the time, as the *Poetics* would otherwise have left a clear trace. This is a sort of projection that cannot give valid results. Therefore, the conditions in which the *Poetics* was so adapted can be reconstructed as an approximation or speculation, but what is important for Arabic tradition is that the *Poetics* failed to affect it, which is a fact that must be explained.

In Old Arabic literature translation was understood quite differently than today. This should be kept in mind. The most frequent form was the *rendering* (*naql*) of a work, implying serious adaptive intervention with the original. The receiving culture was always in the forefront, so that the original text had to be adjusted to the taste and habits of new recipients, as well as to their ideological environment. For instance, a classical work – *Kalila and Dimna* by Abd-Allah Ibn al-Muqaffa' ('Abd Allāh Ibn al-Muqaffa', d. 759) – is so Arabised and Islamised in its translation into Arabic that it seems incredible from the perspective of today's translation standards. The translator added a whole chapter of his own to the work, and infused the noun *Allah* and other elements of Islamisation even though the work had been created in India, in Sanskrit from which it was translated into the pre-Islamic Pahlavi language, etc. Therefore, translators had too free a relation to the original, and this general trend may have influenced the translation of the *Poetics*. However, the difference should be pointed out between a literary work of art – such as *Kalila and Dimna* – and a work of a theoretical nature, since the latter is much less tolerant of interpretations and rewritings. On the other hand, the *Poetics* may have been translated simply because other works of Aristotle – relating to philosophy, particularly logic – were remarkably well received in Arabic-Islamic culture. Namely, owing to their authority, this momentous work of Aristotle's may have been translated out of cultural "courtesy". It is probably no coincidence that the *Poetics* was translated by the philosophers al-Kindi and Ibn Rushd.

However, let us return to interpreting the negative poetic consequences arising from the wrong Arabic "adequates" for the Greek *tragedy* and *comedy*.

This does not concern solely the terms but the very essence they express, as carefully chosen terms in important works usually do in order to carry a certain meaning. Finally, *tragedy* and *comedy* are not only terms but also names of two dramatic forms upon which Aristotle based his *Poetics*. There is no need to explain tragedy and comedy here, as they are generally known, but, for the purpose of asserting their contrast with Arabic literature, it should be noted that they are in the category of drama, which Arabic literature did not have at all. Arabic *madaḥ* is a classical panegyric. Hence, it is a poetic genre containing nothing dramatic: it does not have the structure of dialogue like drama, its plot, etc. The same applies to comedy, whose "adequate" Arabs found in their poetic genre of lampoon (*hijā'*): everything relating to the inadequacy of comparing tragedy and panegyric also applies to the so-called adequates comedy–lampoon.

Trying to discover why Arabs established this incorrect adequacy, I come to the conclusion that they may have done so on the basis of Aristotle's definition of tragedy as a work focusing on sublime feelings and of dramatic characters as coming from the highest social strata, or of comedy as focusing on characters and persons from lower social strata and on non-sublime feelings. Arabic panegyric is also characterised by high pathos and addressed to people who, according to the poet, were sublime and worthy of sublime feelings. Lampoon is saturated with different feelings but not necessarily addressed to characters/persons from the lower or despised social layers; it was frequently addressed to dignitaries the poet wanted to expose to ridicule for various reasons – most often to please his patron and gain material benefit. In any case, the similarity found in sublimity and ridicule is not sufficient for such a clumsy rendering of terminological equivalents. The following should also be noted.

Arabic philologists (and philosophers) dealing with Aristotle's *Poetics* – remaining on the margins of their interests and tradition as it did – basically acted contrary to what should have been expected. Instead of being impressed with the *Poetics* and instead of rendering it in its original form and with a plethora of commentaries, they transferred it as a compendium or as various adaptations. This fact alone is a sufficient indication that Arabs were not impressed with the *Poetics*, since such an attitude would require the highest regard for the text's *authenticity*; its adaptation suggests an insufficient respect of its authenticity and authority. At the same time, adaptations at such a high level, or in such important aspects, prevent the effect of the original, or open wrong directions for its effects. This is exactly what happened to adaptations of Aristotle's *Poetics* in the Arabic tradition. However, what is most important here is the fact, in its own right, that Arabs tried to adapt the *Poetics* to *their tradition*. We saw that these attempts could be so rough that, for example, Greek *tragedy* was substituted with Arabic *panegyric*. Therefore, the *Poetics* was probably rendered because Aristotle had gained a great reputation, the *First Teacher* status, with his philosophy opus, but, unlike his philosophical works, the *Poetics* was subject to a specific revision according to Arabic tradition; it was to be adapted, not adapted to. In addition to the confusions in terminology, this is also attested to by statements of Arabic philologists and philosophers, particularly of al-Qartajanni, who is known as the most affectionate *Poetics* devotee. This refers to the telling belief that Aristotle would have enriched his rules and partly corrected his *Poetics* had he known, among other things, Arabic literature as well. Besides the methodological non-viability of this statement – it is significant that the statement expresses the idea of the need to conform the *Poetics* to Arabic literary tradition. In other words – it is an excellent testimony to the self-confidence of Arabic literary tradition and its almost complete isolation. I must again underline that the subject of my analysis is the Arabic poetic tradition and its poetics: prose forms are basically non-Arabic – they came from different traditions and had different poetics that could be analysed separately.

The facts about the attitude towards Aristotle's *Poetics* suggest an almost extreme self-sufficiency in Arabic tradition: not only was Aristotle's *Poetics* adapted to Old Arabic poetics, but it is often believed that Aristotle himself would have changed many a thing in his *Poetics* had he known Arabic literature. This "twofold" pressure on Aristotle indicates the particularity of Arabic poetics, expressed through a high degree of self-awareness, and its isolation in terms of it preventing influences on itself but certainly aspiring towards influencing other traditions. In no other field of creativity did the Arabic spirit express such a type and degree of egocentricity. In all other fields it displayed curiosity and openness to fruitful communication, which is why it greatly progressed, but in the field of literature, more precisely in poetry, it remained curiously closed to changes from within and almost aggressive in spreading outwards. Owing to this, it became possible – and even desirable in terms of literary theory and literary history – to speak about Islamic poetics and Islamic literature, whose very soul was Arabian and then Arabic poetry. It is hard to say whether this historic fact "damaged" or "deprived" Aristotle's *Poetics* or Arabic literary tradition. The dilemma is too hypothetical, or even false, because the incompatibility of the two poetics has been repeatedly confirmed, along with the impossibility of their interpenetration. This situation can, even today, be subsequently verified through the following obvious points.

Any regret over the absence of Aristotle's influence is groundless, as is the belief that Arabic literary tradition could have influenced him had he been familiar with it. I will present the following evidence supporting my assertions. First, Arabs could not have been unfamiliar with ancient Greek artistic literature, besides Aristotle's *Poetics*, because they were familiar with all his other works, as well as with ancient culture generally. Why then were epic and drama left out?! Still, there is no trace of the effect of ancient artistic literature on Arabs. This means – and is no speculation – that Arabic literary tradition resolutely rejected Greek literature as a foreign body, not considering it even worthy of recorded mention. Second, when translations/renderings of the *Poetics* finally appeared, there was no effect – either in the sphere of theoretical development of literature or in that of literary artistic creativity. Incommunicability was complete. Therefore, these are not speculations but undeniable literary-historical facts. Ibn al-Mu'tazz was the first in the Arabic world to make a classification of figures of speech and tropes, based on the experience of Arabic literature. Editing a Russian translation of Ibn al-Mu'tazz's remarkable work *Kitāb al-badī'* (*Book of the Novel and Strange*) in 1953, Russian Arabist Krackovskij established that Ibn al-Mu'tazz was in no way under Aristotle's influence.[108]

The dawn of a new age

The Aristotelian understanding of art can be related to Arabs only in the modern age, as well as the intense contacts of the two literary traditions. This became possible after a very long historical period, or after overcoming the traditionalism that normative and inductive Old Arabic poetics grew into. Thus there is no confusion in Arabic literature today relating, for example, to terms for drama, tragedy and comedy: Arabic literature has acquired much more suitable terms. Nevertheless, there is the important issue of how traditionalism and normativeness were actually overcome; it is not sufficient to state that there was strong traditionalism and that it served as a barrier to radical literary vicissitudes.

Traditionalism was generated by normative and inductive poetics. This means that traditionalism could be overcome only by the sort of turnabout in which poetics was constructed as deductive, and literary production, in accordance with such poetics, determined as creative, not normative. Modern Arabic poetics was constituted in exactly this way – as deductive – which freed literary art from the chains of traditionalism. Writers no longer committed to consecrate tradition, to create strictly within its thematic and technical norms but were, on the contrary, required to create comparatively great innovative differentiation with respect to works created in tradition. Let us remember – deductive poetics is a broad understanding of literature, refusing to be subsumed under norms and not equating itself with literary exemplars. The moment when poetics is constituted as the broadest experience of literature and literary experience itself, not like the exemplary and inviolable tradition "woven" or "cast" in literary exemplars – as defined by philologists – a comprehensive turnabout can finally happen. On the one hand, it proves necessary to overcome traditionalism, although tradition in a different quality is also respected. For, traditionalism does not represent the broadest understanding of literature: on the contrary, it keeps preventing truly creative breakthroughs, thus reducing art to the authority of exemplars. On the other hand and at the same time, "someone else's" experiences are discovered as precious, becoming compatible with the experience of tradition as well – owing to poetic deduction as the broadest understanding of literary experience. The resistance of traditionalism is finally overcome.

Therefore, modern deductive poetics made true miracles possible in Arabic literature – those inconceivable in the ancient and classicist periods, so that all attempts of advocacy remained futile, such as those penned by al-Qartajanni. Only now did new literary forms enter Arabic literature, including a new literary genre – drama, previously unknown to it. *Free poetry* (without metre and rhyme) flourished, poetry in prose as well, and the Arabic short story was cultivated very successfully. And the novel?! It was developed in the twentieth century and, during the lifetime of one writer, Naguib Mahfouz, it rose to the very top of world novelistic prose: the experience of deductive poetics in Mahfouz's novelistic opus was gilded with the Nobel Prize. It is more than a Nobel Prize: it is recognition for having overcome traditionalism and the deductive poetics that enabled it. If it were less politicised, the Nobel Prize should have been awarded at least once more to this titanic tradition – say, to the poetry of Mahmoud Darwish (Maḥmūd Darwīsh, b. 1941).

Arabic literary tradition resisted changes for too long: entrenched in traditionalism, it could not even dream of the beauty of achievements enabled through fruitful contact with different experiences. Reconstructing the steps that led tradition to the state of ossified traditionalism, the first is undoubtedly the momentum and authority that philology drew from the need to interpret and promote the *Qur'an*'s text. Since the *Qur'an* demonstrated its supernaturalism, or argumentation supporting its divine origin, in the field of language – miraculously pushing apart the borders of its experience, and in stylistics as well, philology decisively turned, through the inertia of its own requests, to poetry, particularly to its wellsprings. Thus antiquity very soon became authority. The highest significance of exemplar was established. This linguistic fact is the source of everything. Namely, it should never be forgotten that the *Qur'an* is the last and completely authentic Revelation that, to an extremely high degree, offers arguments for its divine source precisely in language, the same language from which poetry was created. It is different with other revelations, both in terms of their authenticity and in terms of the supernaturalism and endurance of their respective languages. In the given conditions, philology could not have failed to develop. It strived to promote the wondrous alliance between the language in the sacred Text and those in other texts: they constantly increased one another's importance. For, poetic tradition, promoted by philology, helps to understand the Text and, at the same time, interprets its supremacy while the Text, on its part, indirectly says that tradition is important in order to be able to make a contrast with it. In the context of this cooperation – which is unusual insofar as it is both comparative and contrastive – the story of the exemplary pre-Islamic *al-Mu'allaqāt* displayed on the walls of the Kaaba, as a Shrine, does not sound anecdotal. Namely, tradition has it that these best poems were written out in gold letters on silk fabrics and hung down the Kaaba's walls. If it really happened, then it was epically miraculous; if it is only lore – it is still significant, so little wonder it is dominant. The greatest shrine and the best poetry on it! Admittedly, the poems had been on the Kaaba before the Revelation, before the *Qur'an*, but what remained was their extreme importance, if anything for their having been there: tradition remembered it forever. The Qur'anic Text then made the Kaaba pregnant with meaning, but in its own way, in permanent contrasts: it did not do so on its outer side, by means of suspended silk fabrics; it made it pregnant with meaning within, not primarily by inscriptions but by the human voice that the human soul and heart most convincingly reverberate with.

Whichever the case, this cooperation is as magnificent as it is unusual. True, owing to philology, there developed inductive normative poetics that became the main generator of traditionalism. Yet, it may be comforting that Arabic poetry, taking this direction, reached the truly utter limits of an experience – the experience of technicism, of philotechnic poetry absolutely unmatched in any other tradition. Its too strong attachment to the conditions of the Arabic language and to the refinement of tradition through the form influenced the fact that Old Arabic poetry essentially remained enclosed in one time and one tradition: it never was and never will be successfully translated or rendered into any language, because the most vibrant colours of its attire are always lost in translation. Said in the language of analogy – this poetry and its poetics are endemic.

There is one interesting thing to be noted with regard to the character of Old Arabic poetry and poetics. Namely, this tradition was largely realised on the principles of normativeness, implying that, in itself, it achieved the ideal of imitativeness and, in proportion to it, made relative the concept of originality. All this happened on the principle of contrast with the *Qur'an* based on inimitability and absolute authenticity. However, the unusualness is expressed in the fact that the Arabic tradition, *in relation to all other traditions*, was completely inimitable, remarkably original, resistant even to powerful "charges" such as Aristotle's *Poetics* and ancient Greek literature. Therefore, seen in intercultural proportions and contexts, promoting the inimitability of the sacred Text through its internal imitativeness, this literary tradition amazingly established its own inimitability in relation to other traditional systems, and resilience to their influences. It was thus, at the same time, imitative on one level, and quite original on another.

Philology became exhausted over centuries. In fact, it had fulfilled its mission and could not remain the dominant discipline after that. The age of meaningful theories became a necessity, striving towards the highest degree of universalism. In this regard, it is interesting that the Arabic tradition – more precisely, perhaps, the Arabic world – abounds in historical turnabouts. Namely, it must be said that, in the context of these historical vicissitudes, there is a contradiction at work even today. In the ancient period, and in that of classicism, the Arabic world was widely and creatively open towards other cultures, which is why it progressed extremely fast. At the time – as we have just seen – its literature was, quite disproportionately to the general openness, remarkably closed, egotistic and suspicious of anything new. Today, however, there is an unusual and gloomy inversion at work in this world. Arabic literature has finally become widely and fruitfully open to inter-traditional experience, powerfully spreading its wings, but the Arabic world has remained disturbingly stagnant in almost all other spheres of creative spirit.

In the historic depth of antiquity and on the historical plateau of classicism, literature was determined by the substance of the Text – whether by revising antiquity or by distancing itself, in classicism, from the Text through contrast, having abandoned religious themes. Yet, as we saw in the previous discussion, through the refinement of this principle, there developed a vast system that could be called *Islamic poetics*, or *Islamic literature*. Owing to this new-age poetic turnabout, however, this universalism changed its nature – it converted into a system of general, or Goethean world literature. Today, it is not unusual to hear a term such as *Islamic literature*, but it has no grounds any more. Islamic literature can only be talked about in terms of literary inclusion of a certain circle of motifs or themes (a sort of religious literature), but this actually represents its particularisation, not its universalisation, for there is no Islamic literature today in the same sense in which it existed in the age of classicism: it was connected by the same inductive poetics, operating in the universe of the sacred Text. This is a different type of universalism. The term *literature of Islamic peoples* is also used today. The term is incoherent in terms of literary history and methodology, as it is completely non-immanent. Those using this "integristic" term should explain, for example, what it is that makes Malaysian and Moroccan literatures a literary "community", with this hypothetical community differentiating them, at the same time, from others.

The universe created by the Text is constantly expanding. The meaning of the universalism it initiated is being constantly enriched. Namely, the significant "moment" when the Text deprived poetry of the right to a prophetic mission was a death sentence to poetry in Hegelian terms: it was not capable of carrying and presenting the Truth. However, this was also a declaration of its freedom, which has constantly improved since. Strange as it may seem, it should be noted that this liberation offered the grounds for poetry to finally mature into literature – in terms of its multitude of genres, branching out of forms and great creative achievements. This literature ceased to dream of the totality as imagined by pre-Islamic poetry, and, in turn, it acquired the freedom to *artistically create* behind the horizon in a way philotechnic poetry could not even dream of in the epoch of overripe classicism. The freedom bestowed by the sacred Text most likely has no boundaries, because it – freedom, not ideology – is a precondition of authentic artistic creativity.

However, this is already a New Age, on the margin of the effect produced by the sacred Text, and marginal identities are always of specific importance. This age is still maturing. Its meaning – to paraphrase Hegel – will be fully seen only at the end of its realisation – just as the historical realisations of Old Arabic literature and its poetics are only now transparent to us.

Notes

1 In a work I find epochal, in 1947 E. R. Curtius, rightly I believe, named this literature the literature of the Latin Middle Ages (Ernst Robert Curtius, *European Literature and the Latin Middle Ages*).
2 For more on the philological method, see Svetozar Petrović, *Priroda kritike* [*The Nature of Criticism*], Liber, Zagreb, 1972.
3 See more in Chapter 1.
4 While I was preparing my book *Poetics of Arabic Literature in the USA* for publication in the Arabic language, I faced the problem of literary theory terminology, such that I had to coin terms and explain their meanings. Thus, owing to a severe lack of proper Arabic terminology, I rendered even *poetics* by means of my own term *naẓariyya al-ibdā'*, which actually means *theory of artistic creativity*. (The book is published in Arabic under the title *Naẓariyya al-ibdā' al-mahjariyya*, Dimishq, 1989; in Bosnian under the title *Poetika arapske književnosti u SAD*, ZID, Sarajevo, 1997.)
5 Although the term *ancient* is associative of ancient Greek literature, of the cradle of literature in Western cultural circles, I believe there is no reason not to apply the term *ancient* to Arabic literature in the period discussed here. Moreover, I find this parallel impressive: two quite independent cultures and civilisations had their ancient literatures very close in meaning and function, as well as the poetological achievements in subsequent development of the traditions based upon them.
6 Cf. Ibn Khaldūn, *al-Muqaddima*, Cairo, s. a., p. 505.
7 Quoted from Dr 'Adnān Ḥusayn Qāsim, *al-Uṣūl al-turāthiyya fī naqd al-shi'r al-'arabī al-mu'āṣir fī Miṣr* [*Traditional Basis in Criticism of Contemporary Arabic poetry in Egypt*], Ṭarāblis, 1981, pp. 131–132.
8 Ibn Ṭabāṭabā, *'Iyār al-shi'r* [*Standards of Poetry*], Cairo, 1956, p. 4; quoted from 'Adnān Ḥusayn Qāsim, op. cit., p. 309.
9 Free verse will appear only in the 1950s, even then as a poetic heresy.
10 Cf. I. M. Fil'štinskij, *Arabskaja literatura v srednie veka: VIII–IX vv.*, "Nauka", Moscow, 1978, p. 205.
11 The main work of Abū 'Amr Ibn al-'Alā is *Kitāb marsūm al-Muṣḥaf* [*On al-Muṣḥafa Manifesto*].
12 The main work of Abū 'Ubayda is *Majāz al-Qur'ān* [*Figurativeness of the* Qur'an].
13 The main work of al-Asma'ī is *al-Asma'iyyāt* (named after its author).
14 The main work of Ibn Sallām al-Jumaḥī is *Ṭabaqāt fuhūl al-shu'arā'* [*Classes of Champion Poets*], Brill, Leiden, 1913.
15 The main work of Ibn Qutayba is *al-Shi'r wa al- shu'arā'* [*Poetry and Poets*], Leiden, 1952.

16 Cf. Fil'štinskij, op. cit., p. 205.
17 Ibn Qutayba, *Liber poësis et poëtarum*, ed. M. J. Goeje, Lagduni-Batavorum, 1904, p. 16.
18 After T. S. Eliot's essay *Tradition and the Individual Talent*, published in 1919, there is no need to explain the relationship between tradition and individual talent: this is a commonplace in literary theory. However, the poet's relationship to tradition was separately defined in postmodernism, which uses the intertextuality method and where the poet can either promote or deny tradition.
19 It is almost unbelievable how long-lived requirements set by Ibn Qutaybah and some other philologists were. Namely, the motif of imaginary journey from the ancient *qaṣīda* (travelling on a camel and stopping by a deserted bivouac to sing a passage-prelude of love poetry) has survived into modern times in which we read modern poets writing similar poems about their imaginary journeys, even though they never leave comfortable metropolises where they enjoy the convenience of modern cars and air conditioning.
20 Fil'štinskij, op. cit., p. 214.
21 The semantics of the root *nqd* is very interesting in this case. A derivative of this root (*naqd*, and its plural form *nuqūd*) in contemporary language means money generally, but it etymologically denoted *unforged coins*. A morphological form of this root – *naqd* – denotes literary criticism today. It is also evident that there is a strong semantic link between literary criticism identifying a literary work as non-plagiarism and money as non-forged. Both treat non-forgery as a value.
22 Eva de Vitray-Meyerovitch, "Poetika islama" [Poetics of Islam], in Julija Kristeva, *Prelaženje znakova* [*Traversing of Signs*], Svjetlost, Sarajevo, 1979.
23 A more detailed discussion of the inductive and deductive poetics in Arabic literature can be found in my book *Poetika arapske književnosti u SAD*.
24 The ayah reads:

> O people, verily, We have created you of a male and a female, and we have divided you into peoples and tribes that ye might have knowledge one of another. Truly, the most worthy of honour in the sight of God is he who feareth Him most. Verily, God is Knowing, Cognisant.
>
> (*Qur'an*, 49:13)

25 Cf. Fil'štinskij, op. cit., p. 214.
26 Of course, this refers to the classical period. The modern age has seen brilliant periods and the results of influence on both sides. On the European side, for instance, it is sufficient to mention Goethe or Oriental sources of the infinitely important epoch of Romanticism; on the other side, there emerges the poetic "synthesis" of Khalil Gibran (Khalīl Jubrān, 1883–1931) or of Naguib Mahfouz (Najīb Maḥfūẓ, 1911–2006). However, modern-age interpenetration belongs to a different kind of research.
27 Rene Wellek and Austin Warren, *Theory of Literature*, Nolit, Belgrade, 1965, transl. Aleksandar Spasić and Slobodan Đorđević, p. 162.
28 Ibid., pp. 39–40.
29 Murray Krieger, *Theory of Criticism*, Nolit, Belgrade, 1982, transl. Svetozar M. Ignjačević, p. 215.
30 Qudāma Ibn Ja'far, *Naqd al-shi'r* [*Criticism of Poetry*], ed. al-Jawā'ib al-qisṭanṭīniyya, 1302 AH [1884], p. 17.

Like many other terms in Arabic literature, the term *motif* is originally polysemous and, for the sake of preciseness, its original meanings should be given here. It is the Arabic word *ma'nā*, pl. *ma'ānī*, meaning *theme*, *content*, *meaning*, *motif*. A whole branch of stylistics was even named after it, *'ilm al-ma'ānī*, broadly defined as a set of "rules according to which speech is adapted to a certain speech situation" (Dr Teufik Muftić, *Klasična arapska stilistika* [*Classical Arabic Stylistics*],

El-Kalem, Sarajevo, 1995, p. 29). In the context of my discussion, as well as in that of Arabic philologists, the term *ma'nā* denotes a *motif* in a literary work.

31 Cf. Qudāma Ibn Ja'far, op. cit.

32 Cf. 'Izz al-Dīn Ismā'īl, *al-Usus al-jamāliyya fī al-naqd al-'arabī. 'Arḍ wa tafsīr wa muqārana* [*Aesthetic Grounds in Arabic Literary Criticism: Presentation, Interpretation and Comparison*], 2nd edn, Cairo, 1974, p. 216.

33 Ibn Rashīq, *al-'Umda fī maḥāsin al-shi'r wa ādābih wa naqdih* [*The Mainstay Concerning Poetry's Embellishments, Correct Usage, and Criticism*], quoted from 'Izz al-Dīn Ismā'īl, op. cit., p. 216.

34 Abū Hilāl al-'Askarī, *Kitāb ṣinā'atay al-naẓm wa al-nathr* [*The Book of the Two Skills, Poetry and Prose*], ed. al-Āstāna, 1319 AH [1901], p. 149.

35 Quoted from 'Izz al-Dīn Ismā'īl, op. cit., p. 218.

36 It is interesting to see how Borges, in his artistic story, records the following Arabic poetic perspective: "Alarmed (and not without reason) by the inane versifications of Ibn-Sharaf, Averroës said that in the ancients and the *Qur'an* could all poetry be read, and he condemned as illiterate and vain all desire to innovate" (Borges, *Short Stories*, ed. and transl. Krinka Vidaković Petrov, Rad, Belgrade, 1979, p. 62).

37 Ibid., pp. 20–21.

38 The most famous poet of the Abbasid epoch, Abu Nuwas, for example, sings to a patron (the name Muhammad mentioned in these verses does not refer to the Prophet):

> Neither the Sun nor the Moon bright
> Are worthy of being likened to the Emir
> For if there is some likeness between them,
> There is much more that sets them apart:
> The Sun sets when the night comes
>   And the full Moon puts its crown,
> But Muhammad's light remains forever so bright
>   It can never fade into darkness.
>
> (Abū Nuwās, *Dīwān*, Dār maktaba al-thaqāfa al-'arabiyya, Baghdad, s. a., p. 101)

The official Umayyad panegyrist, al-Akhtal, sings:

> And the Euphrates – when its bed begins to swell
>   And its current rolls many a trunk,
> And on the summer wind its waves break
>   Above the boat they pound against,
> The Euphrates whose clear water rush down the Byzantine massif,
>   Gushing over its steeps –
> Is never more lavish than a patron you entreat,
> Nor more magnificent than a patron appearing before his people.
>
> (*Shi'r al-Akhṭal*, 2nd edn, I, Beirut, 1972, pp. 197–198)

39 Imru' al-Qays sings:

> And many a fair one, concealed behind the purdah, whose tent cannot be sought by others,
> Have I enjoyed myself by playing with, without hastening my departure.
> I passed by the sentries on watch near her, and a people desirous of killing me,
> If they could conceal my murder, being unable to assail me openly.
> I passed by these people at a time, when the Pleiades appeared in the heavens,
> As the appearance of the gems in the spaces in the ornamented girdle, set with pearls and gems.
> Then I came to her, when she had taken off her clothes for sleep,

Except her night garment; and she was standing near the screen of the tent.
Then she said to me, "I swear by God, you have no excuse for what you are doing,
And I cannot expect that your erring habits will ever be removed from your nature."
I went out with her; she walking, and drawing behind us, over our footmarks,
The skirts of an embroidered woollen garment, to erase the footprints.
Then when we had crossed the enclosure of the tribe, the middle of the open plain,
With its sandy undulations and sandhills, was sought by us.
I drew the two side-locks of her head towards me; and she leant towards me;
She was slender of waist, but full in the ankle.
Thin-waisted, white-skinned, not fat in the abdomen,
Her breast-bones shining polished like a mirror.
[...]

(*The al-Mu'allaqāt*, pp. 37–40)

40 Bashshār Ibn Burd, *Dīwān*, I, Cairo, 1950–1957, p. 332.
41 Ibid., pp. 115–119.
42 Cf. Kudelin, op. cit., p. 8.
43 Al-Qāḍī al-Jurjānī, *al-Wasāṭa bayn al-Mutanabbī wa khuṣūmih* [*Mediation between al-Mutanabbi and His Adversaries*], Cairo, s. a., p. 150.
44 It is interesting that the panegyrical opus and fame of Ahmad Shawqi, as the last great panegyric, coincide with the era of the last Egyptian king: after the era of the official panegyric poetry, the Egyptian Republic entered the historical stage.
45 Under *Islamic literature* I always refer to Arabic–Persian–Turkish literature in their classical period.
46 Persian: *madh*, *hajw*, *marsiyye*; Turkish: *medhiyye*, *hicviyye*, *mersiyye*.
47 The importance of language is in its own way attested to by the situation of modern, particularly Arabic literature. Namely, in certain circumstances and in certain literature, it is classified into *Egyptian*, *Syrian*, etc. From the position of the theory of literature and its methodology, such classification is incoherent, even more so than that of the classical period when it was segmented into Umayyad, Abbasid, etc. *Egyptian*, *Syrian* and similar literatures are completely non-immanent, political references that forcefully segment a vast and coherent system such as modern Arabic literature into the borders of political communities. Nonetheless, since it concerns a huge production, which must sometimes be segmented to offer a better overview, this literature can only be talked about as *Arabic literature in Egypt*, in Syria, etc., because Arabic literature can thus express the integrality of the system, while its regionalisation expresses its own conditionality, or imposition for the purpose of making the overview more clear.
48 Cf. Wellek and Warren, op. cit., p. 103.
49 Abd al-Qāhir al-Jurjānī, *Dalā'il al-'i'jāz* [*Intimations of Inimitability*], 2nd edn, al-Manār, 1331 h. [1912], s. l., pp. 196–197.
50 Cf. 'Izz al-Dīn Ismā'īl, op. cit., p. 404.
51 Ibid.
52 'Abd al-Qāhir al-Jurjānī, op. cit., p. 196.
53 Al-Duktūr Aḥmad Kamāl Zakī, *Dirāsāt fī al-naqd al-adabī* [*Studies on Literary Criticism*], Dār al-Andalus, 2nd edn, s. l., 1980, p. 119.
54 Ibn Khaldūn (*The Muqaddimah*, p. 578) and al-Jāḥiẓ used the term *ṣiyāġa* (*al-ṣiyāġa al-fanniyya*) in a similar way (cf. Dr 'Adnān Ḥusayn Qāsim, op. cit., p. 116).
55 Later on, I will use the examples of *naẓīra* and *takhmīs*, as quite particular poetic forms, to illustrate how the condition of different metre and rhyme was abandoned, or how the competitive spirit of technicism culminated in these forms that kept the

same metre and rhyme as the "proto-poem". It was also the pinnacle of a literary tradition facing the alternatives of renaissance salvation or fatal collapse.

56 More on this may be found in my book *Poetika arapske književnosti u SAD*.

57 'Abd al-Qāhir al-Jurjānī, op. cit., pp. 30–31.

58 Cf. 'Izz al-Dīn Ismā'īl, op. cit., p. 324.

59 Ibn al-Athīr, *al-Mathal al-sāir fī adab al-kātib wa al-shā'ir* [*Exemplariness in Literature of Prosaist and Poet*], Būlāq, Cairo, 1282 h. [1865], p. 441.

60 Ibn Rashīq, *al-'Umda fī maḥāsin al-shi'r wa ādābih wa naqdih* [*The Mainstay Concerning Poetry's Embellishments, Correct Usage, and Criticism*], I, 1st edn, s. l., 1907, p. 75.

It should be noted here – as a curiosity, not as an influence – that the word *text* in European languages etymologically indicates *fabrics* (*textum – texture, weaving*).

61 Quoted from Dr 'Adnān Ḥusayn Qāsim, op. cit., p. 317.

62 Ibid., p. 309.

63 Al-Qāḍī al-Jurjānī, op. cit., p. 21.

64 Ibn Sallām al-Jumaḥī, op. cit., p. 3.

65 Al-Duktūr Aḥmad Kamāl Zakī, op. cit., p. 110.

66 Ibid.

67 Called *annual odes* because it took Zuhayr (530–627) a whole year to polish his poem (*ḥawliyya=annual ode*).

68 Dr 'Adnān Ḥusayn Qāsim, op. cit., p. 317.

69 A notable work in this sphere was written by al-Āmidī (d. 981) under the title *al-Muwāzana bayn Abī Tammām wa al-Bukhturī* [*The Balancing, a Comparison of Abu Tammam and al-Buhturi*].

70 Quoted from Dr 'Adnān Ḥusayn Qāsim, op. cit., p. 317. Ibn Rashīq, *al-'Umda fī maḥāsin al-shi'r wa ādābih wa naqdih*, I, 1st edn, s. l., 1907.

71 Cf. ibid., p. 306.

72 Even the name of the poetic form is Arabic: from *khams*=five; *takhmīs* is a gerund derived from a verb, meaning *quintuple*, *make a pentagon*.

73 Under the term *proto-poem* I imply the original lines with which a poetic dialogue is established, while the *meta-poem* implies the additional three lines composing a stanza together with the first two lines.

74 *Takhmīs* was a very popular form in Turkish divan literature in the fifteenth and sixteenth centuries.

75 More on this may be found in my paper "Mostarska *nazira* kao svijest o uobličenoj poetskoj tradiciji" [The Mostar nazira as the awareness of formulated poetic tradition], *Hercegovina*, no. 9, Arhiv Hercegovine Mostar, 1997, pp. 187–192.

Etymologically, *naẓīra* means *a parallel*. The appropriateness of this term could be discussed with regard to it denoting a separate poetic form.

For more on *naẓīra*, see also Dr Fehim Nametak, *Pregled književnog stvaranja bosanskohercegovačkihmuslimana na turskom jeziku* [*Literary Production of BiH Muslims in the Turkish Language*], Sarajevo, 1989; the same author, *Divanska poezija XVI i XVII stoljeća* [*Divan Poetry of 16th and 17th Centuries*], Sarajevo, 1991; Omer Mušić, "Mostar u turskoj pjesmi iz XVII vijeka" [Mostar in 17th century Turkish poem], *Prilozi za orijentalnu filologiju*, no. XIV–XV/1964.65, Sarajevo, 1969, pp. 74–76; Salih Trako and Lejla Gazić, "Dvije mostarske medžmue" [Two Mostar collections], *Prilozi zaorijentalnu filologiju*, no. 38/1988, Sarajevo, 1989, pp. 97–123.

76 The poem of Dervish Pasha Bajezidagić, except its sixth couplet, was translated into Bosnian by Bašagić. (Safvet-beg Bašagić, *Bošnjaci i Hercegovci u islamskoj književnosti. Prilog kulturnoj historiji Bosne i Hercegovine* [*Bosniaks and Herzegovinians in Islamic Literature: A Contribution to Cultural History of Bosnia and Herzegovina*], Sarajevo, 1912.) This translation was also published in *Biserje. Izbor iz muslimanske književnosti*, ed. by Alija Isaković, Zagreb, 1972. The same poem

was also translated into Bosnian by Omer Mušić, op. cit. In the same periodical, Mušić also published his translation of the poem by Dervish effendi Mostarac (Žagrić).

Bašagić translated the poem in the form of a quatrain, rhyming only the second and fourth lines, although the original does not have the form of stanza, while Mušić's translation of the poems has neither rhythm nor rhyme, so that the most important aspects cannot be seen from it, i.e. why the poems are parallel ones and what characterises their form. I therefore did my own translation of the monorhyme poems, using Mušić's philologically reliable translation.

77 Beyân u vasfa gelmez hüsn-i bî hemtâsı Mostar'ıñ
A'ceb mi olsun ey dil, 'âşıkı şeydâsı Mostar'ıñ
Hele olmaz bu dünyâda meğer firdevs-i a'lâda
Hevâ-yi dilkeş ü âb-ı hayât efzâsı Mostar'ıñ
Temâşâ eyleyen kesb-i hayât-ı nev kılur her dem
Müferrihdir iken her kûşe-i zîbâsı Mostar'ıñ
Miyâhiyle fevâkih kesretiyle Şâm-ı sânî
Behişt-i asârdır her ravzâ-i ra'nâsı Mostar'ıñ
Ulüvv-ı şânıyla zât-ül-burûcuñ tâkına beñzer
Ol iki kulesiyle cisr-i müstesnâsı Mostar'ıñ
Aña cift olmağa tâk-ı semânıñ tâkatı yok
Felekdir tâkıdır cisr-i felek-fersâsı Mostar'ıñ
Cihânı arasan halkı gibi kâbil bulunmaz hiç
Kavâbil-i kânîdir şöhret-i cihân arası Mostar'ıñ
Kopar seyf ü kalem ehli içinde mâ-tekaddemden
Olur hâsıl îmdem (?) kâmil ü dânâsı Mostar'ıñ
Yanında tûtîyân-ı Hind olur hâmûş u dem-beste
Bu gün Dervîş sensin bülbül güyâsı Mostar'ıñ

78 Tolu her kûşesinde dilber-i ra'nâsı Mostar'ıñ
A'ceb olmaz çok olsa âşık-ı şeydâsı Mostar'ıñ
Hevâsı mu'tedil Selsebiliñ aynıdır âbı
Hayâta nev bağışlar dağıyla sahrâsı Mostar'ıñ
Nazîrin görmemişdir kimse âlemde añıñ herkes
Nice hâlet virür her kûşe-i zîbâsı Mostar'ıñ
Kalur seyrine her kim gelse çıkmak istemez añdan
Behişt-âsâ olur peder-şehr-i müstesnâsı Mostar'ıñ
Leb-i cûyunda hem sahan-ı safâ nâmında câyı var
Odur hakkâ safâ bahşıyla ruh efzâsı Mostar'ıñ
Miyâhı vefretiyle hak budur kim aynıdır Şâm'ıñ
Gıdâ-i rûhdur hûd-i meyve-i a'lâsı Mostar'ıñ
İki kale arası tâk-ı Kisrâ'dan nişân olmuş
Felek tâkına beñzer cisri bî-hemtâsı Mostar'ıñ
Var ise ma'den-i ilm ü kemâl u ma'rifetdir kim
Değil eksik içinde kâmil ü dânâsı Mostar'ıñ
Değil vassâfıñ ancak Hacı Dervîş anda sultânım
Duâ-gûyândur a'lâsı ednâsı Mostar'ıñ

79 Majdī Wahba wa Kāmil al-Muhandis, *Mu'jam al-muṣṭalaḥāt al-'arabiyya fī al-luġa wa al-adab*, Beirut, 1984.

80 At this point, a contemporary reader will certainly have an association of the postmodernist relationship towards tradition and the citation theory in it. Postmodernist writers also play with tradition they take their citations from, reshaping them or not giving their sources. Of course, postmodernism does not consider this to be plagiarism but a procedure developing appreciation of intertextuality. The dominant pro-

cedure of the artist in Old Arabic literature, just as a very affirmative attitude of the audience towards it, has so many similarities with postmodernism that it could be called the primeval anticipation of postmodernism.

81 Abū Hilāl al-'Askarī, op. cit., p. 196.

82 Quoted from Dr 'Adnān Ḥusayn Qāsim, op. cit., p. 360.

83 Ibn Qutayba, *al-Shi'r wa al-shu'arā'*, quoted from Dr 'Adnān Ḥusayn Qāsim, op. cit., p. 361.

84 al-A'shā lived in the pre-Islamic period, while Abū Nuwās in the Umayyad one.

85 Ibn Ṭabāṭabā, *'Iyār al-shi'r* [*Standards of Poetry*], Cairo, 1956, pp. 77–78.

86 Cf. Dr 'Adnān Ḥusayn Qāsim, op. cit., p. 364.

87 'Abd al-Qāhir al-Jurjānī, *Asrār al-balāġa*, cited in Dr 'Adnān Ḥusayn Qāsim, op. cit., p. 371.

88 Quoted from Dr 'Adnān Ḥusayn Qāsim, op. cit., p. 313.

89 Quoted from al-Marzubānī, *al-Muwashshaḥ*, Cairo, 1965, p. 478.

90 *Qur'an*, 26:220–222.

91 Al-Qarṭājannī, *Minhāj al-bulaġā' wa sirāj al-udabā'* [*Path of the Eloquent and Lamp of the Lettered*]; quoted from al-Duktūr Aḥmad Kamāl Zakī, op. cit., p. 111.

92 Dr 'Izz al-Dīn Ismā'īl, op. cit., p. 403.

93 J. M. Lotman, *Struktura umetničkog teksta* [*The Structure of the Artistic Text*], Nolit, Belgrade, 1976, prev. Novica Petković, p. 178.

94 Dr 'Izz al-Dīn Ismā'īl, op. cit., p. 287.

95 Ibid., p. 299.

96 Ibn al-Nadīm, *al-Fahrast*, I, Leipzig, 1872, p. 35. On first translations of Aristotle's *Poetics*, see more in Dr 'Izz al-Dīn Ismā'īl, op. cit, pp. 287, 299.

97 'Abd al-Raḥmān Badawī, *Fann al-shi'r li Arisṭūṭālīs* [*Aristotle's Poetics*], Maktaba al-nahḍa al-miṣriyya, 1953, p. 56.

98 Quoted from al-Duktūr Aḥmad Kamāl Zakī, op. cit., p. 111.

99 Al-Qarṭājannī, op. cit., p. 118; quoted from Dāwūd Sallūm, *al-Ta'thīr al-yūnānī fī al-naqd al-'arabī al-qadīm* [*Greek Influence in Old Arabic Criticism*], Baghdad, s. a., p. 381.

100 Quoted from Dr Aḥmad Kamāl Zakī, op. cit., p. 111.

101 For more on this, see Esad Duraković, *Poetika arapske književnosti u SAD*.

102 Al-Qarṭājannī, op. cit.; quoted from Dāwūd Sallūm, op. cit., p. 381.

103 In the section entitled "The Authority of Philology and Shu'ubiyyah" of Chapter 6 I discussed this antagonism of precedence in Arabic-Islamic culture and in the sphere of politics as well.

104 Sallūm, op. cit., p. 359.

105 Ṭāhā Ḥusayn, *Ḥadīth al-arbi'ā'* [*Wednesday Talk*], II, 10th edn, Cairo, s. a., p. 12.

106 Cf. 'Izz al-Dīn Ismā'īl, op. cit., p. 287. Borges narrates how Averroës (Ibn Rushd) unsuccessfully searched for adequate terms for *tragedy* and *comedy*, weaving these traditional facts through an excellent postmodernist citation into his story "Averroës' Search": "He suddenly realised the meaning of two mysterious words. With firm and careful calligraphy he added these lines to the manuscript: 'Arisṭū [Aristotle] gives the name of tragedy to panegyrics and that of comedy to satires and anathemas" (Borges, op. cit., p. 62).

107 Khalīl al-Mūsā, "Waḥda al-qaṣīda fī naqd al-Qarṭājannī", in *al-Turāth al-'arabī*, 30, Dimishq, yanāyir 1988, p. 67.

108 'Izz al-Dīn Ismā'īl, op. cit., p. 293.

Bibliography

I have offered the English translation of titles in Arabic and Bosnian to inform readers unfamiliar with Arabic and Bosnian about the themes these works deal with. In addition, since throughout the text I referred to a number of works but in their translation into Bosnian, I list them as such, giving the English titles in brackets.

'Abbās, al-duktūr Iḥsān, *Tārīkh al-naqd al-adabī 'inda al-'Arab* [*Arabic Literary Criticism*], Beirut, 1971.

Abu-Zayd, Nasr, "The dilemma of the literary approach to the Qur'an", *Alif: Journal of Comparative Poetics* 23 (2003): 8–47.

Ahlwardt, Wilhelm, *Bemerkungen über die Aeshtheit der alten arabischen Gedischte*, Greifswald, 1872.

al-Āmidī, *al-Muwāzana bayn Abī Tammām wa al-Buḥturī* [*The Balancing, a Comparison of Abu Tammam and al-Buhturī*], I–II, Cairo, 1961–1962.

Amīn, Aḥmad, *al-Naqd al-adabī* [*Literary Criticism*], Cairo, 1952.

Amīn, Muṣṭafā wa 'Alī al-Jārim, *al-Balāġa al-wāḍiḥa. Al-Bayān wa al-ma'ānī wa al-badī'* [*Clear Rhetoric...*], Cairo, 1965.

Arapska poezija, izabrao Darko Tanasković, Belgrade, 1977.

Aristotel, *O pesničkoj umetnosti* [*On the Art of Poetry*], transl. Miloš Đurić, Belgrade, 1969.

Arberry, Arthur J., *The Koran Interpreted*, Vol. 2, London, 1955.

al-'Askarī, Abū Hilāl, *Kitāb ṣinā'atay al-naẓm wa al-nathr*, [*The Book of the Two Skills, Poetry and Prose*], ed. al-Āstana, 1319 h. [1901], s. l.

Asunto, Rozario, *Teorija o lepom u srednjem veku* [*The Medieval Theory of the Beautiful*], transl. Gligorije Ernjaković, Belgrade, 1975.

Badawī, 'Abd al-Raḥmān, *Fann al-shi'r li Arisṭūṭālīs* [*Aristotle's* Poetics], Cairo 1953.

Badawī, Aḥmad, *al-Buḥturī* [*al-Buhturī*], Cairo, 1956.

Badawī, al-duktūr Aḥmad Aḥmad, *Usus al-naqd al-adabī 'inda al-'Arab* [*Essentials of Arabic Literary Criticism*], Cairo, 1960.

Bajraktarević, Fehim, "Pejzaž u staroj arapskoj poeziji" [Landscape in Old Arabic poetry], *Zbornik u čast B. Popovića*, Belgrade, 1929.

Bart, Rolan, *Književnost. Mitologija. Semiologija* [*Literature. Mythology. Semiology*], Belgrade, 1979.

Barthes, Roland, *Kritika i istina*, transl. Lada Čale Feldman, Algoritam, Zagreb, 2009.

Barthes, Roland, *Le Bruissement de la langue: Essais critiques IV*, Paris, 1984.

Barthes, Roland, *S/Z*, Paris, 1970.

al-Barqūqī, ʻAbd al-Raḥmān, *Sharḥ Dīwān Ḥassān Ibn Thābit al-Anṣārī* [*An Appreciative Explanation of the Collected Poems of Hadrat Hassaan bin Thabit*], Beirut, 1978.

Bašagić, Safvet-beg, *Znameniti Hrvati, Bošnjaci i Hercegovci u Turskoj carevini* [*Distinguished Croats, Bosniaks and Herzegovinians in the Turkish Empire*], Zagreb, 1931.

Bašagić, Safvet-beg, *Bošnjaci i Hercegovci u islamskoj književnosti. Prilog kulturnoj historiji Bosne i Hercegovine* [*Bosniaks and Herzegovinians in Islamic Literature: A Contribution to Cultural History of Bosnia and Herzegovina*], Sarajevo, 1912.

Beker, Miroslav, *Suvremene književne teorije* [*Contemporary Literary Theories*], Zagreb, 1999.

Beker, Miroslav, "Tekst/intertekst" [Text/intertext], in *Intertekstualnost & intermedijalnost*, Zagreb, 1988.

Biserje. Izbor iz muslimanske književnosti [*A Selection of Muslim Literature*]. Odabrao i priredio Alija Isaković, Zagreb, 1972.

Biti, Vladimir, *Pojmovnik suvremene književne teorije* [*Glossary of Contemporary Literary Theory*], Zagreb, 1997.

Borges, H. L., *Kratke priče* [*Short Stories*], ed. and transl. Krinka Vidaković Petrov, Belgrade, 1979.

Boškov, Vančo, "Neka razmišljanja o književnosti na turskom jeziku u Bosni i Hercegovini" [Some thoughts on literature in Turkish in Bosnia and Herzegovina], in *Književnost Bosne i Hercegovine u svjetlu dosadašnjih istraživanja*, Sarajevo, 1977.

Boullata, Issa, "The rhetorical interpretation of the Qur'an: I'jaz and related topics", in Andrew Rippin (ed.), *Approaches to the History of the Interpretation of the Qur'an*, Clarendon Press, Oxford, 1988, pp. 139–157.

Boullata, Issa J., "Retorička interpretacija Qur'ana: I'jaz i srodne teme" [The rhetorical interpretation of the Qur'an: I'jaz and related topics], in Enes Karić (ed.), *Semantika Kur'ana* [*Semantic of the Qur'an*], Sarajevo, 1998.

Brooks, Peter, *Reading for the Plot: Design and Intention in Narrative*, London, 1996.

Brūkalmān, Kārl, *Tārīkh al-adab al-'arabī* [*History of Arabic Literature*], transl. al-duktūr ʻAbd al-Ḥalīm al-Najjār, Cairo, 1977.

Bucaille, Maurice, *Biblija. Kur'an. Nauka* [*The Bible, The Qur'an and Science*], transl. Azra Begić, Starješinstvo Islamske zajednice u SR Bosni i Hercegovini, 2nd edn, Sarajevo, 1979.

al-Buḥturī, *Dīwān*, Beirut, 1966.

Byatt, A. S., *A Whistling Woman*, Vintage, London, 2002.

Chouraqui, André, *Deset zapovijedi danas* [*The Ten Commandments Today*], transl. Jadranka Brnčić and Kruno Pranjić, Zagreb, 2005.

Curtius, Ernst Robert, *Evropska književnost i latinsko srednjovjekovlje* [*European Literature and the Latin Middle Ages*], transl. Stjepan Markuš, Zagreb, 1998.

David-Fox, Michael, Peter Holquist and Alexander Martin (eds), *Orientalism and Empire in Russia*, Kritika Historical Studies 3, Bloomington, IN, 2006.

Dāwūd, al-duktūr Anīs, *Dirāsāt naqdiyya fī al-adab al-ḥadīth wa al-turāth al-'arabī* [*Critical Studies of Modern Literature and Arabic Tradition*], s. l., s. a.

Ḍayf, Shawqī, *Fuṣūl fī al-shi'r wa naqdih* [*Treatises on Poetry and Its Criticism*], 2nd edn, Cairo, 1977.

Ḍayf, Shawqī, *al-'Aṣr al-'Abbāsī al-awwal* [*The First Abbasid Period*], Cairo 1972.

Ḍayf, Shawqī, *al-'Aṣr al-islāmī* [*Islamic Period*], Cairo, 1963.

Ḍayf, Shawqī, *Fī al-naqd al-adabī* [*On Literary Criticism*], Cairo, 1962.

Ḍayf, Shawqī, *al-Fann wa madhāhibuh fi al-shi'r al-'arabī* [*Art and Its Directions in Arabic Poetry*], Cairo, 1960.

Ḍayf, Shawqī, *al-Fann wa madhāhibuh fī al-nathr al-'arabī* [*Art and Its Directions in Arabic Prose*], Beirut, 1956.
Duda, Dean, "Figure u opisu prostora" [Figures in spatial description], in Živa Beničić and Dunja Fališevac (eds), *Tropi i figure* [*Tropes and Figures*], Zagreb, 1995.
Duraković, Esad, "Semiotika prostora u kur'anskome tekstu" [Semiotics of space in the Qur'anic Text], *Ostrvo*, br. 5, Tuzla, 2006.
Duraković, Esad, "Stylistic potentialis of the elative in the Qur'an", *Islamic Studies* 44, 3 (2006), Islamabad.
Duraković, Esad, *Prolegomena za historiju književnosti orijentalno-islamskoga kruga* [*Prolegomenon to Literary History of Oriental-Islamic Circle*], Sarajevo, 2005.
Duraković, Esad, *Muallaqe. Sedam zlatnih arabljanskih oda* [*The al-Mu'allaqat: Seven Golden Arabian Odes*], Sarajevo, 2004.
Duraković, Esad, *Arapska stilistika u Bosni. Ahmed Sin Hasanov Bošnjak o metafori* [*Arabic Stylistics in Bosnia: Ahmed son of Hasan Bosniak on Metaphor*], Sarajevo, 2000.
Duraković, Esad, "Stilske vrednote poglavlja *al-Rahman*" [Stylistic merits of the surah *al-Rahman*], *Takvim za 2001. godinu*, Sarajevo, 2000.
Duraković, Esad, "Ogled o metafori *džennet*" [An essay on the Jannah metaphor], *Novi Izraz*, br. 6, Sarajevo, zima/99.
Duraković, Esad, "Mostarska nazira kao svijest o uobličenoj poetskoj tradiciji" [The Mostar nazira as the awareness of formulated poetic tradition], in *Hercegovina*, no. 9, Mostar, 1997.
Duraković, Esad, *Poetika arapske književnosti u SAD* [*Poetics of Arabic Literature in the USA*], Sarajevo, 1997.
Duraković, Esad and Lutvo Kurić, *Kur'an: stilsko i matematičko čudo* [*The Qur'an: Stylistic and Mathematical Miracle*], Svjetlostkomerc, Sarajevo, 2006.
Dūrākūfītsh, As'ad, *Naẓariyya al-ibdā' al-mahjariyya* [*Poetics of Arabic Literary Émigrés*], Dimishq, 1989.
Džebra, Ibrahim, *U potrazi za Velidom Mesudom* [*In Search of Walid Masoud*], transl. and commentary by Esad Duraković, ZID, Sarajevo, 1995.
Ejhenbaum, Boris, *Književnost* [*Literature*], transl. Marina Bojić, Belgrade, 1972.
Eliot, T. S., *Izabrani tekstovi* [*Selected Texts*], transl. Milica Mihailović, Belgrade, 1963.
Farrūkh, 'Umar, *Tārīkh al-adab al-'arabī* [*History of Arabic Literature*], I–III, Beirut, 1978.
Farrūkh, 'Umar, *Abū Nuwās* [*Abu Nuwas*], Beirut, 1960.
Fayṣal, al-duktūr Shukrī, *Taṭawwur al-ġazal bayn al-jāhiliyya wa al-islām* [*Development of Love Poetry from Pre-Islamic to Islamic Period*], 5th edn, Beirut, s. a.
Fil'štinskij, I. M., *Arabskaja literatura v srednie veka. Arabskaja literatura VIII–IX vekov*, Moscow, 1978.
Fil'štinskij, I. M., *Arabskaja literatura v srednie veka. Slovesnoe iskusstvo Arabov v drevnosti i rannem srednevekovye*, Moscow, 1977.
Fil'štinskij, I. M., *Voprosy periodizacii srednevekovoj arabskoj literatury. Problemi periodizacii istorii literatur narodov Vostoka*, Moscow, 1968.
Gabrijeli, Frančesko, *Arapska književnost* [*Arabic Literature*], transl. Milana Piletić and Srđan Music, Sarajevo 1985.
Ġarīb, Rūz, *al-Naqd al-jamālī wa āthāruh fī al-naqd al-'arabī* [*Aesthetic Criticism and Its Works in Arabic Criticism*], Beirut, 1952.
Gibb, H. A. R., *Arabskaja literatura*, Moscow, 1960.
Gonzalez, Dr Valerie, *Shvaćanja islamske estetike, vizualne kulture i historije*, [*Insights on Islamic Aesthetics, Visual Culture and History*], transl. Nevad Kahteran, Sarajevo, 2006.

Grasi, Ernesto, *Teorija o lepom u antici* [*The Antique Theory of the Beautiful*], transl. Ivan Klajn, Belgrade, 1974.

Grozdanić, Sulejman, *Na horizontima arapske književnosti* [*On the Horizons of Arabic Literature*], Sarajevo, 1975.

Grozdanić, Sulejman, *Stara arapska poezija* [*Old Arabic Poetry*], Sarajevo, 1971.

Grunebaum, Gustav E. von, *Kritik und Dichtkunst. Studien zur arabischen Literaturgeschichte*, Wiesbaden, 1955.

Hartmann, Nicolai, "Estetika" [Aestheticism], in Danilo Pejović (ed.), *Nova filozofija umjetnosti*, Zagreb, 1972.

Ḥasan, al-duktūr Zakī Muḥammad, *Funūn al-islām* [*Islamic Arts*], s. l., 1948.

Ḥasan, Jād Ḥasan, *al-Adab al-muqāran* [*Comparative Literature*], Cairo, 1962.

Hiti, Filip, *Istorija Arapa* [*History of the Arabs*], transl. Petar Pejčinović, Sarajevo, 1967.

Ḥusayn, Ṭāhā, *Ḥadīth al-arbi'ā'* [*Wednesday Talk*], I–III, 7th edn, Cairo, s. a.

Ḥusayn, Ṭāhā, *Fī al-adab al-jāhilī* [*On Pre-Islamic Literature*], 11th edn, Cairo, 1975.

Husayn, Tāhā, *Fī al-shi'r al-jāhilī* [*Pre-Islamic Poetry*], Cairo, 1926.

Ḥusayn Qāsim, al-duktūr 'Adnān, *al-Uṣūl al-turāthiyya fī naqd al-shi'r al'arabī al-mu'āṣir fī Miṣr* [*Traditional Basis in Criticism of Contemporary Arabic Poetry in Egypt*], Ṭarāblis, 1981.

Ibn Abī Rabī'a, 'Umar, *Dīwān*, Beirut, 1961.

Ibn al-Athīr, *al-Mathal al-sāir fī adab al-kātib wa al-shā'ir* [*Exemplariness in Literature of Prosaist and Poet*], Cairo, 1282 A.H. [1865].

Ibn Burd, Bashshār, *Dīwān*, Cairo, 1950–1957.

Ibn Khaldūn, *Muqaddima* [*Prolegomena*], Cairo, s. a.

Ibn Ja'far, Qudāma, *Naqd al-shi'r* [*Criticism of Poetry*], ed. al-Jawā'ib al-qisṭanṭīniyya, 1302 h. [1884].

Ibn al-Mu'tazz, *Ṭabaqāt al-shu'arā'* [*Classes of Poets*], Cairo, 1968.

Ibn al-Mu'tazz, *Dīwān*, Beirut, 1961.

Ibn al-Nadīm, *al-Fahrast* [*Catalogue*], Cairo, 1950.

Ibn Qutaiba, *Liber poësis et poëtarum*, ed. M. J. Goeje, Lagduni-Batavorum, 1904.

Ibn Qutayba, *al-Shi'r wa al-shu'arā'* [*Poetry and Poets*], Leiden, 1952.

Ibn Rashīq, *al-'Umda fī maḥāsin al-shi'r wa ādābih wa naqdih* [*The Mainstay Concerning Poetry's Embellishments, Correct Usage, and Criticism*], I–II, 4th edn, Beirut, 1972.

Ibn Ṭabāṭabā, al-'Alawī, *'Iyār al-shi'r* [*Standards of Poetry*], Cairo, 1956.

Ibrāhīm, Ṭāhā Aḥmad, *Tārīkh al-naqd al-adabī 'inda al-'Arab* [*History of Arabic Literary Criticism*], Beirut, 1937.

Ingarden, Roman, *Doživljaj, umetničko delo i vrednost* [*Experience – Work of Art – Value*], Belgrade, 1975.

Ingarden, Roman, *O saznavanju književnog umetničkog dela* [*The Cognition of the Literary Work of Art*], transl. Branimir Živojinović, Belgrade, 1971.

Irwin, Robert, *Nights and Horses and Desert: An Anthology Classical of Arabic Literature*, Anchor Books, London, 2002.

Irwin, Robert, *1001 noć na Zapadu*, transl. Enes Karić, Tugra, Sarajevo, 1999.

al-Isfahānī, Abū al-Farj, *Kitāb al-aġānī* [*Book of Songs*], I–XXI, Beirut, 1976–1957.

Ismā'īl, 'Izz al-Dīn, *al-Usus al-jamāliyya fī al-naqd al-'arabī. 'Arḍ wa tafsīr wa muqārana* [*Aesthetic Grounds in Arabic Literary Criticism: Presentation, Interpretation and Comparison*], Cairo, 1974.

al-Jāḥiẓ, *Kitāb al-bayān wa al-tabyīn* [*The Book of Eloquence and Exposition*], Baghdad, 1960–1961.

Jakobson, Roman, *Selected Writings, Vol. III: The Poetry of Grammar and the Grammar of Poetry*, ed. by Stephen Rudy, Mouton, The Hague, Paris, 1980.
Jakobson, Roman, *Lingvistika i poetika* [*Linguistics and Poetics*], transl. Draginja Pervaz *et al.*, Belgrade, 1966.
al-Jihād, Dr Hilāl, *Falsafa al-shi'r al-jāhilī* [*Philosophy of Pre-Islamic Poetry*], Dimishq, 2001.
Johns, Anthony, "A humanistic approach to i'jaz in the Qur'an: The transfiguration of language", *Journal of Qur'anic Studies* 13, 1 (2011): 79–99.
al-Jumaḥī, Ibn Sallām, *Ṭabaqāt fuḥūl al-shu'arā'* [*Classes of Champion Poets*], Leiden, 1913.
al-Jurjānī, 'Abd al-Qāhir, *Dalāil al-'i'jāz* [*Intimations of Inimitability*], 2nd edn, 1331 h. [1912], s. l.
al-Jurjānī, al-Qāḍī, *al-Wasāṭa bayn al-Mutanabbī wa khuṣūmih* [*Mediation between al-Mutanabbi and His Adversaries*], Cairo, s. a.
Kajzer, Volfgang, *Jezičko umetničko delo* [*Linguistic Work of Art*], transl. Zoran Konstantinović, Belgrade, 1973.
Kaler, Džonatan, *Strukturalistička poetika* [*Structuralist Poetics*], transl. Milica Mint, Belgrade, 1990.
Katnić-Bakaršić, Marina, *Stilistika* [*Stylistics*], Sarajevo, 2001.
Katnić-Bakaršić, Marina, "Figure kao konektori u tekstu" [Figures as text connectors], in *Radovi*, XII, Filozofski fakultet u Sarajevu, Sarajevo, 2000.
Katnić-Bakaršić, Marina, *Gradacija (Od figure do jezičke kategorije)* [*Gradation (From a Figure to a Linguistic Category)*], Sarajevo, 1996.
Khafājī, Muḥammad 'Abd al-Mun'im, *al-Binā' al-fannī li al-qaṣīda al-'arabaiyya* [*Artistic Structure of Arabic Qaṣīda*], Cairo, 1964.
Khalifa, Rashad, *Qur'an: Visual Presentation of the Miracle*, Tucson, 1982.
Kračkovskij, I. Ju., *Izbrannye sočinenija*, I–III, Moscow–Leningrad, 1956.
Kriger, Mari, *Teorija kritike* [*Theory of Criticism*], transl. Svetozar M. Ignjačević, Belgrade, 1982.
Krymskij, A. E., *Istorija novoj arabskoj literatury, XIX–načalo XX veka*, Moscow, 1971.
Kudelin, A. B., "Motiv v tradicionnoj arabskoj poetike VIII-IX vv.", in *Vostočnaja poetika. Specifika hudožestvennogo obraza*, Moscow, 1983.
Kudelin, A. B., *Klassičeskaja arabo-ispanskaja poezija*, Moscow, 1973.
Leaman, Oliver, *Islamska estetika* [*Islamic Aesthetics*], transl. Nevad Kahteran, Sarajevo, 2005.
Lešić, Zdenko, *Teorija književnosti* [*Theory of Literature*], Sarajevo, 2005.
Lihačov, D. S., *Poetika stare ruske književnosti* [*Poetics of Old Russian Literature*], transl. Dimitrije Bogdanović, Belgrade, 1972.
Lotman, J. M., *Kultura i eksplozija* [*Culture and Explosion*], transl. Sanja Veršić, Zagreb, 1998.
Lotman, J. M., *Struktura umetničkog teksta* [*The Structure of the Artistic Text*], transl. Novica Petković, Belgrade, 1976.
Lotman, J. M., "Problemi opće teorije umjetnosti" [Problems of general art theory], in Danilo Pejović (ed.), *Nova filozofija umjetnosti*, Zagreb, 1972.
al-Ma'arrī, *Obvezivanje neobveznim* [*Unnecessary Necessity*], ed. and foreword Daniel Bučan, Banja Luka, 1984.
al-Ma'arrī, *Poslanica o oproštenju* [*The Epistle of Forgiveness*], ed. and transl. Sulejman Grozdanić, Sarajevo, 1979.
Majnūn Laylā, *Dīwān*, Cairo, 1960.

Mandūr, al-duktūr Muḥammad, *al-Naqd al-manhajī 'inda al-'Arab* [*Arabic Methodological Criticism*], Cairo, 1933.

al-Maqdisī, Anīs, *Taṭawwur al-asālīb al-nathriyya fī al-adab al-'arabī* [*Development of Prose Styles in Arabic Literature*], Beirut, 1936.

al-Maqdisī, Anīs, *Umarā' al-shi'r al-'arabī* [*Coryphaei of Arabic Poetry*], Beirut, 1936.

Margoliouth, D. S., "The origins of Arabic poetry", *Journal of the Royal Asiatic Society*, London, 1925.

al-Marzubānī, *al-Muwashshaḥ*, Cairo, 1965.

Metafora, figure i značenje [*Metaphor, Figures and Meaning*], ed. Leon Kojen, Belgrade, 1986.

Mir, Mustansir, "Some figures of speech in the Qur'an", *Religion & Literature* 40, 3 (Autumn 2008): 31–48.

Mommsen, Katharina, *Goethe i islam*, transl. Vedad Smailagić, Dobra knjiga, Sarajevo, 2008.

Moranjak-Bamburać, Nirman, *Retorika tekstualnosti* [*Rhetoric of Textuality*], Sarajevo, 2003.

Moravski, Stefan, *Predmet i metoda estetike*, preveo Dr Stojan Subotin, Belgrade, 1974.

Muftić, Dr Teufik, *Klasična arapska stilistika* [*Classical Arabic Stylistics*], Sarajevo, 1995.

al-Mūsā, Khalīl, "Waḥda al-qaṣīda fī naqd al-Qarṭājannī" [Unity of qaṣīda in al-Qartajanni's criticism], in *al-Turāth al-'arabī* [*Arabic Cultural Heritage*], No. 30, Dimishq, 1988.

Mušić, Omer, "Mostar u turskoj pjesmi iz XVIII vijeka" [Mostar in 17th century Turkish poem], in *Prilozi za orijentalnu filologiju*, no. XIV–XV/1964.65, Sarajevo, 1969.

Naddaff, Sandra, *Arabesque: Narrative Structure and the Aesthetics of Repetition in the 1001 Nights*, Evanston, IL, 1991.

Najm, al-duktūr Khristū, *Jamīl Buthayna wa al-ḥubb al-'udhrī* [*Jamil Buthayna and Udhri Love*], Beirut, 1982.

Nametak, Fehim, *Divanska poezija XVI i XVII stoljeća* [*Divan Poetry of 16th and 17th Centuries*], Sarajevo, 1991.

Nametak, Fehim, *Pregled književnog stvaranja bosanskohercegovačkih muslimana na turskom jeziku* [*Literary Production of BiH Muslims in the Turkish Language*], Sarajevo, 1989.

Nāṣif, al-duktūr Muṣṭafā, *Dirāsāt al-adab al-'arabī* [*Studies in Arabic Literature*], 3rd edn, Beirut, 1983.

Nicholson, R. A., *A Literary History of the Arabs*, Cambridge University Press, 1979.

Oraić-Tolić, Dubravka, *Teorija citatnosti* [*Theory of the Citation*], Zagreb, 1990.

Petrović, Svetozar, *Priroda kritike* [*Nature of Criticism*], Zagreb, 1972.

al-Qarṭājannī, Ḥāzim, *Minhāj al-bulaġā' wa sirāj al-udabā'* [*Path of the Eloquent and Lamp of the Lettered*], taḥqīq Muḥammad al-Ḥabīb al-Khawja, Tūnis, 1966.

al-Qazwīnī, 'Abd al-Raḥmān al-Khaṭīb, *Īḍāḥ fī al-balāġa* [*Elucidation of Rhetoric*], Cairo, 1899.

al-Qazwīnī, 'Abd al-Raḥmān al-Khaṭīb, *Mukhtaṣar al-Ma'ānī* [*Abridged Work on Tropes*], Cairo, 1965.

Rafīda, Ibrāhīm wa Muḥammad 'Abd al-Mun'im Khafājī, *al-Adab al-'arabī wa tārīkhuh fī al-'aṣr al-umawī wa al-'aṣr al-'abbāsī al-awwal* [*Arabic Literature and Its History in the Umayyad and the First Abbasid Periods*], Cairo, 1966.

al-Rāfi'ī, Muṣṭafā Ṣādiq, *Tārīkh ādāb al-'Arab* [*History of Arabic Literature*], I–III, Beirut, 1974.

Rahman, Yusuf, "The miraculous nature of Muslim scripture: A study of 'Abd al-Jabbar's I'jaz al-Qur'an", *Islamic Studies* 35 (1996): 409–424.

Said, Edward W., *Orientalism*, London, 1978.

al-Sakkākī, Muḥammad Ibn 'Alī, *Kitāb miftāḥ al-'ulūm* [*Key of the Sciences*], 1st edn, Cairo, s. a.

Sallūm, Dāwūd, *al-Naqd al-manhajī 'inda al-Jāḥiẓ* [*Al-Jāḥiẓ's Methodological Criticism*], Baghdad, 1960.

Sallūm, Dāwūd, *al-Ta'thīr al-yūnānī fī al-naqd al-'arabī al-qadīm* [*Greek Influence in Old Arabic Criticism*], Baghdad, s. a.

Al-Shābbī, Abū al-Qāsim, *al-Khayāl al-shi'rī 'inda al-'Arab* [*Arabic Poetic Imagination*], s. l., 1975.

Shahid, Irfan, *Early Islam and Poetry*, University Microfilms International, Ann Arbor, MI, 1976.

Sharḥ al-Mu'allaqāt al-sab' [*Commentary on the Mu'allaqāt*], sharḥ: Ibn al-Ḥusayn al-Zawzanī, Cairo, 1976.

Sharḥ al-qaṣā'id al-'ashar wa dhikr riwāyātuhā [*Commentary on the al-Mu'allaqāt and Their Oral Tradition*], sharḥ Yaḥyā Ibn 'Ali al-Tibrīzī, Cairo, 1933.

Sharḥ al-qaṣā'id al-sab' al-tiwāl al-jāhiliyya [*Commentary on Seven other Pre-Islamic Qasaids*], sharḥ Ibn al-Qāsim al-Anbārī, Cairo, 1963.

Shi'r Ibn al-Mu'tazz [*Poetry of Inb al-Mu'tazz*], III, taḥqīq Ibn Yaḥyā al-Ṣūlī, Baghdad, 1978.

Simić, Vojislav, *Klasična arapska poezija, VI–XVII vek* [*Classical Arabic Poetry 6th–17th c.*], Kruševac, 1979.

Simić, Vojislav, "Višeznačnost ljubavi u poeziji Omer Ibn Abi Rabie – pokušaj tematskog određivanja" [Multiple meanings of love in poetry of Umar Ibn Abi Rabī'ah], *Filološki pregled*, I–II, Belgrade, 1972.

Simić, Vojislav, "Kulturno-istorijska uslovljenost nastanka arapske gradske ljubavane lirike – gazela" [Cultural and historical conditions of the emergence of Arabic urban lyricism – ghazal], *Anali Filološkog fakulteta*, sv. 10, Belgrade, 1970.

Solar, Milivoj, *Uvod u filozofiju književnosti* [*Introduction to the Philosophy of Literature*], Zagreb, 1978.

Solar, Milivoj, *Pitanja poetike* [*Issues of Poetics*], Zagreb, 1971.

Souriau, E., *Odnos među umjetnostima* [*La Correspondance des arts*], Sarajevo, Svjetlost, 1958.

Surio, Etjen, *Odnos među umjetnostima* [*La Correspondance des Arts*], Sarajevo, 1958.

Takhyīl: The Imaginary in Classical Arabic poetics, texts selected, translated and annotated, Geert Jan van Gelder and Marlé Hammond, Oxbow, Oxford, 2008.

Ṭarafa Ibn al-ʿAbd, *Dīwān*, Beirut, 1960.

al-Thaʿālibī, *Abū al-Ṭayyib al-Mutanabbī wa mā lah wa mā 'alayh* [*Abu al-Tayyib al-Mutanabbi: His Credits and Omissions*], s. l., 1915.

The Seven Poems Suspended in the Temple at Mecca, translated from Arabic by F. E. Johnson, Gorgias Press, Piscataway, NJ, 2002.

Todorov, Cvetan, *Poetika* [*Poetics*], Belgrade, 1986.

Tomaševski, B. V., *Teorija književnosti. Poetika* [*Theory of literature: Poetics*], transl. Nana Bogdanović, Belgrade, 1972.

Trako, Salih and Lejla Gazić, "Dvije mostarske medžmue" [Two Mostar collections], *Prilozi za orijentalnu filologiju*, no. 38/1988, Sarajevo, 1989.

Uspenski, B. A., *Poetika kompozicije. Semiotika. Ikone* [*A Poetics of Composition. Semiotics. Icons*], transl. Novica Petković, Belgrade, 1979.

Velek, Rene i Ostin Voren, *Teorija književnosti* [*Theory of Literature*], transl. Aleksandar Spasić and Slobodan Đorđević, Belgrade, 1965.

Vinogradov, V. V., *Stilistika i poetika* [*Stylistics and Poetics*], transl. Predrag Lazarević, Tatjana Šeremet and Milovan Milinković, Sarajevo, 1971.

Vitray-Meyerovitch, Eva de, "Poetics of Islam", in Julija Kristeva, *Prelaženje znakova* [*Traversing of Signs*], Sarajevo, 1979.

Wahba, Majdī wa Kāmil al-Muhandis, *Mu'jam muṣṭalaḥāt al-'arabiyya fī al-luġa wa al-adab*, Beirut, 1984.

Wales, Katie, *A Dictionary of Stylistics*, 2nd edn, London, 2001.

al-Yūsuf, Yūsuf, *Maqālāt fī al-shi'r al-jāhilī* [*Essays on Pre-Islamic Poetry*], Dimishq, 1975.

Zakī, Aḥmad Kamāl, *Dirāsāt fī al-naqd al-adabī* [*Studies on Literary Criticism*], 2nd edn, s. l., 1980.

Zakī, Aḥmad Kamāl, *Ibn al-Mu'tazz al-'abbāsī* [*Ibn al-Mutazz Abbasid*], Cairo, 1964.

Žirmunskij, V. M., *Teorija literatury. Poetika. Stilistika*, Leningrad, 1977.

Zwettler, Michael, *The Oral Tradition of Classical Arabic Poetry*, Columbus, OH, 1978.

Further reading

Books

Abdul-Raof, Hussein, *Arabic Rhetoric: A Pragmatic Analysis*, Abingdon, Routledge, 2006.

Abdul-Raof, Hussein, *Qur'anic Stylistics: A Linguistic Analysis*, LINCOM publishers, Munich, 2004.

Abdul-Raof, Hussein, *Schools of Qur'anic Exegesis: Genesis and Development*, Abingdon, Routledge, 2009.

Abdul-Raof, Hussein, *Theological Approaches to Qur'anic Exegesis: A Practical Comparative-Contrastive Analysis*, Abingdon, Routledge, 2012.

Akhtar, Shabbir, *The Quran and the Secular Mind: A Philosophy of Islam*, Abingdon, Routledge, 2007.

Almond, Ian, *Representations of Islam in Western Thought*, CNS, Sarajevo, 2010.

Beeston, A. F. L., T. M. Johnstone, R. B. Serjeant and G. R. Smith (eds), *Arabic Literature to the End of the Umayyad Period*, Cambridge University Press, Cambridge, 2010.

Bellamy, J.A., *Studies in Near Eastern Culture and History in Memory of E.T. Abdel-Massih*, Centre for Near Eastern and North American Studies, University of Michigan, Ann Arbor, MI, 1990.

Cachia, Pierre (ed.), *Arch Rhetorician or the Schemer's Skimmer: Drawn from ʿAbd al-Ghanī an-Nābulsī*, summarized and systematized by Pierre Cachia, Harrassowitz, Wiesbaden, 1998.

Cotton, Hannah M., Robert G. Hoyland and Jonathan J. Price, *From Hellenism to Islam: Cultural and Linguistic Change in the Roman Near East*, Cambridge University Press, Cambridge, 2012.

Curtis, Michael, *Orientalism and Islam: European Thinkers on Oriental Despotism in the Middle East and India*, Cambridge University Press, Cambridge, 2009.

Ditters, Everhard and Harald Motzki, *Approaches to Arabic Linguistics*, Brill, Leiden, 2007.

Fitzpatrick, Coeli and Dwayne A.Tunstall (eds), *Orientalist Writers*, Gale Cengage Learning, Farmington Hills, MI, 2012.

Fleisch, H., *Arabic Linguistics*, Longman, London, 1994.

Grunebaum, G.E. von, *A Tenth Century Document of Arabic Literary Theory and Criticism Iʿjâz al-Qur'ân*, Jamia Millia Islamia & Creative Books, Delhi, 2004.

Hoffman, Thomas, *The Poetic Qur'ān: Studies on Qur'ānic Poeticity*, Harrassowitz, Wiesbaden, 2007.

Kinberg, Naphtali, *Studies in Linguistic Structure of Classical Arabic*, ed. Leah Kinberg and Kees Versteegh, Brill, Leiden, 2000.
Larkin, Margaret, *The Theology of Meaning: 'Abd al-Qāhir al-Jurjānī's Theory of Discourse*, American Oriental Society, New Haven, CT, 1995.
Macfie, A.L., *Orientalism: A Reader*, Edinburgh University Press, Edinburgh, 2000.
Neuwirth, Angelika, *Scripture, Poetry, and the Making of a Community: Reading the Qur'an as a Literary Text*, Oxford University Press, Oxford, 2014.
al-Qāḍī, Wadād (ed.), *Studia Arabica et Islamica: Festschrift for Ihsan 'Abbas on His Sixtieth Birthday*, American University of Beirut, Beirut, 1981.
Rippin, Andrew, *Approaches to the History of the Interpretation of the Qur'an*, Clarenedon Press, Oxford, 1988.
van Gelder, Geert Jan and Marlé Hammond (eds), *Takhyil: The Imaginary in Classical Arabic*, Gibb Memorial Trust, Cambridge, 2007.
Versteegh, C.H.M., *Arabic Grammar and Qur'anic Exegesis in Early Islam*, Brill, Leiden, 1993.
Versteegh, Kees, Mushira Eid, Alaa Elgibali, Manfred Woidich and Andrzej Zaborski (eds), *Encyclopedia of Arabic Language and Linguistics*, Brill, Leiden, 2005–2007.
Wild, Stefan, *The Qur'an as Text*, Brill, Leiden, 1996.

Articles

Bouman, J., "Fondements de l'autorité du Coran chez al-Bāqillānī", *Monde non-chrétien* 34 (1955): 154–171.
Daneshgar, M. "Qur'ān, Orientalists and Western scholars", *Al-Bayan: Journal of Qur'ān and Hadith Studies* 10, 2 (2012): 5–8.
Hasan Qasim Murad. "The beginnings of Islamic theology: A critique of Joseph van Ess' views", *Islamic Studies* 26, 2 (1986): 191–204.
Ibish, Yusuf, "Life and works of al-Bāqillānī", *Islamic Studies* 4 (1965): 225–236.
Kermani, Navid, "Revelation in its aesthetic dimension", in Stefan Wild (ed.), *The Qur'an as Text*, Brill, Leiden, 1996, pp. 214–224.
Khagga, Muhammad Feroz-ud-Din Shah and Shabbir Ahmad Mansoori, "Orientalistic research methodology towards the Qur'anic text (analytical study)", *Jihāt al-Islām: a Journal of Islamic Studies* 5, 1 (2011): 23–31.
Larkin, Margaret, "The inimitability of the Qur'an: Two perspectives", *Religion and Literature* 20 (1988): 31–47.
Martin, Richard, "The role of the Ba'rah Mu'tazila in formulating the docrine of the apologetic miracle", *Journal of Near Eastern Studies* 39 (1980): 175–189.
Mir, Mustansir, "Baqillani's critique of Imru' al-Qays", in James Bellamy (ed.), *Studies in Near Eastern Culture and History in Memory of Ernest T. Abdel Massih*, Centre for Near Eastern and North American Studies, University of Michigan, Ann Arbor, MI, 1990, pp. 118–131.
Montgomery, James, "Sundry observations on the fate of poetry in the Early Islamic period", in J. Smart (ed.), *Tradition and Modernity in Arabic Language and Literature*, Richmond, Curzon Press, 1996, pp. 49–60.
Vryonis, Speros, "The epic scholarship of Irfan Shahîd: An epic history of the pre-Islamic Arabs and their relations with Byzantium from Constantine the Great to Heraclius and the Islamic conquests of the Byzantine diocese of Oriens", *Byzantion: Revue Internationale des Études Byzantines* 79 (2009): 435–452.

Name index

Abbas, Dr Ihsan (Dr Iḥsān ʿAbbās) 238
Abbasids (750–1258) 52, 74, 84n20, 150, 160, 177, 181, 185–6, 233n38
Abraham 14
Abu Nuwas (Abū Nuwās, 757–814) 160–1, 164, 202, 209–10, 233n38
Abu Tammam (Abū Tammām, 788–40) 235n69
Abu Ubaydah (Abū ʿUbayda, 728–825) 162
Adam 143–4
Agatha 16
Ahlwardt, Wilhelm 116n18
al-Ahmar, Khalaf 161
al-Akhṭal (640–710) 162, 179, 233n38
al-Āmidī (d. 987) 200, 209–10, 235n69
Antara (ʿAntara Ibn Shaddād, d. *c.*615) 107–8, 173, 179
Aristotle 5, 12–13, 16, 19n1, 152, 170, 219–31
Arbery, Artur J. 70
al-Askari (Abū Hilāl al-ʿAskarī, d. 1005) 178, 209
al-Asmai (al-Asmaʿī, 740–828) 161, 179, 183, 198
al-Asmaʿī, Abū ʿAmr Ibn al-ʿAlā (689–770) 162
Assuntoi, Rosario 28
al-Atia (al-ʿAṭīa) 200

Badawi (ʿAbd al-Raḥmān Badawī) 220
Badawi (Aḥmad Badawī) 222
Bajezidagić, Darwish Pasha (d. 1603) 205, 235n76
Bajraktarević, Fehim 238
al-Barqūqī, ʿAbd al-Raḥmān 239
Barthes, Roland 15, 17, 90–1, 115n8
Bašagić, Safvet-beg 235n76
al-Bayati (ʿAbd al-Wahhāb al-Bayyātī, 1926–1999) 64, 197
Beker, Miroslav 239
Benčić, Živa 115n8
Biti, Vladimir 239
Bogdanović, Dimitrije 242
Bogdanović, Nana 244
Borges 233n36, 237n106
Boškov, Vančo 239
Boullata, Issa J. 84n29, 85n38
Brnčić, Jadranka 85n33
Brockelmann 151
Brooks, Peter 14–15, 17
Bucaille, Dr Maurice 85n35
Bučan, Daniel 242
al-Buhturi (al-Buḥturī, 820–97) 235n69
Byatt, A. S. 16

Calvino, Italo 16
Čaušević, Džemaludin 86n40
Chouraqui, André 85n33
Curtius, Ernst Robert 153, 183, 231n1

Dante 171–2
David 24
al-Dawla, Sayf 198
Dawud, Dr Anis (Dr Anīs Dāwūd) 223
Dayf, Shawqi (Shawqī Ḍayf, b. 1910) 239
Darwish (Maḥmūd Darwīsh (1941–2008) 228
Defoe, Daniel 172
Derrida, Jacques 2
Dervish effendi Mostarac (Derviš-efendija Mostarac Žagrić) 205–6, 236
De Vitray-Meyerovitch, Eva 8, 167
Đorđević, Slobodan 232n27
Duda, Dean 115n12
Duraković, Esad 19n5, 85n37

Ejhenbaum, Boris 240
Eliot, T. S. 232n18

Ernjaković, Gligorije 238

Fališevac, Dunja 115n8
al-Farazdaq (641–731) 162, 179, 201, 203
Farrūkh, ʿUmar 240
Faysal (Dr Shukrī Fayṣal) 240
Fil'štinskij, I. M. 231n10, 232n16
Fowles, John 16

Gabrielli, Francesco 18
al-Gaddafi (al-Qadhdhāfī) 148n23
Galland 5
Garib (Rūz Ġarīb) 240
Gavrilović, Zoran 242
Gazić, Lejla 235n75
al-Ghazali (al-Ġazālī, 1058–111) 167, 176, 180
Gibb, H. A. R. 240
Gibran, Khalil (Jubrān Khalīl Jubrān, 1883–1931) 232n26
Goethe 5, 230, 232n26
Gonzalez, Dr Valerie 240
Grasi, Ernesto 241
Grozdanić, Sulejman 115n1
Grunebaum, Gustav von 115n2

Hafez, Shirazi (14th century) 187
Hammond, M. 115n4
al-Harith (al-Ḥārith Ibn Ḥilizza, d. 580) 107
Hartman, Nicolai 241
Hasan (Dr Zakī Muḥammad) 241
Hasan Jad (Ḥasan Jād Ḥasan) 241
Hegel 9, 13, 31, 46–7, 113, 230–1
Hulagu 84n20
Husayn, Qasim (Dr ʿAdnān Ḥusayn Qāsim) 231n7, 234n54, 235n61
Hussein, Taha (Ṭāhā Ḥusayn, 1889–1973) 84n32, 223

Ibn Abi Rabiʿah (ʿUmar Ibn Abī Rabīʿa, 644–712) 154
Ibn Adi (Yaḥyā Ibn ʿAdī, d. 939) 220
Ibn al-ʿAla (Abū ʿAmr Ibn al-ʿAlā', 689–770) 108, 162
Ibn al-Athir (Ibn al-Athīr, 1162–239) 198, 210
Ibn al-Nadim (Ibn al-Nadīm, d. 995) 220
Ibn Burd (Bashshār Ibn Burd, 714–48) 164, 181, 183, 234n40
Ibn Ḥilizza, al-Ḥārith (d. 580) 107
Ibn Hunayn (Isḥāq Ibn Ḥunayn, d. 910) 220
Ibn Jaʿfar (Qudāma Ibn Jaʿfar, 888–948) 174, 232n30
Ibn Khaldun (Ibn Khaldūn, 1332–1406) 66, 161
Ibn Kulthum (Ibn Kulthūm, d. *c.*570) 107–8, 112
Ibn al-Muqaffa, Abd-Allah 177, 225
Ibn al-Muʿtazz (Ibn al-Muʿtazz, 861–908) 211, 227
Ibn Qutaybah (Ibn Qutayba, 828–89) 162–4, 168–9, 194, 200–1, 210–11, 232n19
Ibn Rashiq (Ibn Rashīq, d. 1063) 161, 178, 198, 201
Ibn Rushd (Ibn Rushd, Averroës, d. 1198) 19n1, 220, 224–5, 237n106
Ibn Shaddād, ʿAntara 107–8, 179
Ibn Tabataba 162, 178, 195, 199–201, 210
Ibn Tufail (Ibn Ṭufayl, d. *c.*1185) 171, 210
Ibn Yunus (Abū Bishr Mātā Ibn Yūnus, d. 939) 220
Ibn Yunus, Mata 220
Ibn Zuhayr, Kaʿb (530–627) 52
Ibrahim, Taha (Ṭāhā Aḥmad Ibrāhīm) 241
Ignjačević, Svetozar 232n29
Ingarden, Roman 241
Isaković, Alija 235n76
al-Isfahani (Abū al-Farj al-Isfahānī, 897–67) 241
Ismail, Izz al-Din (ʿIzz al-Dīn Ismāʿīl) 103

al-Jahiz 177
Jakobson, Roman 7, 12, 19n8, 116n22
Jarīr 162
Joseph/Jusuf 23
al-Jumaḥī, Ibn Sallām 162, 200
al-Jurjani, Abdul-Qahir 179, 194, 197
al-Jurjani, al-Qadi 184

Kaʿb Ibn Zuhayr (Kaʿb Ibn Zuhayr, 530/627) 52, 107, 200
Kahteran, Nevad 240
Karić, Enes 84n29, 85n38, 86n42
Katnić-Bakaršić, Marina 28n3
Khafājī, Muḥammad ʿAbd al-Munʿim 242
Khalaf al-Ahmar (Khalaf al-Aḥmar, d. 796) 161
Khalifa, Rashid 75, 85n36
al-Khawja, Muḥammad al-Ḥabīb 243
al-Kindi (Yaʿqūb al-Kindī, d. *c.*870) 220, 224–5
Kojen, Leon 243
Konstantinović, Zoran 242
Kračkovskij, I. Ju. 242
Krieger, Murry 232n29
Kristeva, Julija 19n5, 232

Krymskij, A. E. 16
Kudelin, A. B. 234n42
Kurić, Lutvo 75, 85n37

Labid (Labīd Rabī'a, d. *c*.669) 107, 112, 198
Layla, Majnunb 154
Lazarević, Predrag 245
Leaman, Oliver 242
Lešić, Zdenko 242
Lihačov, D. S. 242
Lotman, J. M. 19

al-Ma'arrī (Abū al-'Alā' al-Ma'arrī, 973–1057) 171–2
Mahfouz, Naguib (Najīb Maḥfūẓ, 1911–2006) 228, 232n26
Majnun Layla (Majnūn Laylā) *see* Qays, Ibn al-Mulawwaḥ
al-Malaika, Nazik (Nāzik al-Malā'ika, b. 1923) 197
Mandur (Dr Muḥammad Mandūr) 243
al-Maqdisi (Anīs al-Maqdisī) 243
Margoliouth 243
Markuš, Stjepan 239
al-Marzubānī (909–94) 237n89
al-Marzūqī (d. 1030) 217
Mas'ūd, Wālīd 19n5
Mihailović, Milica 240
Milinković, Milovan 245
Mint, Milica 242
Moranjak-Bamburać, Nirman 243
Moravski, Stefan 243
Moses 23–6, 28
Moses/Musa/Mūsā 23, 36
Muawiyah 84n20
Muftić, Dr Teufik 232n30
Muhammad/Mohammad 23, 31, 36, 38, 42, 53, 78, 83, 126, 148n26, 153, 233
al-Muhandis, Kāmil 236n79
al-Muqaffa', 'Abd Allāh Ibn (d. 759) 177, 225
al-Musa (Khalīl al-Mūsā) 36
Mušić, Omer 235n75, 236n76
al-Mutanabbi (al-Mutanabbī, 915–65) 198
al-Mu'tazz (Ibn al-Mu'tazz, 861–908) 241

Naddaff, Sandra 14, 18, 19n10
al-Najjar ('Abd al-Ḥalīm al-Najjār) 239
Najm (Dr Khristū Najm) 243
Nametak, Dr Fehim 235n75
Nāṣif, Dr Muṣṭafā 243
al-Naẓẓām (846) 75
Nietzsche 47, 121
Nicholson, R. A. 243

Nuwas, Abu 160–1, 164, 202, 209

Oraić-Tolić, Dubravka 243

Pandža, Muhamed 86n40
Pejović, Danilo 242
Petković, Novica 237n93
Petrović, Svetozar 231n1
Piletić, Milana 240
Plato 46–7, 83n19, 215
Pranjić, Kruno 85n33
Prophet Joseph (Yūsuf) 23
Prophet Moses (Mūsā) 23, 26, 28, 36
Prophet Muhammad 23, 38, 126, 153

al-Qartajanni (Ḥāzim al-Qarṭājannī, 13th century) 216, 220–2, 224, 226, 228
Qays (Imru' al-Qays, d. *c*.540) 64, 89, 92–5, 97–101, 103–5, 107–10, 112, 114–15, 116n18, 120, 129, 147n14, 154, 181, 198, 233n39
Qays Ibn al-Mulawwaḥ 154
al-Qazwīnī (1267–1338) 243

Rabī'a, Labīd (d. *c*.669) 107
Rabi'ah ('Umar Ibn Abī Rabī'a, 644–711) 241
Rafīda, Ibrahim 243
Ramić, Jusuf 85n39, 86n42

Said, Edward 2, 5, 87, 115n5
Sallūm, Dāwūd 223
Šeremet, Tatjana 245
al-Shabbi (Abū al-Qāsim al-Shābbī, 1909–1934) 115n3
Shahid, I. 83n9
Shahrazad 14–15
Shahrayar 14
Shawqi, Ahmad (Aḥmad Shawqī, 1868–1932) 185, 234n44
Simić, Vojislav 244
Solar, Milivoj 244
Spasić, Aleksandar 232n27
Subotin, Stojan 243
Souriau, Etienne 12, 19n3

Tanasković, Darko 238
Tarafa (Ṭarafa Ibn 'Abd al-Bakrī, d. *c*.560) 107, 110, 117n37, 129, 140, 145
Todorov, Tzvetan 7, 12, 19n4
Tomaševski, B. V. 244
Trako, Salih 235n75

'Ubayda, Abū 162

Umayyads (661–750) 33, 52, 74, 154–5, 157, 162, 177, 179–81, 185, 203, 234n47
Uspenski, B. A. 244

van Gelder, Geert Jan 115n4
Vidaković Petrov, Krinka 233
Vinogradov, V. V. 245
Vitray-Meyerovitch, Eva de 8, 19, 167, 232n22

Wahba (Majdī Wahba) 207, 236n79
Wales, Katie 245
Warren, Austin 172, 175, 194
Wellek, Rene 172, 175, 194

Yūnus/Jonah 60
Yūsuf/Joseph 23

Zaki (Aḥmad Kamāl Zakī) 234n53
al-Zawzanī, Ibn al-Ḥusayn 244
Žirmunskij, V. M. 245
Živojinović, Branimir 241
Zwettler, M. 84n25

Subject index

Abbasid dynasty (750–1258) 52, 74, 160, 177
Abbasid epoch 181, 233n38
Absolute Form 64
Absolute Spirit 47
accumulation, of the simile 88
adab (literature) 5, 177–8
al-adab al-muqāran (comparative literature) 178, 201
addition 2, 9, 25, 33, 62, 67, 75, 79–80, 85, 90
aesthetic experience 6, 85n39
aesthetical principle 4, 6, 27, 79, 172, 175
aestheticism 28, 30, 78, 141, 170–1
aesthetics 4, 6, 53, 85n39, 178, 188, 215, 217–18; of identity 217; Islamic 187; of opposition 217; of resemblance 217
al-akhdh (literary borrowing) 192, 207–9, 215
allegory 146n1
alliteration 12
ancient Arabic literature 1, 184; artistic value 1; author's originality in 164–9; de-paganisation of 158; development of 150; drama 5; history of 182; interpretation of imaginativeness in 221; isolation of tradition in 219–27; "materialistic nature" of 2; periodisation of 1; philology of 164–9; text's authenticity of 164–9; *see also* Old Arabic poetry
ancient Arabic poetry 2, 184, 189, 193
ancient Arab-Islamic writing 4
ancient Greek literature 2, 219, 222–3
ancient poetics 163, 165
ancient poetry, de-paganisation of 193
annual ode 200–1
antiquity 2, 67, 125, 160, 163, 165–6, 168, 179–83, 228, 230
apocrypha 24, 72
Apollo poet 174
Arab-Islamic art 5, 13
Arab-Islamic caliphate 157, 170; history of 150
Arab-Islamic poetics 5, 13, 15, 18
Arab spirituality 118
arabesque: associativeness, principle of 101; expression of time 5, 8, 9; mimetic principle of 14; ornamental 6–7; poetics of 4–19; principle of 10; segmentation 106; structure of 8, 10–11, 13–15, 17–18, 26, 81–2, 91, 97, 101, 145, 149, 222; stylization 14
Arabian poetics 30, 144, 149
Arabic-Islamic antiquity 67, 179–83
Arabic-Islamic culture 225; leading works of 4–5; sources of 5
Arabic-Islamic philosophy, development of 152, 170, 220
Arabic-Islamic poetics 5–6, 15
Arabic-Islamic tradition 149–50, 156, 219
Arabic language 4, 14, 50, 65, 118, 201; poetry in 52; structure of 13
Arabic love lyricism 154
Arabic *madaḥ* 225
Arabic nationalism 170
Arabic philological criticism 169
Arabic philology 160, 188, 195; authority of 169–70
Arabic stylistics 158, 187
Arabism, idea of 170
Arabism (*'urūba*) movement 169
arch of imagination 109
archaic language 163–4, 169, 172–3
argumentation 4, 26, 30, 34–6, 69, 228
argumentative 36
Aristotle 12; definition of tragedy 225; as first teacher 152, 219; poetic postulates

12, 16; *Poetics* 5, 13, 152, 219–27; *Rhetoric* 152; theory of mimesis 167
art 5–6, 8–10, 12–14, 16, 22, 27–30, 40, 44–5, 50, 62, 65, 78, 102, 119, 124–5, 151–2, 157–8, 162–3, 168, 172, 175, 177, 194–200, 212–13, 215–18, 221, 225, 227–8
art of poetry 1
artefact resemblance, principle of 215
articulate expression, powers of 54–8, 78, 80–1, 120
artifact 11–12, 61, 89, 92, 116n18, 119, 146, 172, 175, 192, 196, 204, 209, 211, 215, 221
artistic: inferiority 87; originality 165, 183, 192; play 216; prose 19n5, 223; sincerity 192; spatial figurativeness 88; transposition 175
ascetic poems 185
atomistic 8
attitude: of the past 190; of the present 190
attraction for its own sake 78
authentic criticism 166–7
authentic value 166, 169
authentic work 164, 166
authenticity 23–7, 31–2, 35–7, 40–1, 43–5, 47, 57, 64, 72, 76, 79, 116n18, 119, 121–2, 152, 158–9, 164–9, 179, 184, 193, 196–7, 212–15, 217, 223, 226, 229; principle of 179; transhistorical 26
authorship, authenticity of 165–6, 184
autocitationality 28
ayah 32–4, 36, 44–52, 54–6, 61–2, 64–5, 67, 74, 83n7, 119–21, 125, 132–3, 137, 169, 232n24

bacchius poems 151
banalised (*al-mubtadhal*) 184
al-bayān (stylistics) 54, 84n22, 120–1
bayts (couplet) 94, 115n10, 145, 149, 221
Beautiful, the 29, 54–6, 175, 215–18
beauty of expression (*ḥusn al-kalām*) 55, 58, 217
Bedouin realism, pre-Islamic 122
beginning–middle–end, poetic principle of 7–8, 11–12, 14, 221–2
Bible 25
binary grammatical parallelism 12
bio-bibliographies 152
Book of the Novel and Strange 227
Brockelmann's *History of Arab Literature* 151

calligraphy 67, 76–7, 81, 237n106
caravans 95, 98, 181
catalogue presentation, of Arabic literature 151
cause-and-effect sequence, principle of 7
Cave of Hira 62
centrifugal forces 27
centripetal forces 27, 70–4, 145–6
Christian cultural community 52
Christian Europe 176
chronography 95
citationality 23–8
Classes of Champion Poets 200
classical poetics 171, 179
classicism 1, 151, 169–70, 185, 197, 204, 208, 221, 230–1
classicist topos system 191–2
clause of state 49–50
cognitive dominant 82
coherence 65, 91, 97, 102, 104, 106, 222
cohesion 145
cohesive factor 11, 158
commercial panegyric 48
commonplaces 46–7, 60, 74, 84n33, 109, 116n30, 119, 128, 139, 147n13, 160, 164, 171, 183–6, 189, 191, 204, 210, 214, 232n18
communication noise 81
comparative-contrastive analysis 218, 229
comparative relations 130
comparative unit 11
comparison *see al-muwāzana* (comparison)
compendium 224, 226
concept of desire 14
concept of reading for the plot 14
concept of time 8, 19n7
"concrete" poetry 7
conflict with a climax 17
connective 50
connotation 2, 32–4, 38, 46, 48, 50, 83n8, 87, 125–6
connotative nature, of poetic language 58
consequentiality 1, 3, 11, 23, 27, 31, 34, 36, 41, 43, 47, 89
constituent elements of poetics 2
constituents of simile 105, 111–13, 127, 135
constructive principle 6
content 2, 13, 21–4, 27, 30, 34, 36–8, 41, 44, 51–4, 56–8, 60–6, 74, 76, 79, 87, 93, 101, 108–9, 119, 124, 131, 139, 143, 149, 154, 159, 162, 172, 174–5, 178, 186, 192–5, 197–9, 204, 211–12, 221

content–form dichotomy 172, 186, 197
content–form relationship, in ancient poetry 61, 118, 193
contextualisation of form 21–8, 67
contextuality, principle of 21–5, 28, 68, 79, 82
contrast 7–8, 12, 33–4, 39, 53, 67–8, 87, 105, 108, 128, 130, 134, 137, 140, 170–1, 214–15, 217–18, 225, 229–30
corpora, poetic evolution of 87
corpus 4–6, 11, 29, 71, 87–8, 107, 142, 150, 158–60, 168, 173, 193
couplet 11–12, 91, 97, 99–101, 107, 111, 115n10, 128, 130, 145, 147n15, 149, 173, 193, 198, 221, 235n76
creativity, concept of 1–2, 10–11, 23, 108, 118, 148n23, 149, 166, 186, 194, 197, 214, 220, 226–7, 231
criticism: of poetry 101, 159–60, 164–9, 180; concept of 164–5, 167; philological 171
Criticism of Poetry (*Naqd al-shi'r*) 174
cultivation of desire 15
cumulative digressiveness 104
cumulativeness of description 90

Dante's *Divine Comedy* 171–2
deduction 26, 31, 33–4, 36–7, 42, 61–2, 168, 219, 228
deductive nature of the Revelation 49
deductive poetic, principle of 21–8, 61, 138, 168–9, 171, 179, 228, 232n23
denotation 47
denotative description 60
de-paganisation (of ancient poetry) 158–9, 193
derogation, principle of 22
descent of the Revelation 82
description 39, 60, 88–97, 99–110, 112–15, 118, 120–1, 125–36, 141–3, 145–6, 160, 197, 201
descriptive poetry (*waṣf*) 9, 154, 185
desert-Udhri poetry 154
desire 7–8, 13–16, 94, 134, 163, 169, 176, 223
Dictionary of Arabic Literary and Linguistic Terms, The 207
didactic poetry 177
diegesis 14, 16
digressiveness of description 91
discontinuous rifts 44
discourse 12, 14, 87
distance (in the simile) 58, 130, 140
distance of *'i'jāz* 76
divine 4, 8–10, 13, 17–18, 22–5, 30–1, 35–6, 40, 42–3, 48, 55, 57–8, 62–3, 65, 69–70, 72, 75–6, 81, 83n8, 120–3, 125–6, 143–4, 171, 217, 228–9
Divine Comedy 171
divine mediators 43
Divine Structure 72
doctrine of supernaturalism 40, 53, 58, 65–8, 70, 72, 78, 81, 119, 121, 142, 201, 228–9
documentary 89
drama 5; and dramatic literature 8; realisation of inner self on the outer world 9

ecstatic 38, 58
elegy/dirge 47
ellipsis/elliptical 49, 51, 60, 68, 79, 82, 121, 124
emphasis 13, 16, 35, 39–40, 43, 47, 55, 60, 62, 92, 102, 118–19, 129, 133, 140, 144, 146, 151–2, 187, 189, 200, 217
entirety of particularities 6–7
epic 5, 56, 189, 222, 227
epic totality 142
epicentral form 66
epigon/epigonism 64, 157–8, 161–2, 166, 169, 171, 174
epistemological potential of metaphor 59
Epistle of Forgiveness, The 171
epoch of Classicism 1, 185
erotonyms 130–1; in Old Arabic poetry 130–1
"erring follow, the" poets 46
ethic poetry 143, 176, 213, 215
European literary scholarship 151
European Literature and the Latin Middle Ages 183
European Middle Ages 150, 156
European poetry 156
European Renaissance poetics 171
European Romanticism 88
exegesis of the sacred Text 3
exemplar 156, 159, 165, 169, 171, 228
exemplary corpus 88, 159–60
exemplary poem 116n22, 179, 212
expansions of meaning 138
experience: of form 66–7, 96; of literature 168, 221–2, 228
experienced poet 94
explosiveness of the Text 62
exposition 17
expression 5–6, 8–10, 13, 16, 18, 29–30, 37, 41, 44, 49, 53–8, 62, 78, 80–2, 88–9,

100, 109, 113, 119–22, 136, 142, 152, 155, 173, 175, 177, 190, 199, 202, 206, 210–11, 213, 217
external approach 53
extroversion 113–14

fakhr (self-praise) 12
fann al-adab 178
fann al-sh'ir (technique of poetry) 152, 168, 178, 221
Farewell Sermon, ayahs of 62
female rhyme 197
fictionality 47
figurative language 124
figures of description 88–95, 100, 104–5, 112–14, 118, 120, 127, 134–6, 142
flatness 43, 103, 118–20, 143
floral ornamentation 6
folklore poetry 12
foot 94
form 2–3, 5–7, 9–11, 13–15, 17–18, 21–4, 26–8, 30–1, 34, 37–8, 41–2, 45, 50–82
form of cognition 54
"form of emptiness" 77
form of *'i'jāz* 65–75
form–content relationship, in poetry 63, 170–1
form–motif relationship, in "post-Qur'anic" poetry 175
formal value 70
forms of tradition 37
forward movement of the plot 15
fragmentation 13, 17
fragmented poetics 17
French Lieutenant's Woman, The 16
functional style 50

galaxy of signifiers 17
genetic of *'i'jāz* 85n37
genre 9, 47–8, 52, 57, 61–2, 64, 76, 88–9, 96–7, 114, 151–5, 157, 164, 169, 177, 180, 185, 191, 208, 212, 221, 224–5, 228, 231
ghazal (love poetry) 9, 155, 163, 181, 183, 185; types of 154; Umarite and Udhri 189
God of Mercy, The 54
gradation 7, 134, 136; of textual time 99–102
grammatical parallelism 12, 32
Greek literature 2, 219, 222–3, 227, 229

Ḥadīth 67, 237n105
harmoniousness, principle of 8
hijā' 185, 191, 224–5
historical and political periodisation 150, 153
historical contextuality 23, 25
historical time 8
historicism, principle of 165
History of Arab Literature 151
homophonous 144
houri (a Jannah beauty) 59, 127–39, 141, 145
humanism 67–8
hunt poems 166, 185
ḥusn al-kalām (beauty of expression) 217
Hypertext 25, 28n3, 43

ibdā' (creativity) 10
ibtikār (creativity) 10
icons (Not found in the file)
Idea-Of-Beautiful-As-Good 139
ideal woman, concept of 135
ideality 63, 81, 139
identity of intuition and expression 41, 53, 58, 175, 199
If on a Winter's Night a Traveller 16
'i'jāz 4–5, 36, 55, 58, 71–2, 121, 123, 126, 158, 170, 204, 228; argumentation, 69; on centripetal forces of language 70–4; concept of 75; different aspects of 65–82; experience of 66–8, 73; heart of 81; idea of 68; Orientalist attitude to 78; other aspects of 74–5; phenomenon of 74; positioning the Text in the Universe of forms 65–70; promotion of 78; reception of 73; scientific 69, 74
ikhtiyāl (plagiarism) 207–8
imaginative poetry 87, 104, 116n24
imaginativeness, notion of 28, 31, 88, 104, 194, 212, 216, 220–1
imitation 156, 158, 162, 166–7, 221
immanence 2, 223
immanent approach 2–3, 18, 39, 54, 92, 101–2, 106, 114, 150–1, 153, 174, 196
immanent interpretation 22
immanent method 2, 153
immanent periodisation 1
impressionist approach 91, 106, 151
incommunicability 72, 227
Indian poetry 12
individuality 2, 77, 165, 168, 206, 210; of literature 214
induction 33, 40, 42, 61, 179
inductive character of poetry 37
inductive poetics 26, 34, 138, 168–9, 186, 192, 227, 230
inimitability 62–3, 213–14, 229–30

inspiration 5, 32–3, 41, 50, 52, 194, 201–7, 220
interaction between simile correlates 131, 139–40
interpretation 3, 8, 22, 36, 47–8, 59–60, 62–4, 75, 79–80, 90–1, 121, 124–6, 130, 138, 144, 146n1, 159–61, 165, 167, 170–1, 182, 188–9, 197, 199, 211–12, 217–18, 221, 223, 225
intersubjective knowledge 59
intertextuality, principle of 21–8, 43–4, 82, 232n18
al-intiḥāl (plagiarism) 207
intuitive cognition 31
invocation 84, 85n33
Islam 76; meaning of 123; poetics of 167; promotion of 156; spread of 119; values of 51
Islamic enlightenment 153
Islamic epochs 57, 162, 173, 179, 184–5, 201
Islamic literature 188–90, 188–92, 202, 204, 227, 230, 234n45; and Arabian *qaṣīda* 191; components of 191; poetic forms in 191; as supranational and supra-linguistic system 190
Islamic miniature 77
Islamic poetics 18, 205, 227, 230

Jannah and Jahannam 56, 59, 118, 126; poet's belle and houris in 129–36
jinns 32
Judeo-Christian culture 8, 189

kāhin (poet-soothsayer) 29, 32, 50, 53–4, 60–1, 65, 67, 76, 83n8
kāhin poetry 67
kāhins (clergymen) 50, 53, 61
Kalām (God's Oration) 66
Kalila and Dimna 225
Khamriyyāt 185
Kitāb al-badī' see Book of the Novel and Strange

lampoon (*hijā'*), poetic genre of 47, 151, 154, 173, 185, 212, 224–6
Latin language 188
Latin medievalism, literature of 183
Lawḥ Maḥfūẓ 121–3
legalisation of literary theft 207–15
line/verse 12–13, 64, 66, 84n24, 87, 91, 99, 103–4, 194, 197, 208
linear 7–9, 11, 15, 18, 19n7
linearity 14–15
linguistic archaisms 166
linguistic and historic aspect 72
linguistic stylistics 72, 76, 123
linguistic supernaturalism 58, 72
linguistic value 58, 70, 81
literal translation 79
literary adequate translation 79
literary and aesthetic value 4, 22, 33, 45, 52, 56, 58, 78, 81, 86n41, 119, 188
literary borrowing *see al-akhdh* (literary borrowing)
literary émigrés *see* Mahjar
literary history 5, 65, 82, 150–5, 157, 160, 164, 168, 177–8, 183, 185–7, 193–4, 196, 198, 209–10, 215, 227, 230
literary theft *see al-sariqa*
literary thefts: connection between artistically beautiful and 215–19; ethics and religion, issue of 215; legalisation of 211; *Qur'an* and the notion of 216
literary theory 15, 116n18
literary tradition 2, 4–5, 11, 14, 28–9, 87, 91, 107, 119
literature of Islamic peoples 2, 188–9, 230; *see also* Islamic literature
literature of Oriental-Islamic community 4, 17, 53
'lm (positive cognisance) 38
"logic of the past" 165
logical sequence, principle of 7
love lyric prelude 89, 107, 154, 180, 184, 189
love-lyrical prologue 102–3, 184, 189
love poetry 9, 154–5, 160, 163, 173, 181–3, 189, 232n19
lyrical transgressions 155
lyricism 9, 100–1, 154–6, 182, 185; epoch of 154
lyric travelogue genre 97

madaḥ 185, 191, 224–5
Mahjar 47, 174
Mahjar poet 174
majnūn/majnun (poet possessed) 30–5, 67, 194
Majnun–Layla motif 189
Malaysian literature 230
male rhyme 197
Mantle Ode (*Qaṣīda Burda*) 52
maṭbū' (talented) 200
"materialism" of poetry *see* realism
materialist poetry 87
medial character of poet 31
medial function 35

messenger/apostle/prophet 22–4, 30–45, 49, 52, 58, 60, 62, 67–8, 73–5, 78, 126, 149, 153, 155, 162, 177, 212, 230
meta-poet 204
meta-theme 204
metaphors: metaphoric approach 122; metaphoric arch 60, 129, 135, 139; metaphoric context 140; metaphoric mediation 122; metaphoric revolution 118; metaphoric transfer 92–3, 125, 182; metaphoric vertical world order 142–5; processuality of 122, 124, 136–42; sacred 141; "semantic echo" of 139; sub-metaphor 133, 138, 145–6
metre 11, 88, 101, 109, 144–6, 149, 177, 180–1, 193, 196–7, 199–203, 205, 214–15, 221–2, 228
metric organization 56, 180, 205
metrics 12, 56, 180, 196, 205, 208, 220
microstructure 11–12, 102, 111
Middle Ages 151, 156, 164
mimetic principle 14
miniature 67, 77
miracle (supernaturalism of the Qur'anic Text) *see 'i'jāz*
Miracle of the Word 4
mnemotechnic 12
modern poetics 196, 207–9
monometric 199
monorhyme 56, 88, 109, 144–5, 197, 199, 221, 236n76
motifs: autonomous (*al-mukhtaṣṣ*) 11; branching out of 6, 180, 183, 185–6; common (*al-mushtarak*) 184–5, 214; dominant 6, 180, 182; imaginative (*ma'nā takhyīlī*) 210; motif-gold 195; motif-model 179–80; motif sequence 182; motif-topos 184–5; pre-motif 184–5, 191; translation of 80; rational 210; reservoir of 170–4, 179, 184–6, 192, 207–15; set motifs 191; traditional 181–2, 186, 211
Moroccan literature 230
morphological present 137
al-Mu'allaqāt, the 4, 11–12, 71, 87–8, 93, 107, 109, 115n10, 126–7, 133, 159–60, 163, 229
mubtadhal 184–5
mu'jiza 57, 126
multivalence of text 17
Muṣḥaf 70–1
Muslim literature 65, 68, 70, 72, 77
mutakallif (diligent poet) 200
mutashābihāt 82n5
muwashshaḥ (poetic form) 172
al-muwāzana (comparison) 200

al-nabiyy (prophet) 38, 83n8
naqā'iḍ 201, 203, 208; *see also* rebuttals
naqd *see* criticism, of poetry
narration/narrative: arabesque 14, 17; desire 15–16; discourse 14; narrativity 26, 114; present 93, 99–100, 137; space 15; structure 17; texts 15–17, 26
nasīb (lovers' lyrical prelude) 12, 89, 154
nazala (descent of the Revelation) 143
naẓariyya al-ibdā' see poetics
nazīra 203–8
naẓm 54, 62, 70, 76
"nev poetry" 236
non-linear structure 7
non-linear time, philosophy of 11, 15
normative poetics 150–4, 168–9, 229
novel 16, 228

objective 200
obviousness 91–6, 100, 102, 104–5, 110, 118, 120, 126, 140–2
ode 8–9, 12, 29, 95, 111, 200
Old Arabic literature 1–3, 28, 89, 149, 152, 154, 160, 183, 187, 191–3, 195–6, 199, 202, 207–8, 212–13, 219, 223–5, 231; authentic "topographic picture" of 183; poetic postulates of 2–3; reason of the stagnation of 223
Old Arabic poetry: artistically beautiful and literary theft 215–19; authenticity of 116n18; concentration on flatness of the physical 103–6; constituents of the simile 111–13; dawn of a new age in 227–31; de-paganisation of 158–9; development of 164; eroticism in 130–1; figures of description in 88–92; free poetry (without metre and rhyme) 228; gradation of textual time 99–102; history of 160; imaginative 87, 104; "jeweller's aspect" of 195–7; lyrical descriptiveness of 101; materialist 87, 92, 102, 104; motifs and poetic technique 170–4; obviousness and transparency, categories of 92–5; philological classicism and 169; poetics of 90, 149, 193; as poetry of distance 93; preservation of 159; profusion of themes in 88–92; *qaṣīda* of 88–9, 95–6, 100, 114, 161; realism or "materialism" of 87–8; realistic 87; segmentation of textual space in 95–9; self-sufficiency of

Old Arabic poetry *continued*
224; style of 89; supremacy of 170; temporal monotony, effect of 102; themes of 174–9; typicality before description 107–11; value function in 196
One Thousand and One Nights 5–6, 14–17; Western perception of 18
one-who-feels-knowing 39
one-who-knows-through-feelings 39–40
opposition principle 38, 216, 218
oral poetic tradition *see riwāya*
organic unity of poem 221–2
Oriental philology 152, 191
Oriental studies/Orientalist 1–2, 13, 53, 70, 72, 75, 78, 84n32, 86–7, 89–90, 150–2, 160, 190
Oriental-Islamic art 5
Oriental-Islamic cultural community 53
Oriental-Islamic lyric poetry 155–6
Oriental-Islamic ornamentation 11
Oriental-Islamic poetry 12, 15
Oriental-Islamic spirituality 1
Orientalisation 5, 151
Orientology 2
original 15–16, 21–3, 39, 42, 47, 55, 72, 79–81, 121–3, 126, 137, 148n21, 149, 177, 179–80, 202, 204, 207, 210, 214, 225–6, 229–30
originality 22–3, 108, 122, 125, 150, 164–71, 174, 179–86, 190–2, 196, 203, 207–8, 210, 212, 214–15, 229
originality of poetic work 179; concept of 164–6, 212, 214, 229
ornamental arabesque 2, 6–7, 11, 14, 18, 102
ornamentation 6, 11
Ottoman Empire 188
outer borders of the text 15

pagan literature 153
pagan poetry 61, 76
pagan practices 31
Pahlavi language 225
panegyric 47–8, 52, 66, 107, 151, 154, 173, 180–1, 184–5, 204, 212, 224–6, 234n44, 237n106
panegyric poetry 52, 181, 234n44
panoramic view of the world 113
parable 82, 167, 176
paragraph *see* ayah
parallel *see naẓīra*
parallelism 7–8, 11–13, 18–19, 32, 90–1, 97, 114, 145, 190, 220
particle (comparison) 50
path of induction 33, 42
pattern 12, 18, 179–80, 183, 187
People of the Book (*ahl al-kitāb*) 23
periodisation 1–2, 150–4; of Arabic literature 1, 150, 153
Persian poetry 186
perspectives of form 74–5
pessimist poetry 9, 113, 156
philological analysis 116n18, 172
philological commentaries 152
philological criticism 158, 160, 162–3, 165–6, 168–9, 171, 174, 179, 183–4, 186, 192, 196, 200, 207
philological method 151, 165
philological-philotechnical poetics 203
philological poetics 179, 186–92, 202–7; in Islamic culture 186–92; poetics of 203; universalism of 202–7
philological textual analysis 165
philological translation 79, 116n16
philology 28n2, 151–2, 158–86, 188–9, 191, 193, 195–7, 199–200, 207, 210, 223, 228–30
philosophy of time 5
philotechnic 30, 174, 202
philotechnic poetry 30, 192–6, 203–4, 206, 229, 231; forms of 192–6
philotechnical poetics 202, 204
phonetic theme 56
phonetics 50
picturesqueness 127
pillars of poetry 200
plagiarism 164–5, 196, 207–9, 232n21, 236n80
plagiarisms 165, 208
plot 15, 17, 26, 225
poem–reader relation 111
poet-ideologist 45
poet-medium 173
poet-possessed 30–5; by supernatural forces 32
poet-soothsayers 34, 37, 39; negative image of 50
poetic and magic reception 201
poetic authenticity 166
poetic coherence 91, 97, 102, 104, 106, 222
poetic content 53, 60, 192–3, 197, 204, 211
poetic discipline 166
poetic discourse 12; organisation of 12
poetic elements 2, 93, 150
poetic epoch 173

poetic form, concept of 30, 53–4, 61, 109, 149, 154–5, 161, 163–4, 172–3, 176, 180–2, 185–6, 189, 191, 193, 196–7, 201, 203–4, 211–12
poetic function of language 54, 61, 124
poetic heritage, de-paganisation of 159
poetic "hypocrisy" 47
poetic imagination, concept of 217
poetic inductivity and normativeness, principle of 191–2
poetic inspiration and technique 201–2
"poetic instruments" 26
poetic inversion 27, 155
poetic language (articulate expression) 33–4, 57–63; necessity of 59–62
poetic motifs: in Arabic antiquity 179–83; Arabic tradition and 170–4; banalised motifs (*mubtadhal*) 184; common motifs (*mushtarak*) 184; as commonplaces or topoi 183–6; forms of 180; hackneyed status of 185; independent motifs (*mukhtaṣṣ*) 185; and legalisation of "literary theft" 207–15; of love 180; origin of 179–83; reservoir of 207–15; sequences 181; structural schematisation of 184; Umayyad epoch 181, 185; valuation of 179
poetic postulates 1–3, 6, 12, 16, 22, 30, 47, 53, 104–5, 109, 136, 153, 156, 165, 167–8, 189, 203, 217
poetic syntax 32, 79, 109, 114
poetic system 2–3, 187, 209, 214, 218–19, 223
poetic text 43–51, 175
poetic tradition 9, 13, 15–16, 18, 45, 52–3, 61, 149, 161, 164, 168, 170, 186–7, 193, 202, 226, 229
poetic traditionalism 186
poetic translation 116n16, 205
poetics 4–28; of the arabesque 4–19, 106, 221; of composition 15; of film space 116n15; of Islam 19n5, 167, 188–9; of poetry 49; principles 2, 12, 14, 187, 196, 203, 222; repertoire 88, 90, 97; revolutionising 82, 138; of the simile 91, 111, 129, 138; standards 12
Poetics 5, 13, 152, 219–27
poetics of the arabesque 4–19; principle governing 7
Poétique de la prose 7
poetologic methodology 195, 207
poetology 165, 207
poetry 1–3, 6–7, 9–12, 14–15, 29–40, 44–7, 49, 51–75, 77, 82, 87–114, 118–19, 122, 128–31, 133, 136–8, 143–4, 149–62, 164–70, 173–89, 192, 194–201, 203–6, 208, 212–18, 220–2, 227–31; confrontation of *Qur'an* with 60; of distance 93, 105–6, 158, 213; as form of cognition 54; relation with religion 51
polytheistic cults 31
polyvalence 63
positivist periodisation 1
positivity 54, 60, 209, 214; of the simile 111–13
postmodern literature 14, 16, 27
post Qur'anic poetry 175; form–motif relationship in 3, 175
power of speech 55, 119
pre-Islamic poetry 6, 31, 57, 104, 116n18, 118, 129, 133, 138, 144, 149–50, 153, 159, 174, 179–80, 193, 231; characteristics of 129–36; recording of 159
pre-Islamic tradition, poetics of 11
prelude 12, 89, 103, 107, 154, 180, 184, 189, 232n19
present 30, 73, 93, 106
principle 1–3, 5–8, 10–18, 22, 24–5, 27, 35–6, 42, 44–5, 58–61, 66, 68, 71, 73, 87–8, 90–1, 95–7, 101–2, 112, 114, 118, 136, 143–4, 149, 156–8, 184–5, 187, 191, 195–6, 198–200; of arabesque construction 18; of horizontality 45; of spatial sequence 88; of a temporal or logical (cause-and-effect) sequence 7, 15, 18
Prolegomena 66
Prophet faithful, the 30–5
prophethood 35, 57; emotional dimension of 35; forms of 36; significance of 36
Prophet of God 35–8
prose 54, 56–7, 61–2, 66, 78–9, 84n24, 114, 145, 152, 187, 215, 223, 226, 228
prose literary 1, 76, 187
prose styles 76, 169, 177
prosopography 95
"protagonist" of poetics 186
"proto-poem" 203, 205, 235n55
"proto-poet" 204
prototext 24, 43–4
purposeless art 215, 218

al-Qartajanni 216, 220–2, 224, 226, 228
qaṣīda 88–9, 91, 95–8, 100–1, 106–8, 110, 112–14, 130, 137, 142, 154, 161, 163–4, 168, 180–1, 183, 185, 189, 191, 193, 197, 221

Qawl 66
al-Qays', Imru' 64, 89, 92, 94–5, 97, 100, 104–5, 107, 110, 112, 120, 198; love lyric prelude of 103, 154; stories of his loves 114; on woman's psychological states 114
quantitative 193
Qur'anic metaphor: centripetal forces of 145–6; and metaphoric revolution 118–23; past time of the simile and processuality of 136–42; realism of the simile and transfer of 129–36; Text unveiled in language and stylistics 123–9; and vertical world order 142–5
Qur'anic Text: as generator of changes in tradition 154–8; as Great Sacred Text 212; *'i'jāz* of 158; influence on lyric poetry 154; linguistic interpretation of 159; philology of 158–64; poetic tradition 193
Qur'an, poetics of 3–4, 6, 13, 18, 29; autocitation 24–5; confronting poetry at the level of form 53–82; and deformities of earlier prophecies 24; diversity of forms 63–5; on emotional aspects of poets 38–45; grammatical parallelisms in 32; ideological dimension of 31; *'i'jāz*, different aspects of 65–82; intertextuality and contextualisation of 21–8; level of ideology in 30–53; necessity of poetic language and form 59–62; poet possessed and Prophet faithful 30–5; primeval Revelation 23, 26–7; Prophet of God 35–8; recitation of 77; and resourcefulness of tradition 45–53; on significance of God's gift to man 55; stylistic supernaturalism of 53–9; on symbiosis between poetry and religion 31; text citations 24; translation of 80; wisdom of 45–53; as Word of God 53

rasūl (prophet) 35, 39
rāwī see rhapsodist
Reading for the Plot 14–15
realism 87–8, 92–4, 101, 103, 105–6, 108, 110–11, 113, 118, 122, 129–36, 221
realistic poetry 87
rebuttals 203
reception: of form 58; of *'i'jāz,* 73
recurrent theme 164
reductionist reading of the Text 84n33
redundancy 12, 178
reference 8, 28, 69, 85, 135, 159, 176, 181
referential 88, 95
reflexive poetry 113
reification 129, 131, 134, 142, 148n23
relief of topoi 184, 192
religion, relation with poetry 51
Renaissance 1, 13, 67–8, 171, 186, 191, 206, 220; Renaissance poetics 171
rendering (*naql*) 224–7
repetitiveness 6–8, 50, 180, 184; of elements 6
Republic, The 46
resolution 15, 17
resourcefulness of tradition 44–53
Revelation 13, 23–5, 35, 37–41, 47–9, 51–4, 56–8, 61–3, 74, 82, 83n7, 131, 158, 164, 218, 229; concept of form in 63; poetics of 37, 39–40, 49, 52, 57, 62; from World of Divine Beyondness 62
rhapsodist 161
Rhetoric 152
rhetoric/rhetorical 65–7, 69, 92, 99, 113, 119, 177, 179, 219–20, 223
rhyme and rhythm 6, 11–12, 18, 33, 54, 56–8, 61–2, 66, 70, 76, 78, 84n24, 101, 109, 114, 145–6, 177, 180–1, 193, 196–7, 200, 203, 205, 214, 222, 228, 234n55, 236n76; key element of 197; prose characterised by 57–8
rhythmical alternation 8
rhythmic and melodious qualities 126–7
rithā' 191
riwāya 208
Robinson Crusoe 172
Romanticism 31, 88, 232n26
Russian folklore poetry 12

sacred 3, 24–5, 27–8, 30, 38, 43–8, 50–2, 55, 61, 64, 71–2, 139, 141, 144, 149, 173, 188, 205, 213–19
sacredness of tradition 43
Saidian "Orientalist orientalisation of Orient" 151
ṣāiġ (poet-jeweller) 194
saj' 54, 57, 61–2, 70, 76
ṣan'a (poetic mastery) 199–200, 203
Sanskrit language 225
ṣarf, concept of 75
al-sariqa 207, 209, 211–12
segmentation 6–7, 11, 90–1, 101–2, 104–6, 109, 115n10, 118, 145–6, 251; of elements 6; principle of 118; of textual space 95–9; of time 101–2
self-praise 9, 12, 107
self-referential 14

semantic indentation 79
semantic unit 145, 199, 221–2
semantics 36, 38–40, 80, 84n33, 110, 138–9, 148n25, 195, 232n21
semi-couplet (single line) 111, 145
semiotic stylisation of time 102
semiotics: semiotic sign 48, 98, 111, 123; semiotic stylistic relevance of space 97; semiotic stylistics 97; of space 48–9, 97–8, 101
sequence 6–8, 11–13, 15, 18, 67, 88, 91, 96, 101–2, 104, 109, 114, 130–1, 181, 199
Seven Golden Odes of Arabia 4, 6, 29, 66, 71, 142
sha'ara (know through feelings) 39–40, 83n13
shā'ir (poet-soothsayer) 32, 38–9, 46; condemnation of 53; notion of subjectivism 41
shaytan 33–4, 37, 47, 50, 202, 216
shi'r (poetry) 32, 57, 152, 177
shi'riyya 1
short story 228
Shu'ubiyyah (*shu'ūbiyya*) movement 169–70, 223
simile 127–8, 130, 147n13; as architects of positivity 111–13; realism of 129–36; transparency of the world in 142–5; and travelogue airiness of the world 113–14; undertaking segmentation 145–6
simile correlate 111, 131, 135, 139–40
similitude 139–40, 157
ṣiyāġa (technique of poetic creation) 194, 199, 203, 234n54
soothsayer 29, 31–2, 34–6, 39
soothsaying and religious poetry 52, 156, 194
space 6–8, 15, 27, 37, 47–9, 70, 72, 74, 77, 88–90, 93, 95–102, 106. 109, 111, 116n15, 122, 136, 143, 148n23, 166, 170, 189, 203, 205–6, 214, 233n39
spatial arabesque 96
spatial distance 93
spatial sequence 88; principle of 7
spatial structure 7
structural unit 11, 91, 115n10
structuralist poetics 5
structure 7–8, 10–15, 17–18, 24–7, 49, 51, 54–5, 57, 72, 81, 89, 91, 96–7, 99–102, 106, 119, 140, 145, 149, 180–1, 184–5, 198–9, 203, 206, 222, 225
style: style-generating fragmentation 17; stylisation, 14, 23, 99, 102; stylistic dominant, 87–8, 137–8, 144, 149, 182; stylistic means, 80, 82, 89, 98, 111, 113, 120–1, 123, 128–9, 133–4, 136–8, 144, 183, 187, 205, 218; stylistic supernaturalism, 53–9, 65, 72, 75, 142; stylistic value, 55, 70, 81, 212; stylistics, 53–5, 76, 97, 119, 121, 123–9, 138, 157–8, 178, 187, 218, 223, 228, 232n30
stylistic supernaturalism, of text and tradition 53–9
subjective inwardness/inner self 9, 113
subjectivity 41–3, 141
Sufi poetry 104, 156, 176
suggestiveness 34, 58–60
supernatural forces 30, 32, 47
supernaturalism: doctrine of 75; of poetry 40; of the Text 65, 70, 75, 119, 142
supra-linguistic system 189
surah (a chapter in the *Qur'an*) 13, 18, 45, 50, 54–6, 58, 60, 64–5, 67, 74, 80, 119, 120–1, 125, 132, 137
symmetry 7
syntax of prepositions 83n17
system of artistic creativity 2

Tablet Well-Preserved 122
tafsīr (exegesis of the *Qur'an*) 22, 47
tajwīd (singingly delivery of the *Qur'an*) 77
takhayyul see imaginativeness, notion of
takhmīs (poetic form) 203–4, 206, 234n55
tardiyyāt see hunt poems
tathqīf (cultivation of poetry) 199
tautology 12
Tawrāt 26
téchnē 152, 161
technique of composition 4–5
Tekst/intertekst 239
temporal sequence 7, 15, 18
temporality/non-temporality 137, 148n21
Text's *'i'jāz* 69–70, 72, 75
textual environment 28
textual journey 95
textual space 95–100, 116n15
textual time 99–102
textuality 14, 22, 25, 28, 56, 62
theft, concept of 210, 212–13
thematic diversity of poem 87–9, 163, 193
thematic indiscipline 193
thematic schematisation 184
thematic unity of poem 87
theme 11–12, 18, 53–4, 56, 61, 63, 88–92, 96–8, 107–9, 114, 128, 156, 160, 163–4, 166, 172–9, 185, 193–4, 203

theory of citationality 23–8
theory of creativity 10, 23
"three-part" 163, 168, 176
time 8
tools 12, 105, 108, 129, 137
topography 93, 95, 116n16
toponym 93–5, 97–8
topos 184–5, 191–2
tradition 2–6, 9–16, 18, 21–2, 26–82; Arabic-Islamic concept of 167; of Vertical 43
traditional reservoir 109
traditional value 30, 63, 167
transcendental approach 59
transfiguration 27–8
transformation 28, 30, 126, 180, 183, 211–12; of motifs 180, 211
transhistorical value 68
translation 4, 19n1, 39, 49, 58, 72–3, 79–82, 85n33, 86n40, 87, 108, 122, 125, 132, 148n25, 205, 224–5, 227, 229, 236n76; of meaning 80
transparency 91–6, 100, 102, 106, 110–11, 114, 119–21, 123, 136–8, 140, 142–5, 152
transposition 23, 26, 37–8, 88, 94, 105, 109, 113, 155, 157, 175–6, 212–13, 216–17
travelogue airiness of the world 113–14
travelogue character of the qaṣīda 101, 114, 137
travelogue-description simile 142
travelogue genre 89, 97
trope 33, 70, 78, 82, 117n34, 121, 126, 140, 146n1, 227
truth 16, 22–3, 27–8, 31–9, 43, 47, 51, 53, 60, 67, 82, 149, 155, 174–6, 212–13, 215–18, 230; ideological concept of 212
Turkish language 187–9, 203
typicality/typifying 107–11, 181
typification of space 95

Udhri poetry 156, 160, 181
Ugro-Finnish folklore 12
Umarite love poetry 160
Umarite lyricism 155
Umarite poetry 154, 156–8
Umayyad dynasty (661–750) 52, 74, 153–5, 157, 177
universalism of deduction 42
Universe of forms 53, 64–71, 82
unusualness 195, 197, 202, 229
urban hedonist 154
urban-hedonist love poetry 154

value 1–2, 4, 5–6, 8, 14, 21–2, 27, 30, 33, 42, 45, 51–2, 55–6, 58, 60–3, 65, 67–70, 73–4, 78, 81, 86–8, 106, 110–12, 119, 122, 126, 128–9, 133–4, 136, 139–41, 143, 152–5, 160, 162–70, 172–5, 179–80, 184, 186, 188, 191–2, 194–6, 200–1, 207, 210–16
value judgement 2, 6, 63, 65, 87, 101, 151, 160, 165, 168, 170–1, 195, 201, 203–4
Vertical (divine world order) 48–9, 123, 142–5
vertical communication 55
vertical (sacred) deduction 37, 42, 62
vertical deduction, principle of 37, 42
Vertical, principle of 35
visualisation of space 95

al-waḥda al-'uḍwiyya see organic unity of peom
Waḥy (Revelation) 62
walk-on roles of theme 98
waqfiyah 78
weighing, aesthetic 10
Western culture 4–5, 9–10, 152, 219
Western literature 7, 17
Western poetics 7, 14–15, 18
Whistling Woman, The 16
wine poems (*khahmriyyāt*) 185
Word-of-God-about-Truth 53, 157
work of art 5, 12, 22, 27, 40, 157, 168, 172, 175, 194, 198–9, 215, 217, 221, 225
World of Divine Beyondness 62

zajal 172
zajal (poetic form) 172
al-zaman al-dā'irī 8
zuhdiyyāt see ascetic poems